I0885488

Conflict of Laws

Fifth Edition

Maebh Harding

Routledge
Taylor & Francis Group
LONDON AND NEW YORK

Fifth edition published 2014
by Routledge
4 Park Square, Milton Park, Abingdon, Oxon OX14 4RN
605 Third Avenue, New York, NY 10017

Routledge is an imprint of the Taylor & Francis Group, an informa business

© 2014 Maebh Harding

The right of Maebh Harding to be identified as author of this work has been asserted by her in accordance with sections 77 and 78 of the Copyright, Designs and Patents Act 1988.

All rights reserved. No part of this book may be reprinted or reproduced or utilised in any form or by any electronic, mechanical, or other means, now known or hereafter invented, including photocopying and recording, or in any information storage or retrieval system, without permission in writing from the publishers.

Trademark notice: Product or corporate names may be trademarks or registered trademarks, and are used only for identification and explanation without intent to infringe.

First edition by Abla Mayss published by Cavendish Publishing 1994
Fourth edition by Ruth Hayward published by Cavendish Publishing 2006

British Library Cataloguing in Publication Data
A catalogue record for this book is available from the British Library

Library of Congress Cataloging in Publication Data
Harding, Maebh.
Conflict of laws / Maebh Harding, Senior Lecturer in Law, University of Portsmouth. – Fifth Edition.
page cm
ISBN 978-0-415-69505-3 (hbk) – ISBN 978-0-415-69506-0 (pbk) –
ISBN 978-1-315-88683-1 (ebk) 1. Conflict of laws–England. I. Title.
KD680.H37 2014
342.42'042—dc23

2013011597

ISBN: 978-0-415-69505-3 (hbk)
ISBN: 978-0-415-69506-0 (pbk)
ISBN: 978-1-315-88683-1 (ebk)

Typeset in Joanna
by RefineCatch Limited, Bungay, Suffolk

Outline Contents

Detailed Contents

Preface

This edition of *Conflicts of Law* is offered as a primer for students who are new to the English study of conflicts of law. It provides a basic overview of the main concepts, and points the students to more critical writings of established commentators. Many of the chapters provide a very basic overview of domestic English law so that students from other legal backgrounds can understand the context in which English conflict of law rules operate.

As the European Union continues to expand its harmonisation programme of conflicts of law rules, the discipline becomes more relevant to academic lawyers working in fields that were previously untroubled by the possibility of the application of foreign law. It is hoped that this version of *Conflicts of Law* may be of interest to students and academics from a non-commercial law background and that the inclusion of a great emphasis on Family Law may provide a different viewpoint on the subject.

Acknowledgements

Thanks are due to my colleagues at the University of Portsmouth for their support for and interest in the Private International Law Units I co-ordinated during my time there. I am particularly grateful to Greg Osborne for his tales from a previous life in practice and his endeavours to keep litigation out of the Texan courts. I am very appreciative of the help received from the editors at Routledge in the updating of this work and particularly the patience of Damian Mitchell. I owe a debt of gratitude to my husband, Stephen, for his support.

Table of Cases

B

C

D

E

H

I

J

K

L

M

S

T

U

V

Table of Legislation

A

B

C

D

N

P

Table of International Legislation and Treaties

Treaties and Conventions

A

B

E

M

N

R

Decisions

Directives

Regulations

Resolutions

International Legislation

Australia

France

India

USA

Table of Figures

Chapter 1

Introduction to Conflict of Laws

Chapter Contents

Key Issues:

- Introduction to the subject
- Sources of the conflict of laws rules
- How the conflict of laws rules are applied in cases
- The legal philosophy behind choice-of-law rules

1.1 Introduction

The 'conflict of laws' refers to part of English domestic law which comes into operation whenever the English court is faced with a case involving one or more foreign elements. This may occur when an element of the dispute happened in a foreign country, for example when an English tourist is injured in a road accident in Spain. It may also occur where one of the parties has a strong link to another country. For example, where an Englishwoman seeks a divorce from a German spouse who lives in Germany, or where an English company issues proceedings against a company incorporated in New York. In such cases, the English court may have to consider whether England is the best place for the dispute to be heard. If the English court decides to hear the case, it may consider whether it is appropriate to decide the dispute according to a foreign law. The dispute may have a stronger connection to a foreign legal system than to the English legal system. For example, a contract between two parties may stipulate that all disputes between the parties should be determined by New York law.

The conflict of laws is also referred to as **private international law**. Every modern legal system has its own domestic rules of private international law. The rules of private international law in France may differ from the rules of private international law in place in Greece; much like the land law of Greece differs from the land law of France. Today, there is also some international and European Union (EU) regulation of private international law. Private international law should not be confused with public international law. Public international law concerns the rules that govern relations between sovereign states rather than private individuals.

This book is primarily concerned with the rules that guide the English courts when seised of a case which involves a foreign element. These conflict of laws rules are used to solve three key questions:

1. Does the English court have jurisdiction to hear the case?
2. What system of law should be applied to determine the dispute: English law or a foreign law?
3. When should the English court recognise and enforce a foreign judgment?

1.2 Jurisdiction

The first question which must be decided is whether the English court has the power to hear a case which has a foreign element. The question of jurisdiction raises a number of issues. What connection to England is required for the English court to have competence to rule on disputes involving foreign elements? Should the presence of the parties in the UK be enough or must there be some stronger link between the parties and the English legal system? In what circumstances should the English courts be permitted to decline jurisdiction?

The role of the parties in deciding what court should have jurisdiction must also be examined. Should the parties be able to choose the jurisdiction to hear their case? Is it acceptable for a claimant to 'shop around' and choose the jurisdiction that is likely to give the most favourable ruling?

These questions are fully examined in Chapters 3 and 4. Issues of jurisdiction are determined by rules of English law or by EU regulations such as Brussels I.[1]

1.3 Applicable Law

Once the jurisdiction of the English court has been established, the court must decide whether the substance of the dispute should be determined by English law or by a foreign law. For example, in determining whether a contract between a French party and an English party is legally binding, should the court apply English Law or French Law? The English court decides what system of law to apply using 'choice of law' rules.

The 'choice of law' rules are subject matter specific. For example, the law governing the validity of a contract is the law chosen by the parties. So when deciding whether a contract between a French party and an English party is legally valid, the courts will look to the law specified by the contract. If the contract states that all disputes should be regulated by French law, the English courts will apply French law. French law is the **applicable law**. However, the law governing legal ownership of a house is the law of the country in which the property is situated. When the English court hears a dispute involving a question of title to land situated in South Africa, the choice-of-law rules require the English court to apply South African law to determine that title. South African law is the applicable law.

Some choice-of-law rules stem from English domestic law, others from EU regulations. A key question is to what extent parties should be permitted to choose the law applicable to their dispute. For example, is it possible for English citizens to choose foreign law in order to avoid the provisions of English law?

Another current issue is whether all disputes must be decided by reference to the law of a nation state. Should parties instead be able to choose a set of international principles such as the UNIDROIT Principles of International Commercial Contracts? These questions are considered in Chapters 7 and 8.

1.4 Recognition and enforcement of foreign judgments

The final question examined in this book is the recognition and enforcement of foreign judgments in England. This question arises where the parties litigate abroad and then seek to have judgment enforced in England. For example, if a claimant has obtained a judgment against an English defendant in a Turkish court for damages for negligence, they may decide to enforce the judgment against the defendant's assets in England.

The English courts automatically recognise and enforce foreign judgments of EU Member States subject to certain safeguards. Other foreign judgments are recognised and enforced under the rules of English domestic law. If a foreign judgment is not recognised in England, fresh proceedings may have to be issued in the English courts.

The recognition and enforcement of English judgments in other EU Member States is governed by EU regulation Brussels I[2] which is examined in Chapter 5. In all other cases, whether or not a foreign country will recognise and enforce an English judgment is a matter for the domestic law of that country. For example, whether or not an English judgment will be enforceable in China is a

1 Council Regulation (EC) No 44/2001 [2001] OJ L12/1.
2 Council Regulation (EC) No 44/2001 [2002] OJ L12/1.

matter for Chinese law. The question of whether or not an English judgment will be recognised and enforced abroad is outside the scope of this book.

The recognition and enforcement of foreign judgments raises two critical questions. To what extent should the recognising or enforcing court be permitted to re-examine the judgment of the first court? An enforcing court may be obliged by domestic or international law to ensure that foreign judgments comply with public policy and human rights concerns to avoid injustice. However, in-depth scrutiny of a foreign judgment could amount to a rehearing of the case. This would cause considerable delay and expense to both parties and could be perceived to be undermining the ruling of the first court. A second question is to what extent judgments by non-judicial bodies such as arbitration tribunals or agreements reached through mediation should be enforceable in other countries? These questions are considered in Chapter 5.

1.5 Sources of conflict of laws rules

1.5.1 English law

Originally, all three 'conflict of laws' questions were determined by English domestic law, but today the area is subject to increasing international and European regulation. English domestic law still regulates some aspects of private international law. For example, the English courts will determine whether a foreign marriage is valid in England by reference to common law rules,[3] and the Family Law Act 1986 determines whether foreign divorces obtained outside the EU will be recognised as changing a person's marital status in England.[4]

English domestic law also applies to resolve **intra-UK conflict of laws issues**. Although Scotland, Northern Ireland, Wales and England are all part of the United Kingdom, they are each a distinct legal area or jurisdiction. Where a case involves cross-border issues between, for example Northern Ireland and England, English conflicts of law rules apply to determine if the English court should hear the case. While the substantive law of all four jurisdictions is often the same, it may be the case that the substantive law of one jurisdiction is very different on a particular issue to that of another UK jurisdiction. For example, the remedies available for breach of contract are different in Scots law to those available under English law. In a disputed case, an English court will look to English conflict of law rules to determine which domestic law should apply.

1.5.2 International treaties

In some areas of the law, the UK has signed up to international treaties governing conflict of laws issues. These treaties can work by unifying the internal laws of the signatory states on a given topic. For example, the Montreal Convention of Unification of Certain Rules for International Carriage by Air 1999 provides uniform rules in relation to the international carriage of persons or goods by air.

Alternatively an international treaty may implement a co-operative procedure which requires mutual recognition of foreign rulings or statuses. These treaties do not interfere with substantive domestic law. For example, arbitration proceedings that take place in England are governed by the Arbitration Act 1996. This Act also governs how English arbitral awards are enforced in England. The UK is a signatory to the New York Convention.[5] The Convention allows signatory countries to retain their domestic rules and processes for recognising arbitral awards. However, the Convention requires signatory states to enforce foreign arbitral awards, as if they were domestic arbitral awards. This allows English arbitral awards to be automatically enforced in other signatory countries and

3 See Chapter 8.

4 See Chapter 9.

5 UN Convention on the Recognition and Enforcement of Foreign Arbitral Awards 1958.

requires the English courts to enforce foreign arbitral awards made in other signatory countries even though the substantive rules governing the foreign arbitration tribunal may be very different to English rules.

By signing an international treaty, the UK makes a commitment to adhere to the principles of the treaty. Where other states make the same commitment, this ensures a level of consistency in how cross-border issues are treated. This commitment may be qualified where a state opts out of certain provisions of an international treaty.

The conflicts of law rules embodied in international treaties do not come into force in England until incorporated into English domestic law. For example, the New York Convention was brought into force by the Arbitration Act 1975.[6]

1.5.3 European Union regulation of the conflict of laws

The European Union is an economic and political partnership between 27 European countries. Central to this partnership is the creation of a common market which enables goods, services, money and people to move freely within the European Union. The principles of mutual trust and mutual recognition are promoted by the European Union as essential to maintaining the common market. Recently the free circulation of judgments in civil and commercial matters has become a stated objective of the EU.[7]

European Union Member States have transferred some of their law-making powers to the EU through a series of international treaties. The goals and policies of the European Union and its law-making competencies are now consolidated and outlined in two treaties: the Treaty on European Union (TEU)[8] and the Treaty on the Functioning of the European Union (TFEU).[9] Since 1997, the EU has had express powers to create legislation in the field of judicial co-operation in civil law cases.[10] As a result the EU has created a number of regulations to harmonise the conflict of laws rules of EU Member States. This has been referred to as the 'Europeanisation' of the conflict of laws.

The EU regulations are binding on all EU Member States. This means that regulation of conflict of law issues at EU level changes the domestic conflict of law rules of Member States. However, Denmark, Ireland and England have negotiated a protocol to limit the application of EU measures relating to judicial co-operation in civil law cases. Denmark does not take part in the measures at all and so EU regulations harmonising private international law are not generally binding in Denmark.[11] Ireland and England can choose whether to opt into such measures.[12]

The Court of Justice of the European Union (CJEU)[13] is the ultimate arbitrator on the interpretation of EU regulations. Member States can send a matter of interpretation to the CJEU for preliminary ruling under Art 267 of the TFEU. A 'preliminary ruling' means that the European Court of Justice (ECJ) interprets the way in which a particular provision of the EU regulation is intended to apply without going into the merits of the dispute in question. Such a decision is then binding on all national courts.

6 Which has now been consolidated by the Arbitration Act 1996.
7 Brussels I recast; Regulation (EU) No 1215/2012 [2012] OJ L351/1, recital (6)
8 Consolidated Version of the Treaty on European Union [2010] OJ C83/13.
9 Consolidated Version of the Treaty on the Functioning of the European Union [2010] OJ C83/47.
10 Art 65 of the Treaty Establishing the European Community (EC Treaty) [1997] OJ C340/03. This power is now found in Art 81 of the TFEU.
11 Protocol No 5 1997 annexed by the Treaty of Amsterdam to the EC Treaty. This protocol is maintained by Protocol No 1 annexed to the Treaty of Lisbon [2007] C306/165.
12 Protocol No 4 1997 annexed by the Treaty of Amsterdam to the EC Treaty. This protocol is maintained by Protocol No 1 annexed to the Treaty of Lisbon [2007] C306/165.
13 Made up of the European Court of Justice (ECJ) and the General Court (EGC), which was formerly known as the Court of First Instance before the implementation of the Lisbon Treaty.

1.6 How conflict of law issues arise in English cases

In the English legal system, it is generally up to the parties to raise conflict of laws issues.

1.6.1 Jurisdiction

Disputes over jurisdiction can arise before proceedings take place. Under the English legal system, a claimant must serve the defendant with a claim form in order to initiate proceedings.[14] If a claimant wishes to serve a claim on a defendant who is not present in the UK he may have to seek the permission of the court. In this case he must prove a basis for jurisdiction. The question of jurisdiction can also be raised by the defendant after acknowledgment of service. If the defendant does not raise any jurisdictional issues after acknowledgment of service he is deemed to have accepted the jurisdiction of the English courts.[15] In certain circumstances the English court must refuse jurisdiction of its own motion, such as where another Member State has exclusive jurisdiction under an EU regulation.[16]

1.6.2 Applicable law

Once the matter of jurisdiction has been settled, the next question is whether the court should apply foreign law. The English court will not apply foreign law automatically. It is up to the party seeking to rely on foreign law to show that the English conflict of law rules point to the application of foreign law. The conflict of law rules determining which system of law is applicable are subject matter specific. The court must decide the substance of the case in order to apply the correct rule. This process is called **characterisation** or **classification**. If the court determines that the substantive issue in the case is a matter relating to contract, the applicable law is the law chosen by the parties.[17] If it is a matrimonial remedies case, the applicable law is the law of the forum.[18]

It is also up to the party wishing to rely on foreign law to prove the content of the foreign law. For example, if the matter concerns a remedy for breach of contract and one party is relying on the application of French law, he must prove to the court what remedies are available under French law for breach of contract and which is appropriate here. Foreign law is treated as a matter of fact by the English courts; the court is not expected to know the content of foreign laws in the way that it ascertains and applies the law of England.[19] The parties may call expert witnesses to produce reports and testify in court as to the content of the foreign law. Section 4(3) of the Civil Evidence Act 1972 allows a previous reported decision on the meaning of the foreign law to be introduced as admissible evidence.[20] Where the content of foreign law cannot be satisfactorily proved, the English court will apply the relevant rule of English domestic law.[21]

---

14 CPR rule 7(2).

15 CPR rule 11(5).

16 See for example Art 29 Brussels I.

17 Art 3, Council Regulation (EC) 593/2008 [2008] L177/6, (Rome I).

18 See, for example, *B v S* [2012] EWHC 265 (Fam) [10].

19 This differs from the approach in civil law countries, where the court will apply foreign law on its own motion. See further T Hartley 'Pleading and Proof of Foreign Law: The Major European Systems Compared' (1996) 45 *International and Comparative Law Quarterly*, 271–292; R Hausmann, 'Pleading and Proof of Foreign Law – a Comparative Analysis' [2008] *The European Legal Forum*, 1–14.

20 *Phoenix Marine Inc v China Ocean Shipping Co and another* [1999] 1 Lloyd's Rep 682.

21 *Szechter v Szechter* [1971] P 286, 296.

1.6.3 Recognition and enforcement of foreign judgments

A party seeking the enforcement of a foreign judgment must make an application to the English court for an order for enforcement.[22] The issue of recognition of a foreign judgment may arise at any stage in proceedings where the English courts are asked to take note of the result of a foreign judgment.

1.7 Some technical issues relating to applicable law

1.7.1 Classification/characterisation

The choice-of-law rules are subject matter specific, so much depends on how an issue is classified or characterised. In general, classification is a relatively straightforward process. Two key problems can be identified. First, the dispute might fall into more than one category, such as the requirement for a parent to give consent for a marriage which could be seen as relating to the formalities for a marriage or relating to the essential validity of marriage.[23] Second, the dispute may be of a type unknown to English law.[24]

Raiffeisen Zentral Osterrich v Five Star General Trading LLC[25] concerned the assignment of a marine insurance policy on a ship. The policy was governed by English law and issued by French insurers. It was alleged the policy had been assigned to the claimants, who had lent the money to purchase the insured vessel. The court had to determine whether the assignment was valid, thus entitling the claimant to make a claim under it. If the assignment was characterised as a contractual issue, it would be governed by English law. This would render the assignment valid. If the assignment was considered as a matter relating to property law, it would be governed by the law of the domicile of the insurers. The insurers were domiciled in France. Under French law, the assignment was not valid. The right to claim was wholly dependent on how the issue was characterised. In this case the assignment was treated as a matter of contract law. Lord Mance took a pragmatic view, stating that 'the conflict of laws does not depend (like a game or even an election) upon the application of rigid rules, but upon a search for appropriate principles to meet particular situations'.[26]

Many commentators have suggested rules of classification in order ensure uniformity.[27] There is, however, no consistent approach to classification in English law.[28] Where the choice-of-law rule stems from EU legislation, the CJEU has the ultimate say on whether a dispute falls into the subject matter scope of an EU regulation – in other words, how matters should be classified for the purposes of EU law.[29]

1.7.2 Connecting factors

Once the relevant choice-of-law rule has been established this will point the court to a factor that connects the dispute to the legal system of a particular country. This is called a 'connecting factor'.

22 S 4 Civil Jurisdiction and Judgments Act 1982.
23 *Ogden v Ogden* [1908] P 46.
24 *The Colorado* [1923] P 102.
25 [2001] QB 825.
26 Ibid [29].
27 WE Beckett, 'The Question of Characterisation (Qualification) in Private International Law' (1934) 15 *British Yearbook of International Law*, 46–81.
28 See further C Forsyth, 'Characterisation Revisited: An Essay in the Theory and Practice of the English Conflict of Laws' (1998) 114 LQR 141–161.
29 For example *LTU v Eurocontrol* [1976] ECR 1541; Case C-464/01 *Gruber v BayWa AG* [2005] ECR I-439, [2006] QB 204; C220/95 *Boogaard v Laumen* [1997] ECR I-1147, [1997] QB 759.

Some connecting factors point to the law of the place where an event or transaction took place, such as the place of formation of a contract or the place of celebration of a marriage. Other connecting factors point to a law that is connected to a person that is part of the dispute, such as the law of their domicile or habitual residence.

In many legal systems, a person is assigned a personal law which defines his or her legal status and legal capacity. This is the legal system to which the person is considered to be most closely connected. In common law systems, a person's personal law is the law of his domicile. In civil law systems personal law refers to the law of a person's nationality, and in some legal systems personal law is determined by a person's religion. These connecting factors are generally fixed and not easily changed. This means that even where an individual moves abroad and remains there for many years they may continue to be governed by the personal law assigned to them at birth.

In recent years the idea of a personal law has become less relevant. As people become more internationally mobile it becomes inappropriate to consider them to be irreversibly connected to one legal system for life. In EU law, the law of a person's habitual residence has gained favour as the law to determine a person's capacity to marry, or their status as a married or divorced person. This is a connecting factor that is more easily changed than domicile or nationality. In English law, personal law based on domicile remains relevant in matters of family law and personal capacity.

Connecting factors are discussed further in Chapter 2. As connecting factors are often referred to in Latin, it is helpful to have a glossary of examples:

Lex loci contractus: the law of the place where the contract was made.
Lex loci solutionis: the law of the place where the contract is to be performed.
Lex loci celebrationis: the law of the place where the marriage was celebrated.
Lex loci delicti: the law of the place where the tort was committed.
Lex domicilii: the law of the place where a person is domiciled
Lex patriae: the law of the nationality
Lex situs: the law of the place where the property is situated.
Lex fori: the law of the forum, that is, the domestic law of the court in which the case is heard.

1.7.3 Public policy

It is a general principle of the conflict of laws that a rule of foreign law which should govern as the applicable law, as the most appropriately connected rule may be disregarded if its application would be contrary to public policy. This allows the court to avoid the application of a foreign law if the substantive content of the rule or the result that would be reached by its application is objectionable to the forum. This doctrine is commonly accepted in the conflict of laws but its boundaries are not easily defined.

The English court has refused to enforce contracts in restraint of trade,[30] contracts breaking the laws of a friendly country,[31] and an incapacity existing under a penal foreign law, such as the inability of persons divorced for adultery to remarry, so long as the innocent spouse remains single.[32] The English court has also refused to recognise a marriage of a child under the age of

30 *Rousillon v Rousillon* (1880) 14 Ch D 351.
31 *Regazzoni v Sethia* [1958] AC 301.
32 *Scott v AG* (1886) 11 PD 128.

puberty.[33] The English court will also refuse to apply foreign law where to do so would undermine international human rights protections.[34]

The EU regulations allow the English court to refuse to apply foreign laws that are manifestly incompatible with public policy.[35] The English court will substitute the equivalent rule of English law in place of the foreign rule violating public policy.

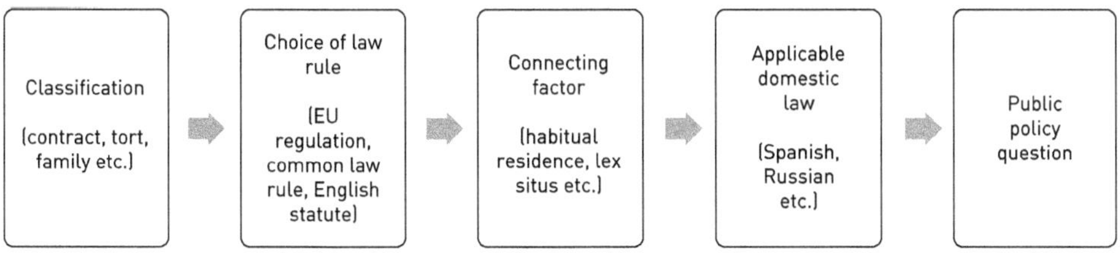

Fig 1.1 The process of choosing applicable law.

1.7.4 The Doctrine of *renvoi*

Where the conflicts of law rules point to the application of foreign law it is generally the domestic law of that county that will be applied. For example, if the rule points to the application of Norwegian law as the law of the defendant's habitual residence, the English court will apply the rules that Norwegian courts would apply to domestic cases.

However, it could be argued that the English court should consider how the conflicts of law rules of the foreign system would treat the case.[36] It may be that the Norwegian court would not apply its domestic law to the dispute but instead apply the law of the defendant's country. This reference to the law of a second country is called the doctrine of *renvoi*.

The doctrine has been discussed in some English cases relating to succession and the title of personal property situated abroad, but has received little support. In *Islamic Republic of Iran v Berend*[37] the court had to consider the ownership of a fragment of limestone carving from the ancient city of Persepolis. The defendant bought the artefact in Paris and later sent it to auctioneers in London to be sold. The Republic of Iran brought proceedings to recover the fragment as it was a national moment that belonged to Iran. The relevant English conflict of laws rule pointed to French law as the applicable law to govern title of this piece of personal property. Under French domestic, law, the artefact would belong to the defendant. The Republic of Iran argued that if the case were governed by French conflict of laws rules, the French courts would apply the law of the place of origin of the artefact to determine title and this would give ownership to the Republic of Iran. The court considered whether it should use the doctrine of *renvoi* to determine the case according to French conflict of law rules. Eady J stated that *renvoi* could be a useful tool to further policy objectives but that there was no good reason to introduce it in the particular case.[38]

The EU regulations expressly exclude the application of the doctrine of *renvoi* in cases regulated by EU choice-of-law rules.[39]

---

33 *Mohamed v Knott* [1969] 1 QB 1.
34 *Williams & Humbert Ltd v W&H Trade Marks (Jersey) Ltd* [1986] AC 368, 379.
35 Eg, Art 41, Rome I and Art 26 Rome II.
36 A V Dicey, *A Digest of the Law of England with Reference to the Conflict of Laws* (London 1896) 77.
37 [2007] EWHC 132 (QB).
38 Ibid [31]
39 Eg Art 20 Rome I, Art 24 Rome II.

1.8 The legal philosophy behind conflict of laws rules

The conflict of laws is the study of how the courts treat cases with a foreign element. Before commencing this study, the question must be posed: what justification does the court have for treating cases with a foreign element differently to cases with no foreign elements? This question has been addressed by many legal commentators over the centuries.

Most theories centre on the legitimacy of choice-of-law rules rather than on the basis of jurisdiction. The assumption of many theorists is that if one system of choice of rules is universally accepted, jurisdiction will become irrelevant. It would not matter where a dispute was brought; the same law would be applied by all jurisdictions.[40] In reality, because each state retains different conflict of law rules, jurisdiction may actually be determinative of how the dispute is resolved.[41]

When examining the justification for choice-of-law rules, two questions must be answered.

1. Should a court apply foreign law at all?
2. Where several legal systems are connected to a dispute, why should one particular applicable law be favoured over the others?

1.9 Justifications for the application of foreign law

Early theorists justified the application of foreign law as protecting state interests. Ulricus Huber, a seventeenth-century German jurist, laid down three principles which came to be regarded as the basis for the English system of the conflict of laws.[42] Huber argued that the laws of each state have force within its territory but not beyond. These laws bind all persons found within the territory whether their presence is permanent or temporary.[43] A court applies foreign law on the basis of **comity**. This principle allows courts to apply foreign law out of respect for the law of other nations. This allows laws to retain their effect provided that they do not prejudice the powers or rights of another state or its subjects. Huber reinforces the idea that law is only strictly binding within the territory of a nation and is applied in other states only by the tacit consent of that state. Inherent in the principle of comity is the hope that other courts will return the favour, out of mutual interest in preserving state interests. Under Huber's doctrine of comity, the law of other states was only given effect to the extent that it did not interfere with national state interests. Where the foreign law conflicts with forum state interests, it will not be applied.

Huber's principle of comity formed the basis for the 'vested rights' theory of choice of law. This theory was central to English jurist AV Dicey's system of the conflict of laws.[44] Writing in the late nineteenth century, Dicey justified the application of foreign law as allowing a right acquired under the law of a one country to be recognised in another state provided that it was not contrary to the public policy of that country.[45] Dicey's theory separates private rights from the foreign law that created them. Courts uphold rights of private individuals acquired under foreign law unless to do so would be contrary to domestic public policy. This theory framed the justification for choice-

40 Preventing forum shopping was one of the reasons for the introduction of an EU regulation for harmonised rules for applicable law on divorce. This has not been adopted by the UK. Council Regulation (EU) 1259/2010 [2010] OJ L343/10 (Rome III).

41 T Hartley, *International Commercial Litigation* (Cambridge University Press 2009) 5–8.

42 See further, DJ Llewelyn Davies, 'The Influence of Huber's De Conflictu Legum on English Private International Law' (1937) 18 *British Yearbook of International Law* 49–78, which contains an English translation of the work.

43 U Huber, 'De Conflictu legum deverarum in diversis imperiis' in *Praelectiones Juris Romani et Hodierni* Vol 11 Book 1 (1689).

44 AV Dicey, *A Digest of the Law of England with Reference to the Conflict of Laws* (London 1896). Huber was also influential on traditional American commentators, Story and Beale. See J. Story, *Commentaries on the Conflict of Laws* (1834) 19–21.

45 AV Dicey, *A Digest of the Law of England with Reference to the Conflict of Laws* (London 1896) 22–38.

of-law rules in terms of justice between the parties. The court was not applying foreign law out of a sense of respect for other states, but out of a requirement to uphold private rights. It would be unjust to treat parties who entered into a contract unsupported by consideration in Italy as if they had contracted under English law, and accordingly declare their contract void for lack of consideration.[46] These accrued contractual rights should only be ignored if respecting them undermined forum state interests. The theory allowed more deference to foreign law than under the doctrine of comity.

These two justifications for the application of foreign law – **justice between the parties** and **respect for state interests** – are still relied upon today in English case law and in EU legislation.

References to comity can still be found in English judgments.[47] In such cases, the decision to uphold a foreign law may not serve the private interests of the parties. For example, a marriage carried out abroad may be held to be void even where both parties intended to be bound, if the ceremony did not comply with the formal requirements of the place in which it was celebrated. The rule is upheld partly to protect the interests of a foreign country and partly in the expectation that the favour will be returned.

The principle of **mutual trust** is the keystone of EU regulations harmonising conflict of law rules.[48] As with comity, this principle requires courts to give effect to the laws and rulings of other EU Member States. Some commentators have argued that the ECJ has gone too far in prioritising mutual trust between Member States above the need to find justice between the parties to the dispute.[49]

Choice-of-law rules are also justified on the basis of justice between the parties or upholding the expectations of the parties. Respecting the autonomy of parties to a dispute is an important concern in many EU regulations.[50]

1.10 Which law to apply?

Once it has been established that it is legitimate to apply a foreign law in some circumstances, the next question is which law to apply.

There are two approaches to this question. The most traditional approach in English conflict of laws is to choose the legal system that is most appropriately connected to the dispute, with little regard for the content of the rules or the substantive result in the case. This is referred to as a 'conflicts justice' approach. The second approach, favoured by US commentators, looks to the content of the rules and seeks to apply the law that will give the best result in the case – the 'substantive justice' approach.

1.10.1 Conflicts justice approach

The traditional method of the conflict of laws is to select a legal system that is geographically connected to the dispute. This idea of a strict list of geographical connecting factors dates back to the work of Savigny, a nineteenth-century German jurist.[51] Savigny noted that as the laws of nation states could differ significantly from each other on particular issues, it was vital to fix the limits of

---

46 *Re Bonacina* [1912] 2 Ch 394.

47 *Agbaje v Agbaje* [2010] UKSC 13; *Schmitt v Deichmann* [2012] EWHC 62 (Ch); *Travers v Holley* [1953] P 246; *Igra v Igra* [1951] P 404.

48 Eg recital (16) Brussels I.

49 L Walker and P Beaumont 'Shifting the Balance achieved by the Abduction Convention: The contrasting approaches of the European Court of Human Rights and the European Court of Justice' (2011) 7 JPIL 231–250; A Briggs, 'The Death of Harrods. *Forum on Conveniens* and the European Court' [2005] 121 LQR 535.

50 Eg recital (11) Rome I; recital (31) Rome II.

51 Fredrich Von Savigny, *A Treatise of the Conflicts of Laws and the Limits of Their Operation in Respect of Space and Time* (translation) (2nd ed, Edinburgh 1880).

each legal system, to decide when one state's authority to decide a dispute ended and another began.[52] If disputes could be attached to a national system by a series of fixed rules it would always be possible to determine the correct law to apply to a dispute. He sought to establish a system where it was possible to look at any dispute with foreign elements and assign it to the correct legal system.[53]

Savigny focused on categories of disputes or legal relationships and sought to identify the state to which the legal relationship or dispute belonged. He assigned decisive importance to the geographical location of certain elements – **the connecting factors**. This precluded any pre-choice examination of the content of the laws and placed the laws of the forum and foreign law on an equal footing. Conflict of laws rules should not choose the result of the case, as different societies have different value judgements on how to resolve legal disputes. According to Savigny, the geographical connection of the dispute to a particular legal system gave the choice of law legitimacy. Substantive outcome is irrelevant except where it conflicts with the public policy of the forum.

Today, EU regulations and English conflict of law rules still rely on a series of geographical connections. This does not completely exclude judicial examination of the fairness of the substantive outcome of the case. The EU regulations allow the court to depart from strict adherence to the list of connecting factors where the dispute is manifestly more closely connected with another country.[54] It is also possible to avert an unfair result by refusing to apply the applicable law on the basis of public policy.

1.10.2 Substantive justice approach

In the USA, conflicts of law rules initially followed the traditional 'conflicts justice' approach.[55] Over time, a number of US jurists questioned the legitimacy of this approach and suggested that instead of seeking to apply the most geographically connected system of law, the court should instead look to apply a law that would give a just result. This development is referred to as the American Revolution in conflicts of law.

David E Cavers[56] compared the traditional conflicts of law system to a slot machine programmed to select the applicable law based on territorial contracts without regard to the content of the laws. This prevented intelligent result-based choices.

Walter Wheeler Cook[57] highlighted the need to consider legislative purposes and policy before a wise choice between conflict rules could be made. He characterised the choice-of-law problem as one of choosing between competing rules, not competing legal orders in the abstract. Referring to case law, he argued that when the court applied foreign law it was actually trying to fashion a remedy that took into account foreign law, but approximated to the forum's own idea of fairness.

Brainerd Currie[58] argued that conflict cases should be dealt with in the same way as domestic cases. The court should look to the statutes to be applied to see if they were intended to apply to cases with a foreign element. Then the court should look to the interest of each state involved in pursuing the underlying purpose of each competing rule. Where the purposes of the statutes conflicted the forum should apply its own law. Currie argued that foreign law should only be applied where the forum had no interest in applying its own law or if the interest of the forum state

52 Ibid 48.
53 Ibid 70.
54 Eg Art 4.3 Rome I and Art 4.3 Rome II.
55 First Restatement of Conflicts of Laws (1934).
56 DE Cavers, 'A Critique of the choice of Law Problem', (1933) 47 Harv L Rev 173–208.
57 WW Cook, 'The Logical and Legal Bases of the Conflict of Laws' (1924) 33 Yale LJ 457–488.
58 B Currie, *Selected Essays on the Conflict of Laws* (Duke University Press 1963), 177–187.

was much less than that of the other competing state. Currie was indifferent to the private interests of the individuals in the conflict.

For example, a vulnerable individual in State A and a corporation in State B enter into a contract. Under the law of State A, the contract is invalid; the policy is that vulnerable individuals should be protected from making unwise contractual decisions. Under the law of State B, the contract would be upheld; the policy is to ensure the certainty of commercial transactions. This is a conflict of values. If the case is heard in State B, the contract will be upheld. If it is heard in State A, the contract will be void.

Robert Leflar[59] argued that the courts should give the real reasons for their choices rather than hiding behind mechanical rules and the language of conflicts justice. He proposed five factors that the courts should consider when resolving conflicts problems – predictability, maintenance of international and interstate order, simplification of the judicial task, advancement of the judicial task and the application of the 'better rule' of law. The 'better law' approach was later criticised as merely a cover for applying *lex fori*. Judges could generally be expected to think that their own law was preferable to foreign law in terms of fairness.

Some of the ideas of these commentators were given expression in the Second Restatement of Conflicts of Laws published by the American Law Institute in 1969. Section 6 of the restatement expressly steers the courts away from an approach based purely on geographical connections to an approach that considers policy and justice concerns.

1.11 Further reading

P McEleavy, 'The Brussels II Regulation: How the European Community has moved in Family Law' (2002) 51 *International and Comparative Law Quarterly* 883–908.

T Hartley 'Pleading and Proof of Foreign Law: The Major European Systems Compared' (1996) 45 *International and Comparative Law Quarterly* 271–292.

AJE Jaffey, 'The Foundations of Rules for the Choice of Law' (1982) 2 *Oxford Journal of Legal Studies*, 368–392.

SC Symeonides, *The American Choice of Law Revolution: Past, Present and Future* (Brill: Martinus Nijhoff Publishers, 2006).

A Schulz, 'The Accession of the European Community to the Hague Conference on Private International Law' (2007) 56 ICLQ 938–949.

59 R Leflar, 'Choice Influencing Considerations in Conflict Law' (1966) 41 NYU L Rev 267–327; R Leflar 'Conflicts of Law: More on Choice influencing Considerations' (1966) 54 Cal L Rev 1584–1598.

Chapter 2

Connecting Factors

Chapter Contents

Key Issues:

- Introduction to connecting factors
- Domicile
- Habitual residence
- How connecting factors are used in EU regulations

2.1 Introduction

As people become more internationally mobile, they create connections with a number of different countries. It is now quite common for an individual to move abroad to go to university or to work for a few years. This individual is connected both to the country of his birth and the country to which he has moved. In private international law these connections are referred to as 'connecting factors'.

Connecting factors help the courts to quantify a person's connection to a country. While it seems obvious that an English person who has established his permanent home in England is most appropriately governed by English law, the situation of a German person living in Greece may not be so clear. It is not immediately obvious how strongly connected the German person is to the Greek legal system. Has he been there for a long time? Does he intend to become part of Greek society or is he just passing through? Private international law uses a list of defined 'connecting factors' to measure an individual's connection to a particular country in order to establish jurisdiction and to determine applicable law.

This chapter will examine the most common connecting factors used in English conflict of laws. In each case, it will look at how the connection is acquired and whether the connection is easily changed.

2.2 Domicile

The English common law has traditionally used the concept of domicile as a key connecting factor in private international law. Domicile refers to an individual's one and only permanent home.

The common law concept of domicile was developed during the nineteenth century when people were less internationally mobile than they are today. Most people lived and died in the same place and in most cases were only ever connected to one legal system. The task of identifying an individual's permanent home was, in general, very straightforward. In the words of Lord Cranworth:

> If you do not understand your permanent home, I'm afraid that no illustration drawn from foreign writers or foreign languages will very much help you to it.[1]

However, it is rather more difficult to establish an individual's one permanent home when he has lived in a number of countries. In the twenty-first century, as individuals become more internationally mobile, the common law definition of domicile has become an increasingly artificial concept, far removed from the practicalities of modern life. In *Agulian v Cyganik*,[2] Longmore LJ described domicile as an antiquated notion and suggested that its use as a connecting factor should be reconsidered.[3]

1 *Whicker v Hume* (1858) 7 HL Cas 124, 160.
2 [2006] EWCA Civ 129.
3 Ibid [58].

In the 1980s a new statutory definition of domicile[4] was developed and this is now used in all cases involving civil and commercial disputes. This includes matters falling under Brussels I,[5] Rome I[6] and Rome II.[7] The old common law definition of domicile is still used to establish jurisdiction under Brussels II *bis*[8] and for a variety of family law and taxation matters.

This section will look at how a **common law domicile** is acquired and lost. It will then go on to examine the definition of **statutory domicile**.

2.2.1 Common law domicile

The English common law domicile can be defined as the country in which an individual has his home and intends to live permanently.[9] It is made up of two components that must be proved: the location of the individual's home and the individual's intention. Domicile is a relatively permanent connecting factor which is not easily changed.

Three rules are helpful in understanding how the common law concept of domicile is acquired and changed:

(a) Everyone is born with a domicile which they keep throughout life unless they acquire a new one.
(b) An individual can only have one domicile at any time.
(c) An individual can never be without a domicile.

When an English court needs to establish an individual's common law domicile it will use English law[10] unless a statutory exception applies.[11]

The concept of common law domicile is used today for determining the capacity of an individual to enter into marriage[12] or a contract.[13] Common law domicile is also used to ascertain jurisdiction over divorce proceedings[14] and proceedings for financial relief[15] and other areas of family law.[16] Common law domicile is used to establish liability for taxation of foreign income and jurisdiction over bankruptcy proceedings.[17] The law governing inheritance of moveable property is governed by the law of the testator's domicile at the date of his/her death.[18] The concept of common law domicile is used by Brussels II *bis* as one of the alternate grounds of jurisdiction.[19]

---

4 S 41(2) Civil Jurisdiction and Judgments Act 1982.
5 Regulation (EC) No 44/2001 on jurisdiction and the recognition and enforcement of judgments in civil and commercial matters [2001] OJ L12/1 (Brussels I).
6 Regulation (EC) No 593/2008 on the law applicable to contractual obligations [2008] L177/6 (Rome I).
7 Regulation (EC) No 864/2007 on the law applicable to non- contractual obligations [2007] OJ L299/40 (Rome II).
8 Art 3(2) Regulation (EC) No 2201/2003 concerning jurisdiction and the recognition and enforcement of judgments in matrimonial matters and matters of parental responsibility [2003] OJ 338/1 (Brussels II *bis*).
9 Private International Law Committee, *First Report* (Cmd 9068, 1954) [6].
10 *Re Martin* [1900] P 211.
11 Eg under s 46(5) of the Family Law Act 1986, a party to a marriage is considered to be domiciled in a foreign country if he is domiciled there within the meaning of English law or within the meaning of the family law of that country.
12 See Chapter 10.
13 *Baindail v Baindail* [1946] P 122, 128 (CA).
14 Where Brussels II *bis* does not apply, s 5 Domicile and Matrimonial Proceedings Act 1973.
15 S 15 Matrimonial and Family Proceedings Act 1984.
16 S 55A Family Law Act 1986; s 54 of Human Fertilisation and Embryology Act 2008; s 1 Inheritance (Provision for Family and Dependants) Act 1975.
17 S 265 Insolvency Act 1986.
18 *Somerville v Somerville* (1801) 5 Ves 750.
19 See *NDO v JFO* [2007] EWHC 1274 (Fam).

2.2.2 Domicile of origin

A person's **domicile of origin** is acquired at birth and depends on the marital status of his parents. If a child is born into a marital family, his domicile of origin will be the same as the domicile of his father at the time of the birth. This may not be the same as the country of the child's birth. For example, if a child is born in France to an English domiciliary, the child will have an English domicile of origin.

A child born to parents who are not married at the time of his birth will acquire his mother's domicile of origin.[20]

A person will retain his domicile of origin for life unless he acquires a different domicile either by choice or by dependency. A person's domicile of origin is given great importance under the English common law. It is more difficult to lose a domicile of origin than it is to lose a domicile of choice.[21] If a person loses a domicile of choice the domicile of origin will revive to fill the gap.[22]

2.2.3 Domicile of dependency

If a person does not have legal capacity, his domicile may be dependent on the domicile of the person who is legally responsible for his well-being. This is known as the domicile of dependency. Before 1974, a woman acquired the domicile of her husband upon marriage. Her domicile then changed as the domicile of her husband changed. The 'dependent wife's domicile' was abolished by s 1 of the Domicile and Matrimonial Proceedings Act (DMPA) 1973. Today wives acquire an independent domicile in the same fashion as any other individual. Children under the age of 16 and mentally incapacitated adults remain subject to a domicile of dependency.

A dependent person does not have legal capacity to change their permanent home. Therefore, they cannot acquire a new domicile by choice. The domicile of children under the age of 16 changes with the domicile of the person on whom they are legally dependent.[23] This means that if this parent acquires a domicile of choice in a new country, the child's domicile will also change. This could occur where the whole family moves permanently to another country for employment reasons.

At common law, the domicile of a **child born to married parents** changes with that of his **father** as long as his father is alive, and the parents are living together. This reflects the presumption that, at common law, the husband of the child's mother is presumed to be the child's father. If a marital child's father dies, the child's domicile will become dependent on his mother's domicile. Section 4 of the Domicile and Matrimonial Proceedings Act 1973 provides that where a child's married parents are living apart, the child's domicile shall be that of his mother if he has his home with her and no home with his father. This could occur where married parents live apart or where they divorce.[24]

If a **child is born to unmarried parents**, his domicile will change according to the domicile of his mother. If his mother dies, the child will retain the domicile his mother had at the time of her death.[25] This rule would seem to apply where a child is born to a couple who are in a civil partnership.

Where a child reaches the age of 16, or marries,[26] he becomes capable of having an independent domicile.[27] The child will retain his domicile of dependence as a domicile of choice. In

---

20 *Udny v Udny* (1869) LR 1 SC & Div 441.

21 See *Winans v Attorney General* [1904] AC 287; *Liverpool Royal infirmary v Ramsay* [1930] AC 588; *Cyganik v Agulian* [2006] EWCA Civ 129.

22 *Udny v Udny* (1866–69) LR 1 SC. 441.

23 S 3 Domicile and Matrimonial Proceedings Act 1973.

24 *Petitioner Williams* (1977) SLT (Notes) 2.

25 S 4(3) Domicile and Matrimonial Proceedings Act 1973.

26 The minimum age for marriage in England is 16; S 2 Marriage Act 1949. However, the rule could be applicable where a child domiciled abroad marries in that country; *Mohamed v Knott* [1969] 1 QB 1.

27 S 3 Domicile and Matrimonial Proceedings Act 1973.

Henderson v Henderson,[28] a man was born to a father with Scottish domicile. Before Henderson reached the age of majority, his father acquired a domicile of choice in England. The court held that on the age of majority, Henderson was domiciled in England.[29]

If a child is adopted, the child's domicile will become dependent on his adoptive father if the adoptive parents are married or on the domicile of his adoptive mother where the adoptive parents are unmarried.[30] It is unclear what will occur to the child's domicile if adopted by a single man,[31] or by a same-sex couple.[32]

Section 54 of the Human Fertilisation and Embryology Act 2008 allows the court to make a parental order transferring legal parenthood from a surrogate mother to intentional parents. Such an order allows the child to be treated in law as the child of the applicants. It would seem that in most cases a parental order will mean that the child's domicile will become dependent on that of his intentional parents. Again it is unclear what will occur if the order is made in favour of a same-sex couple.

Adults who lack mental capacity[33] retain the domicile that existed on the date that the incapacity began. Their domicile becomes immutable. Where the onset of mental incapacity occurred while a person was still a child the domicile of that person remains dependent on parental domicile.[34]

The idea of dependent domicile was criticised in the Law Commission Report in 1987. The rules were considered to discriminate between legitimate and illegitimate children. It was also felt that the rules inadequately dealt with cases where children were abandoned or taken into the care of the local authorities or where the parents died.[35] In addition, the rules of children's dependent domicile can be criticised as failing to take into account changes to family law in the UK such as the introduction of civil partnership and developments in assisted human reproduction.

In 1987 it was suggested that a child should be domiciled in the country with which he is most closely connected at that time.[36] In most cases this would mean that the child would have the same domicile as the child's parent with whom he lived.[37] The proposed reforms were never implemented in the UK and were formally abandoned in 1996.[38]

In 2006 the Scottish Parliament reformed the rules for domicile for children[39] following suggestions from the Scottish Law Commission.[40] According to Scots law, a child will have the same domicile as his parents where the parents are domiciled in the same country and the child has a home with at least one of them. Where this is not the case, the child shall be domiciled in the country with which the child has for the time being the closest connection. As these provisions abolish any reference to marriage they are more suited to an age of civil partnership and artificial reproduction.

For most international regulation relating to children, habitual residence is the preferred connecting factor.[41]

---

28 *Henderson v Henderson* [1967] P 77.
29 Ibid 82.
30 S 67 Adoption and Children Act 2002.
31 S 51 Adoption and Children Act 2002.
32 S 50 Adoption and Children Act 2002.
33 Within the meaning of s 2 of the Mental Capacity Act 2005.
34 Law Commission, *Private International Law: The Law of Domicile* (Law Com 168, 1987), [6.2]–[6.4]
35 Ibid [3.2].
36 Ibid [4.13].
37 Ibid [4.16].
38 Hansard HC vol 269 cols 488.489w, 16 Jan 1996.
39 S 22 Family Law (Scotland) Act 2006.
40 Scottish Law Commission, *Report on Family Law* (Scot Law Com No 135, 1992).
41 Brussels II *bis*; Hague Convention on Protection of Children and Co-operation in Respect of Intercountry Adoption 1993; Hague Convention on Civil Aspects of International Child Abduction 1980.

2.2.4 Acquiring a domicile of choice

A domicile of choice is acquired when an individual moves from his country of origin to **reside in another country** with the **intention of remaining there permanently**. This might happen where an English person moves to Spain upon retirement to live out the rest of their days in a better climate. A domicile of choice is based on the combination of residence and intention. **Both the elements of residence and intention** must be satisfied before English law can recognise a change in domicile.

2.2.4.1 Residence

Residence in the new homeland is a question of fact. In *IRC v Duchess of Portland*[42] residence was defined as 'physical presence in that country **as an inhabitant of it**'.[43] This means that more than mere physical presence is required. Presence in a country for the purposes of a holiday or a flight transfer does not amount to residence. The length of residence is not crucial. In *Re Flynn*[44] Errol Flynn had spent limited periods of time in Jamaica, where he was in the process of building a house. Megarry J held that, although Flynn's movie star career took him to many parts of the world, Jamaica had become his 'centre of gravity'.[45] Accordingly, he had acquired a Jamaican domicile of choice.

Although the length of residence is not crucial, it must be proved that residence occurred after the age of majority. In *Harrison v Harrison*,[46] a husband was born in South Africa with an English domicile of origin. He married his wife in New Zealand when he was 20 years old. The husband planned to set up a business in New Zealand training his own horses, and live there permanently. He decided to travel to England for a period of training. The couple arrived in England on 27 March 1951, and, while still in England, the husband turned 21, the age of majority in 1951. The court held that the husband had not acquired a domicile of choice in New Zealand. He had the intention to make New Zealand his permanent home, but he had not lived in New Zealand since he had reached the age of majority.

Illegal residence in a country can satisfy the residence requirement. In *Mark v Mark*[47] a Nigerian husband and wife divided their time between England and Nigeria. The wife's right to remain in the UK had expired and her stay in England had become illegal. The wife sought a decree of divorce from the English courts. Section 5(2)(a) of the DMPA 1973 gave the court jurisdiction if she had acquired an English domicile of choice. Thorpe LJ held that as this was a family law case, an area where the courts have discretion, the court could decide whether or not the element of illegality should preclude the acquisition of a domicile of choice.[48] In the House of Lords, it was held that illegality of the stay might be a relevant factor when considering whether the wife had the intent to remain in England permanently but her presence in England was a matter of fact.[49]

It is possible for an individual to be resident in several countries at the same time but it is only possible to have one domicile. In *Plummer v Inland Revenue Commissioners*,[50] a taxpayer tried to establish that she was domiciled in Guernsey. She only spent brief periods in Guernsey and maintained her main residence in England. Hoffman J held that although domicile could be established from a very short period of residence[51] it was difficult to draw an inference of a permanent intention to settle

42 [1982] Ch 312.
43 Ibid 318–319.
44 [1968] 1 WLR 103.
45 Ibid 119.
46 [1953] 1 WLR 865.
47 [2005] UKHL 42.
48 Ibid 38.
49 *Witkowska v Kaminski* [2006] EWHC 1940 (Ch).
50 *Plummer v IRC* [1988] 1 WLR 292.
51 *IRC v Duchess of Portland* [1982] Ch 312.

where the person divides their time between two countries. In such a case, a domicile of choice can only be acquired in the country of chief residence.[52]

2.2.4.2 Intention

A person acquiring a domicile of choice must have the intention **to reside in the new homeland permanently or indefinitely**.[53] Factors the court can consider as evidence of this intention include whether the language of the country has been learned,[54] exercising the right to vote and making a will relating only to assets held in the country in question.[55] Residence that is intended to be only for a limited period of time or for a particular purpose does not satisfy the necessary intention to acquire a domicile of choice.[56]

The courts have differed in their approach to establishing if the necessary intention exists to acquire a domicile of choice. In early cases, the courts looked for a strong positive intention to acquire a domicile of choice that could be objectively ascertained.

In *Ramsey v Liverpool Royal Infirmary*,[57] George Bowie, who was born in Glasgow in 1845 with a Scottish domicile of origin, had moved to Liverpool in 1892. When he first came to Liverpool, he lived in lodgings, but when his brother died 21 years later, he moved into his house, where he lived with his sole surviving sister until she died in 1920. He remained there until he died, unmarried, in 1927. He remained in England for the last 36 years of his life, except for one short visit to the USA and one trip to the Isle of Man on holiday. He expressed a determination never to return to Glasgow. In fact, he did not even attend his mother's funeral, and he arranged for his own burial in Liverpool.

The House of Lords unanimously held that when Bowie died he was domiciled in Scotland. The court held that there was no positive intention to acquire English domicile; Bowie remained in England out of indifference.[58] In the absence of evidence of an intention to acquire English domicile, Bowie retained his Scottish domicile.

A similar approach was taken in *Winans v AG*,[59] where Lord Macnaghen held that the intention to change a domicile of origin 'is not to be inferred from an attitude of indifference or a disinclination to move increasing with increasing years'.

The two House of Lords decisions seemed to establish a trend that the requirement of intention to remain indefinitely would not be satisfied if there was even a vague hope of returning to the country of origin.

Other cases took a more flexible approach to the understanding of an 'intention to remain permanently or indefinitely'. *In the Estate of Fuld (no 3)*[60] Scarman J observed that no intention was present where a man intends to return to the land of his birth upon a clearly foreseen and reasonably anticipated contingency, for example the end of a job. However, if he only entertained a vague possibility of going home, such as if he won the lottery, such a state of mind can be considered to provide intention to reside indefinitely.[61]

In *IRC v Bullock*[62] Mr Bullock, whose domicile of origin was Canadian, came to England in order to join the Royal Air Force. While still in service, he married an English woman. He wished to return to Canada after leaving the RAF, but did not do so, because his wife disliked the idea.

---

52 *Plummer v IRC* [1988] 1 WLR 292, 296.
53 *Bell v Kennedv* (1868) LR 1 Sc & Div 307, 321.
54 *Irvin v Irvin* [2001] 1 FLR 178.
55 *Morgan v Cilento & Others* [2004] WTLR 457.
56 *Udny v Udny* (1866–69) LR 1 SC 441, 458; *Cramer v Cramer* [1987] 1 FLR 116.
57 [1930] AC 588.
58 Ibid 593.
59 [1904] AC 287, 291.
60 [1968] P 675, 684–685.
61 See also *Re Furze* [1980] 3 All ER 838.
62 [1976] 2 All ER 353.

Nevertheless, if his wife were to predecease him, it was his intention to return to Canada. The Court of Appeal held that although the establishment of a matrimonial home in a new country was an important factor in deciding whether that new country had become the permanent home, it was not conclusive. Mr Bullock had maintained a firm intention to return to Canada should he survive his wife, which was not unlikely to occur. Therefore, he had no intention of establishing a permanent home in England and had not acquired a domicile of choice there.[63]

In *Cyganik v Agulian*,[64] the Court of Appeal returned to the approach of looking for a strong positive intention to acquire the domicile of choice. The deceased was from Cyprus but had lived in London on and off for 43 years. He had a business in London but retained strong links with Cyprus. The deceased had not actually expressed his intention as to whether he intended to make England his permanent home or ultimately return to Cyprus. He told different people different things. In the last years of his life he became engaged to be married and showed no intention of retiring from his business in England. After he died, his fiancée applied for financial provision under s 1 of the Inheritance Act 1975. Mummery LJ noted that when establishing the domicile of an individual at his death the court must look back over the whole of the deceased's life.[65] In this case the deceased had clearly been domiciled in Cyprus until the age of 55. The issue in the case was whether his engagement was sufficient evidence to show that he had changed his mind about his permanent home. The deceased had retained a Cypriot domicile in spite of long-term residence in England, and the birth of two children there.[66] The court held that in these circumstances the engagement did not transform his domicile status.

This approach, that a strong positive intention is required to discard the domicile of origin and acquire a domicile of choice, has been followed in several recent cases. In *Davies v Morris*,[67] emails from the deceased stating that he intended to reside in Belgium indefinitely were not considered to be evidence of intent to acquire Belgian domicile.[68] In *Holliday v Musa*[69] it was held that the longer the residence and the more it becomes home, the more likely the inference that there is the intention to reside permanently and indefinitely. However, there must be a clear intention of settling finally in the new domicile and abandoning the domicile of origin.[70]

2.2.5 Abandoning a domicile of choice

It is not possible to change a domicile of origin without acquiring a domicile of choice. The domicile of choice will adhere until a domicile of choice is acquired.[71] However, it is possible for a person to abandon their domicile of choice without acquiring a new one.[72] In order to abandon a domicile of choice a person must cease to reside there *and* cease to intend to reside there permanently.[73]

In *Morgan v Cilento*,[74] the deceased acquired a domicile of choice in Queensland, Australia[75] where he lived with his wife. He owned a restaurant business there and had built his dream home. He retained a home in London for occasional work and travelled to London regularly for medical treatment. There he started a relationship with another woman. He was considering divorcing his

63 See also *Hoskins v Matthews* [1856] 8 De GM & G 13; *Donaldson v Donaldson* [1949] P 363.
64 [2006] EWCA Civ 129.
65 Ibid [46].
66 Ibid [50].
67 [2011] EWHC 1773 (Ch).
68 Ibid [71].
69 [2010] EWCA Civ 335.
70 Ibid [23].
71 *Bell v Kennedy* (1868) LR 1 Sc & Div 307.
72 *Henwood v Barlow Clowes International Ltd* [2008] EWCA Civ 577 [148].
73 *Re Flynn* [1968] 1 WLR 103, 115.
74 [2004] EWHC 188 (Ch).
75 Ibid [73].

wife when he died in London. The court held that he had not abandoned his domicile of choice in Queensland as he had not yet made up his mind to abandon his life in Australia.

Once a domicile of choice is abandoned, the domicile of origin revives until another domicile of choice is acquired.[76] The revival of the domicile of origin is a matter of law. There is no need for the person to have any intention to reside in his domicile of origin.[77]

In *Udny v Udny*,[78] the court had to determine the domicile of the respondent's father at the time of his (the respondent's) birth. His father had been born in Scotland but had left Scotland and taken a lease of a house in London. He visited Scotland frequently but had no residence there. The court held that he had acquired a domicile of choice in England. In 1844, he sold the lease and his personal possessions and left London for France to avoid his creditors. But he did not intend to reside permanently in France. He formed a liaison with the respondent's mother who, in 1853, gave birth to the respondent in London. He married her and went back to Scotland, where he thought he would be safe from his creditors.

The House of Lords held that the respondent's father had lost his domicile of choice in England when he left to go to France and that his domicile of origin had revived. He had no intention to acquire a domicile of choice in France and so when the son was born his father was domiciled in England.[79]

In *Henwood v Barlow Clowes International Ltd*[80] the jurisdiction of the English court over a bankruptcy claim was challenged on the basis that the debtor was not domiciled in England and Wales. Henwood was originally domiciled in England and Wales but acquired a domicile of choice on the Isle of Man. He left the Isle of Man in 1992 and went to Mauritius to take up an offer of employment and leased a property on an experimental basis. The court held that Henwood had abandoned his domicile of choice on the Isle of Man in 1992. He himself asserted that he no longer had the intention to reside there permanently or indefinitely. The question to be decided was whether he had acquired a new domicile of choice in Mauritius or whether his domicile of origin had been revived.

The Court of Appeal stated that it would be absurd to suggest that he had immediately acquired a domicile of choice in Mauritius. He was only resident there on a trial basis.[81] Once Henwood had abandoned his domicile on the Isle of Man, Henwood's domicile was his domicile of origin.[82]

In 1987 the Law Commission suggested that an adult's domicile of choice should continue until he acquired a new domicile.

2.2.6 Proving a change of domicile

In *Re Flynn*, it was noted that the court cannot read a man's mind but merely draw inferences from what he has said and done during his life.[83] The burden of proving a change in domicile falls on the person alleging that the change has occurred.[84]

Case law differs on the standard of proof needed to prove a change in domicile. Older cases lean towards a heavy burden of proof beyond the civil standard of a strong intention to acquire a new domicile. For example, in *Moorhouse v Lord*[85] 'clear and unequivocal proof was required'. In

76 *Tee v Tee* [1973] 2 All ER 1105.
77 *Henwood v Barlow Clowes International Ltd* [2008] EWCA Civ 577 [119].
78 (1869) LR 1 Sc & Div 441.
79 This meant that the son could be legitimated under Scottish law.
80 [2008] EWCA Civ 577.
81 Ibid [14].
82 Ibid [118].
83 *Winans v Attorney General (No 1)* [1904] AC 287, 288; *Re Flynn* [1968] 1 WLR 103, 107.
84 *Re Flynn* [1968] 1 WLR 103, 115.
85 (1863) 10 HL Cas 272, 286.

Winans v Attorney General (No 1)[86] Lord Macnaghton suggested that a heavy burden of proof to prove the change with perfect clearness and satisfaction existed.[87]

In later cases the civil standard of proof on the balance of probabilities was used. For example, in *Re Fuld (No 3)*[88] Scarman J held that the criminal standard was inappropriate and there must simply be enough evidence of change that the conscience of the court is satisfied.[89] This was followed in *Buswell v IRC*.[90]

In 1987 the Law Commission recommended that the normal civil burden of proof on the balance of probability should apply.[91]

In *Cyganik v Agulian*[92] Mummery J again referred to the need for a clear case to be established that domicile had changed.[93] In *Henwood* the court drew attention to the inbuilt flexibility of the standard of proof to take the seriousness of an allegation into account. Accordingly the more serious an allegation the more substantial will need to be the evidence to prove it on a balance of probabilities.[94] Perfect clearness and satisfaction[95] were again required but the court also stated that the evidence required in a particular case will depend on the application of common sense to the particular circumstances.[96]

2.2.7 Criticisms of common law domicile

There have been many attempts to modernise the use of common law domicile in England but with the exception of the abolition of dependent domicile for married women in 1974, no significant changes have been made. In 1954, the First Report of the Private International Law Committee identified two problems with the concept of common law domicile.[97] It was felt that too much importance was given to the domicile of origin. The heavy burden of proof required to prove that a domicile of origin had changed meant that people retained a domicile when they had no real connection to that place. The rule that the domicile of origin revives to fill a gap causes the same problem.

The second problem identified was the quality of intention required to prove a change in domicile. It was unclear if a strong positive intention to acquire a new domicile was needed or if a more flexible approach could be used.

The Committee recommended that these defects be cured by abolishing the doctrine of the revival of the domicile of origin and establishing rebuttable presumptions as to a person's domicile. A person should be presumed to intend to live permanently in the country in which he had his home.[98] The proposals of the 1954 report faced strong political opposition from the supporters of foreign businessmen who feared that the proposed reforms would make them liable for increased income tax and estate duties and were never implemented.[99]

The Private International Law Committee looked again at domicile and reported in 1963.[100] A businessman's exception to the presumptions of domicile was suggested but it was concluded that the changes were hardly worth making if businessmen were excluded.[101]

86 [1904] AC 287.
87 Ibid 291.
88 [1968] P 675.
89 Ibid 685.
90 *Buswell v IRC* [1974] 1 WLR 1631, 1637.
91 Law Commission, *Private International Law: The Law of Domicile* (Law Com 168, 1987) 43.
92 [2006] EWCA Civ 129.
93 Ibid [49].
94 [2008] EWCA Civ 577 [88]. This case quoted *Re H and others (minors) (sexual abuse: standard of proof)* [1996] AC 563, 586–587. This approach to the burden of proof was clarified in *Re B* [2008] UKHL 35.
95 [2008] EWCA Civ 577 [85].
96 Ibid [94].
97 Private International Law Committee, *First Report* (Cmd 9068, 1954) [8]–[9] and [14].
98 Ibid [15].
99 Hansard HL vol 214 cols 240–243, 12 Feb. See further, M Mann, 'The Domicile Bills' (1959) 8 ICLQ 457.
100 Private International Law Committee, *Seventh Report (Law of Domicile)* (Cmd 1955, 1963).
101 Ibid [17] and [34(6)].

In the 1980s the Law Commission looked whether common law domicile should be retained as a connecting factor.[102] It recommended that common law domicile should be retained but that the rules relating to domicile of children should be changed. In addition it was suggested that a domicile of choice should continue until another domicile of choice was acquired.[103] The Law Commission put forward a draft bill but this was never taken forward. In 1996 plans to reform the law of domicile were formally abandoned.[104]

In 2002, the Treasury invited comment on the use of domicile for tax purposes.[105] No changes were made.[106] McEleavy argues that a complete overhaul of the concept of domicile is necessary but that no political will to do so currently exists.[107] As common law domicile is used for different reasons in a variety of distinct areas of law, any attempts to reform the concept or its use tend to be sunk by conflicting policy concerns.

2.2.8 Statutory domicile

Domicile was used as the primary connecting factor under the Brussels Convention 1968.[108] Domicile was not defined for the purposes of this Convention. To do so would go beyond the scope of the Convention and impose uniform substantive law.[109] The basic concept of domicile was similar in the laws of the original contracting states.[110] It described the place where the person primarily lived. The text of the Convention left England and Ireland free to use their domestic concepts of domicile. However, the working party felt that this would create an imbalance in the application of the Convention as the common law definition was substantially different. Ireland and England would assume jurisdiction in many cases where the laws of the other Member States would hold that the person was domiciled at their residence within a different Member State. Ireland and England were specifically requested to come up with a new definition of domicile for the purpose of the Brussels Convention which reflect the concept of domicile 'as understood in the original States of the EEC'.[111]

Brussels I[112] uses domicile as defined by national law as an important connecting factor in establishing jurisdiction over civil and commercial matters. The rules of Brussels I will, in general, only apply where the defendant is domiciled in an EU Member State.[113] Article 59 allows courts to use a national definition of domicile when deciding if the person is domiciled in that Member State. If the defendant is not domiciled in the same country as the court seised, the court shall apply the law of another Member State.[114] For example, if the English courts decide that the claimant is not domiciled in England but may be domiciled in France the court must use French law to determine if the person is in fact domiciled in France as a matter of French law.

102 Law Commission, *Private International Law: The Law of Domicile* (Law Com WP 88, 1985); Law Commission, *Private International Law: The Law of Domicile* (Law Com 168, 1987).

103 Law Commission, *Private International Law: The Law of Domicile* (Law Com 168, 1987).

104 Hansard HC vol 269 cols 488–489w, 16 Jan 1996.

105 *Reviewing the Residence and Domicile Rules as they Affect the Taxation of Individuals: A Background Paper* (HM Treasury & Inland Revenue, 2003), www.hm-treasury.gov.uk/media/A37/8B/adres273kb03.pdf (accessed 24 May 2013).

106 HM Revenue and Customs, 'Residence, domicile and the remittance basis' (HMRC6 revised 2010) 12–21.

107 P McEleavy, 'Regression and Reform in the law of Domicile' (2007) ICLQ 453–462, 462.

108 Arts 2–4, Brussels Convention [2008] OJ C27/1.

109 P Jenard, 'Report on the Convention on jurisdiction and the enforcement of judgments in civil and commercial matters' [1979] OJ 59/1, 15.

110 P Schlosser, 'Report on the Convention on the Association of the Kingdom of Denmark, Ireland and the United Kingdom of Great Britain and Northern Ireland to the Convention on jurisdiction and the enforcement of judgments in civil and commercial matters and to the Protocol on its interpretation by the Court of Justice' [1979] OJ C59/71 [71].

111 Ibid [73].

112 Council Regulation (EC) No 44/2001 of 22 December 2000 on jurisdiction and the recognition and enforcement of judgments in civil and commercial matters, [2001] OJ L12/1.

113 Recital (8); Arts 2–4. Arts 22 and 23 may apply where the defendant is not domiciled in a Member State. See Chapter 3.

114 Art 59(2).

Section 41(2) of the Civil Jurisdiction and Judgments Act (CJJA) 1982 introduced a statutory definition of domicile of private individuals into English law. This definition is used for cases falling under the Brussels Convention, Lugano Convention or the Brussels I regulation.[115]

There are marked differences between the common law definition of domicile and the statutory definition of domicile under s 41(2). A individual is domiciled in the United Kingdom within the meaning of s 41(2) if he is resident in the UK and the nature and circumstances of his residence indicate that he has a substantial connection with the United Kingdom. There is no need to establish a permanent home under the Act. Under this definition it is also possible for an individual to have more than one domicile.

The same criteria apply to determine whether an individual is domiciled in a part of the UK, i.e. Northern Ireland, Scotland or England and Wales; however, the presumption of three months' residence cannot be used for this purpose.

The question of determining statutory domicile is one of fact. *Canada Trust Co v Stolzenberg* (No 2)[116] established that the burden of proof is on the claimant to show a good arguable case that the defendant is domiciled in the jurisdiction. Furthermore, the court looks at domicile at the time of issue, not service of the claim form.[117] In *Petrotrade Inc v Smith*[118] Thomas J held that where the defendant would have returned to Switzerland after a few days of his arrest had it not been for the condition imposed as a term of his bail that he must remain in the UK, there was no good arguable case that he was domiciled in the UK for the purposes of the Brussels Convention. Furthermore, his enforced presence in the UK did not indicate a 'substantial connection' with the country as required by s 41 of the CJJA 1982.

The Heidelberg Report[119] of 2007 highlighted the great scope in the definitions of domicile in the national laws of the Member States. It was suggested that a definition based on objective criteria such as length of residence would be preferable to this disparity. This would make it easier for courts to establish if the defendant was domiciled in another Member State and avoid the application of foreign law. The proposals for reforming Brussels I retained use of national law for determining the domicile of private individuals.[120] However, in Brussels I recast, it is clear that domicile will be defined autonomously.[121]

2.2.9 Domicile of corporations

Under Art 60 of Brussels I, a company or other legal organisation is domiciled in the place where it has its statutory seat or central administration or principal place of business. Article 60(2) assists the English courts when they must decide if a company is domiciled in England on the basis of its statutory seat. In such a case 'statutory seat' means the registered office, place of incorporation or the place under the law of which the company was formed.

Under Art 22(2) the courts of the Member State must use their internal law to determine the seat of a company for the purposes of exclusive jurisdiction. For English courts this is defined by s 43 of the Civil Jurisdiction and Judgments Act 1982. A company will be considered to have its seat in the UK for the purposes of Art 22(2) if it was incorporated or formed under the law of a part of the United Kingdom or its central management and control is exercised in the United Kingdom.

In *King v Crown Energy Trading AC*,[122] the meaning of 'principal place of business' and 'central administration' under Art 60 was examined in the context of a company with offices in several countries.

115 The Civil Jurisdiction and Judgments Order 2001 (SI 2001/3929).
116 [2002] 1 AC 1.
117 *Provimi Ltd v Aventis Animal Nutrition SA* [2003] 2 All ER (Comm) 683.
118 [1999] 1 WLR 457.
119 Hess, Pfeiffer and Schlosser, *Report on the Application of Regulation Brussels I in the Member States* (Study JLS/C4/2005/03), 85.
120 COM (2010) 0748.
121 Brussels I recast, Recital (15).
122 [2003] IL Pr 28.

Common law domicile of choice

- Residence as an inhabitant of the country.
- Intention to make a permanent home in that country.
- Only one domicile possible.

s 41(2) Domicile

- Residence as a fact.
- Substantial connection with the country.
- More than one domicile possible.

Figure 2.1 Contrasting common law domicile of choice with statutory domicile

The court considered that the same approach could be adopted in relation to determining a company's principal place of business and the place of its central administration. The fact that a company carried out most of its business from a particular place did not necessarily mean that was its 'principal place of business'; that expression meant finding the place which was at the centre of operations. Here, 'that place' was found to be London, as most of the company's key executives were listed as being based at the London office, though they travelled between the offices in different countries.

2.3 Habitual residence

Habitual residence is used as a basis of jurisdiction under Brussels II *bis*.[123] Habitual residence is also commonly used in EU regulations as the primary connecting factor when designating the applicable law.[124] The connecting factor of habitual residence is also used by the Hague Conference[125] in many international Conventions. Habitual residence is also used in domestic English statutes.[126]

The meaning of habitual residence varies according to the context in which it arises. Within EU legislation, habitual residence means the place where the person has established his permanent or habitual centre of interests. This is assessed on a case-by-case basis. For EU purposes habitual residence has to be ascertained 'in the light of the aim and scheme of the Community legislation concerned'. Thus in cases relating to employment rights, the place of employment has been emphasised whereas in cases involving the habitual residence of children, importance is given to the best interests of the child.

The English definition of habitual residence is to give the phrase its ordinary meaning as a matter of fact. Habitual residence means a voluntary residence, for an appreciable period of time with a degree of settled purpose.[127]

123 Arts 3, 8 and 9.
124 Eg Rome I Arts 4–7. Rome II, Art 4(2) and Art 5. Rome III Art 8.
125 Such as the Hague Convention on the Civil Aspects of International Child Abduction and Protocol of 23 November 2007 on the Law Applicable to Maintenance Obligations.
126 S 47(3) Adoption and Children Act 2002; s 3 Family Law Act 1986.
127 *Kapur v Kapur* [1984] FLR 920, 926.

2.3.1 EU meaning of habitual residence

Habitual residence has now been adopted as a key connecting factor for choice of law in many EU regulations. The phrase 'habitual residence' is given an autonomous and uniform meaning. The CJEU has considered the meaning of the phrase 'habitual residence' in EU legislation in a number of cases.

In *Magdalena Fernández* v *Commission*, the ECJ held that a person's habitual residence was the place which the person has established as the permanent or habitual centre of his interests.[128] Thus a temporary change of residence did not affect habitual residence.

In *Swaddling v Adjudiciation Officer*[129] the ECJ contrasted the autonomous EU meaning of habitual residence with the English treatment of the term. The ECJ confirmed that in EU law, habitual residence refers to a person's habitual centre of interests.[130] This is to be determined by a national court on a case-by-case basis. In cases involving employment rights, account should be taken in particular of the employed person's family situation; the reasons which have led him to move; the length and continuity of his residence; the fact that he is in stable employment; and his intention as it appears from all the circumstances.

In contrast the requirement in English case law, for the claimant to have the settled intention of residing in the United Kingdom and have resided there for an appreciable period, were precluded by EU regulation.[131] Member States were not permitted to make entitlement dependent on the completion of an appreciable period of residence there.

In *Adanez-Vega*,[132] a case concerning employment benefits, the ECJ again referred to the establishment of a habitual centre of interests.

The meaning of 'habitual residence' as a basis for jurisdiction was considered in the Borras report.[133] It was felt that this connecting factor represented a genuine connection between the person and the Member State.[134] Habitual residence was widely accepted as a connecting factor by the Member States and would apply in most cases.[135] It was also consistent with the idea that a person would expect to be governed by the rules of the place where they take legal action. Borras referred to the autonomous meaning given to habitual residence by the ECJ as 'the place where the person had established, on a fixed basis, his permanent or habitual centre of interests, with all the relevant facts being taken into account for the purpose of determining such residence'.[136]

The English courts have accepted that for the purposes of Brussels II *bis*[137] an autonomous meaning of habitual residence exists which is different to the meaning given to 'habitual residence' in domestic law.[138]

In *Marinos v Marinos*,[139] Mumby J considered the meaning of habitual residence within the context of Brussels II *bis*. The case concerned an English wife who was a British flight attendant and a Greek husband. The couple had moved to Greece and stayed with family. The children went to school in Greece but the wife worked out of the UK and spent about equal time in the UK and Greece. She filed for divorce. Mumby J held that for the purposes of EU legislation 'habitually resident' meant 'the place where the person had established, on a fixed basis, his permanent or habitual centre of interests, with all the relevant facts being taken into account for the purpose of

128 C452/93 P, *Magdalena Fernandez* v Commission [1994] ECR I-4295 [22].
129 C90/97 [1999] ECR 1-1075 [29].
130 Ibid [29].
131 Council Regulation (EEC) No 1408/71 of 14 June 1971.
132 C372/02 *Adanez-Vega* [2004] ECR I-10761 [37].
133 Borras, Explanatory report on the Convention, drawn up on the basis of Art K.3 of the Treaty on European Union, on Jurisdiction and the Recognition and Enforcement of Judgments in Matrimonial Matters, [1998] OJ C221/27.
134 Ibid [30].
135 Ibid [31].
136 Ibid [32].
137 Implemented by s 2(1) of the Family Law Act 1986.
138 *C v FC (Brussels II: Free-Standing Application for Parental Responsibility)* [2004] 1 FLR 317 [98]; *L-K v K (No 2)* [2007] 2 FLR 729 [35].
139 [2007] 2 FLR 1018.

determining such residence'.[140] He noted that the previous ECJ case law had focused on workers' rights, so place of work had been influential. In this case, the place of the matrimonial home was also an important factor. He noted that the determination of habitual residence was highly fact specific.[141]

For the purposes of EU legislation, a person can only have one habitual residence and in this sense it was very different from the English definition of habitual residence.[142] All relevant legislation referred to one place of habitual residence. When someone was undertaking a planned, purposeful and permanent relocation from one country to another, there was nothing in Community law to prevent the acquisition of a new habitual residence contemporaneously or virtually contemporaneously with the loss of the previous habitual residence.[143]

In *Z v Z (divorce; jurisdiction)*[144] Ryder J reiterated that for the autonomous EU definition of habitual residence, the length of residence was not determinative. Instead the court should focus on the individual's centre of interest.[145] This need not be permanent but must be habitual and stable. A person could only have one habitual residence and intention was important.

The meaning of 'habitual residence' in Brussels II *bis* was considered by the ECJ in C523/07 *Re Proceeding Brought by A*.[146] This case concerned the jurisdiction of the Finnish courts to approve the decision of the Finnish national authorities to take three children into care. The children had previously been in state care in Finland. Subsequently they had been habitually resident in Sweden before returning to Finland for a holiday. While in Finland the family applied for social housing and the children were again taken into care. The jurisdiction of the Finnish authorities was challenged by their mother, who claimed that the children were Swedish nationals who had permanent residence in Sweden.

The court noted the need for provisions of EU law to be given an autonomous and uniform meaning throughout the EU.[147] The court drew attention to the need for meanings to be determined within the context of the objective pursued by the legislation in question and referred to recital 12 of Brussels II *bis*.[148] In light of this objective it was not possible to transpose the previous meanings given to habitual residence onto Art 8(1) of Brussels II *bis*. The habitual residence of a child must be established on the basis of all the circumstances specific to each individual case.[149] In addition to presence in the Member State some level of permanence and some level of integration in a social and family environment must be shown.[150] The duration, regularity, conditions and reasons for the stay on the territory of a Member State and the family's move to that State, the child's nationality, the place and conditions of attendance at school, linguistic knowledge and the family and social relationships of the child in that State must be taken into consideration.[151] The court indicated that a short presence in a Member State during which time the child spent a lot of time travelling about was an indication that no habitual residence existed.[152]

In *Mercredi v Chaffe*[153] the ECJ gave further guidance on how habitual residence was to be determined for children under Arts 8 and 10 of Brussels II *bis*.[154] The court approved the test laid down

---

140 Ibid [34], [36].
141 Ibid [73]. See also *Munro v Munro* [2007] EWHC 3315 (Fam), [2008] 1 FLR 1613.
142 Ibid [38], [40]–[43]
143 Ibid [89]–[90].
144 [2010] 1 FLR 694.
145 Ibid [40],[41], [44].
146 [2009] ECR I 2805.
147 Ibid [34].
148 Ibid [34]–[35].
149 Ibid [36]–[37].
150 Ibid [37].
151 Ibid [39].
152 Ibid [41].
153 C497/10 PPU, *Mercredi v Chaffe* [2011] 1 FLR 1293.
154 Ibid [47]–[57].

in *A* and held that to ensure that the best interests of the child are given the utmost consideration, habitual residence must be taken to mean the place which reflects some degree of integration by the child in a social and family environment.[155]

The national court should consider the conditions and reasons for the child's stay on the territory of a Member State, and the child's nationality.[156] Habitual residence must reflect an adequate degree of permanence.[157] As the integration into family and social environment is crucial, the factors to be taken into account in the case of a child of school age are thus not the same as those to be considered in the case of a child who has left school and are again not the same as those relevant to an infant.[158] An infant necessarily shares the social and family environment of the circle of people on whom he or she is dependent. Consequently, where, as in the main proceedings, the infant is in fact looked after by her mother, it is necessary to assess the mother's integration into her social and family environment.[159] There is no requirement for minimum duration but the court must consider the intention of the person with parental responsibility to establish a permanent or habitual centre of interests with the child in another Member State.[160]

The habitual residence of children is further explored in Chapter 13.

2.3.1.1 Habitual residence of companies

Article 23 of Rome II defines the habitual residence of companies for the purposes of Rome II. The habitual residence of companies and other bodies, corporate or unincorporated, is the place of central administration. The habitual residence of a natural person acting in the course of his or her business activity is his principal place of business.

2.3.2 English meaning of habitual residence

The English meaning of habitual residence is used in cases relating to the Hague Convention on the Civil Aspects of International Child Abduction given force by the Child Abduction and Custody Act 1985. These cases fall outside the Brussels II *bis* regulation.[161] The Convention applies to any child who was habitually resident in a Contracting State immediately before any breach of custody or access rights.[162] In order to make an order under the Hague Convention the court must determine if the child is habitually resident in a Contracting State.

For some divorce cases, habitual residence is used to determine if the court has jurisdiction to grant financial relief.[163] Habitual residence is also the jurisdictional basis for declarations of parenthood[164] and other orders relating to children.[165]

The English meaning of habitual residence is the same as the meaning given to ordinary residence.[166] The words are given their ordinary meaning. Habitual residence means a voluntary residence, with a degree of settled purpose.[167]

In determining a person's habitual residence, under a domestic statute, the English courts apply English law. In *Re A (Abduction: Habitual Residence)*[168] Cazalet J found that a US serviceman and his family

155 Ibid [47].
156 Ibid [10].
157 Ibid [51].
158 Ibid [53].
159 Ibid [55].
160 Ibid [50].
161 Art 60, Brussels II *bis*. The Convention also applies when the child is habitually resident in a non-EU State.
162 Art 4.
163 S 15 Matrimonial and Family Proceedings Act 1984.
164 S 55A Family Law Act 1986.
165 S 2 Family Law Act 1986
166 *Kapur v Kapur* [1984] FLR 920; *Shah v Barnet London Borough Council* [1983] 1 All ER 226.
167 *Kapur v Kapur* [1984] FLR 920, 926.
168 [1996] 1 WLR 25.

were habitually resident in Iceland during a posting there and not in Michigan as the serviceman alleged. Under the law of Michigan, the family was considered to be habitually resident in Michigan even if there was no presence there because the presence in Iceland was as part of an overseas military posting. Cazalet J interpreted the term 'habitual residence' in the Child Abduction and Custody Act 1985 as requiring physical presence under English law. Accordingly, when the family was settled in Iceland there was no habitual residence in Michigan.

As habitual residence is not considered to be a term of art but rather to reflect the natural meaning of the phrase it is considered to have the same meaning in all English statutes where it is used.[169] No consideration is given to the purpose of the statute in question. In *Ikimi v Ikimi*[170] Thorpe LJ found that it was essential that the term 'habitual residence' was accorded the same meaning in all family law statutes. Therefore the phrase has the same meaning in the context of jurisdiction for financial relief and under the Child Abduction and Custody Act 1985.[171] The courts have a degree of flexibility in determining habitual residence depending on the context in question.

In contrast to the EU meaning given to habitual residence, under the English definition of habitual residence a person can have more than one habitual residence.[172] In *Ikimi*[173] the couple had two marital homes and divided their time between them. Thorpe LJ held that the test should be flexible. In *Ikimi v Ikimi*, the claimant had spent five periods of time abroad during the relevant time where she was seeking to establish habitual residence in the UK. Thorpe LJ found there was just about sufficient residence in England to found jurisdiction.

In *Armstrong v Armstrong*[174] the husband was habitually resident in South Africa but worked as a deep-sea diver in the North Sea for considerable periods of time. He had a residence in England that he used as a stopping-off point on the way to jobs. The court held that he did not show a sufficient degree of continuity to be properly described as habitually resident in the UK.[175]

It is also possible for an individual to have no habitual residence. A person may cease to be habitually resident in a single day if he quits the country with a settled intention not to return but to take up habitual residence elsewhere. By contrast, habitual residence in the second country is not acquired on arrival but only after a period that demonstrates that the residence has become habitual and is likely to continue to be habitual depending upon the relevant facts and circumstances.

In *Nessa v Chief Adjudication Officer*[176] it was held that 'habitual' had to be given its normal meaning as being for an appreciable amount of time. A woman who had lived all her life in Bangladesh was not habitually resident in the UK, where she had just arrived at Heathrow. It would only be appropriate to classify someone as habitually resident from the moment of arrival if that approach was necessary to give effect to a piece of legislation where it was important that there was no gap between residences in different countries.

This requirement that an appreciable period of time is required to establish habitual residence has been confirmed in several cases.[177]

In *W v H (Child Abduction: Surrogacy) (No 1)*[178] a child was born in England to a surrogate mother to whom it had no genetic connection. The child's intentional parents were habitually resident in California. The child had no habitual residence in either California or England.[179]

---

169 *Re J (Abduction: Custody Rights)* [1990] 2 AC 562, 578–579.
170 [2001] 2 FLR 1288.
171 Ibid [31].
172 Ibid [35].
173 [2001] 2 FLR 1288.
174 [2003] EWHC 777 (Fam).
175 Ibid [30].
176 [1999] 2 FLR 1116, 1121.
177 *Shah* [1983] 2 AC 309, 342; *Re J* [1990] 2 AC 562, 758.
178 [2002] 1 FLR 1008.
179 Ibid [25].

In *Mark v Mark*,[180] it was established that illegal residence could be enough to establish 'habitual residence' in England.

In *DT v LBT*[181] a woman moved to Italy while in a highly abusive relationship. It was held that a person is to be taken as acting voluntarily in adopting habitual residence in a country unless their presence there is enforced. Bowing to pressure or agreeing with extreme reluctance does not make presence involuntary.[182]

In M v M[183] Millett LJ held that a man can be habitually resident in a place even though he has no intention of remaining there permanently or indefinitely. All that is necessary is that he should be able to say: 'I have settled down here and made this my home for the present, although in due course I do or may intend to settle elsewhere.'[184]

The 'settled intention' needs only to be an intention to settle and remain in a country for a period, such as working abroad under a fixed-term employment contract. There is no requirement that a person intends to remain permanently or indefinitely. In *CJ v KJ*[185] a mother and child resided in the United States on visitor visas with no right to return. Sumner J held that they had habitual residence in the USA. He held that habitual residence arises where a person settles voluntarily in a particular country for a settled purpose whether of short or long duration, or even on a trial basis.[186]

In *A v A (Child Abduction)*[187] a family went to Australia on immigration visas. The wife then returned to England to arrange shipment of the family furniture to Australia, but she retained the tenancy of a council-owned property as a 'back up' if the family decided to return to England after

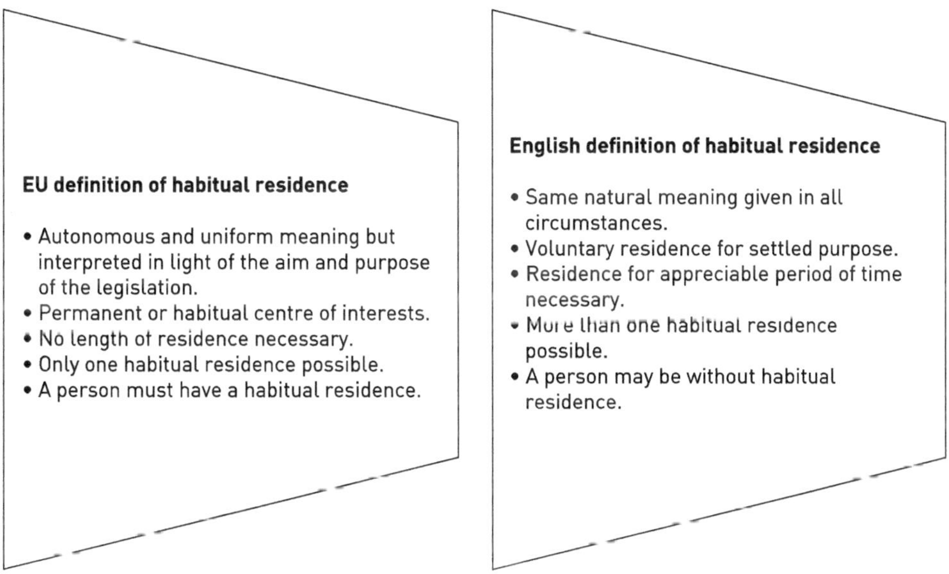

Figure 2.2 Contrasting the EU definition of habitual residence with the English definition of habitual residence

180 [1999] 1 WLR 1937.
181 [2011] 1 FLR 1215.
182 Ibid [31].
183 [1997] 2 FLR 263.
184 Ibid 275.
185 [2006] 2 FLR 1.
186 Ibid [53].
187 [1993] 2 FLR 225

all. The shipment of the furniture to Australia was found to be evidence of the necessary 'settled intention' to establish habitual residence in Australia.

2.4 Further reading

P Carter, 'Domicile: The case for radical reform in the United Kingdom' (1987) 36 ICLQ 71.
J Fawcett, 'Result selection in domicile cases' (1985) 5 OJLS 378.
R Fentiman, 'Domicile revisited' (1991) CLJ 445.
S Harder, 'Domicile of children: the new law in Scotland' (2006) 10 *Edinburgh Law Review* 386.
T Kruger, 'Dual nationality = double trouble?' (2011) 7 JPIL 601–626.
P McEleavy, 'Regression and reform in the law of domicile' (2007) ICLQ 453–462.
P Rogerson, 'Habitual residence: the new domicile?' (2000) 49 ICLQ 86.

Chapter 3

Jurisdiction of the English Courts in Commercial Disputes

The EU Regime

Chapter Contents

Key Issues:

- Overview of the EU Framework on Jurisdiction
- Current rules of Brussels I
- Jurisdiction agreements in the international legal order
- *Lis pendens* rules under Brussels I
- Changes to jurisdiction and *lis pendens* under Brussels I recast

3.1 Introduction

The jurisdiction of the English Courts to hear disputes in civil and commercial matters is governed by two different sets of rules. This chapter focuses on the question of jurisdiction of the English courts in the context of the Brussels I Regulation[1] and the Lugano Convention.[2] The rules ascribe jurisdiction where a civil and commercial dispute involves defendants domiciled within the European Union (EU) or in Norway, Switzerland or Iceland.

A defendant who is a non-EU domiciliary will generally be subject to national rules of jurisdiction but this is subject to certain exceptions explored in this chapter. Chapter 4 deals with the traditional rules governing jurisdiction of the English courts in cases that fall outside the European regime. These rules apply where the defendant is not domiciled in a Member State and no other jurisdictional provision of Brussels I applies to give the court jurisdiction,[3] for example a New York domiciliary present in England.

European regulation of the rules governing jurisdiction in civil and commercial matters began at an intergovernmental level[4] with the Brussels Convention in 1968.[5] This Convention has since been replaced by the Brussels I regulation. However, case law interpreting the Brussels Convention is still good law on the interpretation of many of the provisions of the current regime and will be referred to throughout this chapter.

The instruments making up the current EU regime are as follows:

The Brussels I regulation

The Brussels I regulation governs the allocation of jurisdiction in all EU Member States. The regulation came into force on 1 March 2002. Although Denmark has opted out of Brussels I using its powers under the 1997 Protocol No 5 on the position of Denmark,[6] an agreement reached between the EU and Denmark in 2006[7] extends the provisions of Brussels I to Denmark. This agreement entered into force on 1 July 2007.[8]

The current Brussels I regulation has recently been revised and will be replaced by Brussels I recast,[9] which will apply from 10 January 2015. The changes that this will make to the law are highlighted throughout the chapter.

1 Council Regulation (EC) No 44/2001 [2001] OJ L12/1.
2 Convention on jurisdiction and the enforcement of judgments in civil and commercial matters signed in Lugano on 30 October 2007 [2007] OJ L339/3.
3 Specifically Arts 22 and 23.
4 See Chapter 1.
5 Convention on jurisdiction and the enforcement of judgments in civil and commercial matters (consolidated version) [2008] OJ C27/1.
6 This protocol is maintained by Protocol No 1 annexed to the Treaty of Lisbon [2007] C306/165.
7 Council Decision 2006/325/EC.
8 Denmark has opted out of Brussels I recast so the provisions of Brussels I will continue to apply.
9 Regulation (EU) No 1215/2012 [2012] OJ L351/1.

Brussels I was implemented in the UK by the Civil Jurisdiction and Judgments Order 2001[10] which modified the Civil Jurisdiction and Judgments Act 1982. A modified version of the rules in Brussels I, referred to as the Modified Regulation, is used to deal with the allocation of jurisdiction between different parts of the United Kingdom (England and Wales; Scotland; and Northern Ireland). These rules are found in Schedule 4 of the Civil Jurisdiction and Judgments Act 1982 and are examined at the end of this chapter.

The Lugano Convention

The Lugano Convention 1988[11] governs the allocation of jurisdiction between EU Member States and Norway, Switzerland and Iceland. It is closely based on the text of the Brussels Convention of 1968 and started out as an agreement between the then members of the European Community (EC) and the European Free Trade Association (EFTA). The Lugano Convention was implemented in the UK by the Civil Jurisdiction and Judgments Act 1991.

In 2007 a revised Lugano Convention was signed and approved.[12] This 'new Lugano Convention' is closely based on the text of Brussels I. This new Convention comes into force after deposition of ratification documents by the EU and the other state. This Convention is now in force between the EU and Norway,[13] the EU and Switzerland[14] and the EU and Iceland.[15] It brings the allocation of jurisdiction in Norway, Switzerland and Iceland fully in line with the rest of the EU regime.

Where the English court has jurisdiction under the EU regime, a claim form can be served on the defendant out of the jurisdiction without the permission of the court under Civil Procedure Rule 6.33.[16]

Brussels I and the Lugano Convention also regulate recognition and enforcement of the judgments of the courts of Member States and Norway, Iceland and Switzerland. These aspects are examined in Chapter 5.

This chapter will deal with the provisions of Brussels I that govern allocation of jurisdiction. Any variations in the provisions of the Lugano Convention will be indicated as and when necessary.

3.2 Interpretation of the EU regime

The Court of Justice of the European Union (CJEU) has jurisdiction to rule on the interpretation of any provision of Brussels I.[17] This helps to ensure that Brussels I is consistently applied and interpreted in all Member States. The CJEU will rule on the meaning of a provision of Brussels I after a reference for preliminary ruling under Art 267 of the Treaty on the Functioning of the European Union (TFEU) from a court in a Member State. This reference may occur in the middle of a dispute. A 'preliminary ruling' means that the CJEU interprets the way in which a particular provision of the Brussels Regulation is intended to apply without going into the merits of the dispute in question. Such a decision is binding on all national courts. Where a question on the interpretation of a provision of Brussels I is raised in a dispute in the Supreme Court, such a matter must be referred to the CJEU. The Court of Appeal may also refer such questions to the CJEU.

---

10 SI 2001/3928.

11 Convention on Jurisdiction and the Enforcement of Judgments in Civil and Commercial Matters. Done at Lugano on 16 September 1988 [1988] OJ L 319/9.

12 Council Decision 2009/430/EC.

13 1 January 2010.

14 1 January 2011.

15 1 May 2011.

16 For more details on service of claim forms see Chapter 4.

17 Art 267 TFEU ex Art 234 TEC. See further Chapter 1.

In contrast, the interpretation of the Lugano Convention by the CJEU is only binding on EU Member States and not on Switzerland, Iceland or Norway. Protocol 2 of the Lugano Convention requires the courts in Switzerland, Iceland and Norway to have regard to the principles laid down in the decisions of the courts of other Contracting States, rulings of the CJEU and decisions under the Brussels Convention, Lugano Convention 1988 and Brussels I.

Judgments of the ECJ on the Brussels Convention are strong authority as to how Brussels I should be interpreted.[18] National courts may also refer to the explanatory reports accompanying each legislative instrument as an aid to interpreting provisions: for example, the Jenard-Moller Report on the Lugano Convention 1988,[19] the Pocar Report on the Lugano Convention 2007[20] and the Schlosser Report on the Brussels Convention.[21]

Schedule 4 of the Civil Jurisdiction and Judgments Act 1982, which uses a moderated form of Brussels I to allocation jurisdiction within the UK, is not subject to interpretation by the CJEU as it forms part of UK domestic law.[22]

3.3 Scope of the EU regime

3.3.1 Excluded matters

Brussels I is limited in scope to civil and commercial matters,[23] irrespective of the nature of the court or tribunal before which the action is brought. Revenue, customs and administrative matters are expressly excluded by Art 1(1). Article 1(2) expressly excludes the following matters from the scope of the regulation: **the status or legal capacity of natural persons, rights in property arising out of a matrimonial relationship, wills and succession, bankruptcy and liquidation, social security**[24] and **arbitration**.[25]

3.3.2 Interpretation of 'civil and commercial'

The phrase 'civil and commercial matters' is left undefined by Brussels I. Case law has established that this phrase is to be given an autonomous meaning and should not rely on the classification used under national law.

In *LTU v Eurocontrol*,[26] Eurocontrol, which was a public company in the business of supplying services for the purposes of air traffic control in Western Europe, claimed charges owed to them by LTU. The ECJ held that the question to be asked was whether the claim in question arose from Eurocontrol's exercise of its public powers, that is, traffic control measures. If so, then the claim would not be within the ambit of 'civil and commercial matters'. But if the claim arose out of activities not specific to Eurocontrol's public function, such as the purchase of food for consumption by the company's staff or the acquisition of furniture for staff offices, then it would be covered by the Brussels Convention.

Similarly in *Netherlands v Ruffer*,[27] the ECJ ruled that the concept 'civil and commercial matters' did not extend to a claim made by the Netherlands State for the recovery of costs incurred in the

18 See for example Case C281/02 *Owusu v Jackson* [2005] QB 801.
19 [1979] OJ C59/1.
20 [2009] OJ C319/1.
21 [1979] OJ C59/71.
22 C346/93 *Kleinwort Benson Ltd v Glasgow City Council* [1995] ECR I-615.
23 Art 1.
24 The meaning of this exclusion was discussed in C271/00 *Gemeente Steenbergen v Luc Baten* [2002] ECR I-10527.
25 The interaction between arbitration and Brussels I is explored in some detail in Chapter 6.
26 [1976] ECR 1541.
27 [1980] ECR 3807.

course of removing a vessel's wreck from a public waterway. This ruling was again based on the ground that the Netherlands was acting in its capacity as the public authority in charge of administering public waterways in accordance with the provisions of an international Convention. Thus the claim was not civil or commercial but related to the exercise of a public function.

In *Sonntag v Waidmann*,[28] the ECJ held that where the standard or duty of care required of a public authority is that applicable to all individuals, then a claim for the breach of such a duty is within the ambit of 'civil and commercial matters'. In this case, Sonntag, a schoolteacher employed by the German government, took a group of schoolchildren on a trip to the Italian Alps. One of the children fell and died. Sonntag was prosecuted and convicted on a charge of homicide before the Italian courts. The next of kin of the victim joined in the criminal proceedings as *parties civiles*, claiming damages which the Italian courts ordered Sonntag to pay. An order for the enforcement of this judgment was granted by the German court of first instance and was confirmed by the Court of Appeal. On appeal to the Federal Court of Justice of Germany, the *Bundesgerichtshof*, Sonntag and the State Government contended, *inter alia*, that the judgment of the Italian court ordering the payment of compensation was not a 'civil matter' and therefore did not fall within the meaning of Art 1 of the Brussels Convention. The ECJ ruled that, as the standard of care required of Sonntag was that applicable to all individuals, whether it be schoolteachers, state employees or ordinary individuals, his liability would be treated as ordinary civil liability, thus falling within the scope of the Brussels Convention.

Sonntag shows that 'civil and commercial matters' is an autonomous concept and the court will look at the content of the claim. Even though this claim was brought in criminal proceedings it was considered to be civil, despite the fact that the notion of *parties civiles* in criminal proceedings is not known in the national law of all Member States. Although Sonntag was a public servant his actions were civil as the duty of care breach was not specifically related to the exercise of his public functions.

3.4 Exclusive jurisdiction (Art 22)

Brussels I is based on the general principle that a defendant should be sued in the court of the country of his domicile.[29] This is often the most appropriate venue in which to bring proceedings as the defendant is not required to leave his domicile to defend himself and his assets are generally located in that jurisdiction. However, in certain cases, outlined in Art 22,[30] there is a clear geographical link between the subject matter of the dispute and one particular Member State. In these situations the court of that Member State will have exclusive jurisdiction regardless of the domicile of the defendant. For example, where the subject of the dispute is the ownership of a farm in Germany it will not matter that the defendant is domiciled in France, as the German courts have exclusive jurisdiction under Art 22(1). This includes cases where the defendant is not domiciled in the European Union.[31]

Exclusive jurisdiction is given to the courts of Member States in the following situations:

Immovable property. Where the main issue in proceedings concerns ownership or rights of possession in immovable property or concerns a tenancy the courts of the Member State in which

28 [1993] ECR 1-1963.
29 Art 2.
30 These appear, unchanged, in Art 24 of Brussels I recast.
31 Opinion 1/03 [2006] ECR I-1145, [149]. C343/04 *Oberösterreich v CEZ* [2006] IL Pr 25, [21]; cf *Chaudhary v Bhatter* [2009] EWCA Civ 1176; T Carney, 'Exclusive jurisdiction – third party states' [2009] *European Legal Forum* 246–252.

the property is situated shall have exclusive jurisdiction.[32] There is one exception. Where the proceedings concern a six-month tenancy and the landlord and tenant are domiciled in the same Member State, the Member State in which they are both domiciled will have exclusive jurisdiction. This would include the situation where an English landlord rents a holiday villa in Spain to an English tenant. These provisions are examined more fully in Chapter 9.

Status or decision-making powers of companies and associations: Where the issue in proceedings related to the internal workings of a company or other legal entity, the Member State in which that company has its seat will have exclusive jurisdiction.[33] This includes disputes concerning the validity of the constitution of a company or the nullity or dissolution of companies or the validity of decisions taken by governing organs. The seat of a company is defined by the national conflict of laws rules of each court.[34]

Public registers: Where the proceedings have as their object the validity of entries in public registers, the courts of the Member State where the register is kept shall have exclusive jurisdiction.[35]

Intellectual property: Where the subject matter of the proceedings is concerned with the registration or validity of intellectual property rights that require registration or deposit, the Member State in which registration has taken place or is deemed to have taken place has exclusive jurisdiction.[36] Where registration has been applied for the courts of that Member State will have exclusive jurisdiction.

Enforcement of judgments: Where the proceedings are concerned with the enforcement of judgments, then the courts of the Member State in which the judgment is sought to be enforced shall have exclusive jurisdiction.[37]

Where the geographical connections in Art 22 point to a non-EU Member State, no exclusive jurisdiction is given to the third country state by Brussels I. However, the English courts have indicated that in such cases they will stay proceedings in favour of the third country state.[38] It is unclear if this is compatible with Brussels I. This practice is compatible with Brussels I recast if there are pending proceedings in the third country state and the provisions of Arts 33 and 34 are satisfied.[39]

3.5 Jurisdiction by appearance (Art 24)

By virtue of Art 24,[40] the courts of a Member State before whom a defendant enters an appearance shall have jurisdiction. This appearance must represent a step towards defending the case on its merits, showing the defendant's acceptance of the jurisdiction. An appearance merely to contest jurisdiction will not confer jurisdiction by appearance. Jurisdiction by appearance will not prevail over a court with exclusive jurisdiction under Art 22. Thus if a dispute over rights in a property in Member State A is taken in Member State B, it does not matter that the defendant has appeared in Member State B to defend the case. Member State A has exclusive jurisdiction and Member State B must decline jurisdiction.

---

32 Art 22(1).
33 Art 22(2). This provision was considered in C144/10 *BVG v JP Morgan* [2011] 1 WLR 2087.
34 See Chapter 2.
35 Art 22(3).
36 Art 22(4). This is further explored in Chapter 9.
37 Art 22(5).
38 *Ferrexpo AG v Gilson Investments Ltd* [2012] EWHC 721 (Comm).
39 See below.
40 Art 26 of Brussels recast.

Jurisdiction by appearance will override a jurisdiction agreement giving exclusive jurisdiction to another Member State. This is because a jurisdiction agreement confers jurisdiction based on the parties' consent to that jurisdiction. Where one party had taken proceedings in a different jurisdiction and the defendant has consented to that jurisdiction by appearing to contest the claim, there is no need to enforce the exclusive jurisdiction agreement. The wishes of the parties are being respected. This line of reasoning was confirmed by the ECJ in *Elefanten Schuh v Jacquin*,[41] where Art 18 of the Brussels Convention was held to override an earlier agreement conferring jurisdiction on the courts of another Contracting State.

Jurisdiction by appearance will also override the protective measures of Arts 15 to 21. However, under Brussels recast, the court must inform a defendant policyholder, beneficiary of an insurance contract, consumer or employee of his right to contest the jurisdiction of the court and the consequences of entering or not entering an appearance before assuming jurisdiction by the appearance of the defendant.

3.6 Protective measures (Arts 8–21)

The European regime sets out a number of protective provisions regulating jurisdiction in three specific types of contract: notably, contracts relating to insurance,[42] certain consumer contracts[43] and individual contracts of employment.[44] These provisions are designed to protect certain categories of persons, who are presumed to be the weaker party in the contractual relationship. This protection is manifested in two ways across all three types of contract. First, where there is no jurisdiction agreement, the weaker party must be sued in the court of their domicile. However, the stronger party can be sued in a greater variety of jurisdictions, including the court of the weaker party's domicile. This shows a presumption that the court of the weaker party's domicile is the most protective of his interests.

Second, there is a limitation on the use of jurisdiction agreements between the parties. Thus the autonomy of the parties to the jurisdiction agreement is limited in order to protect the weaker party.

The rules of protective jurisdiction work in conjunction with the protective choice-of-law rules under Rome I[45] to ensure that the weaker party to a contract is protected both by the choice of jurisdiction and by the choice of applicable law.

The rules under Arts 8 to 21 are exclusive, subject to Art 22 and Art 24. This means that when dealing with one of the three species of protective jurisdiction, jurisdiction is dictated solely by the special regime for that type of contract.[46] The rules of Arts 8 to 21 only apply where the defendant party is domiciled in a Member State or has a branch agency or other establishment in one of the Member States.[47] If the English courts are making a determination of jurisdiction based on these articles they will look to s 44 of the Civil Jurisdiction and Judgments Act 1982 to define the domicile of a branch, agency or establishment.[48]

When reviewing Brussels I, the Commission noted that this limitation deprived EU claimants of the protections offered to them by EU rules where they brought proceedings against defendants

41 [1981] ECR 1671.
42 Arts 8–14.
43 Arts 15–17.
44 Arts 18–21.
45 Council Regulation (EC) 593/2008 [2008] L177/6. These are treated in detail in Chapter 7.
46 *Glaxosmithkline v Jean-Pierre Rouard* [2008] ECR I-3965.
47 This issue is explored below.
48 See Chapter 2.

based outside the EU.[49] An extension of the protective rules of jurisdiction to non-EU domiciliaries was proposed.[50] Under Brussels I recast, the protective rules of jurisdiction relating to employees and consumers will apply where the defendant employer or professional is not domiciled within the EU.[51]

3.6.1 Jurisdiction in matters relating to insurance (Arts 8–14)

Articles 8 to 14 of Brussels I apply to matters relating to insurance. These rules favour the policyholder, beneficiary or insured rather than the insurer.

Under Art 8 of Brussels I, the policyholder can sue the insurer either in the courts of the State where the insurer is domiciled, or in the courts of the State where the policyholder is domiciled. If the policyholder is also suing a co-insurer then this can be done in the courts of the State where the leading insurer is being sued. In addition, in the case of liability insurance, or insurance of immovable property, the policyholder can also bring proceedings in the courts of the State where the harmful event occurred.[52] Thus an English domiciliary who is a policyholder of insurance on a property in Spain can sue an Italian insurer in Spain for refusal to pay out when his property catches fire. He could also sue the Italian insurer in England or Italy under Art 8.

In contrast, the policyholder may only be sued in the courts of the state where he is domiciled.[53] Thus, in the above example the English policyholder may only be sued in England. This provision does not affect the right to bring a counterclaim in the court in which the original claim is pending. So in the above example the Italian insurer could serve a defence in the Spanish courts with a counterclaim that the policyholder had set the house on fire himself.

The meaning of the Brussels Convention equivalent to Art 12 was examined by the Court of Appeal in *Jordan Grand Prix v Baltic Insurance Group*.[54] The claimant in the original action was an English company which ran a Formula One racing team. It agreed to make bonus payments to its employees if it finished in the top six of a world championship, and it insured that contingent liability with the defendant insurer, a Lithuanian company. The latter had a managing agent in Belgium, CIU. Q Ltd, an Irish Company, of which D and G, both domiciled in Ireland, were directors, agreed with the claimant to sponsor the team and to pay a certain sum if the team finished in the top six. The claimant's primary claim was that the requisite insurance cover was effected with the defendant through CIU and with the participation of another Belgian intermediary, SRI. The claimant also had a secondary claim against SRI. In the event, the team finished fifth, but the insurer refused to pay, alleging that the bonus scheme and sponsorship agreement were not genuine and that the claimant and Q Ltd were parties to a conspiracy to defraud the insurer.

The claimant (policyholder) brought proceedings in the English court against the insurer, claiming the sum due under the policy. The defendant (insurer) served a defence and a counterclaim alleging conspiracy and fraud. The counterclaim was made against various individuals associated with the claimant and against Q Ltd and SRI. Before the counterclaim had been served on Q Ltd, Q Ltd served proceedings in the Belgian court against the defendant, SRI and CIU, and then applied to the English court for a declaration that the court did not have jurisdiction to entertain the counterclaim against them. As they had not brought the primary claim, this was not a counterclaim against them.

49 COM (2009)174 final, 5.
50 COM(2010) 748 final [3.1.2]
51 See Arts 18 and 21 of Brussels 1 recast.
52 Art 10.
53 Art 12.
54 [1998] 3 All ER 418.

The Court of Appeal held that the word 'counterclaim' in Art 11 was limited to a counterclaim against the original claimant. The basic principle underlying the last part of Art 11 was that, by becoming a litigant within the jurisdiction, a claimant submitted to the incidents of such litigation, including liability to a counterclaim. Additionally, the words 'the policyholder, the insured or a beneficiary' in Art 11 were not intended to be an exhaustive list of those capable of taking advantage of this provision, but rather elaborated the meaning of 'defendant'. Accordingly, the declaration sought by Q Ltd was granted.[55]

3.6.1.1 Restrictions on jurisdiction agreements

An agreement on jurisdiction can displace the rules of Arts 8 to12 but such an agreement must comply with one of five requirements in Art 13 that ensure the protection of the policyholder.

- **The agreement is entered into after the dispute has arisen.** This gives the policyholder the chance to consider whether this jurisdiction is in his favour on the facts of the dispute.
- **The agreement allows the policyholder, the insured or a beneficiary to bring proceedings in courts other than those indicated in Arts 8–13.** This gives the weaker party more choice rather than less.
- **The agreement is concluded between a policyholder and an insurer, both of whom are at the time of conclusion of the contract domiciled or habitually resident in the same Member State, and which has the effect of conferring jurisdiction on the courts of that State even if the harmful event were to occur abroad, provided that such an agreement is not contrary to the law of that State.** This ensures that the policyholder will have the protection of the jurisdiction of his domicile/habitual residence.
- **The agreement is concluded with a policyholder who is not domiciled in a Member State.** This does not apply if the insurance is compulsory or is related to immovable property in a Member State. This provision extends the protections on jurisdiction agreements to non-EU domiciliaries where the subject of the agreement is immovable property in a Member State or mandated by the law of a Member State.
- **The agreement relates to a contract of insurance which covers one or more of the risks connected with carriage by air or sea as set out in Art 14 of the Brussels Regulation.**

3.6.2 Jurisdiction over consumer contracts (Arts 15–17)

Articles 15 to 17 of Brussels I contain special provisions for jurisdiction over certain consumer contracts. Article 15(1) defines the 'consumer' as a person who concludes the contract 'for a purpose which can be regarded as being outside his trade or profession'. A 'consumer contract' is defined to include a contract for the sale of goods on instalment on credit terms; **OR** a contract for a loan repayable by instalments or for other forms of credit to finance goods; **OR** any other contract (i.e. not restricted to supply of goods or services) concluded with a person who pursues commercial or professional activities in the Member State of the consumer's domicile, or **by any means, directs such activities to that Member State and the contract falls within the scope of such activities.** The extent of those 'activities' directed to the Member State of the consumer's domicile may prove to be a crucial question.[56] This provision includes a contract made though a website which the consumer accessed in his or her domicile.[57]

---

55 See also *Dollfus Mieg et Compagnie v CDW International Ltd* [2004] IL Pr 12.
56 C190/11, *Mühlleitner v Yusufi* [2012] IL Pr 46.
57 This is further examined in Chapter 6.

The consumer may bring proceedings against the other party to the contract, **either** in the courts of the State where the defendant is domiciled **or** in the courts of the state in which the consumer is domiciled. Article 15(2) allows the consumer to sue the other party in the Member State in which that party has a branch, agency or establishment. Thus a consumer domiciled in England who made a contract in Spain with a Spanish domiciliary could sue in England or Spain.

In contrast, if a consumer is to be sued, then proceedings can only be brought in the courts of the State in which the consumer is domiciled.

3.6.2.1 Restrictions on jurisdiction agreements

Jurisdiction agreements are restricted by Art 17 to three situations in order to protect the weaker party. The parties can only agree to the jurisdiction of a different Member State where:

(a) the jurisdiction agreement is entered into after the dispute has arisen **OR**
(b) the jurisdiction agreement allows the consumer to bring proceedings in courts other than those indicated in Arts 15–16; **OR**
(c) both parties to the jurisdiction agreement are domiciled or habitually resident in the same Member State on whose courts jurisdiction is conferred so long as such an agreement is not contrary to the law of that state.

In *Benincasa v Dentalkit*[58] the defendant (an Italian company specialising in the sale of dental hygiene equipment) entered into a franchising contract with the claimant (an Italian national) for the claimant to set up and operate a shop in Germany, trading in goods supplied by the defendant. The claimant set up a shop, paid the defendant an initial agreed sum and made several purchases of products, for which he never paid. He then ceased trading. He brought proceedings in the German court seeking to have the franchising contract and all subsequent contracts declared void and argued that, as he had not commenced trading, he should be regarded as a consumer and therefore he should be permitted to bring the action in Germany, where he was domiciled.

The ECJ ruled that the concept of a 'consumer' within the meaning of the Brussels Convention had to be construed strictly to mean a private, final consumer. It did not extend to a person who concluded a contract with the intention of pursuing a trade or profession either at the present time or in the future. Hence the claimant could not be classed as a consumer.

Benincasa was distinguished in *Standard Bank London Ltd v Apostolakis (No 1)*.[59] Here, the bank made foreign exchange contracts with A, a married couple resident in Greece, who wished to make profits from using their money under such contracts. The couple were a civil engineer and a lawyer. Transactions made by the bank on A's behalf amounted to US$7 million, but the bank then withdrew from the agreed transactions when the drachma was devaluated. The court was asked, *inter alia*, whether the contracts were consumer contracts; it was contended that the sheer scale of the money involved meant that A, acting for profit, acted as a trader in foreign exchange; EU law required consumer contracts to be concluded for the purpose of 'satisfying a person's private consumption needs', as was the case in *Benincasa*. Longmore J found that those words were used in the specific factual context of *Benincasa* and the ECJ could not have intended those words to be a substitute for the wording of the Brussels Convention. A had made 'consumer contracts'; the scale was not determinative, they were merely using their income in a way they hoped would be profitable. The judge continued, 'the evidence is all to the effect that it was outside their trade or profession that the contracts were being made.'

58 [1997] IL Pr 559.
59 [2001] IL Pr 766.

Only the original consumer can rely on the protective provisions of Arts 15 to 17. In *Shearson Lehmann Hutton Inc v TVB GmbH*,[60] a German consumer had entered into contracts with Hutton Inc, American brokers, for financial services and advice. His investment was a near total loss. The consumer was thought to have a claim against Hutton Inc, based, *inter alia*, on their failure to indicate the risks involved in such transactions. Rather than suing them himself, he elected to assign his right to sue to a German company, TVB. TVB brought an action in the German court. The defendant contested the jurisdiction of the German court. The issue was referred to the ECJ. It was held, *inter alia*, that protective jurisdiction did not apply in this instance. The claimant in this case was not a private consumer, though the assignee of a consumer's claim, and was not entitled to avail itself of this protective jurisdiction.

<table>
<tr><th colspan="2">Jurisdiction over consumer contracts (Arts 15–17)

1) Contract must be between a consumer and a professional.

2) Contract must be for the sale of goods on instalment credit terms OR a contract for a loan OR be within the scope of commercial activites directed to the consumer's domicile.</th></tr>
<tr><td>Where no jurisdictional agreement is made:

The consumer can be sued in the courts of his domicile only.
The professional can be sued in the court of his domicile OR in the court of the consumer's domicile.</td><td>Proceedings may only be taken the courts of another MS by jurisdiciton agreement:

The agreement is entered into after the dispute arises.
OR
The agreements allows the consumer to bring proceedings in another court.
OR
The consumer and the professional are habitually resident in the same MS and the agreement confers jurisdiction on that Member State.</td></tr>
</table>

Fig 3.1 A closer look at jurisdiction over consumer contracts.

3.6.3 Jurisdiction over individual contracts of employment (Arts 18–21)

Article 19 of Brussels I allows an employee employed under an individual contract of employment to sue his employer in the state in which the employer is domiciled or in the Member State where the employee habitually works or last did so. If the employer is not domiciled in a Member State but has a branch, agency or other establishment in one of the Member States the employer will be deemed to be domiciled in that Member State as long as the dispute arises out of the operations of that branch.

The meaning of 'place of habitual work' was addressed by the ECJ in *Rutten v Cross Medical Ltd*,[61] where the employee carried out his work in the Netherlands, the UK, Belgium, Germany and the USA. The ECJ ruled that 'place of habitual work' referred to the place where the employee has established **the effective centre of his working activities**, and where, or from which, he in fact performs the essential part of his duties.[62]

60 [1993] ECR 1-130.
61 [1997] IL Pr 199.
62 Ibid 214.

In *Herbert Weber v Universal Ogden Services Ltd*,[63] an employee worked on an installation over the continental shelf adjoining one Contracting State and also in the territory of another Contracting State. The ECJ laid down a number of factors to consider in establishing the 'place of habitual work'. Work on the installation would be regarded as undertaken in the Contracting State to which the continental shelf was adjacent. Second, where work is undertaken in more than one Contracting State the place where the employee 'habitually works' is where he performs his essential work for the employer. Third, if the employee performs the same activities in more than one Contracting State, account should be taken of the whole duration of the employment relationship, to identify where the employee habitually works. Fourth, if other criteria fail, the place of habitual work is where the employee has worked the longest. Fifth, if the facts indicate the subject matter of the dispute is more closely connected with another place, that place will be the relevant one. Finally, the ECJ indicated that, if none of these criteria enable a national court to identify the habitual place of work, the employee could choose to sue the employer in either the courts of the place where the business which engaged him is situated, or in the courts of the Contracting State of the employer's domicile.

This case is now reflected in Art 19(2)(b) of Brussels I, which states that if the employee does not habitually work in any one country he may sue his employer in the courts for the place where the business which engaged the employee is or was situated.

In contrast, the employee can only be sued in the Member State where the employee is domiciled, although this provision does not apply to the employer's counterclaim to an action by the employee.[64] In *Swithenbank Foods Ltd v Bowers*,[65] a former employer claimed that an employee had breached an implied term of his contract of employment. The employee was domiciled in France, and so the English courts had no jurisdiction to hear the claim.

In *Samengo-Turner v J & H Marsh & McLennan (Services) Ltd and others*[66] the Court of Appeal granted an anti-suit injunction to prevent proceedings by an employer for breach of a bonus agreement from going ahead in the state of New York. The employees were domiciled in England. The court held that bonus agreements, which were the subject of the dispute, were part of the employees' employment contracts. It further held that the United States companies bringing the suit, which were in the same group as the English company which had employed Samengo-Turner, were employers for the purposes of Brussels I. Their enforcement of the bonus contracts should be subject to the same jurisdictional restraint as the English company who initially employed Samengo-Turner would have been, if it had enforced the bonus contract.

Article 21 of Brussels I restricts the use of jurisdiction agreements between an employer and employee. Such an agreement is only valid if:

1. it is entered into after the dispute arises, **OR**
2. it allows the employee to bring the action in an additional jurisdiction to those specified in Arts 18 to 20.

3.7 Jurisdiction agreements

Article 23 of Brussels I confers exclusive jurisdiction to a chosen court in cases where there is a jurisdiction agreement to submit disputes exclusively to the courts of a particular Member State.

---

63 C37/00, *Herbert Weber v Universal Ogden Services Ltd* [2002] QB 1189.
64 Art 20.
65 [2002] 2 All ER (Comm) 974.
66 [2007] EWCA Civ 723.

Jurisdiction is based solely on the autonomy of the parties. There is no need for the chosen court to have any geographical connection to the dispute. Such an agreement may be an invaluable part of negotiations between the parties. Some venues may be speedier or may advantage one party over the other. Parties may choose a neutral venue or agree not to litigate in a particular venue that advantages one party over the other.

Article 23 states that 'if the parties, one or more of whom is domiciled in a Member State, have agreed that a court or the courts of a Member State are to have jurisdiction to settle any disputes which have arisen or which may arise in connection with a particular legal relationship, that court or those courts shall have exclusive jurisdiction', provided that the jurisdiction clause is either:

- in writing or evidenced in writing; OR
- in a form which accords with practices which the parties have established between themselves; OR
- in international trade or commerce, in a form which accords with a usage of which the parties are or ought to have been aware and which in such trade or commerce is widely known, and regularly observed by parties, to the contracts of the type involved in the particular trade or commerce concerned.

Jurisdiction agreements cannot exclude the courts of a Member State which has exclusive jurisdiction under Art 22 of Brussels I. In cases of protective jurisdiction, additional requirements apply which are laid down in Arts 8 to 21 and examined above.

Where a valid jurisdiction agreement in favour of a Member State exists, if another EU State is seised it must decline jurisdiction.

3.7.1 Formal requirements

The meaning of 'in writing or evidenced in writing' was clarified by the ECJ in *Tilly Russ v Nova*,[67] where it was held that the jurisdiction clause must be contained in a document signed by both parties. In this case, the contract had expired and the terms of the contract required renewal to be in writing. The parties had continued to rely on the terms of the written contract after it had expired. This did not undermine the validity of the written jurisdiction clause. In *Iveco Fiat v Van Hool*,[68] the ECJ adopted the view that if the law applicable to the contract allowed the parties to renew the original contract other than in writing, then the jurisdiction clause in the original contract would continue to be effective, provided that neither party objected.

In *Powell Duffryn v Petereit*,[69] the ECJ held that a jurisdiction clause governing disputes between a company and its shareholders, and contained in the constitutional documents of the company, satisfied the formal requirements of 'writing or evidenced in writing'. Equally, where the jurisdiction clause was agreed orally and the written confirmation was later received by the party without raising any objection then, according to *Berghoefer v ASA*,[70] the agreement would satisfy the requirement of 'evidenced in writing'. Nevertheless, following the ECJ ruling in *Galeries Segoura v Bonakdarian*,[71] a contract concluded orally subject to the general conditions of sale which incorporate a jurisdiction clause would not satisfy this requirement unless the seller's written confirmation was accompanied by a notification of the general conditions and these were accepted by the purchaser in writing.

67 [1984] ECR 2417.
68 [1986] ECR 3337.
69 [1992] ECR 1-1745.
70 [1985] ECR 2699.
71 [1976] ECR 1851.

Electronic forms of communication are now dealt with by Art 23(1) of Brussels I, which accords 'any communication by electronic means which provides a durable record of the agreement' equivalence with writing. This means that emails will constitute writing.

Schedule 4 of the Civil Jurisdiction and Judgments Act 1982 which allocates jurisdiction within the UK does not have the requirement of writing for jurisdiction agreements.

If the agreement on jurisdiction does not satisfy the requirement of 'writing or evidenced in writing', it may still be valid if it 'accords with practices which the parties have established between themselves' or with 'trade usage'. The first alternative requires a trading relationship between the parties. Thus in *Tilly Russ v Nova*, where the shipper and carrier concluded a contract for the carriage of goods orally and, subsequently, the carrier issued a bill of lading incorporating the jurisdiction clause, it was held that the clause was effective, provided that the parties had a continuing trading relationship governed by the carrier's general conditions; the latter containing the jurisdiction clause.[72]

In the absence of such a trading relationship, the jurisdiction clause may remain valid if it is made in the course of international commerce in accordance with a usage widely known to, and regularly observed by, parties to contracts of the type involved in the particular trade concerned, and the parties ought to have been aware of the practice. The meaning and application of this provision was clarified by the ECJ in *Mainschiffahrts-Genossenschaft v Les Gravieres Rhenanes*.[73] The case concerned a charter party concluded between the claimant, domiciled in Germany, and the defendant, domiciled in France. Following completion of negotiations, the claimant forwarded a letter of confirmation incorporating a jurisdiction clause in favour of the Wurzburg courts to the defendant. A reference to that clause was also made on invoices which the claimant paid without challenging them in any way. In this case, the fact that the defendant did not react to the letter of confirmation or to the invoices would be deemed to constitute consent to the jurisdiction clause because they were common in the trade.

The ECJ went further to give guidance to national courts as to how they should determine a) whether a contract came under a head of international trade or commerce, b) whether there was a practice in that branch of international trade or commerce in which the parties were operating and c) whether the parties were or ought to have been aware of that practice. It should first be considered whether a contact, concluded between two companies domiciled in different Contracting States, came under the head of international trade. Second, the question of whether a practice existed must not be determined by reference to the law of one Contracting State; nor should it be determined in relation to international trade in general, but rather the branch of trade in which the parties in question were operating must be examined. Finally, actual or presumptive awareness of such a practice would be established where, in particular, the parties had had trade relations between themselves or with parties in the same sector or where, in that sector, a particular course of conduct was generally and regularly followed when a contract of the type in question was concluded.[74]

It is not enough that the usage or custom exists; it must be widely known and 'regularly observed by parties to the contracts of the type involved in the particular trade or commerce concerned'. In *Trasportie Castellati Spedizione Internationali SpA v Hugo Trumpy SpA*,[75] the clause was in small print on the reverse of bills of lading, signed by the shipper and carrier on the face. The court, *inter alia*, had to decide whether a trade custom incorporating such clauses into the contract existed and, if so, whether it was necessary for the parties themselves to be aware of the custom. The ECJ determined that the awareness of the parties was necessary, but,

72 See also *Middle East Tankers and Freighters Bunker Services SA (Offshore) v Abu Dhabi Container Lines PJSC* [2002] 2 Lloyd's Rep 643.
73 [1997] IL Pr 411.
74 See also *OT Africa Line Ltd v Hijazy and Others* [2001] 1 Lloyd's Rep 76.
75 [1999] ECR 1-1597.

> There will be actual or presumed awareness of this usage by the contracting parties, profession traders in branch of international trade in question, where, in this branch, a certain course of conduct is sufficiently known, by reason that it is generally and regularly followed in the conclusion of a certain type of contract, such as to be capable of being regarded as an established practice.[76]

The ECJ also had to consider whether awareness of the consignees of the bills of lading was required and held that it was the awareness of the original contracting parties which was required.[77]

The requirement of consensus was addressed by the English courts in *IP Metal v Ruote*,[78] where the claimants and defendants entered into seven contracts for the sale of quantities of aluminium. The telexes confirming the sales contained a clause nominating English law as the applicable law and England as the competent forum. In reliance on that clause, the claimants brought an action against the defendants in relation to six contracts. An action in relation to the seventh contract had already been commenced by the defendant in the Italian court. The defendants then applied to the English court for a stay of proceedings on the ground that there was no agreement, nor sufficient consensus in relation to jurisdiction. Waller J rejected this argument and held that, in the context of metal trade, as was the case here, it was common form that the terms would go without saying and that there would then be a confirmation of those terms by telex immediately thereafter. Unless the defendants made it clear that they were not prepared to accept a particular term, they must be taken to have agreed to it. Therefore, the jurisdiction clause was valid.

3.7.2 Material validity

The ECJ has stated that the purpose of the formal requirements imposed by Art 23 is to ensure that consensus between the parties is in fact established.[79] However, there are no requirements imposed by Brussels I regarding the material validity of the choice of court agreement. Thus as long as the formalities are complied with it is presumed that the clause is materially valid. This was confirmed by the English Court of Appeal in *Deutsche Bank v Asia Pacific Broadband Wireless Communication*.[80]

Sanicentral GmbH v René Collin[81] suggests that such clauses cannot be found to be materially invalid by application of national law. In this case the jurisdictional clause in question violated French law and would ordinarily be found void. However, it did comply with the formal requirements of the Brussels Convention. The court found the clause to be valid.

The Hess, Pfeiffer and Schlosser Report[82] reviewing the application of the Brussels Regulation in 2007 revealed that Member States often apply their national laws in order to determine the material existence of consent. A solution has now been adopted under Brussels I recast[83] which states that the substantive validity of a jurisdiction agreement is to be governed by the law of the chosen state. This means that the material validity of a choice of court clause in favour of Poland must be ascertained according to Polish law. Recital 20 of Brussels I recast leaves it open to the Polish courts to refer the matter to the law of another country through the doctrine of *renvoi*,[84] in accordance with national conflict of laws rules.

76 Ibid [160(4)].
77 See also C387/98 *Coreck Maritime GmbH v Handelsveem BV* [2000] ECR 1-9337.
78 [1993] 2 Lloyd's Rep 60.
79 C387/98 *Coreck Maritime GmbH v Handelsveem* [2000] ECR I- 09337 [13].
80 [2008] EWCA Civ 1091 [23].
81 C25/79 *Sanicentral GmbH v René Collin* [1979] ECR 3423.
82 Hess, Pfeiffer and Schlosser, *Report on the Application of Regulation Brussels I in the Member States* (Study JLS/C4/2005/03).
83 Art 25(1).
84 See Chapter 1.

Jurisdiction agreements are most often found as a 'choice of court' clause in a contract. However, the validity of a choice of court clause is not dependent on the material validity of the contract in which it is found. Such a clause has been held by the ECJ to confer exclusive jurisdiction on the designated court even where the action is to seek a declaration that the contract containing the clause is void.[85] Brussels I recast makes it clear that the validity of a jurisdiction agreement cannot be contested solely on the ground that it is part of a contract that is not valid.[86]

3.7.3 Exclusivity of jurisdiction

An *exclusive* jurisdiction agreement gives jurisdiction to one court only. A statement that 'All disputes arising under this contract shall be referred to the English courts' would be considered as 'exclusive'. However, what if the clause stated, 'Disputes arising under this contract may be referred to the English courts or any other court with jurisdiction', or 'Disputes arising under this contract shall be determined by the French or English courts'?

Where the jurisdiction clause indicates that disputes 'may' be referred to the courts of a specified Member State, this does not appear to be an obligation; that is, it seems 'non-exclusive', merely giving the parties a further choice of forum in addition to any others which may have jurisdiction under Brussels I. However, the wording of Art 23(1) of Brussels I states that 'jurisdiction given to a court shall be exclusive unless the parties have agreed otherwise'.

Whether a jurisdiction clause is exclusive or non-exclusive is a matter of construction to be determined by the law governing the contract. In *Insured Financial Structures Ltd v Elecktrocieplownia Tychy SA*[87] the clause stated that 'Each party agrees to the non-exclusive jurisdiction of the courts of (Poland) in connection with any disputes arising out of this agreement.' The Court of Appeal had to consider whether this clause gave exclusive jurisdiction to the Polish courts under Art 17 of the Lugano Convention in a way which reflected the parties' intentions. It was clear that the intention was to give jurisdiction to the Polish courts in addition to any other courts identified by the provisions of the Lugano Convention. Such a clause could give jurisdiction to a court which would not otherwise have jurisdiction. However, it did not exclude the jurisdiction of other courts with jurisdiction under the Lugano Convention.

If the contract does not specifically name the state or states to whose courts jurisdiction is given it may be questioned whether the parties have truly chosen a forum. In *Meeth v Glacetal*[88] it was enough that those states could be identified by reference to the domicile of a particular defendant. In *Coreck Maritime*,[89] the ECJ gave a preliminary ruling that the chosen forum did not necessarily have to be apparent only from the wording of the jurisdiction clause. It was enough that the choice could be identified from the statement in the clause of the objective factors which indicated the parties' intention. The 'statement' in this case was a clause in the bill of lading stating, 'Any dispute arising under this bill of lading shall be decided in the country where the carrier has his principal place of business. . .'. Though it had been alleged that there was difficulty in determining who the carrier referred to, so that the clause did not express an intention towards a particular court, the ECJ said that it was for the national court to decide who the carrier was on the facts. The ECJ also pointed out that it should be possible for the national court to determine the address of that carrier's principal place of business. Only if these factors could not be determined would the clause be invalid. Therefore, where the court can fill in the gaps, the parties will be considered to have

85 *Benincasa v Dentalkit* [1997] IL Pr 559.
86 Art 25(5).
87 [2003] QB 1260.
88 C23/78 *Meeth v Glacetal* [1978] ECR 2133.
89 C387/98 *Coreck Maritime GmbH v Handelsveem* [2000] ECR I- 09337.

expressed intention but where the choice is impossible to establish on the facts the parties will not be considered to have expressed intention.

3.7.4 Scope of the jurisdiction clause

A jurisdiction clause will not necessarily cover all disputes between the parties. A clause in a contract to purchase radiators referring 'all disputes arising out of this contract to the exclusive jurisdiction of the English courts' would not require a dispute between the contracting parties on an entirely unrelated issue to be subject to the exclusive jurisdiction of the English courts. It is for the national court to interpret the clause in order to determine whether the dispute in question comes within its scope.[90]

In interpreting the scope of the exclusive jurisdiction clause in *British Sugar plc v Fratelli Babbini di Lionell Babbini & Co SAS*,[91] Seymour J looked to what was commercially sensible. The clause in this case did not indicate whether it covered only national disputes or international disputes also. The clause, indicating that all contractual disputes should be tried in Italy, was held to cover all disputes regardless of where they arose.

In *Skype Technologies SA v Joltid Limited and others*[92] the clause read as follows: 'Any claim arising under or relating to this agreement . . . the parties submit to the exclusive jurisdiction of the English courts.' A common-sense approach was advocated.[93]

3.7.5 Jurisdiction agreements with third country elements

The opening sentence of Art 23 of Brussels I stipulates that 'one or more of the parties' must be domiciled in a Member State. At the time of the agreement on jurisdiction it is uncertain as to which of the parties will be the defendant and which of them will be the claimant in future disputes. Hence, if one or more of the parties is domiciled in a Member State, then provided that their agreement complies with the formal requirements of Brussels I, the courts designated in the agreement shall have exclusive jurisdiction over the actions.

3.7.5.1 Non-domiciliary agreements

If none of the parties is domiciled in a Member State, but there is an exclusive jurisdiction agreement in favour of the court of Member State, this agreement will give jurisdiction to the Member State court under Brussels I.[94] Article 23(3) of Brussels I provides that where such an agreement exists the courts of other Member States will have no jurisdiction, unless the court chosen has declined jurisdiction.[95] If other courts would have jurisdiction to hear the case under Art 5 or 6 of Brussels I, the jurisdiction will give the chosen court exclusive jurisdiction over these courts. If no court would have jurisdiction under the rules of Brussels I, the jurisdiction agreement will preclude the courts of other Member States from taking jurisdiction under their national rules.[96] For example, if two New York domiciliaries have an exclusive jurisdiction agreement in favour of the English courts, a German court, if seised would decline jurisdiction based on Art 23. The German court could only establish jurisdiction under its own domestic law if the English courts had declined jurisdiction.

90 *Knorr-Bremse Systems for Commercial Vehicles Ltd v Haldex Brake Products GmbH* [2008] FSR 30.
91 [2005] 1 All ER (Comm) 55.
92 [2009] EWHC 2783 (Ch).
93 See also *Fiona Trust & Holdings Corporation v Privalov* [2007] 2 Lloyd's Rep. 267; [2007] EWHC 39 (Comm).
94 Opinion 01/03 [2006] ECR I-1145 [67].
95 Brussels I recast treats all jurisdiction agreement the same regardless of the domicile of the parties. Art 25.
96 C387/98 *Coreck Maritime GmbH v Handelsveem* [2000] ECR I-09337.

3.7.5.2 Agreements where jurisdiction is given to a non-Member State

Article 23 of Brussels I refers only to agreements where 'a court or the courts of a Member State are to have jurisdiction', thus an agreement to litigate in the court of a non-Member State falls outside the Brussels Regulation.

This becomes an issue when a court with jurisdiction under Art 2 or 5 of Brussels I is seised of such a dispute. Should that court decline jurisdiction because of an exclusive jurisdiction agreement in favour of a non-EU State? This point is highly controversial and is as yet unresolved.

The text of Brussels I only permits courts to decline in favour of agreement specifying another Member State. Should the court extend this to agreements in favour of third countries? This is referred to as 'reflexive effect'. This possibility was alluded to by the Advocate General in *Owusu v Jackson*[97] but neither approved nor rejected.

In *Coreck Maritime*[98] the ECJ suggested that in such a case the court should assess the validity of the clause by reference to national law. In *Opinion 1/03*[99] the court suggests that an agreement in favour of a non-EU court would not displace Art 2 jurisdiction based on the domicile of the defendant. This would allow an EU court to hear a case contrary to a choice of court agreement and to issue a judgment that could conflict with the judgment from the chosen court.

In *Konkola Copper Mines Plc V Coromin*[100] Colman J reserved the right to stay English proceedings in favour of an exclusive jurisdiction clause in favour of Zambia on the basis of Art 23. It is unclear if this is compatible with Brussels I. This practice is compatible with Brussels I recast if there are pending proceedings in the third-country state and the provisions of Arts 33 and 34 are satisfied.[101]

This problem of exclusive jurisdiction agreement in favour of third countries was considered in the review of Brussels I. The solution proposed was the EU's adoption of the Hague Convention on Choice of Court Agreements.[102]

3.7.5.3 The Hague Convention of 30 June 2005 on Choice of Court Agreements

The Hague Convention on Choice of Court Agreements is an international Convention. So far only Mexico has acceded to the Convention, although it has been signed by the USA and the EU. It does not need to be ratified by individual Member States[103] although Denmark remains outside the Convention. If the EU ratifies the Convention it will come into force between the EU and Mexico and any other countries that ratify the Convention.

The Hague Convention applies to international cases involving exclusive choice of court agreement in civil and commercial matters. The Hague Convention applies only to situations involving an exclusive choice of court agreement. Article 5 states that where such an agreement is present, the chosen court will have exclusive jurisdiction over the dispute. This court will adjudicate whether or not the exclusive jurisdiction agreement is valid. The chosen court cannot decline jurisdiction.

Article 6 states that a non-chosen court will not have jurisdiction to rule unless the agreement is found to be void by the chosen court or the chosen court has decided not to rule. If it is first seised it must decline jurisdiction until the chosen court has ruled on the matter.

Brussels I will take priority over the provisions of the Hague Convention.[104] Where both parties are resident in the EU and agree on an EU court, Brussels I will regulate the dispute. Brussels

97 [2005] QB 801.
98 C387/98 *Coreck Maritime GmbH v Handelsveem* [2000] ECR I- 09337.
99 [2006] ECR I-1145.
100 [2005] EWHC 898 (Comm). See also *Winnetka Trading Corp v Julius Baer International Ltd* [2008] EWHC 3146 (Ch).
101 See below.
102 COM (2009) 174 final.
103 *Opinion 01/03* [2006] ECR I-1145.
104 Art 26(6) Hague Convention.

I will also apply where either party is resident in an EU Member State and the court of an EU Member State is chosen. The impact study on the possible ratification of the Hague Convention ordered by the Commission[105] suggests that where two parties resident in the EU choose a third-country state, this agreement will fall outside Art 23 of Brussels I and the Hague Convention rules will apply.[106]

3.8 The primary basis of jurisdiction under Article 2

Under Art 2 of Brussels I,[107] where a defendant is being sued on a matter covered by Brussels I and is domiciled in a Member State, the action must be brought in the courts of that State. This is the general rule of Brussels I which operates in the absence of choice, protective jurisdiction or exclusive jurisdiction. Hence, a service of claim form issued under the traditional rules of jurisdiction explored in Chapter 4 cannot be served on a defendant domiciled in a Member State where the English courts do not have jurisdiction under Brussels I.

English courts must currently accept jurisdiction where the defendant is domiciled in England. This is so irrespective of any opinion by the English judges in that case that the dispute could be determined more appropriately by a court outside England.[108] However, the English courts have declined jurisdiction under Art 2 where an exclusive jurisdiction agreement exists in favour of a non-EU State[109] or where one of the exclusive jurisdiction grounds of Art 22 is present in a non-EU State.[110] The ECJ has yet to rule on whether these actions are compatible with Brussels I. Such stays will be possible under Brussels I recast where proceedings are pending in the third country and the requirements of Art 33 or 34 are satisfied.

The defendant's domicile is the point on which the EU regime's jurisdictional rules hinge. In contrast, the claimant's domicile has no relevance to jurisdiction under the general rule.[111]

The concept of domicile is left undefined by EU law. Brussels I merely indicates which system of national law would apply to determine the defendant's domicile.[112] The courts should apply the law of the state in which the defendant claims to be domiciled. **In English law the definition of domicile in ss 41–46 of the Civil Jurisdiction and Judgments Act 1982 applies in relation to civil and commercial disputes**.

The question of determining a defendant's domicile is one of fact. *Canada Trust Co v Stolzenberg (No 2)*[113] established that the burden of proof is on the claimant to show a good arguable case that the defendant is domiciled in the jurisdiction. Furthermore, the court looks at domicile at the time of issue, not service of the claim form.[114]

With regard to a corporation or association's domicile, Art 60(1) of Brussels I indicates that the corporation or association is domiciled 'at the place' where it has its statutory seat or central administration or principal place of business.[115]

---

105 GHK Consulting, 'Study to inform an Impact Assessment on the Ratification of the Hague Convention on Choice of Court Agreements by the European Community' (2007), available online at: http://ec.europa.eu/justice/civil/files/ia_choice_courts_agreement_en.pdf (accessed 9 May 2013). See Annex 4.

106 Ibid, 101.

107 Found in Art 4 of Brussels I recast.

108 C281/02 *Owusu v Jackson* [2005] QB 801.

109 *Konkola Copper Mines Plc v Coromin Ltd* [2005] EWHC 898 (Comm).

110 *Ferrexpo AG v Gilson Investments Ltd* [2012] EWHC 721 (Comm).

111 *Universal General Insurance Co (USIG) v Group Josi Reinsurance Co SA* [2000] ECR 1-5925.

112 Art 59.

113 [2002] 1 AC 1.

114 *Provimi Ltd v Aventis Animal Nutrition SA* [2003] 2 All ER (Comm) 683.

115 See further Chapter 2.

New proposals for reform to Brussels I have suggested the development of an autonomous meaning for domicile.[116] In Brussels I recast, it is clear that domicile will be defined autonomously.[117]

3.9 Special jurisdiction (Arts 5–7)

In certain cases, the general rule that a defendant must be sued in the court of his domicile is supplemented by Arts 5 to 7 of Brussels I. These confer 'special jurisdiction' on the courts of another Member State in addition to the state where the defendant is domiciled in a number of situations. While the bases of jurisdiction under Art 5 rely on the existence of a factual connection between the subject matter of the dispute and the court specified, the bases under Art 6 address cases where there is a multiplicity of defendants or a multiplicity of liability actions. Before dealing with the various heads available, it is important to note that the courts with special jurisdiction have no discretion under Brussels I to refuse jurisdiction. This will change under Brussels I recast where the criteria of Art 33 or 34 are satisfied. The special jurisdiction grounds, where available, enable a claimant to forum shop as more than one Member State may have jurisdiction. It will, therefore, be crucial for claimants to consider which is a more advantageous forum before commencing an action.

3.9.1 Contract

Article 5(1) of Brussels I provides the first alternative basis of jurisdiction. It states that, in matters relating to a contract, a defendant may also be sued 'in the courts for the place of performance of the obligation in question'. If that place is in Belgium, for instance, then the Belgian courts will also have jurisdiction even where the defendant is domiciled in England, giving the English courts jurisdiction under Art 2.

3.9.1.1 Matters relating to contract

Due to differences between national legal systems, the phrase 'matters relating to contract' has been given an autonomous EU meaning. The concept covers any relationship which is contractual whereby the defendant has voluntarily undertaken to fulfil an obligation towards the claimant, but subject to the privity rule. In *Martin Peters BmbH v Zuid Nederlandse AV*[118] the meaning covered the obligation to pay money arising from a relationship between an association and its members.

Where a dispute between the parties is as to the existence of the contract itself then, by virtue of *Effer SpA v Kantner*,[119] such a dispute is also within the meaning of this concept. The English Court of Appeal has applied this principle to a case where the claimant denied the existence of the contract. In *Boss Group Ltd v Boss France SA*[120] the claimant, an English company, terminated a contract of exclusive distributorship of its products with the defendant, a company domiciled in France. The defendant considered the act to be a breach of the contract and commenced proceedings against the claimant in France, claiming damages. The claimant then commenced proceedings in England under Art 5(1), seeking a declaration that no contract had existed between the parties. The Court of Appeal held, *inter alia*, that the word 'contract' in Art 5(1) could not be read as including only cases where the existence of the contract was unchallengeable or unchallenged. Article 5(1) provision was not confined to actions to enforce or to obtain recompense for the breach of a contract; and since the

116 Hess, Pfeiffer and Schlosser, *Report on the Application of Regulation Brussels I in the Member States* (Study JLS/C4/2005/03), 85.
117 Recital (15).
118 [1983] ECR 987.
119 [1982] ECR 825.
120 [1996] 4 All ER 970.

defendant had sought to enforce the contract in France, this was sufficient to establish that the claimant's claim was a matter relating to contract.

Despite the wide meaning this phrase has been given by the ECJ, it would seem to be restricted to cases where there is a direct undertaking between the parties to the dispute. In *Jacobe Handte GmbH v Traitement Mécano-Chimiques des Surfaces*,[121] the ECJ held that an action by a buyer against the manufacturer, rather than the vendor of a defective product, did not come under the provision of Art 5(1). This type of remedy is allowed under French Law, where it is classified as a contractual remedy and is called an *action directe*. In general terms, under this type of remedy, a purchaser of a product which is found to be defective can sue the manufacturer directly, irrespective of the lack of contractual relationship between them. Moreover, the Court of Appeal held in *Barclays Bank v Glasgow City Council*[122] that the phrase 'matters relating to a contract' required either an actual relationship or consensual relations closely akin to a contract.

Nevertheless, in *Agnew v Lansfosakringsbolagens*[123] a majority in the House of Lords held that Art 5(1) was sufficiently wide to cover an action for the breach of the duty to make a fair presentation of the risk by not giving full disclosure and for misrepresentation during the negotiation of a contract of reinsurance. This was despite the fact that, under English law, the defendants' obligations were extra-contractual. Thus, the scope of Art 5(1) might be regarded as unclear.[124]

3.9.1.2 Place of performance of the obligation

In *Industrie Tessili v Dunlop*[125] the ECJ gave some guidance as to how the place of performance of the obligation in question was to be ascertained. In that case, the ECJ ruled that the place of performance of the obligation in question was to be determined by the law which governed that obligation. That law would be ascertained by the national court before which the matter was brought, in accordance with its own private international law rules. Where, however, the place of performance had been indicated by the parties in a clause which was valid by the law applicable to that contract then, under *Zelger v Salinitri (No 1)*,[126] such a clause would generally be upheld.

In *De Bloos v Bouyer*,[127] the ECJ held that the phrase referred to the contractual obligation which formed the basis of the claimant's action and not to any other obligation under the contract. Therefore, where a claim was brought by a seller of goods for non-payment by the buyer then, clearly, the obligation in question was that of the buyer to pay the agreed price. Conversely, where the buyer brought an action against the seller for non delivery of goods, then the obligation in question was that of the seller to deliver the 'place of performance of the obligation in question'.

Brussels I[128] now states that unless the parties have agreed otherwise the place of performance of the obligation in question is:

- in the case of the **sale of goods**, the place in a Member State where, under the contract, the goods were delivered or should have been delivered;
- in the case of the **provision of services**, the place in a Member State where, under the contract, the services were provided or should have been provided; and
- if the contract is not one for the sale of goods or supply of services the court must go back to the general test under Art 5(1)(a).

121 [1992] ECR 1-3967.
122 [1994] 2 WLR 466.
123 [2001] 1 AC 223 relating to Art 5(1) of the Lugano Convention.
124 See also C265/02 *Frahuil SA v Assitalisa SpA* [2004] ECR I-1543.
125 [1977] 1 CMLR 26.
126 [1980] ECR 239.
127 [1977] ECR 1497.
128 Art 5(1)(b).

3.9.1.3 Multiple obligations and negative obligations

Where the subject of the dispute entails more than one obligation then, according to the ECJ in *Shenavi v Kreischer*,[129] the phrase refers to the principal obligation as determined by the national court seised of the dispute. This principle was subsequently applied in *Union Transport v Continental Lines*.[130] The claimant brought an action in England against the defendant, a Belgian company, for failure both to nominate and to provide a vessel to carry a cargo of telegraph poles from Florida to Bangladesh under a charter party agreement. Thus the claimant alleged breach of two obligations: the first was to nominate a vessel, and the second was to provide that vessel to load the cargo. The House of Lords held that the principal obligation in this case was the obligation to nominate the vessel. Since this obligation was to be performed in England, where the claimants were to receive the nomination, the English court had competent jurisdiction under Art 5(1) of the Brussels Convention. It was irrelevant that Florida was the place where the vessel would have been made available for the purposes of loading the cargo.[131]

Where a contractual obligation is a negative one, not subject to geographical limits, ascertaining 'the place of performance' may be problematic; this issue was referred to by the ECJ in *Besix SA v Wassereinigungsbau Alfred Kretzchmar GmbH*.[132] Under the terms of a contract, two companies undertook not to commit themselves to other partners; in relation to an alleged breach of this agreement, the question arose as to jurisdiction under Art 5(1). The ECJ ruled that Art 5(1) was not applicable because the 'place of performance' could not be determined in relation to an exclusivity agreement with geographical limits. The absence of such limits meant there were 'a multiplicity of places for its performance' and accordingly jurisdiction could only be determined by Art 2 of the Brussels Convention.

3.9.2 Tort

Article 5(3) of Brussels I provides for special jurisdiction in matters relating to tort, delict or quasi-delict, to the effect that a person domiciled in a Member State may also be sued 'in the courts for the place where the harmful event occurred'.[133]

The meaning of 'tort, delict or quasi-delict' was considered by the ECJ in *Kalfelis v Schroder, Munchmeyer, Hengst and Co*,[134] where it was held that the phrase must be given an independent EU meaning and cover all proceedings which were brought against a defendant for any liability that did not involve contractual matters. For example, in *Casio Computer Co Ltd v Sayo (No 3)*[135] knowingly assisting a breach of trust came within Art 5(3) on the facts. In *Verein Fur Konsumenteninformation v Karl Heinz Henkel*[136] the ECJ held that an action for an injunction, to prevent the use of unfair terms in consumer contracts, came within the meaning of Art 5(3).

Whether the proceedings concern 'matters relating to tort' or 'matters relating to contract' cannot be determined by reference to the classification of the action under national law. For instance, where proceedings concern 'matters relating to tort', a claimant cannot invoke the jurisdiction of the French courts under Art 5(1), on the basis that the action can be framed in contract under French internal law. Similarly, where the action relates to a contractual matter, an English court cannot be jurisdictionally competent under Art 5(3) simply because English internal

---

129 [1987] ECR 239.
130 [1991] 1 All ER 161.
131 See also *Raiffeisen Zentralbank Osterrich AG v National Bank of Greece SA* [1999] 1 Lloyd's Rep 408.
132 [2002] ECR I-1699.
133 These provisions are found in Art 7(2) of Brussels I recast.
134 [1988] ECR 5565.
135 [2001] IL Pr 694.
136 C167/00, *Fur Konsumenteninformation v Karl Heinz Henkel* [2002] ECR I-8111.

law classifies it as a matter relating to tort. Where the proceedings against the defendant are partly related to tort and partly related to contract, a court which has competent jurisdiction in tort under Art 5(3) can only deal with that part of the proceedings which is not contractual.

The Court of Appeal has held that where a claim may be based alternatively in contract and in tort, the claim will be regarded for the purposes of the Convention as being contractual in nature, as the test in *Kalfelis* states that tort is anything that is not related to contract. The action in *Source Ltd v TUV Rheinland Holding*[137] was brought on the basis of both the defendants' contractual obligation to use reasonable skill and care in carrying out the inspections, and their breach of duty in the form of a negligent misstatement. The Court of Appeal held that the claimant's alternative claim in tort was excluded from the special jurisdiction in Art 5(3).

In *Raiffeisen Zentralbank Österreich AG v National Bank of Greece*[138] the claimants sought to bring proceedings in England for breach of contract or alternatively negligent misstatement. It was contended that England had jurisdiction under Art 5(1) as the place where the contractual obligations were to be performed or under Art 5(3) as the place where the harmful event occurred. Tuckey J interpreted *Source* to mean that the court with jurisdiction over the contract claim has jurisdiction over the alternative tort claim as well.

3.9.2.1 Place of the harmful event

The key geographical connection under Art 5(3) is 'the place where the harmful event occurred or may occur'. This phrase was interpreted by the ECJ in *Bier BV v Mines de Potasse d'Alsace SA*.[139] Here the claimant, a Dutch market gardener, alleged that the defendants, a company domiciled in France, had polluted the waters of the Rhine in France. The pollution of these waters, which he used for the purposes of irrigation, resulted in damage to his plants. He brought an action in the Dutch court as the court for the place where the harmful event occurred. The jurisdiction of the Dutch court was contested and the matter was referred to the ECJ, which ruled that Art 5(3) was intended to cover both the place where the damage occurred and the place where the event giving rise to the damage occurred. Hence, according to this decision, a claimant suing in tort may have as many as three options. He or she may choose to bring the action in any of the following courts:

(a) in the courts for the place where the defendant is domiciled (Art 2);
(b) in the courts for the place where the damage occurred (Art 5(3)); or
(c) in the courts for the place where the event giving rise to the damage took place (Art 5(3)).

The question of identifying the place where the harmful event occurred was again referred to the ECJ in the case of *Shevill v Presse Alliance SA*,[140] which related to the tort of defamation. In a simplified account of the facts, the claimants, Shevill, domiciled in the UK, along with three other companies established in different Member States brought an action against the defendant, Presse Alliance, alleging libel as a result of an article published in the newspaper *France Soir*, which suggested that the claimants were involved in a drug-trafficking network. The action in the English court was for damages on the ground that the claimants had suffered harm in France and in the other states, as well as in England. The claimants subsequently limited their claim to damages for the harm suffered in England. The newspaper was mainly distributed in France (237,000 copies) but with a small circulation in English (230 copies). The defendants contested the jurisdiction of the English court on the ground that the harmful event within the meaning of

137 [1997] 3 WLR 365.
138 [1999] 1 Lloyd's Rep 408.
139 [1976] ECR 1735.
140 C68/93 *Shevill v Presse Alliance SA* [1995] 2 AC 18.

Art (3) had occurred in France and not in England. The House of Lords referred a number of questions to the ECJ.

The ECJ ruled that the harmful event occurred either in the place where the publisher was established, which was France, as the place the harmful event originated; or the place where the damage occurred. As this case was one of international libel through the press, the damage occurred in the places where the publication was distributed, and in which the victims were known. Therefore, the courts of each Member State in which the defamatory publication was distributed, and in which the victims suffered injury to their reputation, had jurisdiction, but only to the extent of harm suffered within those jurisdictions.[141] The end result of this case law is that, in international libel cases, Art 5(3) confers jurisdiction on the courts of the place where the publisher is established or on the courts for the places where the harm was suffered. However, with regard to the harm suffered, the courts of each place have jurisdiction only to the extent of damages suffered within that place.[142]

The place of the harmful event in connection with the tort of negligent misstatement was considered by the English court in *Domicrest Ltd v Swiss Bank Corp*,[143] where Rex J held that this place was where the misstatement originated. In his view, the place from which the misstatement was put into circulation was as good a place in which to found jurisdiction as the place where the misstatement was acted upon, even if receipt and reliance were essential parts of the tort. Indeed, it was the representor's negligent speech, rather than the hearer's receipt of it, which best identified the harmful event which set the tort in motion, and no distinction was to be drawn between a written document, an oral communication or other instantaneous communication. In *Alfred Dunhill Ltd v Diffucion International de Maroquinerie de Prestige SARL*,[144] an action for misrepresentation was held to come within Art 5(3), not Art 5(1), and that the 'harmful event' occurred where the misrepresentations were made, not where they were received, in England by an English company.

3.9.2.2 Direct damage and indirect damage

The question arises as to whether 'the place where the damage occurred' embraces cases involving direct and indirect economic loss, as opposed to personal injury or damage to property. Suppose that a parent company, domiciled in France, suffers loss as a consequence of its German subsidiary becoming insolvent after acting on the defendant's negligent advice. The German subsidiary has suffered economic loss in Germany as a direct result of the negligent advice and should be able to bring proceedings in Germany. Would the French courts have jurisdiction under Art 5(3) on the basis of the indirect loss suffered by the French parent company? This question was addressed by the ECJ in *Dumez France SA and Tracoba SARL v Hessiche Landesbank*,[145] where similar facts were the subject matter of the proceedings. The ECJ expressed the view that Art 5(3) applies to allocate jurisdiction to the courts for the place where the *direct damage* occurred to the immediate victim and does not cover cases of indirect damage.

The dividing line between direct and indirect damage was examined in *Marinari v Lloyds Bank plc*,[146] where the claimant, domiciled in Italy, had received a set of promissory notes issued in the Philippines in favour of a company trading in Lebanon. The notes, which had an exchange value of $752 million, were deposited with Lloyds Bank in England. The bank, suspecting that the notes were of dubious origin, informed the police, who arrested the claimant and confiscated the notes. Following criminal proceedings in England, the claimant was acquitted, but the notes

141 See further *Bus Berzelius Umwelt Service AG v Chemconserve BV Reakt* [2004] IL PR 9.
142 See further Chapter 8.
143 [1998] 3 All ER 577.
144 [2002] IL Pr 13.
145 C220/88 *Dumez France SA and Tracoba SARL v Hessische Landesbank* [1990] ECR I-49.
146 C364-93 *Marinari v Lloyds Bank plc* [1995] ECR I-2719.

were not returned. Subsequently, he brought an action in the Italian courts, claiming damages to the value of the notes. The Italian action was brought in reliance on Art 5(3), on the ground that he suffered financial loss in Italy as a result of the conduct of the bank staff which had taken place in England. He argued that the Italian courts had jurisdiction, since it was in Italy that the harmful consequences had occurred. The ECJ rejected this argument and ruled that the Italian courts did not have jurisdiction. As in *Dumez*, the ECJ drew a distinction between the place where the direct damage had occurred – that is, England – and Italy, where the alleged consequential loss was felt. The place where the damage occurred under Art 5(3) must be taken to cover only the place of direct damage and did not include the place where the consequential financial loss was suffered.

A similar approach was taken in *Zuid-Chemie BV v Philippo's Mineralenfabriek NV/SA*,[147] where a Dutch fertiliser manufacturer took delivery of defective fertiliser ingredients in Belgium. They were used to make fertiliser in the Netherlands. This fertiliser was sold to customers but was unusable. The fertiliser company undertook proceedings in the Netherlands. The Dutch court sought clarification on where the damage had occurred. The ECJ held that the 'place where the damage occurred' was the place where the damage caused by the defective product actually manifested itself.[148] In this case this was in the Netherlands, where the defective product was processed into fertiliser. The ECJ did not have to consider the indirect financial damage caused by the sale of ineffective fertiliser.

3.9.2.3 Restitutionary claims

While the primary basis of jurisdiction under Art 2 encompasses restitutionary claims such as claims for unjust enrichment, breach of fiduciary duty, *quantum meruit*, payment, or breach of constructive trust. It is less clear whether the special bases of jurisdiction under Arts 5(1) and (3) embrace such claims. The ECJ has not addressed this question to date.

Two controversial English judgments highlight the difficulties with classifying such claims. *Kleinwort Benson Ltd v Glasgow City Council*,[149] which concerned a relatively new type of financial transaction known as interest rate swap agreements, arose under the modified Convention allocating jurisdiction within the UK. In plain terms, such a transaction consists of an agreement between two parties, whereby one party pays the other sums of money over a period of months or years. The sums in question are calculated by reference to the difference between a fixed rate of interest and the current rate of interest from time to time. The main feature of the agreement is that it is a futures contract, whose financial outcome depends on future movements in interest rates. A number of local authorities, including Glasgow City Council, used these contracts in 1982 in an attempt to improve their financial income. The facts of the case are as follows: Glasgow City Council entered into seven transactions with Kleinwort. In 1991, the House of Lords held that all such transactions were void for lack of capacity on the part of the local authorities.[150] Consequently, Kleinwort brought an action against Glasgow City Council in the English court, claiming restitution of the sum of £807,230, being the balance standing to the credit of the City Council under the transactions, on the basis of unjust enrichment. The defendant challenged the jurisdiction of the English court on the ground that it was domiciled in Scotland and, therefore, the action should be brought in the Scottish courts pursuant to Art 2 of the modified Convention.

The claimant contended, *inter alia*, that the English courts had jurisdiction under Art 5(1), or alternatively under Art 5(3) since the claim was for restitution in respect of money paid to the

---

147 C189/08 *Zuid-Chemie BV v Philippo's Mineralenfabriek NV/SA* [2009] ECR I-6917.
148 Ibid [27].
149 [1997] 4 All ER 641.
150 *Hazell v Hammersmith and Fulham London Borough Council* [1992] 2 AC 1.

defendant under a contract which was a nullity, because one of the parties did not have capacity to enter into it; and that England was 'the place of performance of the obligation in question' or 'the place where the harmful event occurred'. The Court of Appeal held that the correct approach was to determine whether the defendant should broadly be regarded as being sued in a matter relating to a contract. It was incorrect to ask whether the claim would be classified as contractual under domestic law. Hence, a contract was a consensual arrangement intended both to create legal relations and be legally enforceable, and that included a void contract. As for the phrase 'place of performance of the obligation in question', this meant the intended place of performance of the supposed obligation. Accordingly, the English court had jurisdiction under Art 5(1) to adjudicate the claim of the claimant for restitution in respect of money paid under the terms of the interest rate swap contracts. The Court of Appeal then found it unnecessary to decide whether a claim of this type also fell under Art 5(3). A reference to the ECJ for a preliminary ruling was rejected on the basis that the ECJ does not have jurisdiction to give rulings on the modified Convention.

On appeal to the House of Lords, the decision of the Court of Appeal was reversed and it was held that the claim fell under neither Art 5(1) nor Art 5(3). The House of Lords took the view that a claim could only fall within Art 5(1) if it was based on a particular contractual obligation, the place of performance of which was within the jurisdiction of the court. On the facts, however, the claimant's claim was for the recovery of money paid under a supposed contract which had never existed in law. Thus, the claim was not based on contractual obligation, but rather on the principle of unjust enrichment. Since no express provision was made in respect of such claims in Art 5(1), the defendants must be sued in the courts of their domicile. With regard to Art 5(3), again the House of Lords held that the claim did not fall within its ambit, for such a claim did not, apart from in exceptional circumstances, presuppose either a harmful event or a threatened wrong. Accordingly the English court did not have jurisdiction to entertain the action.

The question of classifying restitutionary claims also arose in *Atlas Shipping v Suisse Atlantique Société d'Armement Maritime SA*,[151] which concerned an implied constructive trust created by memoranda. The claimants, brokers on behalf of the sellers, sought to recover from the buyers the commission they were due as a result of the sale of two vessels. The claimant had no contractual relationship with the buyers, but the latter had the right to deduct 2 per cent commission from the purchase price under the terms of the contracts. The claimants contended that, by necessary implication, where the deduction was taken, the buyers had contracted with the sellers to pay the identified commission to the brokers. Consequently, the buyers and sellers had created a trust, of which the buyers were trustees and the claimants were the beneficiaries. The buyers were domiciled in Switzerland but the claimants brought the action in England, in reliance on Art 5(1). The buyers contested the jurisdiction of the English court on the ground that they were not sued in matters relating to contract but rather by reason of a constructive trust created by memoranda. Nevertheless, Rix J held that the obligation, which was being enforced in this case, was the obligation owed by the buyers to the sellers to pay the brokers. It made no difference that the contractual promise had been given with the intention of creating an irrevocable trust in favour of a third party; the obligation in question was contractual. Indeed the buyers were being sued 'in matters relating to a contract'; the obligation in question was the alleged promise given by them that they would pay over the deduction in the form of commission to the brokers; and the place of performance of that obligation was England. Thus the claimant's claim was within both the spirit and letter of Art 5(1).

151 [1995] 2 Lloyd's Rep 188.

3.9.3 Maintenance

This section of Brussels I has been replaced by the Maintenance Regulation (Council Regulation (EC) No 4/2009). This will be examined in greater detail in Chapter 11. However, as Denmark has opted out of the Maintenance Regulation, this section will continue to apply.[152] The new Lugano Convention contains a similar section to Art 5(2) that will apply to maintenance claims.

Article 5(2) allows a person domiciled in a Member State to be sued in the place where the maintenance creditor is domiciled or habitually resident. This means that the person to whom maintenance is owing, the weaker party, may take proceedings in the court of their own domicile.

Brussels I does not apply to matrimonial property or decisions relating to marital status, but it does apply to maintenance. As claims for maintenance are often combined with the main proceedings for divorce, Art 5(2) further provides that in such cases the court which has competent jurisdiction in respect of the main proceedings (determined by Brussels II *bis*) also had jurisdiction in respect of maintenance claims. This is the case, provided that jurisdiction over the main proceedings is not assumed merely on the basis of one of the parties' nationality.

The new Lugano Convention gives jurisdiction to the courts entertaining parental responsibility proceedings if the matter of maintenance is ancillary to those proceedings.

It must be noted that the inclusion of 'matrimonial proceedings ancillary to proceedings of status' under Art 5(2) has given rise to problems of interpretation, especially when considered in light of matters relating to 'rights in property arising out of a matrimonial relationship' which are excluded from the ambit of Brussels I.

In *Van de Boogard v Laumen*,[153] the ECJ explained how to draw the distinction between decisions regulating matrimonial property excluded under Art 1 and those relating to maintenance under Art 5(2). The ECJ drew a distinction between those aspects of a decision which regulated matters of maintenance and those which regulated the matrimonial relationship of the parties, stating that maintenance provisions were those designed to enable one spouse to provide for himself or herself. Alternatively, if the needs and resources of each of the spouses are taken into consideration in the determination of the amount, the decision is concerned with maintenance.[154]

Where, on the other hand, the decision is solely concerned with dividing property between the spouses, it will then be related to a matrimonial property and cannot be enforced under Brussels I. This issue is further explored in Chapter 11, where the EU regulation of matrimonial property is discussed.

The term 'maintenance creditor' was interpreted by the ECJ in *Farrel v Long*[155] to cover not only persons applying for owing maintenance, but also persons bringing a maintenance action for the first time. Article 5(2) does not extend to a public body seeking to recover money paid to a maintenance creditor such as the English Child Support Agency.[156]

3.9.4 Civil claims in criminal proceedings

Article 5(4) of Brussels I allows a claimant making a civil claim for damages or restitution which is based on an act giving rise to criminal proceedings to sue in the courts seised of the criminal proceedings, provided that such a court can entertain the civil claim under its own law. This provision is not likely to be operative in England, for English law does not generally confer jurisdiction upon criminal courts to deal with civil claims. Article 5(4) covers cases such as *Sonntag*

152 There is no equivalent section in Brussels I recast. See recital (10).
153 [1997] IL Pr 278.
154 Ibid 306.
155 [1997] IL PR 343.
156 *Freistaat Bayern v Jan Blijdensteine* [2004] ECR I-981.

v Waidmann,[157] where the deceased's next of kin were allowed to join in the criminal proceedings in the Italian court for the purposes of claiming civil compensation.

3.9.5 Branch agency or other establishment

Article 5(5) allows a defendant to be sued where the dispute arises out of the operation of a branch, agency or other establishment, 'in the courts for the place in which the branch agency or other establishment is situated'. This phrase also has huge significance in establishing jurisdiction under the protective jurisdiction provisions in Arts 8–14.[158] At first glance, this provision appears to embrace a wide extension of jurisdiction, likely to cover any dispute arising out of the operation of any secondary establishment.

Initially the ECJ had given the phrase 'branch, agency or other establishment' a narrow Community meaning. For instance, in *De Bloos v Bouyer*[159] an exclusive distribution agreement was granted by Bouyer, a French company, to De Bloos, a Belgian company, for the marketing by the latter of the former's products in a number of Contracting States. De Bloos brought an action in the Belgian courts, claiming breach of contract and seeking dissolution of the distribution agreement. The jurisdiction of the Belgian court was invoked on the ground that De Bloos should be regarded as a branch, agency or other establishment within the meaning of Art 5(5). The ECJ, however, rejected this view and held that one of the essential characteristics of this concept was that the branch or agency had to be subject to the direction and control of the parent body.

Similarly, in *Blankaert and Willems v Trost*[160] the ECJ held that an independent commercial agent who could also represent other rival firms and who merely conveyed orders to the parent body without being involved in the performance of the contracts, could not be classed as a branch agency or other establishment. Furthermore, in *Somafer SA v Saar-Ferngas AC*,[161] an action was brought against the defendant, a French company, in the German courts. The defendant company had its registered office and principal place of business in France, but its notepaper also had a business address in Germany. This business was not registered as a branch in Germany and was carried on only by one of the defendant's employees. The ECJ ruled that, for an action to come within the meaning of Art 5(5), it had to be shown that the branch, agency or other establishment had a fixed permanent place of business, was subject to the direction and control of the parent body, and acted as an extension of the parent body.

Nevertheless, in the subsequent case of *Sar Schotte GmbH v Parfums Rothschild SARL*[162] the ECJ appears to have moved towards adopting a wider meaning for the concept. The claimant, a German company, supplied goods to a French subsidiary of another German company. Following a dispute over the quality of the goods supplied, the claimant brought an action in the German courts on the basis of Art 5(5), that is, the German parent company was considered as a branch, agency or other establishment of the French subsidiary, for it had conducted business with the claimant on behalf of the subsidiary. The ECJ confirmed this view and ruled that the vital question was to look at the way in which the two companies were behaving and how they presented themselves to third parties. A third party should be able to rely on the representation given.

In order to invoke jurisdiction under Art 5(5), it needs to be established that the claim arose out of the 'operation' of the branch, agency or other establishment itself. The word 'operation' was

157 [1993] ECR 1-1963.
158 See above.
159 [1977] 1 CMLR 60.
160 [1981] ECR 819.
161 [1978] ECR 2183.
162 [1987] ECR 4905.

given an independent EU meaning by the ECJ in *Somafer SA v Saar-Frngas AG*.[163] This includes actions relating to the management of the branch, agency or other establishment. Such actions include those concerning the situation of the building, the local engagement of staff, torts committed in the course of the branch's activities, and undertakings entered into in the name of the parent and which are to be performed in the place where the branch, agency or other establishment is situated.[164]

In *Lloyd's Register of Shipping v Sociéte Campenon Bernard*[165] the ECJ went further to decide that it was not necessary for the operation giving rise to the dispute to take place in the state where the secondary establishment was situated. The case concerned a contract between the claimant, a French company, and the defendant, an English company with various branches in a number of states, including France and Spain. The contract, which was concluded in France through the defendant's subsidiary therein, was to be performed in Spain. The defendant was to examine steel through their branch there. Following a dispute, the claimant brought an action in the French courts on the basis of Art 5(5). The defendant contested the jurisdiction, contending that since the steel was to be examined in Spain, that is, the place where the undertaking was to be performed, the requirements of the provision were not satisfied. Nonetheless, the ECJ took the view that such an undertaking would form part of the operation of a secondary establishment within the meaning of the provision, even though it was to be performed outside the Member State where such an establishment was situated.

More recently, in *Anton Durbeck GmbH v Den Norske Bank ASA*[166] a claim was made against a bank for wrongful interference with a cargo of bananas on board a ship, which resulted in the cargo being a constructive total loss. The ship had been purchased with a loan from the bank's London office, with the vessel as security for the loan. The London branch, with the approval of the head office in Norway, had enforced the security by seizure of the ship in Panama. At first instance, it was held that Art 5(5) did not give jurisdiction to the English courts as the loss was caused by the seizure in Panama. The Court of Appeal found that Lloyd's Register robbed 'the geographical limit in the *Somafer* case . . . of such authority as it might otherwise have had', thereby agreeing that it was not necessary for the operation giving rise to the dispute to take place in the Contracting State where the secondary establishment was situated. What was actually required for jurisdiction under Art 5(5) was a nexus between the branch and the dispute which would render it natural to describe the dispute as one which has arisen out of the activities of the branch. Where the claim is in contract, that nexus can be derived from the negotiations between the claimant and the branch which gave rise to the contractual obligation.[167]

It was not considered desirable to formulate a test for tortious liability, but rather to determine the issue by reference to the facts of the individual case. In this case, the dispute had arisen out of the activities of the London branch because the loan was negotiated by the London branch, which also made the decision to enforce the security. Thus Art 5(5) gave the English courts jurisdiction against the defendant company.

3.9.6 Trusts, salvage and shipping

Article 5(6) of Brussels I provides for special jurisdiction in relation to trusts to the effect that the courts of the Member State in which the trust is domiciled will also have jurisdiction. In order for

163 [1978] ECR 2183.
164 Ibid [13].
165 [1995] ECR 1-96.
166 [2003] QB 1160.
167 Ibid 1173.

this provision to be invoked, the trust must have been created by the operation of a statute or by a written instrument or created orally and evidenced in writing.

Article 5(7) provides for special jurisdictional rules in relation to remuneration for the salvage of a cargo.

Article 7 provides special jurisdiction in actions relating to liability from the use or operation of a ship.

3.9.7 Multiple defendants

Article 6 of Brussels I provides further alternative bases for jurisdiction which are designed both to reduce the expense and inconvenience of litigating in different Member States and to avoid the risk of irreconcilable judgments resulting from separate proceedings in different States.[168]

Article 6(1) applies when a defendant is one of a number of defendants to the same claim or where there are several closely connected claims against different defendants. Under Art 2 each defendant would have to be sued in a separate action in the state of their domicile. Article 6(1) allows a person domiciled in an EU State to be sued in the courts of the Member State where any of the other defendants is domiciled provided the claims are 'closely connected'.[169] The purpose of Art 6(1) is to prevent irreconcilable judgments. It is necessary to show that there is a connection between the claims made against each defendant which renders it expedient to hear the claims in the same venue.[170] The claims cannot merely relate to the same set of facts.[171] Otherwise claimants would be encouraged to join EU domiciliaries to actions merely to be able to bring proceedings in a particular EU court.

Reunion Européenne SA and Others v Spliethoff's[172] concerned a consignment of peaches that had been shipped from Australia to Rotterdam and then onwards to France. When they arrived in France they were overripe as the cooling system on the ship had failed. The claimants brought proceedings against the Australian suppliers, the Dutch company that carried the goods and the Dutch master of the vessel that shipped the goods in the French courts. The French courts had jurisdiction to hear the claim against the Australian company under national rules of jurisdiction. The question was whether the Dutch transport company and the Dutch ship master could be sued in the French courts as co-defendants. The ECJ ruled that the matter was tortious. The damage to the fruit had occurred sometime during the transport. The court held that the Dutch courts had jurisdiction under Art 5(3) as the place where the damage occurred as that was the last place where the cargo was under the defendants' control.

The ECJ considered whether Art 6(1) allowed the EU domiciliaries against whom a claim had been brought under Art 5(3) to be sued in another Member State that is seised of the same action under its national rules. It was held that as the Australian company was not domiciled in the EU the other defendants could not be sued in the French courts under Art 6(1).[173] Furthermore, the claims were not connected within the meaning of Art 6(1).

The time for determining the domicile of the 'anchor' defendant is the date of issue of the claim and not the date when the claim form was served.[174] In *Reisch Montage AG v Kiesel Baumaschinen Handels GmbH*[175] the ECJ held that Art 6(1) could be relied on where the case against the anchor defendant was inadmissible under provision of national procedural law.

---

168 Arts 7 and 8 of Brussels recast.

169 *King v Crown Energy AG* [2003] IL Pr 28; *Andrew Weir Shipping Ltd v Wartsila UK Ltd* [2004] EWHC 1284 (Comm).

170 C98/06 *Freeport Plc v Arnoldsson* [2007] ECR 1-8319.

171 See also *Kalfelis* case [1988] ECR 5565.

172 [1998] ECR I-6511.

173 Ibid [67].

174 *Canada Trust Co v Stolzenberg (No 2)* [2002] 1 AC 1; *Petrotrade Inc v Smith* [1999] 1 WLR 457.

175 C103/05 *Reisch Montage AG v Kiesel Baumaschinen Handels GmbH* [2006] ECR I-6827.

The ECJ has limited the application of Art 6(1) in cases where the initial claim was based on one of the protective jurisdiction provisions. In *GlaxoSmithKline*[176] an employee had sued in France, where his first employer was domiciled, and he applied to join his other employer who was domiciled in the UK as a co-defendant relying on Art 6(1). The court stated that the provisions of s 5 were exclusive and did not incorporate a rule allowing claims against multiple defendants to be joined. This decision was criticised as disadvantaging employees who might, as a result, have to bring proceedings in different courses and run the risk of irreconcilable judgments. This seemed contrary to the spirit of protective provisions of Brussels I.[177]

When Brussels I was reviewed the decision in *GlaxoSmithKline* was identified as problematic.[178] The Commission advocated permitting employees to bring actions against multiple defendants under Art 6(1).[179] This possibility had existed under the Brussels Convention and it benefited employees. In Brussels I recast employees are permitted to join proceedings against employers.[180]

By virtue of Art 6(2), a person domiciled in a Member State may be sued as a third party in an action on a warranty or guarantee, in the courts seised of the original proceedings. This is so unless such proceedings were instituted in order to avoid the jurisdiction of the court which would otherwise be competent in the case.

Article 6(3) allows a counterclaim arising from the same contract or facts on which the original claim was based to be brought in the court in which the original claim is pending.

Under Art 6(4), invoked in matters relating to a contract, if the action may be combined with an action against the same defendant is related to a right *in rem* in immovable property, the defendant may also be sued in the court where the property is situated.

3.10 Residual jurisdiction under Article 4

If the dispute is one of a civil and commercial nature which is not caught by any of the above provisions of Brussels I, Art 4 applies. Article 4 states that where a defendant is not domiciled in a Member State the jurisdiction of the courts of each Member State shall, subject to Arts 22 and 23, be determined by the national law of that Member State. The ground of jurisdiction under national law may be much broader than those permitted under Brussels I. For example, under English law mere presence in England will give the English courts jurisdiction,[181] whereas in France the French courts will have jurisdiction where one of the parties is a French national.[182]

During the review of Brussels I, it was suggested that harmonisation of the rules of residual jurisdiction was needed. Consumers were left without protective jurisdiction against third-state defendants and access to justice was unequal.[183] These proposals were criticised by the House of Lords,[184] who counselled that a flexible approach should be taken.

In 2010 the Commission put forward proposals to harmonise the residual rules of jurisdiction and extend the rules of Brussels I to cases where defendants were not domiciled in a Member State.[185]

176 C462/06 *GlaxosmithKline v Rouard* [2008] ECR I-3965.
177 Z Tang, 'Multiple Defendants in the European Jurisdiction Regulation' (2009) 34 E L Rev 80–103; J Harris 'The Brussels I Regulation, the ECJ and the rulebook' (2008) 124 LQR 523–529.
178 COM (2009) 174 final.
179 COM (2010) 748 final [3.1.6].
180 Art 20 (1).
181 See further Chapter 3.
182 Art 14, Code Civil.
183 COM (2009) 174 final, 5.
184 The European Union Committee of the House of Lords: Green Paper on the Review of the Brussels Regulation Report with Evidence, (2009) HL paper 148.
185 See also K Takahashi, 'Review of the Brussels I Regulation: A Comment from the Perspectives of Non-Member States' (2012) 8 JPIL 1–15.

This would have meant an end to national rules of jurisdiction for civil and commercial matters.[186] The European Parliament considered that the proposals were premature and that a stronger case was needed.[187] It suggested that the Commission should also attempt to revive the attempts by the Hague Conference to create an international judgments Convention.

Brussels I recast extends the rules of the regulation to claims against non-EU domiciliaries where the claimant is a consumer or an employee. A consumer may bring proceedings against the other party to a contract in the courts of his own domicile regardless of the domicile of the other party.[188] An employee may bring proceedings against an employer in the courts where he habitually carried out his work regardless of the employer's domicile.[189] As under Brussels I, the EU regime will apply, regardless of the defendant's domicile, where there is an exclusive jurisdiction agreement in favour of an EU Member State[190] or where the courts of a Member State are considered to have exclusive jurisdiction.[191] The jurisdiction of the courts of each Member State to hear such claims when the claimant is not a consumer or an employee is governed by national rules.[192]

3.11 Provisional measures (Art 31)

Article 31 of Brussels I allows a court to decide on provisional, protective measures where there is a genuine connection between the protective measure and the territory of the Member State such as the fact that the defendant has assets there.[193] There is no need for the Member State granting the protective measure to have jurisdiction over the substance of the dispute. A protective or provisional measure is one which protects the status quo such as a temporary freezing order.[194]

In the review of Brussels I it was noted that the case law on the real link between the measure sought and the territorial jurisdiction was unclear.[195] No changes were made to Brussels I recast in relation to this problem.

3.12 *Lis pendens* and related actions

Under Brussels I, it is possible for more than one Member State court to have jurisdiction for the same action. In a case where concurrent proceedings relating to the same cause of action are taking place, a strict 'first in time rule' applies. The EU regime currently gives no discretion to a court to stay proceedings where the court has jurisdiction and is the first court seised.[196]

3.12.1 Mandatory stay of proceedings

Article 27 of Brussels I applies where proceedings involving the **same cause of action** and the **same parties** are brought in courts of two different Member States. Any court other than the one first seised must stay its proceedings of its own motion. The stay will be for a limited period of time,

186 COM (2010) 748 final [3.1.2].
187 European Parliament resolution of 7 September 2010 on the implementation and review of the Brussels I Regulation (2009/2140(INI)) [15].
188 Art 18(1).
189 Art 21(2).
190 Art 25.
191 Art 24.
192 Art 6(1).
193 C99/96 *Mietz v Intership* [1999] ECR I-2277.
194 C99/96 *Mietz v Intership* [1999] ECR I-2277; C104/03 *St Paul Dairy v Unibel* [2005] ECR I-3481.
195 COM (2009) 174 final.
196 This contrasts with the flexibility of the English traditional rules explored in Chapter 4.

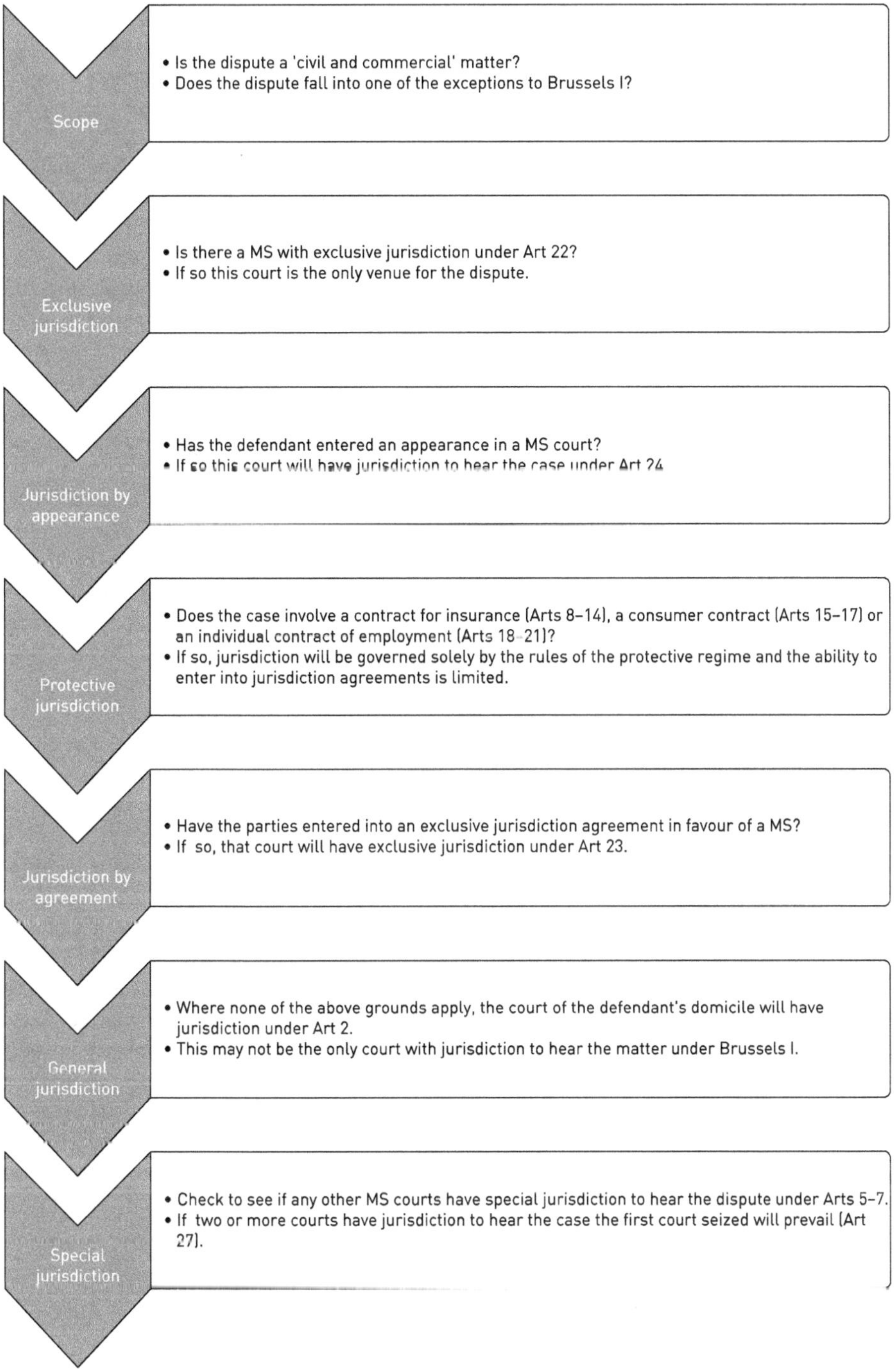

Fig 3.2 Checklist for determining jurisdiction under Brussels I.

until the court first seised establishes whether or not it has competent jurisdiction over the parties and the cause of action. If the first court claims jurisdiction, then the second court has an obligation to decline jurisdiction. In this sense the first in time rule set down under *lis pendens* is rigid and inflexible. The object of the provisions is to prevent parallel proceedings from taking place in two different Member States, thereby avoiding the risk of irreconcilable judgments.[197]

Article 27 applies to concurrent proceedings in Member States only. However, there is no requirement that either party should be domiciled in a Member State for the *lis pendens* rule to apply. In *Overseas Union Ltd v New Hampshire Insurance Co*[198] the defendant, a company incorporated in the USA, carried on business in England and in France. The claimants were three companies, two of which were incorporated in England and the third in Singapore. Following the defendant's initiation of proceedings in France, the claimants sought a declaration, relating to their rights against the defendant, from the English court. The Court of Appeal was satisfied that the proceeding involved the same parties and the same cause of action. The question of whether the *lis pendens* rule applied where one of the parties was not domiciled in the EU was referred to the ECJ. The ECJ ruled that the *lis pendens* rule applied to any proceedings before a court of a Contracting State, regardless of the parties' domicile.

What is meant by the notion 'the same cause of action'? In *Gubisch Maschinenfabrik v Giulio Palumbo*,[199] the court ruled that this phrase had an autonomous EU meaning and gave the phrase a wide interpretation. The case concerned a dispute over a contract of the sale of a machine by a German seller to an Italian buyer. The seller brought an action for payment of the price in the German court. The buyer brought an action in the Italian court, seeking the annulment of the contract and/or rescission of the contract on the basis of delay in the delivery of the machine. The ECJ held that Art 21 of the Brussels Convention extended to a case where one party brought an action in the courts of one Contracting State claiming annulment or rescission of a contract when another action for the enforcement of the contract was simultaneously pending in the courts of another Contracting State. In *The Maciej Ratay*,[200] an action seeking to establish the defendant's liability in contract for causing loss to a cargo was held to have the same object as earlier proceedings brought by the defendant for a declaration that he was not liable for that loss.

In *Boss Group v Boss France*[201] the Court of Appeal held that proceedings of a provisional nature and proceedings adjudicating the merits of the case were not classed as the same cause of action. In *Mecklermedia Corp v DC Congress*[202] it was held that a claim based on the infringement of a trademark registration was not the same as a passing off action.

In *Gantner Electronic GmbH v Basch Exploitatie Maatschappij BV*,[203] the ECJ held that defence grounds raised did not need to be taken into account, in determining whether claims brought between two parties before the courts of different Contracting States had the same subject matter. The nature of proceedings was fixed before defence submissions were made. This case was distinguished in *Secret Hotels 2 Ltd v EA Traveller Ltd*,[204] where the parties had raised two different claims on identical issues in Cyprus and England. Both claims could be set off against each other. The court held that this was different to the scenario in *Gantner*, where the set off was one-sided. However, the court held that even if this was not the case, *lis pendens* applied under Art 28 of Brussels I (examined below).

---

197 *Bank of Tokyo-Mitsubishi Ltd v Baskan Gida Sanayi Ve Pazarlama AS* [2004] 2 Lloyd's Rep 395.
198 [1992] 2 WLR 586.
199 [1987] ECR 4861.
200 [1995] 1 Lloyd's Rep 302.
201 [1997] 1 WLR 351.
202 [1997] 3 WLR 479.
203 [2003] ECR 1-4207.
204 [2010] EWHC 1023 (Ch).

Article 27 also requires that the concurrent proceedings must be *between the same parties*. Thus where two sets of proceedings do not involve the same parties, Art 27 cannot come into operation. In *Mecklermedia Corp v DC Congress*,[205] Mecklermedia was not considered to be the same party as Mecklermedia's licensee. However, the ECJ held in *Drouot Assurances v Consolidated Metallurgical Industries*[206] that where an insurer, by virtue of its right of subrogation, brings or defends an action in the name of its insured, the insurer and insured must be considered to be one and the same party. But Art 27 cannot have the effect of precluding the insurer and the insured from asserting their respective interests before the courts as against the other parties concerned by the proceedings. Where the interests of the insurer can be considered as identical to and indistinguishable from those of its insured is for the national courts to ascertain.

Article 27 of Brussels I ascribes priority to the court 'first seized' of the proceedings. In *Zelger v Salinitri (No 2)*,[207] the ECJ interpreted the term to require the action to be 'definitely pending'. The question of whether a court is 'definitely seised' at the time when a claim is issued or the time it is served must be determined in accordance with the law of the state to which the court in question belongs. From the information placed before the ECJ in this case, it appeared that in all six original Member States (that is Belgium, France, Germany, Italy, Luxembourg and the Netherlands) a court would only be definitely seised when the claim was served.

Today, Art 30 states that a court is deemed to be seised at the time where the document issuing proceedings is lodged at the court, as long as the claimant later takes the steps required to have service of claim effected.

Article 29 applies where two Member States have exclusive jurisdiction over the same dispute. In such a case the court first seised has jurisdiction and the second court must decline jurisdiction.

The mandatory 'first in time' rule for concurrent proceedings involving the same cause of action and the same parties remains under Brussels I recast.[208]

3.12.2 Torpedo tactics and exclusive jurisdiction agreements

Article 27 does not distinguish between an action taken because of a genuine belief that that Member State has jurisdiction and a deliberate attempt to frustrate litigation by taking an action in a jurisdiction that clearly does not have jurisdiction.

This practice is particularly resented where the parties have a contractual clause on exclusive jurisdiction and have agreed that they will bring proceedings in only one court. Suppose the parties have agreed in their contract to refer their dispute to the exclusive jurisdiction of the English court. In breach of the agreement, one of the parties commences proceedings in the Greek court. The other party then brings an action in the English court in accordance with the jurisdiction agreement. If Art 27 is prioritised, the English proceedings would have to be stayed. Conversely, if the exclusive jurisdiction agreement is prioritised and the parties are held to their agreement, the Greek proceedings would have to be stayed.

The ECJ has held that the 'first in time' rule must apply even where the first proceedings were brought in a court with no jurisdiction to deliberately delay proceedings.[209] The second court seised must wait until the first court has declined jurisdiction before proceeding. This practice is known as

205 [1997] 3 WLR 479.
206 [1998] IL Pr 391.
207 [1984] ECR 2397.
208 Arts 29 and 31(1).
209 C116/02 *Gasser v Misat* [2003] ECR I-14693.

a 'torpedo' and can cause substantial delay and expense. It can be used as a tactic to gain an unfair commercial advantage and encourage settlement.

In *Gasser v MISAT*,[210] Gasser, an Austrian company, had supplied children's clothes to Misat, an Italian company over a period of years. Misat brought an action against Gasser in the Italian courts claiming that the contract between them had terminated. Gasser brought an action in the Austrian courts for payment of outstanding invoices. It further claimed that the relationship was subject to an exclusive jurisdiction agreement favouring the Austrian courts. The Austrian courts stayed proceedings until the Italian courts had ruled on jurisdiction in accordance with the *lis pendens* rule. Gasser appealed, and the following questions, *inter alia*, were sent by the Higher Region Court of Austria to the ECJ.

Can the court with exclusive jurisdiction rule without waiting for the first court to decline jurisdiction? Here the ECJ ruled that there could be no short cut to the *lis pendens* rule even where the second court appeared to have exclusive jurisdiction. The ECJ held that the court second seised must stay proceedings of its own motion until the jurisdiction of the court first seised has been established and, where it is so established, must decline jurisdiction in favour of the latter.

What if the court first seised takes an excessive amount of time to come to a decision? Here it was argued that a failure to give timely judgment could infringe Art 6 of the ECHR. Thus Brussels I should be interpreted in compliance with the ECHR, allowing the *lis pendens* rule to be avoided if used abusively to prolong litigation. The ECJ reiterated that there was no short cut around the *lis pendens* rule. There was no statutory exception based on length of proceedings. The principles of mutual trust and certainty required the court second seised to wait for the first court to rule.

The ruling in *Gasser* has been greatly criticised.[211] It allows one party to deliberately violate an exclusive jurisdiction agreement in an effort to frustrate proceedings in the agreed jurisdiction. Although the court without jurisdiction should eventually decline jurisdiction, this can cause considerable delay and cost.

JP Morgan Europe Ltd v Primacom[212] is an example of 'torpedo' tactics. In this case, a loan facility agreement existed between the parties which was subject to an exclusive jurisdiction clause in favour of the English courts. Primacom failed to pay the interest on the agreement and then took proceedings in the German courts, alleging that the original agreement was immoral in a deliberate attempt to frustrate proceedings in England. JP Morgan took proceedings in England, *inter alia*, to prevent Primacom from disposing of its assets. Primacom sought a stay of proceedings on the basis of Art 27. The English courts granted the stay until the German courts declined jurisdiction, although they noted that it would be difficult to see how any claim that the German courts had jurisdiction could be sustained.

Attempts by the English courts to use anti-suit injunctions to prevent proceedings being brought in EU Member States without jurisdiction to delay proceedings were found to be incompatible with Brussels I.[213]

During the review of Brussels I, concerns were voiced that Art 27 did not adequately protect exclusive jurisdiction agreements. The Commission noted that while there were no statistics available to ascertain whether 'torpedo' tactics were frequent they were particularly resented when the first proceedings were brought for a declaration of non-liability.[214] This could effectively prevent proceedings on the merits from being heard by a competent court.

---

210 [2003] ECR I-14693.

211 T Hartley, 'The European Union and the Systematic Dismantling of the Common Law of Conflict of Laws' (2005) 54 ICLQ 813–828; P Briza, 'Choice-of-Court Agreements: Could the Hague Choice of Court Agreements Convention and the Reform of the Brussels I Regulation be the Way Out of the *Gasser-Owusu* Disillusion?' [2009] 5 JPIL 537; Y Baatz, 'Who Decides on Jurisdiction Clauses? *Erich Gasser v. MISAT*' (2004) *Lloyd's Maritime and Commercial Law Quarterly* 25.

212 [2005] EWHC 508.

213 *Turner v Grovit* [2005] 1 AC 101; see further Chapter 4.

214 COM (2009) 174 final, 6.

In 2010, the Commission suggested that a time limit should be placed on the court first seised to decide on its jurisdiction. In addition, courts seised of the same matter should exchange information.[215] The Commission also proposed that where the parties have entered into a choice of court agreement to have their dispute heard by an EU court, the chosen court must be given priority to decide on its jurisdiction, regardless of whether it is first or second seised. Any other court must stay proceedings until the chosen court has established or declined jurisdiction.[216] It was hoped that this change to Brussels I would increase the effectiveness of choice of court agreements and eliminate the incentives for abusive litigation in non-competent courts.

An exception to the *lis pendens* rule is made in Brussels I recast, where there is an exclusive choice of court agreement in favour of a Member State court.[217] The court designated in the exclusive choice of court agreement has priority to decide on the validity and scope of the exclusive jurisdiction agreement and can proceed irrespective of whether a non-designated court seised of the same proceedings has stayed matters.[218] Where there are conflicting exclusive jurisdiction agreements the general *lis pendens* rule will still apply.[219] In addition, the general *lis pendens* rule will still apply where the exclusive jurisdiction agreement does not comply with the restrictions on jurisdiction agreements under the protective rules of jurisdiction relating to insurance, employment and consumer contracts.

3.12.2.1 Where there are proceedings pending in a jurisdiction outside the EU regime

Brussels I is silent as to the problem of concurrent proceedings pending before the courts of a Member State and the courts of a non-Member State. Under the English traditional rules,[220] the English courts may stay proceedings in favour of another court on the basis that the other court is better placed to hear the dispute. This power, known as *forum non conveniens*,[221] is often used where proceedings are pending in the other court and there is a risk of conflicting judgments.

In *Owusu v Jackson*[222] the ECJ ruled that where the court has jurisdiction under Art 2 of Brussels I, jurisdiction cannot be refused on the basis of the common law doctrine of *forum non conveniens*. In *Owusu*, the English courts could not stay proceedings in favour of the Jamaican courts even though the accident that was the subject of the dispute had occurred in Jamaica and it would be more convenient for witnesses and evidential matters to have the trial there.

Owusu did not directly deal with the question of whether a Member State court could decline Brussels I jurisdiction or stay proceedings because proceedings are already under way in a third country and there is a risk of irreconcilable judgments. Avoiding irreconcilable judgments is one of the key purposes of the Brussels I *lis pendens* rule under Art 27.

The issue was explored in *Catalyst Investment Group Ltd v Lewisohn and others*.[223] In this case, fraud proceedings were under way in Utah. The claimant sought a declaration from the English courts that it was not liable for fraud and had committed no breach of contract. The defendant challenged the jurisdiction of the English court on the basis that a reflexive interpretation of Art 27 of Brussels I allowed the English courts to stay proceedings pending a decision from the Utah courts. Barling J rejected this argument, holding that there was no support from the existing authorities that Art 27 should be given reflexive effect. He held that while there was some support in favour of the court

215 COM (2010) 748 final [3.1.5].
216 Ibid [3.1.3].
217 Art 31(2).
218 Recital (22).
219 Ibid.
220 Examined in Chapter 4.
221 See Chapter 4.
222 [2005] QB 801.
223 [2009] EWHC 1964 (Ch).

upholding an exclusive jurisdiction agreement in favour of a third country[224] the same could not be said for a strict first in time basis. He held that to do so would reintroduce *forum non conveniens* by the back door contrary to the ruling in *Owusu*.

Under Brussels I recast,[225] where a Member State court is seised either under the general rule as the court of the defendant's domicile,[226] or under the rules of special jurisdiction[227] **and** proceedings are pending before the court of a third state involving the same cause of action and between the same parties the Member State may stay proceedings in certain circumstances.

In order for a stay to be granted it must be shown that the court of the third state will give a judgment that can be recognised and enforced in the Member State[228] **and** that the Member State court is satisfied that a stay is necessary for the proper administration of justice.[229] When deciding if the stay is necessary for the proper administration of justice the Member State court should consider whether the third state would have exclusive jurisdiction if the provisions of Brussels I recast were given reflexive effect.[230]

A similar power exists to stay proceedings where proceedings are pending in a third-country state which do not relate to the same cause of action but are related causes of action.[231] In such cases the Member State court may stay proceedings on the same grounds if it is expedient to hear the related claims together to avoid the risk of irreconcilable judgments.

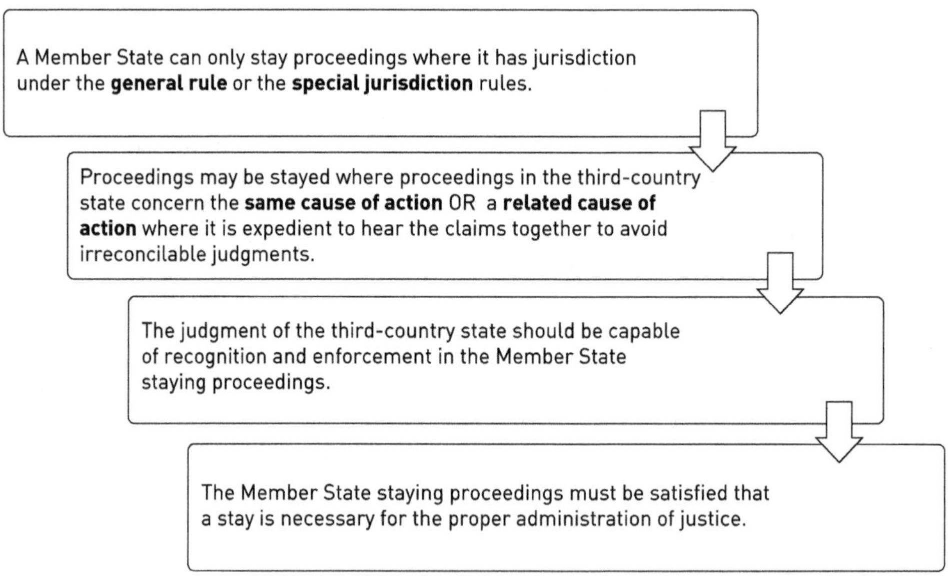

Fig 3.3 Staying actions under Brussels I recast where proceedings are pending in a third country.

224 C387/98 *Coreck Maritime GmbH v Handelsveem* [2000] ECR I- 09337. See above.
225 Art 33.
226 Art 4 Brussels I recast.
227 Arts 7–9 Brussels I recast.
228 Art 33(1)(a).
229 Art 33(1)(b).
230 Recitals (23) and (24).
231 Art 34.

3.12.3 Discretionary stay of proceedings under Brussels I

Article 28 allows a court to stay its proceedings where the cause of action, *not the same but related*, is pending in another State first seised of the matter. This power is optional where the court is second seised. In *Cronos Container NV v Palatin*[232] a stay of English proceedings was sought in favour of proceedings in Luxembourg. The actions were found to be related and the English court to be first seised. Accordingly a stay could not be granted.

'Related proceedings' are proceedings which are closely connected so that it is expedient to hear them together to avoid the risk of irreconcilable judgments resulting from separate proceedings. The meaning of the concept of 'related actions' has been considered in a number of cases. For instance, in *Sarrio v KIA*[233] the House of Lords held that there should be a broad common-sense approach to the question of whether actions are related. Thus a claim based on negligent misrepresentation and one of sums for non-performance of the contract were 'related actions', since the same allegation about the role of the defendant in the negotiations for the sale of the claimant's business underpinned the litigation in both jurisdictions and raised a risk of irreconcilable judgments.[234] However, in *Mecklermedia Corp v DC Congress*[235] the action in the English court was for passing off, and the action in the German court was for the infringement of the German trade mark registration. These were held to be not related in that there was no risk of irreconcilable judgments.

In *Miles Platts Ltd v Townroe Ltd*,[236] proceedings were commenced in a French court for the appointment of an expert to investigate whether components sold were defective. Proceedings were also commenced in England for damages for losses incurred by the alleged defects in the components. The Court of Appeal refused to grant a stay of the English proceedings in favour of the French court; these were not 'related proceedings'. The French proceedings were interim rather than substantive and would only determine whether the components were defective but were not concerned with tracing who was responsible for any defects. The English proceedings related to whether the defendant company had been involved in electroplating the components and so was liable for any defects. The proceedings were not so closely connected that it was expedient to hear and determine them together to avoid the risk of irreconcilable judgments.

In *Abko*,[237] proceedings had been instituted in copyright law, in relation to the same films. These were not related actions, because the English proceedings related only to UK copyright and the French proceedings had no concern with the UK breach.

Under Brussels I recast the discretionary power to grant a stay remains.[238] In addition, the second court seised may decline jurisdiction where the law allows the actions to be consolidated.[239]

3.13 Jurisdiction within the UK

Section 16 of the Civil Jurisdiction and Judgments Act 1982 determines which jurisdiction within the UK should hear a particular set of proceedings. A modified form of Brussels I is used, which is found in Sched 4. According to s 16, the Sched 4 rules apply if the following three conditions are satisfied:

---

232 [2003] 2 Lloyd's Rep 489.
233 [1998] 1 Lloyd's Rep 129.
234 See also *Blue Nile Shipping Co Ltd v Iguana Shipping and Finance Inc* [1998] IL Pr 440.
235 [1997] 3 WLR 479.
236 [2003] IL Pr 47.
237 *Abko Music and Records Inc v Jodorowski* [2003] ECDR 3.
238 Art 30(1).
239 Art 30(2).

(1) the issue must concern allocation of jurisdiction within the UK (i.e. England and Wales, Scotland and Northern Ireland);
(2) the subject matter of the proceedings must be within the scope of Art 1 of the Brussels Regulation; and
(3) the defendant must be domiciled in the UK or the dispute must come within the scope of Art 22 of the Brussels Regulation.

The rules in Sched 4 operate in a similar manner to the rules of Brussels I outlined above. The UK courts must have regard to the decision of the CJEU in relation to the meaning of Brussels I when interpreting Sched 4 but cannot refer matters to the CJEU for preliminary ruling.[240] There are some small differences which have been noted above. For example, for the purposes of allocation jurisdiction within the UK there is no requirement that a jurisdiction agreement is in 'writing'. The doctrine of *forum non conveniens* is still in operation in relation to Sched 4.[241]

3.14 Further reading

A Briggs, 'The subtle variety of jurisdiction agreements' [2012] *Lloyd's Maritime and Commercial Law Quarterly* 364–381.
P Briza, 'Choice-of-court agreements: Could the Hague Choice of Court Agreements Convention and the reform of the Brussels I Regulation be the way out of the *Gasser-Owusu* disillusion?' [2009] 5 JPIL 537.
R Fentiman, 'Civil Jurisdiction and Third States: Owusu and After' (2006) 43 *Common Market Law Review* 705–734.
L Gillies, 'Clarifying the "philosophy of article 15" in the Brussels I Regulation: *Pammer v Reederei Karl Schluter GmbH & Co KG* (C-585/08) and *Hotel Alpenhof v Heller* (C-144/09)' (2011) ICLQ 557–564.
U Grusic, 'Jurisdiction in employment matters under Brussels I: a reassessment' (2012) 61 ICLQ 91–126.
T Hartley, 'The European Union and the systematic dismantling of the common law of conflict of laws' (2005) 54 ICLQ 813–828.
B Hess, 'The Brussels I Regulation: recent case law of the Court of Justice and the Commission's proposed recast' (2012) 49 *Common Market Law Review* 1075–1112.
J Mance, 'Exclusive jurisdiction agreements and European ideals' (2004) 120 LQR 357–365.
L Merrett, 'The enforcement of jurisdiction agreement within Brussels regime' (2006) 55 ICLQ 315–336.

240 *Kleinworth Benson Ltd v Glasgow City Council* [1997] 4 All ER 641.
241 *Cumming v Scottish Daily Record and Sunday Mail Ltd* [1995] EMLR 538.

Chapter 4

Jurisdiction of the English courts in Commercial Disputes

The Traditional Rules

Chapter Contents

Key Issues:

- Civil Procedure rules for service within the jurisdiction
- Civil Procedure rules for service outside the jurisdiction
- Jurisdiction clauses
- *Forum non conveniens*
- The anti-suit injunction

4.1 Introduction

This chapter will examine the English rules of jurisdiction, i.e. whether the English court has the power to hear a case which has a foreign element. These rules are common law based but have been modified by legislation and are now embodied in the Civil Procedure Rules. Today, EU regulation of jurisdiction in civil and commercial matters through Brussels I[1] means that these traditional rules have a limited application. The traditional rules apply only to cases where the defendant is domiciled in a country that is outside the European Union and is not a party to the Lugano Convention,[2] and where no other rules Brussels I apply.[3] This would include defendants domiciled in the USA, Australia, Canada, China etc. The EU regulation of jurisdiction in civil and commercial matters is examined in Chapter 3.

This chapter will examine jurisdiction *in personam* in civil cases. Jurisdiction *in personam* refers to the jurisdiction of a court to require a person to do something, such as pay damages to another party. The judgment is binding only on specific people who are parties to the case. There is a second type of jurisdiction know as jurisdiction *in rem*. This refers to the jurisdiction of the court to make a judgment that can be enforced on a piece of property. In such cases, the property is seized and sold by order of court to satisfy the claim brought. Such an order is binding on the whole world. In English law, jurisdiction *in rem* only exists in relation to ships and will not be examined in this book. The jurisdiction of the English courts to hear matrimonial matters and matters relating to children will be examined in Chapters 10 to 13.

It is a fundamental principle of the conflict of laws that the legitimacy of the court to hear an action against a defendant is based on some geographical connection between the defendant and the forum. The traditional English rules of jurisdiction focus on correct service of a claim form giving the court jurisdiction. A defendant can be served with a claim form if present in England. If the defendant is not present in England, permission from the court must be granted in order to serve a claim form. In such cases, it must be proved to the court that a suitable connection between the dispute and the English courts exists. An English court will also have jurisdiction where the defendant voluntarily submits to the jurisdiction of the English courts.

The English traditional rule allowing service of a claim form on a defendant who is merely present in the jurisdiction means that disputes can be brought in the English courts where there is little connecting the dispute to the forum. This basis of jurisdiction may seem exorbitant, particularly where one party is trying to take advantage by bringing proceedings in England rather than another more appropriate forum. This practice is known as **forum shopping**. In order to avoid unfairness, the English traditional rules allow the court to stay proceedings in England where the defendant can prove that England is an unsuitable forum and that another more suitable forum

1 Council Regulation (EC) No 44/2001 OJ L12/1.

2 Convention on jurisdiction and the enforcement of judgments in civil and commercial matters signed in Lugano on 30 October 2007 [2007] OJ L339/3.

3 Arts 22 & 23 give an EU Member State exclusive jurisdiction regardless of the domicile of the parties. See Chapter 3.

exists. This is known as the doctrine of *forum non conveniens*. This traditional remedy is only available if jurisdiction is based on the traditional rules and jurisdiction falls outside the remit of EU legislation. The interaction of *forum non conveniens* with Brussels I is explored below.

Where proceedings are brought in a foreign court and England is clearly the more appropriate forum, the traditional rules allow the defendant to apply to the English courts for an injunction to restrain foreign proceedings. This remedy is unavailable where the foreign proceedings in question are taking place in an EU Member State and jurisdiction is based on Brussels I.

4.2 Service of claim forms

In England, proceedings are commenced when the court issues a claim form at the request of a claimant. The claimant will fill in a form containing details of the claim and submit this to the court. The court then issues the claim form and sends the claimant a notice of issue.[4] The court will serve the claim form on the defendant if the defendant is present in the jurisdiction.[5] Where the defendant is not present in the jurisdiction, the claimant must seek permission from the court to have the claim form served on the defendant.[6]

4.3 Defendant's presence in England

If the defendant is domiciled in an EU State, jurisdiction must be based on the rules of Brussels I. This includes all claims against English domiciliaries. In other cases, the English court has the power to hear a case under the traditional rules when a claim form is served on a defendant physically present in England. The application of this principle varies, depending on whether the defendant is an individual or a corporation.

4.3.1 Individuals

A claim form may be served on any individual who is present in England, however short the visit may be. For example, in *Maharanee of Barona v Wildenstein*,[7] a case pre-dating Brussels I, the claimant, an Indian princess residing in France, brought an action in England against the defendant, an art expert also residing in France. The claim form was served on the defendant while he was in England on a one-day visit to the Ascot races. The court held that service was valid and the claim should not be struck out merely because the defendant was only on holiday in England.

4.3.2 Corporations

Where a corporation is domiciled in England or another EU Member State, jurisdiction will be governed by Brussels I. A company is considered to be domiciled in England if it was incorporated or formed under the law of a part of the United Kingdom or its central management and control is exercised in the United Kingdom.[8] It will also be considered to be domiciled in England if this is its principal place of business.[9] The traditional rules will apply only if the company is not domiciled

4 CPR 6.3–6.29.
5 CPR 6.4.
6 CPR Part 6 (IV).
7 [1972] 2 All ER 689.
8 S 43 of the Civil Jurisdiction and Judgments Act 1982.
9 See further Chapter 2.

in an EU Member State. This will include companies that are incorporated in a non-EU country and have a place of business in England that is not a headquarters or principal place of business. In such situations, if the company is served with a claim form at its **place of business**, the English courts will have jurisdiction over the dispute based on the traditional rules.[10]

The question of whether a foreign company has established a place of business in England has been examined in several cases.

In *South India Shipping Corporation Ltd v Export-Import Bank of Korea*,[11] the claimant company was incorporated in India and brought a claim in England against the defendant bank, which was incorporated in Korea. The Bank rented an office in London for the purpose of maintaining relations with banking and financial institutions in the UK and Europe. Banking transactions were not concluded from the London office, nor was the office registered as a place of business under the Companies Act 1948, then in force. The claim form was served at the office in London. The defendants contended that they had not established a place of business in England and so the claim form had not been duly served. The Court of Appeal held that a company was said to have established a place of business in England if it carried out part of its business activities there. It was not necessary for those activities to be more than incidental to the main purpose of the company. It was immaterial that the defendant had neither concluded any banking transactions in London nor had banking dealings with the general public. A business activity was being carried out at the offices in London and the claim form was properly served.

In *Re Oriel Ltd*,[12] the Court of Appeal held that a *specific* location in England, where the company *habitually* carried out business, was necessary to show that a company had a place of business in England. In this case, the company was registered on the Isle of Man but its two directors resided in a house in England and it was alleged that this residence was a 'place of business'. The court held that in this case the house was not a place of business as there was no evidence of any overt or covert activity of the company at those premises. While a private residence could be a place of business, the mere presence of company directors at a private home in England followed by the company's entry into business dealings would not be sufficient to establish the home as the company's place of business.

In *Cleveland Museum of Art v Capricorn Art International SA & Anor*,[13] Capricorn Art dealers agreed to lend an ancient reliquary to the Cleveland Museum of Art. The reliquary had been stored in a vault in London which was part of the private residence of a London art dealer. When the reliquary arrived at the museum, part of it was missing. Capricorn brought proceedings in Ohio and before the trial started the Cleveland Museum issued proceedings in London, serving the claim form on the London storage premises. Capricorn claimed that the London premises were a private dwelling and not an art gallery of any kind. The reliquary had been stored there on an informal basis as a matter of convenience.

The court held that Capricorn regularly used the house for storing and showing work to private buyers and controlled access to the vault and so had established a place of business at the house. It was immaterial that there was no nameplate on the premises or any other indication to the public that the dealers were based there.

4.4 Service outside the jurisdiction

Where the defendant is not physically present in England, the claimant seeking to issue proceedings in England must apply to court for permission to serve the claim form out of the jurisdiction in

10 CPR 6.3(2).
11 [1985] 2 All ER 219.
12 [1985] 3 All ER 216.
13 [1990] 2 Lloyd's Rep 166; [1990] BCLC 546.

specific cases.[14] The application for permission will be made without notice to the defendant. The power to grant permission is discretionary and will only be granted if the case is a proper one for service out of the jurisdiction. Once permission has been granted the claimant bears the responsibility of ensuring that the claim form is properly served in the foreign jurisdiction.[15]

In order to obtain permission, the claimant must show (1) that one of the grounds laid out in paragraph 3.1 of Practice Direction 6B is satisfied.[16] This will open a 'jurisdictional gateway' to the English courts. Some of these grounds are very similar to the court's jurisdiction under Brussels I and will not be examined in this section.[17] Other grounds are particular to English law and are examined below. Once this gateway is opened the English court will decide, at its discretion, whether or not to grant permission. The claimant must satisfy the court that it is proper to allow service out of the jurisdiction. In order to do this, the claimant must also show (2) that his claim has merits and (3) that England is an appropriate forum (*forum conveniens*) to hear this claim.[18]

4.4.1 Gateways to jurisdiction under the CPR

In order for leave to be granted, the claimant must show that the claim satisfies one of the gateways to jurisdiction listed in Practice Direction 6B paragraph 3.1. These grounds require a link to be established between the dispute and England before the court can exercise its discretion to allow the claim form to be served. The burden of proof is on the claimant to make a **good arguable case** that its claim falls into one of the classes of case for which permission may be given.

In *AK Investment CJSC v Kyrgyz Mobil Tel Ltd and others*[19] the Privy Council held that in this context 'good arguable case' meant that one side had a much better argument than the other on the material available to the court.[20] This is a lower standard of proof than the balance of probabilities but is justified on the basis that jurisdictional issues ought, generally, to be decided with due despatch, without hearing oral evidence in order to avoid expense and delay.[21]

4.4.1.1 Contract

If the claim is related to a contact, permission to serve can be granted where (1) **the formation of the contract occurred in England**[22] or (2) **where the contract is governed by English law**.[23] The English courts may also hear the dispute if the contract contains a choice of court clause stating that the English courts will have jurisdiction to hear any disputes in connection with the contract.[24] This is examined below in the section on jurisdiction agreements.

English law is used to determine where the contract was concluded. This contains a series of arbitrary rules depending on what method of communication was used to conclude the contract. A contract formed by postal communications is concluded where the letter of acceptance was posted.[25] In contrast, where a contract is formed using instantaneous communication such as

14 CPR 6 (IV).
15 CPR 6.40 (3). The claimant may wish to comply with the Service Regulation, Council Regulation (EC) 1393/2007 [2007] OJ L324/79.
16 CPR 6.36.
17 E.g. 6B PD 3.1 (1) where the claimant must show that he is seeking a remedy against a person domiciled in the jurisdiction.
18 CPR 6.37(1)(b).
19 [2011] UKPC 7.
20 Ibid [71].
21 See further *Canada Trust Co and others v Stolzenberg and others (No 2)* [2002] 1 AC 1,13; *Bols Distilleries BV v Superior Yacht Services* [2006] UKPC 45 [28].
22 6B PD 3.1 (6)(a) and (b).
23 6B PD 3.1 (6)(c).
24 6B PD 3.1 (6)(d).
25 *Henthorn v Fraser* [1892] 2 Ch 27.

telephone, email, fax, text message or telex, the contract is considered to have been made where the acceptance is received.[26] This acceptance must be final and not marked 'subject to modification'. In *Brinkibon Ltd v Stahag Stahl GmbH*[27] the House of Lords held that a seller's telex[28] which had modified the terms of the buyer's offer was actually a counter-offer and not an acceptance. This meant that the contract was not made in England, where the seller's telex was received, but in Australia, where the buyer's confirmation of the modification was received.

The question of where receipt occurs when a person sends an email, instant message or text message or concludes a contract through a website requires some examination. If 'receipt' is taken to mean actual communication to the intended recipient, the place of contract will depend entirely on the recipient's location, which may not be foreseen by the sender of the acceptance. This would mean that an American businessman reading an English company's texted acceptance while on business in China would have a contract made in China.

An alternative approach to determining the place of contract for the purposes of satisfying the CPR grounds was taken in *Apple Corps Ltd v Apple Computers Inc.*[29] In this case, the court considered the effect of draft agreements signed by one party and subsequent telephone conversations. Mann J felt that the circumstances were such that it was difficult to pinpoint specific instances of offer and acceptance; to do so would be forced and might not represent the true intentions of the parties. Mann J looked to the commercial reality of the negotiations. He held that neither party had wanted to give the other an advantage in terms of jurisdiction and governing law. He concluded that a good arguable case could be made that the contract had been made both in England and in California.[30] As England was one of the places in which the contract was formed, the CPR ground was satisfied.

The English court may assume jurisdiction over a defendant outside the jurisdiction where the contract is governed by English law.[31] Whether a contract is governed by English law is now determined by EU regulation Rome I[32] and this matter is examined in Chapter 7.

In *Cecil v Bayat*,[33] the dispute concerned an oral agreement, in which the defendants allegedly promised the claimants a share in a company, set up to create a telecommunications network in Afghanistan, in return for the claimants taking responsibility for the technical aspects of the project. The defendants argued that the parties had merely been in negotiations and no contract had been formed. The court had to consider whether a good arguable case that the causes of action satisfied one of the gateways existed. The court held that the evidence that some understanding had been reached was enough to establish a good arguable case that a contract existed, which had been formed in England.[34]

Where the issue in the dispute is whether or not a valid contract actually exists, the court may grant leave to serve the claim where the putative contract would comply with the conditions already examined.[35]

4.4.1.2 Tort

Where the claim is founded in tort, the court may grant leave to serve a claim form where damage occurred in England or where damage sustained resulted from an act committed in the

26 *Entores v Miles Far East Corpn* [1955] 2 QB 327.
27 [1983] 2 AC 34.
28 An ancient form of fax machine.
29 [2004] EWHC 768 (Ch).
30 Ibid [43].
31 6B PD 3.1 (6)(c); *Cecil v Bayat* [2010] EWHC 641 (Comm) [84].
32 Regulation (EC) No 593/2008 [2008] OJ L177/6.
33 [2010] EWHC 641 (Comm).
34 Ibid [76]–[81].
35 6B PD 3.1 (8).

jurisdiction.[36] These grounds are very similar to those laid down in Brussels I, and CJEU jurisprudence is relevant to how they are interpreted by the English courts.[37]

In *Booth v Phillips and Others*,[38] the court considered a case where damage had occurred in two locations. The claimant's husband had died in Egypt due to the alleged negligence of his employers. The defendant argued that the damage occurred in Egypt, where the husband had been killed. This was the only element of damage that should be considered as it was the damage element that was needed to complete the cause of action.[39] The widow submitted that she had also sustained damage in England in her own right, by reason of her loss of dependency on the deceased and, in her capacity as his executrix, in relation to funeral expenses. It was held that, for the purposes of granting leave to serve the claim form, the court should consider the damage sustained by the claimant. It was sufficient that some of the damage was sustained in England even if most of the damage occurred elsewhere. The loss of dependency was determined to be damage sustained in England, where the claimant would live and suffer the loss. A similar finding was made in relation to the funeral expenses.[40]

In *Saldanha v Fulton Navigation Inc*[41] an Indian engineer was injured aboard a ship anchored off the coast of Wales. He was later taken to hospital in London to be treated for his injuries. He issued proceedings against the owners of the ship in the English courts and was granted permission to serve the claim form out of the jurisdiction. The jurisdiction of the English courts was contested on the basis that the injury should not be deemed to have taken place in England but in the Marshall Islands, where the ship was registered. The court held that for the purposes of 6B PD 3.1 (9) the injury had taken place in the territory of England and Wales.[42] In any event, the considerable amount of pain and suffering that the defendant endured while hospitalised in England was sufficient to found jurisdiction.

Where the cause of action is the tort of defamation, ascertaining where the damage took place and where the defamatory act occurred can be complex. These issues are examined in more depth in Chapter 8.

4.4.1.3 Property

Leave to serve a claim form on a defendant outside the jurisdiction is permissible where the whole subject matter of the claim relates to land situated within the jurisdiction.[43] This is very similar to the rule in Brussels I that the courts in the Member State where the land is situated have exclusive jurisdiction over proceedings relating to ownership or tenancies of that property.[44] The English courts have no jurisdiction under the traditional rules to entertain claims relating to property rights in immovable property outside the jurisdiction.[45] The rules of jurisdiction relating to property are further examined in Chapter 9.

4.4.1.4 Defendant is a 'proper party'

Leave to serve a claim form may also be obtained if there are two defendants, one of whom has already been duly served with the claim form or will be duly served in the future and the claimant wishes to serve the second defendant, who happens to be outside the jurisdiction.[46] The purpose of

36 6B PD 3.1 (9).
37 Art 5(3); *Bier v Mines de Potasse d'Alsace* (Case 21/76) [1976] ECR 1735.
38 [2004] 2 Lloyd's Rep 457.
39 In order to show negligence in English law a duty of care must exist which is breached resulting in damage.
40 [2004] 2 Lloyd's Rep 457 [44].
41 [2011] EWHC 1118 (Admlty).
42 Ibid [16]
43 6B PD 3.1 (11).
44 Art. 22(1) Brussels I.
45 *British South Africa Co v Companhia de Mocambique* [1893] AC 602.
46 6B PD 3.1 (3).

this ground is to alleviate the inconvenience where a dispute involving more than one defendant is heard in a number of venues. It also helps to avoid the risk of irreconcilable judgments. Originally the first defendant or the 'anchor defendant' had to be served within the UK, but today the CPR makes it clear that the anchor defendant may be served within the jurisdiction or outside the jurisdiction.

Under the 'proper party' gateway no territorial connection between the cause of action and the jurisdiction of the English courts is required. The courts are cautious in exercising this power to bring foreign defendants to England.[47] The second defendant must be a **proper and necessary** party to the claim.

AK Investment v Kyrgyz Mobil Tel[48] concerned the enforcement of a Kyrgyzstan judgment against a Russian company incorporated on the Isle of Man. The Russian company counterclaimed and obtained permission to join thirteen defendants to the counterclaim and serve them outside the jurisdiction. Six of these defendants applied to have the order for service outside the jurisdiction set aside. The Privy Council considered whether they were necessary or proper parties to the proceedings. Although this case involved Manx law, Lord Collins was quite clear that his comments applied equally to the English rules under the CPR.[49] The court asked whether, if both parties had been within the court's jurisdiction, they both would have been proper parties to the action.[50] If the claims against both defendants involved one single investigation or a common thread, both parties would be proper parties to the action. This will be the case, for example, when claims gave rise to common questions of fact or arise out of the same series of transactions.[51]

4.4.1.5 Others

Other grounds of jurisdiction enable the court to grant leave to serve a claim form in action relating to the execution of trusts[52] and enforcement of a judgment or arbitral award.[53]

4.4.1.6 Merits of the issue to be tried

In order to prevent vexatious litigation, as well as showing that the claim falls into one of the gateways, the claimant must also show that 'his claim has a reasonable prospect of success'.[54]

In *Seaconsar Far East v Bank Markazi Jomouri Islami Iran,*[55] Lord Goff held that it was sufficient for the claimant to establish that there was a serious issue to be tried, rather than needing to show an arguable case on the merits.[56] The claimant is required to show that there is a substantial question of fact or law, or both, arising on the facts disclosed by the parties at pre-trial stage.

In *Swiss Reinsurance Co Ltd v United India Insurance Co*[57] it was argued that the 'reasonable prospect of success' test outlined in the CPR differed from the traditional 'serious issue' test examined in *Seaconsar*. Gross J found that applying the *Seaconsar* test or the wording of the CPR achieved much the same result.[58]

In *AK Investment CJSC v Kyrgyz Mobil Tel Ltd and others*[59] the court held that the claimant must satisfy the court that there is a serious issue to be tried on the merits, such as a substantial question of law

47 *The Goldean Mariner* [1990] 2 Lloyd's Rep 215, 222.
48 [2011] UKPC 7.
49 Ibid [67].
50 Ibid [87].
51 E.g. *United Film Distribution v Chhabria* [2001] EWCA Civ 416.
52 6B PD 3.1 (12).
53 6B PD 3.1 (10).
54 Now found in CPR 6.37(1)(b).
55 [1994] 1 AC 438.
56 Ibid 457.
57 [2003] EWHC 741 (Comm).
58 Ibid [27].
59 [2011] UKPC 7.

or fact or both. There must be a real (as opposed to fanciful) chance of success.[60] There is no serious issue to be tried where the claim was 'bound to fail' or 'hopeless'.[61]

4.4.1.7 *Forum conveniens*

The court must not give permission to serve the claim form unless it is satisfied that England is the proper forum to hear the claim. (*forum conveniens*).[62] The question of whether the English court is the appropriate forum is a matter within the discretion of the judge.[63] This discretion allows the English court to ensure that one party is not seeking to gain an unfair advantage by bringing proceedings in an inappropriate forum. Such attempts at forum shopping could delay proceedings and incur significant costs for the defendant.

When **applying for leave** to serve a claim form outside the jurisdiction, the burden of proof is on the **claimant** to prove that England is *forum conveniens*. The defendant may only become aware that the claimant is intending to litigate in England once the claim form has been served. At this stage the defendant may apply to set aside service of proceedings contesting the English court's jurisdiction.[64] Where the defendant seeks to have **service set aside** the onus remains on the **claimant** to prove that England is an appropriate forum to hear the case, as for example in *SMAY Investments Ltd v Sachdev*,[65] where Patten J confirmed that where the defendant is contesting an order for service outside the jurisdiction it is up to the claimant to demonstrate that England is the proper place in which to bring the claim.

Where the **defendant has been properly served** outside the jurisdiction it is open to the defendant to apply for a **stay in proceedings** on the basis that there is a more appropriate forum to hear the case. In such a scenario, the defendant is not questioning the service of the claim form or jurisdiction of the court but rather requesting that proceedings be transferred to a more appropriate forum. It is important not to confuse the two actions. Where the defendant applies for a stay **it is up to the defendant** to satisfy the court that the case should be transferred.[66] This doctrine of *forum non conveniens* is examined in detail below.

The classic formulation of how the court should deal with the issue of the appropriate forum is outlined in *Spiliada Maritime Corpn v Cansulex Ltd*.[67] In this case, an application was made to set aside leave to serve proceedings, on the basis that England was not the appropriate forum to hear the case and the courts of British Columbia were more appropriate. Lord Goff distinguished between a situation where the claimant has served proceedings in England as of right, and cases where an application has been made to serve proceedings out of the jurisdiction.[68] In both situations the court should look to identify the forum in which the case can be suitably tried for the interests of all the parties and for the ends of justice.[69] However, in cases where the claimant has served proceedings out of right, the defendant must apply for a stay of proceedings and a more formal two-stage test outlined in *Spiliada* applies.[70] This test requires the court to determine the most appropriate forum and then to consider if there are special circumstances that require the case to be heard in England. This two-part test is examined in the section examining stays of action based on *forum non conveniens* below.

60 Ibid [71].
61 Ibid [103].
62 CPR 6.37(3).
63 *AK Investment CJSC v Kyrgyz Mobil Tel Ltd and others* [2011] UKPC 7 [139].
64 CPR Part XI.
65 [2003] EWHC 474 (Ch).
66 Ibid [45].
67 [1987] AC 460.
68 Ibid 481.
69 Ibid 480.
70 Ibid 477.

In *Cecil v Bayat*,[71] an application for leave to be set aside, the High Court attempted to identify the natural forum with which the action had the most real and substantial connection.[72] Most of the parties' dealings had taken place in the USA, but the project was directed and managed from England and the vast majority of witnesses were based in England. The court stated that England would clearly be the most appropriate forum if it were not for the fact that related proceedings had already taken place in the USA in which extensive pleadings, disclosure of documents and depositions had been provided. A forum in the USA would be more appropriate if such a forum was available. The court was satisfied that in this case, the claimants had established that a US forum was not available and this satisfied the court that England was the most appropriate forum.[73]

In *AK Investment CJSC v Kyrgyz Mobil Tel Ltd and others*,[74] an application was made to set aside proceedings on the Isle of Man on the basis that this was not the most appropriate forum. Kyrgyzstan was an available forum, and the issue had a closer connection to Kyrgyzstan. The Privy Council stated that the court should consider whether a competing forum was a forum in which the case could be suitably tried for the interests of all the parties and for the ends of justice.[75]

It was suggested by the Court of Appeal in *VTB Capital plc v Nutritek International Corp and others*[76] that when the defendant is challenging service of proceedings outside the jurisdiction, on the basis that England is not an appropriate forum, the two-part *Spiliada* test does not apply. Instead there is a single burden on a claimant to show that England was clearly or distinctly the appropriate forum.[77]

> Instead of asking first whether England was the 'natural forum' and then, even if it is not, asking whether England is nevertheless the appropriate forum for other reasons, there is only one overall question to be answered: has VTB established that England is clearly or distinctly the appropriate forum?[78]

This one-stage approach was followed in *Alliance Bank JSC v Aquanta Corporation and others*.[79] This complex international fraud dispute centred around loan agreements governed by English law. The claimant was a Kazakh bank who sought permission to bring proceedings in England. Burton J set aside permission to serve outside the jurisdiction on the basis that the claimant had not established that the English court was clearly and distinctly the most appropriate.[80] He held that the case had an overriding Kazakh feel as almost all the events took place in Kazakhstan, Kazakh law had an important role to play and a substantial quantity of documents relevant to the case were in Kazakhstan. This aspect of the ruling was upheld by the Court of Appeal adopting the *VTB* restatement of the test.[81]

The Supreme Court approved the one-stage *forum conveniens* test in *VTB Capital plc v Nutritek International Corp and others*.[82]

71 [2010] EWHC 641 (Comm).
72 Ibid [144].
73 Ibid [156].
74 [2011] UKPC 7.
75 Ibid [143].
76 [2012] EWCA Civ 808.
77 Ibid [130].
78 Ibid [131].
79 [2012] EWCA Civ 1588.
80 Ibid [75].
81 [2012] EWCA Civ 1588. [91].
82 [2013] UKSC 5, [44] and [99].

4.5 Jurisdiction by agreement

Where the parties have agreed to the jurisdiction of the English court, the English court will have jurisdiction over the dispute even if the defendant is not present in the jurisdiction and has little or no connection to the jurisdiction.

Agreement can be shown by submission to the English court or by a jurisdiction agreement. Leave to serve a claim for outside the jurisdiction will generally be refused if the parties have agreed to the jurisdiction of another court.

4.5.1 Submission

By submitting to the English court's jurisdiction, the defendant acts in such a way that a future challenge to the jurisdiction of the English court will not be entertained.

Where the defendant is outside the jurisdiction s/he may instruct a solicitor to accept service in England on his or her behalf.[83] Where the solicitor accepts service without disputing jurisdiction[84] the defendant has led the claimant to believe that he is happy to accept the jurisdiction of the English courts and he will be prevented from challenging jurisdiction later. In order to later dispute jurisdiction, an acknowledgment of service must be filed and the defendant must apply to court for an order stating that the court has no jurisdiction.[85]

Where a defendant enters an appearance in the English courts to defend the case on its merits, he will be precluded from challenging the jurisdiction of the courts at a later stage. In such a case the defendant will be considered to have accepted the jurisdiction of the English courts.[86] Where the defendant merely appears in court to contest the jurisdiction of the court s/he will not be considered to have accepted jurisdiction.[87]

In *SMAY Investments Ltd v Sachdev*,[88] it was claimed that some of the defendants had submitted to the jurisdiction of the English courts. When returning acknowledgment of service, Sachdev had ticked the 'intention to defend' box on the form. However, he had served an affidavit on the claimants stating that he intended to contest jurisdiction. The court was satisfied that the defendant had not waived his right to challenge jurisdiction.

By issuing proceedings the claimant submits to the court's jurisdiction to hear a counterclaim against him which is related to the original claim.

4.5.2 Jurisdiction clauses

The English courts may hear a dispute if a jurisdiction agreement to take proceedings in England exists between the parties.[89] This may be either an exclusive jurisdiction agreement or a non-exclusive jurisdiction agreement.[90] Where the defendant is outside the jurisdiction, leave must be sought to serve the claim form but leave will most likely be granted.

Indeed in *Gulf Bank v Mitsubishi Heavy Industries*,[91] Hobhouse J held that where there was a jurisdiction clause granting jurisdiction to the English courts, the discretion of the court should, *prima facie*, be exercised in favour of giving effect to that clause by permitting service out of the jurisdiction.

---

83 CPR 6.8.
84 *Manta Line Inc v Seraphim Sofianites* [1984] 1 Lloyd's Rep 14.
85 CPR 11(1).
86 *Marketmaker Technology Ltd v CMC Group Plc* [2008] EWHC 1556 (QB).
87 CPR 11(5). *Williams and Glyn's Bank v Astro Dinamico* [1984] 1 All ER 760.
88 [2003] EWHC 474 (Ch).
89 6B PD 3.1 (6)(d).
90 See Chapter 3.
91 [1994] 1 Lloyd's Rep 323.

The principle underlying this ground is that the parties to the contract should be bound by their agreed choice of jurisdiction unless there is some strong reason to the contrary.

Leave to serve outside the jurisdiction will generally be refused where the parties have agreed that any dispute arising between them shall be referred to the exclusive jurisdiction of a foreign court. In most cases this will be because the requirement that England is the *forum conveniens* has not been satisfied. In *Mackender v Feldia*,[92] a case that pre-dates EU legislation on jurisdiction, the contract in dispute contained an exclusive jurisdiction clause in favour of the Belgian court. The Court of Appeal held that as the parties had agreed that the dispute would be decided in Belgium the court should not exercise its discretion to grant leave to serve the claim form.[93]

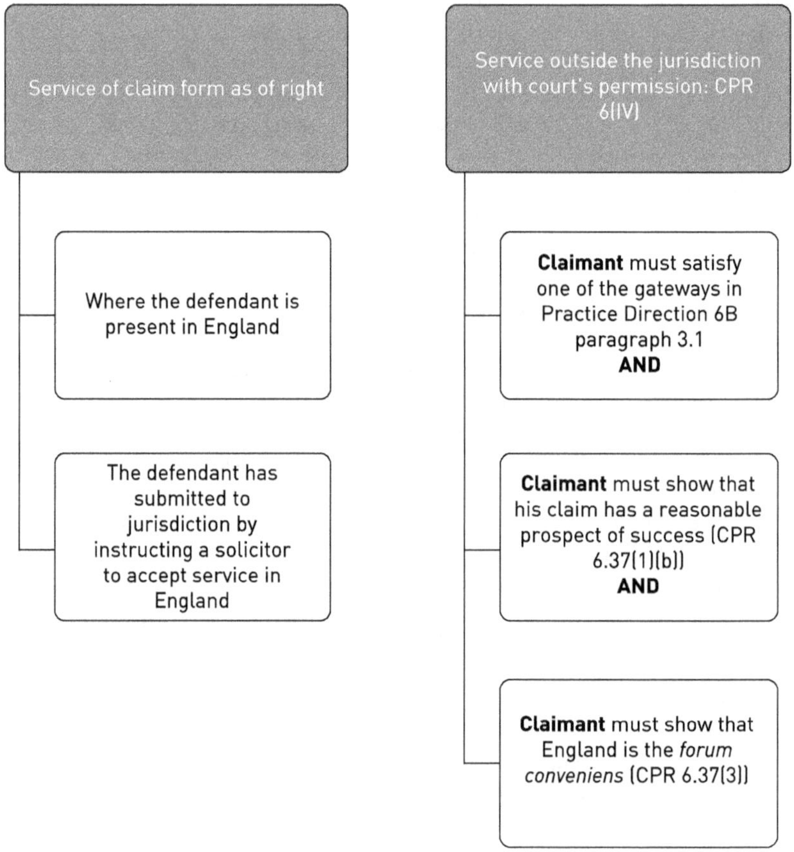

Fig 4.1 Establishing English jurisdiction.

4.6 Staying proceedings in the English Courts

The English traditional rules allow any claimant to invoke English jurisdiction, provided that the defendant has been properly served with a claim form. This appears to allow the claimant to forum

92 [1967] 2 QB 590.
93 Ibid 598.

shop for the best remedy available and can empower the English courts to hear cases which have little connection to England, particularly if the defendant has been served while present in England. Forum shopping occurs where the claimant bypasses the natural forum that is most connected to the dispute and brings his action instead in a more alien forum which gives him a benefit that would not be available in the natural forum or disadvantages the defendant.[94] For example, a claimant may choose to bring proceedings in England because the level of damages may be higher than on the continent.

Under English law, forum shopping is limited by two discretionary remedies that may be invoked by the defendant. The English court has inherent jurisdiction, reinforced by s 49(3) of the Senior Courts Act 1981, to stay an action in England or to restrain foreign proceedings by injunction whenever it is necessary to do so to preserve justice. The discretionary power to stay proceedings in England may be invoked by a defendant on the basis of (1) the doctrine of *forum non conveniens* or (2) because the proceedings are in breach of a jurisdiction agreement

An anti-suit injunction to prevent proceedings proceeding elsewhere may be invoked on the ground that the foreign proceedings are vexatious and oppressive. This is examined in the next section.

4.6.1 *Forum non conveniens*

The obligation on the **claimant** to establish that England is the most appropriate forum when applying for service outside the jurisdiction has already been examined. This section is concerned with **application by the defendant for a stay of proceedings** on the basis that England is not the most appropriate forum and the proceedings should take place elsewhere.

Initially the doctrine of *forum non conveniens* was rather limited in English law. The English courts would not exercise the discretion to stay proceedings in England unless the proceedings were vexatious and oppressive.[95] However, in the 1970s and 1980s the courts moved to a broader approach to the exercise of this discretion.[96]

The definite test to be satisfied before the court will exercise its discretion to order a stay of action on the basis of *forum non conveniens* was set out in *Spiliada Maritime Corpn v Cansulex Ltd*.[97] The test has two stages.

The defendant must first prove to the satisfaction of the court that **England is not the most appropriate forum for the case**. This is done by showing (1) there is another available forum, (2) this forum has competent jurisdiction to hear the claim and (3) that the forum is more suitable than England to hear the claim in the interests of all parties and the ends of justice.[98] When considering if another available forum is more suitable the court will weigh up whether this other forum has the most real and substantial connection to the claim. This may exist where the other forum is more convenient for witnesses and the places where the parties reside and carry out business or where the other forum is less expensive for both parties or where the foreign law applicable to the dispute can be more easily applied by the other forum.[99] The degree of weight accorded to each consideration varies depending on the circumstance of the case.

Once the defendant has shown that the other forum is *prima facie* the more appropriate forum to hear the action, the burden of proof switches to the claimant to show that there are **special circumstances that require the case to proceed** in England.[100] The fact that a stay of proceedings would deprive the claimant of a legitimate personal advantage available in the English

94 See *Chaplin v Boys* [1971] AC 356 per Pearson LJ.
95 See *St Pierre v South American Stores Ltd* [1936] 1 KB 382.
96 E.g. *MacShannon v Rockware Glass Ltd* [1978] AC 795; *The Abidin Daver* [1984] AC 398.
97 [1987] AC 460,
98 Ibid 477.
99 Ibid 478.
100 Ibid 477–478.

courts will not generally deter the court from granting a stay, if substantial justice will be done in the most appropriate forum.[101]

The courts engage in a delicate balancing exercise, weighing up not only the geographical factors connecting the dispute to different forums, but also the advantages and disadvantages posed to each party and the interests of justice.

In *Limit (no 3) Ltd and Ors v PDV Insurance Co*[102] the Court of Appeal stressed the discretionary nature of the *Spiliada* test, stating that whether or not the test is satisfied is largely a matter for the trial judge and an appellate court should be slow to interfere.

4.6.1.1 Establishing the appropriate forum

The first stage of the *Spiliada* test involves the consideration of geographical connecting factors to determine the most appropriate forum.

Where there is no territorial connection to England and a strong territorial connection to another available forum, the courts are likely to find that the other forum is more appropriate. In *Ceskoslovenska Obchodni Banka AS v Nomura International plc*,[103] the dispute concerned the internal management of a Czech company in the sale of other Czech companies. All parties to the transactions were Czech companies or companies with a strong presence in the Czech Republic. The strong territorial connection with the Czech Republic made it the only appropriate forum for the case.[104]

English courts have attached considerable weight to the availability of witnesses and additional expense, delay and inconvenience when establishing the appropriate forum.

In *Bristow Helicopters Ltd v Sikorsky Aircraft Corp*[105] a stay of proceedings was refused as England was the most appropriate forum. The subject of the dispute was a helicopter accident which had claimed the lives of everyone onboard. The blades of the helicopter had been previously damaged in a lightning strike, but had been repaired and certified as safe to use. The English claimant owners and operators of the helicopter took proceedings against both the manufacturers of the helicopter and the company who had repaired and certified the part. These were both American companies. The personal representatives of the deceased crew and passengers applied to have the English proceedings stayed so as to allow the personal representatives to take proceedings in Connecticut against the manufacturers of the helicopter.

The court held that England was the most obvious and appropriate forum for the action. The accident had occurred there; the helicopter was run by an English company; the service log for the helicopter was in England; expert witnesses had already been instructed in England; and the preparations were at an advanced stage.[106]

Lubbe & Others v Cape plc[107] involved over 3,000 claimants who brought proceedings for personal injury and death against an English company which owned subsidiary companies in South Africa. The claims related to exposure to asbestos in South Africa, while mining and processing asbestos and selling asbestos-related products. The House of Lords held that South Africa was clearly a more appropriate and more closely connected forum than England.

Where proceedings between the same parties arising out of the same dispute are simultaneously pending in the English courts and in the courts of another country, an application for a stay of proceedings may be made. Unlike Brussels I, which applies a strict first in time rule requiring the second seised court to stay proceedings, under the English rules, granting a stay is up to the

101 Ibid 478.
102 [2005] EWCA Civ 383.
103 [2003] IL Pr 20.
104 Ibid [12].
105 [2004] EWHC 401 (Comm).
106 Ibid [27].
107 [2000] 1 WLR 1545.

court's discretion. The existence of pending proceedings either in England or in another jurisdiction may affect the first stage of the *forum non conveniens* test. The court may decide that the forum where proceedings are pending is for reasons of convenience the most appropriate forum.

In *Cleveland Museum of Art v Capricorn Art International SA & Anor*,[108] the case involving the loan of an ancient reliquary to a museum in Ohio, which had arrived with a piece missing, how the reliquary had been packed and unpacked was a matter of key importance. A stay of proceedings was granted in England because there were proceedings pending in Ohio which were more convenient to the 11 witnesses who had been called to give evidence. The loan agreement was also governed by Ohio law.

If an exclusive jurisdiction agreement exists, the courts will find that the chosen forum is the most appropriate forum.[109] If a non-exclusive jurisdiction agreement exists, this will not preclude another forum from being deemed more appropriate unless proceedings are already pending in the chosen forum.

In *Import Export Metro Ltd and Another v Compania Sud Americana de Vapores SA*[110] proceedings had been commenced in England and there existed a non-exclusive jurisdiction clause and choice of law clause in favour of England. The defendant applied for a stay of proceedings on the basis that in spite of the non-exclusive jurisdiction clause, Chile was the more appropriate forum. Gross J held that in cases where proceedings had commenced in accordance with a non-exclusive jurisdiction clause, strong reasons must be present that go beyond a mere matter of convenience and show that, in the interests of justice, the proceedings should take place in another forum. On the facts it appeared that England had been chosen precisely because it was a neutral forum.[111]

4.6.1.2 Special circumstances that require the case to be heard in England

Where the defendant has established that the English court is not the most appropriate forum, the second stage of the *Spiliada* test allows the claimant to argue that the English proceedings should continue even though England is not the most appropriate forum. At this second stage the courts will consider not only the geographical factors that connect the proceedings with the foreign or the English forum but also the question of whether justice will be done in the foreign forum. The claimant must show that if the English courts were closed to him by a stay of proceedings, there is a risk that **substantial justice would not be done** in the foreign courts.[112]

The fact that the claimant will lose a personal or juridical advantage if forced to contest proceedings in another jurisdiction is not sufficient to prevent the stay being granted. It must be shown that the disadvantage is so serious that it means that substantial justice will not be done in the foreign courts.

For example, in *Lubbe & Others v Cape plc*,[113] where South Africa was found to be the most appropriate forum, the claimants established that no source of funding was available in South Africa to enable the claimant to pursue their personal injury claims. If these proceedings were stayed in favour of the more appropriate forum in South Africa, the claimants would be unlikely to obtain professional representation and the expert evidence essential to justly deciding the claims. This would amount to a denial of justice.[114] The House of Lords held that the special and unusual circumstances of these proceedings provided a compelling reason for refusing to stay proceedings at the second stage of the *Spiliada* test.

---

108 [1990] 2 Lloyd's Rep 166; [1990] BCLC 546.
109 See section on jurisdiction agreements.
110 [2003] 1 Lloyd's Rep 405.
111 A similar approach was taken in *Antec International Ltd v Biosafety USA Inc* [2006] EWHC 47 (Comm).
112 *Spiliada* [1987] AC 460, 482.
113 [2000] 1 WLR 1545.
114 Ibid 1559.

Mere allegations that foreign courts are inefficient or suffer from procedural delays will not be sufficient to prevent the stay from being granted, where the foreign forum is more appropriate.

In *Ceskoslovenska Obchodni Banka AS v Nomura International plc*,[115] the courts found the Czech Republic to be the most appropriate forum. The claimants argued that justice was unlikely to be achieved in the Czech courts as they had little experience of hearing commercial cases of this scale, they lacked proper procedures for disclosure and cross-examination and proceedings took a long time.[116] The court held that while the English system would probably be quicker, substantial justice would be done in either jurisdiction and so the case should be heard in the most appropriate jurisdiction as determined under the first stage of the *Spiliada* test.[117] The action was stayed in favour of the Czech courts. A similar approach was taken in *SMAY Investments Ltd v Sachdev*.[118]

4.6.2 Jurisdiction Agreements

Under Brussels I,[119] where an exclusive jurisdiction clause exists in favour of a Member State court, all other Member State courts must decline to hear the case.[120] Under the English rules, where the claimants sue in England, in breach of an exclusive jurisdiction clause, the defendants may apply for a stay of proceedings. The English court is not required to uphold the exclusive jurisdiction clause but may exercise its discretion to grant the stay. Where it is shown that an exclusive jurisdiction clause exists, the courts will *prima facie* rule that a stay should be granted because of the desirability of holding parties to their agreements. The existence of the exclusive agreement will mean that the foreign forum is *prima facie* more appropriate. This satisfies the first stage of the *Spiliada* test. The burden is then on the **claimant** to show why a stay should not be granted. The courts will often apply the second stage of the *Spiliada* test to determine this matter. In general, the English court will exercise its discretion to stay proceedings to uphold a choice of court clause.

4.6.2.1 The agreed forum is *prima facie* the most appropriate

In *The Eleftheria*[121] the claimants issued proceedings in England for damages for breach of a contract of carriage that was part of a bill of lading. The defendants had discharged their goods in Rotterdam rather than transporting them to Hull, because of labour problems in Hull. The defendants were properly served with proceedings. They applied for a stay of proceedings on the basis that an exclusive jurisdiction clause existed in the bill of lading which required all disputes to be referred to a Greek court. The court held that the English court was not bound to grant such a stay of proceedings but the court's discretion should be exercised in favour of granting a stay unless a strong case for not doing so is shown. The burden is on the claimant to show why a stay should not be granted. In exercising its discretion, the court should take into account all the circumstances of the particular case. For instance, the court should address such questions as which is the most convenient country for the evidence, which is the cheapest, whether the dispute is governed by a foreign law, how close are the connections of the parties to the relevant countries, whether the defendant genuinely desires to have the trial in the foreign country or whether he is only seeking a procedural advantage in England. The court must also consider whether the claimant would receive a fair trial in the foreign country.[122]

115 [2003] IL PR 20.
116 Ibid [15]–[17].
117 Ibid [18].
118 [2003] EWHC 474 (Ch).
119 Art 23.
120 See Chapter 3.
121 [1970] P 94.
122 Ibid 99–100.

In *The Eleftheria* the court found that although there were some factors suggesting that the case should be heard in England, the claimants had not established a good cause why they should not be held to their agreement. The defendants had a very real connection to Greece and Greek law determined the dispute.

In *Hamed El-Chiaty v Thomas Cook Ltd*[123] the court upheld an oral agreement to take proceedings in Egypt. The claimants, an Egyptian tourist company, contracted with the defendants, an international travel company registered and based in England, to construct a cruise ship. In return the defendants agreed to help finance the construction of the vessel and to charter it for use on their package tours. A series of contracts were made and the applicable law was agreed to be Egyptian. There was no jurisdiction clause. However, the defendants claimed that during negotiations, the parties had orally agreed that any disputes would be subject to the exclusive jurisdiction of the Egyptian courts. Following the failure of the defendants to supply the agreed minimum number of tourists, the claimants brought an action in the English court. Hirst J held that the oral agreement was effective and granted a stay. Egypt was the natural forum for the case and it was up to the claimant to show good cause why the exclusive jurisdiction agreement should not be upheld. The claimant had not managed to satisfy the second stage of the *Spiliada* test and so the stay was granted.

A non-exclusive jurisdiction clause will also create a *prima facie* case that the agreed forum is the appropriate forum for litigation and that a stay of English proceedings may be granted. In *The Rothnie*[124] the defendants entered into a contract to carry out repair and maintenance work on the claimant's ship in Gibraltar.[125] The contract was subject to the defendant's standard terms and conditions, which expressly provided that the contract was to be governed by the law of Gibraltar and that any disputes were subject to the non-exclusive jurisdiction of the courts of Gibraltar.[126] Proceedings were initially started in England and later in Gibraltar. The court applied the *Spiliada* two-stage test.[127] It was held that the fact that the parties had agreed that a certain forum had jurisdiction, albeit non-exclusive, created a strong *prima facie* case in favour of that forum being the appropriate one. The claimant had not persuaded the court that proceedings should proceed in England in the interests of justice.

However, in *BP Plc v AON Ltd (No 1)*[128] Colman J held that the existence of a non-exclusive jurisdiction clause prevented either party from contesting the jurisdiction of the named agreed forum – in this case Illinois.[129] However, the non-exclusive jurisdiction clause did not prevent either party from bringing proceedings in an alternative forum. This is the key difference between an exclusive jurisdiction clause and a non-exclusive jurisdiction clause. The claimant is not required to establish strong reasons for bringing a claim in England where there is a non-exclusive jurisdiction clause in favour of another forum, if there are no proceedings pending in that jurisdiction. It is enough for the claimant to show that the balance of fairness points to England as the most appropriate forum.

4.6.2.2 Refusal to stay proceedings

Discretion to refuse a stay has been exercised in cases where it is shown that justice will not be done in the agreed foreign forum.

123 [1992] 2 Lloyd's Rep 399.
124 [1996] 2 Lloyd's Rep 206; [1996] CLC 1062.
125 Today, Gibraltar is treated as another Member State of the EU under the Civil Jurisdiction and Judgments Act 1982 (Gibraltar) Order 1997/2602. *Forum non conveniens* arguments will not be permitted.
126 Ibid 1064.
127 Ibid 1068–1069.
128 [2005] EWHC 2554 (Comm).
129 Ibid [21].

In *Carvalho v Hull Blyth (Angola) Ltd*,[130] the defendants, a company registered in England, carried on business in Angola through subsidiaries in which the claimant owned a 49 per cent shareholding. In a contract made in Angola, at a time when Angola was a Portuguese province, the claimant, who was then living there, agreed to sell his shareholding to the defendant. The price was payable in four instalments. The contract contained an exclusive jurisdiction clause in favour of the Angolan courts. When the defendant failed to pay the fourth instalment, the claimant brought an action in the English court. The defendants applied for a stay. The Court of Appeal held that the jurisdiction clause in favour of the Angolan courts could not be relied upon, because under the revolutionary government the Angolan court was no longer a Portuguese court applying Portuguese municipal law. It was not the same court as had been agreed upon. In any event, due to the political and legal changes in Angola the claimant satisfied the court that it was 'just and proper' to refuse the stay.

An exclusive jurisdiction clause in favour of a foreign jurisdiction will not be upheld if the stay of English proceedings would lead to separate additional proceedings on the same facts. In *Citi-March v Neptune Orient Lines*[131] the claimants contracted with the first defendant, a company incorporated and carrying out business in Singapore for the carriage of consignments of clothing to London. The bills of lading incorporated an exclusive jurisdiction clause in favour of the courts of Singapore. Following delivery in London, it was found that a quantity of the goods were missing. The claimant commenced proceedings in the English court against the first defendant and three other companies, based in England, which had stored the goods on their premises prior to delivery. The first defendant applied to have service of the English proceedings set aside on the basis of the exclusive jurisdiction clause. Colman J held that if the jurisdiction clause was upheld, therefore requiring the claimants to pursue their claim in Singapore, it was probable that separate proceedings against the three companies would have to be pursued in England. This would lead to a clear risk of inconsistent decisions on the facts. The claimants would also lose the benefit of a composite trial and would be precluded from having the benefit of all four defendants. Therefore, a strong reason had been shown in favour of ignoring the jurisdiction clause and maintaining the action in the English court.

4.6.3 *Forum non conveniens* under Brussels I

The primary purpose of Brussels I is certainty of jurisdiction within the EU. Where one Member State has jurisdiction under Brussels I, it is required to rule. Where more than one Member State has jurisdiction, a strict first in time rule applies under Art 27.[132] The discretion of the traditional rules to transfer the case to a more appropriate forum does not exist under Brussels I. Where Brussels I grants jurisdiction to the English courts, this cannot be declined. This is the case even where a third country is a more appropriate forum.

Initially in *Re Harrods (Buenos Aires) Ltd*[133] the Court of Appeal held that pursuant to s 49 of the Civil Jurisdiction and Judgments Act 1982, *forum non conveniens* remained applicable to cases where to decline jurisdiction was not inconsistent with the Brussels Regulation. In *Re Harrods*, an action was brought for the winding up of an English incorporated company. The company's registered office was in England, but its business was carried on and it was managed and controlled exclusively in Argentina. Article 2 of the Brussels Convention applied by virtue of the company's domicile in England. However, the defendant argued that the English proceedings should be stayed, because

130 [1979] 1 WLR 1228.
131 [1996] 2 All ER 545; [1996] 1 WLR 1367.
132 The rules of Brussels I are explored in Chapter 3.
133 [1991] 4 All ER 334.

Argentina was the most appropriate forum for the trial of the action. He also claimed that Art 2 did not have a wide mandatory effect where the only conflict was between the courts of a Brussels Convention country and the courts of a non-Brussels Convention country. Unexpectedly, the Court of Appeal upheld this argument and granted a stay of the English proceedings. A fundamental distinction was drawn between cases where the alternative forum was in a non-Contracting State and cases where it was in a Contracting State. The Brussels Convention was intended and designed to regulate relations between Brussels Convention countries. Accordingly, the court retained its discretion under s 49 of the Civil Jurisdiction and Judgments Act 1982 to stay or dismiss the action on the grounds of *forum non conveniens* where the more appropriate forum was in a non-Contracting State.

The ECJ gave a ruling in *Owusu v Jackson*[134] depriving the English courts of their perceived right to control forum shopping by way of *forum non conveniens* where a defendant is domiciled in England. Application of *forum non conveniens* was held to potentially undermine the predictability of the jurisdictional rules of the Brussels Convention, in particular Art 2. This would undermine the principle of legal certainty. The ECJ also referred to the fact that the doctrine of *forum non conveniens* was not universally accepted in the Member States, which meant its application in an Art 2 situation went against the objectives of the Brussels Convention. Accordingly, Art 2 was mandatory in nature, regardless of the fact that is application might make the claimant's action logistically difficult and expensive, and the enforceability of the judgment might be in question.

The decision in *Owusu* made it clear that the English courts could not decline jurisdiction granted to them by Art 2 of Brussels I on the basis of *forum non conveniens*. In *Mahme Trust Reg v Lloyds TSB Bank Plc*[135] the court held that it could not decline jurisdiction using *forum non conveniens* where jurisdiction was granted to the English courts under Arts 2 and 5 of the Brussels Convention. In *Alberta Inc v Katanga Mining Ltd*[136] the court ruled that *forum non conveniens* could not be used where England had jurisdiction under Art 2 as the Bermudan company in question had its central administration in London.

Brussels I allows England to decline jurisdiction if relating proceedings are pending in an EU Member State or if the exclusive jurisdiction grounds of Art 22 points to another EU Member State or if there is an exclusive jurisdiction agreement in favour of an EU Member State. *Owusu* did not directly address whether it was still open to the English courts to decline jurisdiction where related proceedings were pending in a third country, or where the exclusive jurisdiction grounds of Art 22 pointed to a third country or where there was an exclusive jurisdiction agreement in favour of the third country. To decline jurisdiction in such cases could be seen as upholding the goals of Brussels I to prevent parallel proceedings and irreconcilable judgments. It would also give Brussels I reflexive effect, treating the third county as if it were another EU Member State. The English courts have declined jurisdiction in favour of the third country in such cases.[137]

The provisions of Brussels I recast introduce a discretionary power allowing EU Member States to stay proceedings in favour of a third-country state.[138] This power is only available where the EU Member State has jurisdiction under the general rule of Brussels I, as the state of the defendant's domicile,[139] **OR** where the EU Member State has special jurisdiction to hear the case under Arts 5 to 7.[140] In such cases, proceedings can be stayed if (1) proceedings on the same cause of action or a related cause of action are already pending in the court of the third country state **AND** (2) A

134 [2005] QB 801.
135 [2004] EWHC 2180 (Ch).
136 [2008] EWHC 2679 (Comm).
137 *Catalyst Investment Group Ltd v Lewisohn and others* [2009] EWHC 1964; *Chaudhary v Bhatter* [2009] EWCA Civ 1176; *Konkola Copper Mines Plc v Coromin* [2005] EWHC 896 (Comm); *Winnetka Trading Corp v Julius Baer International Ltd* [2008] EWHC 3146 (Ch).
138 Brussels I recast, Regulation (EU) No 1215/2012 [2012] OJ L351/1, Arts 33–34.
139 Art 2 Brussels I, Art 4 Brussels I recast.
140 Arts 7–9 of Brussels I recast.

Forum non conveniens

- **Defendant** must show that England is not the most appropriate forum and that a more appropriate forum exists.
- The stay will be refused where the **claimant** shows special circumstances that require the case to be heard in England.

Exclusive jurisdiction agreement

- **Defendant** must show that an exclusive jurisdiction agreement exists in favour of another court. The court chosen in the agreement will be *prima facie* the most appropriate forum.
- The stay will be refused where the **claimant** shows that justice will not be done in the agreed foreign forum.

Fig 4.2 Staying actions in the English courts.

judgment of the third country state would be capable of recognition and enforcement in the Member State declining jurisdiction **AND** (3) the stay is required for the proper administration of justice.[141]

This discretionary power to stay proceedings is less flexible than the English doctrine of *forum non conveniens*. The Member State court can only grant a stay where proceedings are already pending and it is in the interests of justice to stay proceedings. The parties are assured that the judgment will be enforceable in an EU Member State. It is not possible, under Brussels I recast, for a court to stay proceedings in favour of a third state where the EU Member State has exclusive jurisdiction[142] or where the court has jurisdiction under the provisions of Brussels I recast designed to protect vulnerable parties such as consumers and employees[143] or jurisdiction by appearance.[144]

The doctrine of *forum non conveniens* is still available under the modified form of Brussels I which allocates jurisdiction between England and Wales, Northern Ireland or Scotland.[145]

4.7 Anti-suit injunctions

Where a claimant has taken proceedings abroad, the defendant may apply to the English court for an anti-suit injunction to restrain the foreign proceedings. The injunction operates *in personam*. It is granted against the claimant, not the foreign court itself. However, an anti-suit injunction always requires caution because it involves interference with the process or potential process of a foreign

141 See Figure 3.3 in Chapter 3.
142 Arts 24 and 25.
143 Arts 10–23.
144 Art 26.
145 Sched 4 of the Civil Jurisdiction and Judgments Act 1982; *Cumming v Scottish Daily Record and Sunday Mail Ltd* [1995] EMLR 538.

court. Anti-suit injunctions are no longer permitted where the foreign court is bound by Brussels I; instead the English court must wait for the other court to decline jurisdiction.[146]

Where proceedings are taken abroad in breach of an exclusive jurisdiction clause in favour of the English courts, this creates a contractual right not to be sued elsewhere. In such cases the English courts have the discretion to grant an anti-suit injunction to enforce the exclusive jurisdiction agreement, and this will usually be exercised. The relationship between jurisdiction agreements and anti-suit injunctions is explored below.

In cases where there is no jurisdictional agreement, traditionally the test for granting an anti-suit injunction was based on the *Spiliada* principles[147] and injunctions were granted where the balance of convenience indicated that England was the most appropriate forum. Today the test is more stringent. In order for the injunction to be granted **England must be the natural forum** for the case **AND** it must be shown that the foreign proceedings are **vexatious and oppressive**.[148] The courts must also consider whether granting the anti-suit injunction is compatible with the respect for the workings of other courts through the doctrine of **comity**.

4.7.1 Natural forum

In the leading case of *Société National Industrielle Aérospatiale (SNIA) v Lee Kui Jack*[149] a Brunei businessman was killed in a helicopter crash in Brunei. The helicopter had been manufactured in France by SNIA, which had a subsidiary in Texas through which it sold helicopters. At the time of the crash, the helicopter was owned by an English company and operated and serviced by its Malaysian subsidiary under a contract to a Brunei subsidiary of an international oil company. Proceedings against the French manufacturer and the Malaysian service company were brought both in Brunei and in Texas. The claimant brought an action in Texas in the hope of attaining higher damages. The jurisdiction of the Texas courts was based on the fact that the manufacturer had sold its helicopters through its Texan subsidiary in Texas. The defendants applied for an injunction restraining the Texan proceedings because it was highly unlikely that the Malaysian company could be brought before the Texan courts and therefore SNIA would have to claim a contribution from that company in some other forum. This meant that the Brunei courts were the more appropriate forum.

The Privy Council held that as the accident happened in Brunei, the deceased and the claimants were resident there and the law governing the claim was the law of Brunei, Brunei was the natural forum for the action. The proceedings in Texas were considered oppressive because the defendants might be unable to pursue their own contributions claim against the Malaysian company. Accordingly the injunction was granted.

The case of *Morris v Davies*[150] concerned the will of a British citizen ('X') who had died in France after living abroad in France and Belgium since 2001. His executor sought a grant of probate in the English courts. The validity of the will depended on whether the deceased was an English domiciliary at the time of death or whether he had acquired French or Belgian domicile. The grant of probate was challenged by the deceased's relatives who would inherit if the deceased had died intestate.

The defendants submitted to the English court and did not contest jurisdiction. Midway through English proceedings, before the question of the defendant's domicile had been determined, the defendants brought proceedings in the Belgian courts for a declaration that the will was null and void. The executor sought an anti-suit injunction to suspend the proceedings in Belgium.

146 *Turner v Grovit* [2005] 1 AC 101. See Chapter 3.
147 *Castanho v Brown and Root (UK) Ltd* [1980] 3 WLR 991.
148 *Société National Industrielle Aérospatiale (SNIA) v Lee Kui Jack* [1987] AC 871.
149 Ibid.
150 [2011] EWHC 1272 (Ch).

The court held that England was the natural forum for these proceedings. Although X had lived in France and Belgium since 2001, he had retained a British passport and driving licence, he spoke no Flemish or Dutch, his funeral was in England, he retained a property in England and approximately 75 per cent of his assets were in England.[151]

4.7.2 Vexatious or oppressive behaviour

In *Société National Industrielle Aérospatiale (SNIA) v Lee Kui Jack*,[152] the Privy Council held that in determining whether the foreign proceedings were 'vexatious and oppressive' the court must consider whether granting an injunction would not unjustly deprive the claimant of advantages available to him in the foreign forum. The injustice to the defendant if the claimant was allowed to pursue foreign proceedings would outweigh the injustice to the claimant if he was not allowed to proceed.[153]

Star Reefers Pool Inc v JFC Group Co Ltd[154] provides an excellent analysis of 'vexatious or oppressive behaviour'. The defendant, JFC, was a Russian company which had brought declaratory proceedings in Russia that it was not bound by two guarantees. The claimant, Star Reefer, had obtained summary judgment against JFC under the guarantees for the sum of $16 million in the English courts. JFC had challenged the jurisdiction of the English courts in these proceedings, lost and then failed to make an appearance. Teare J had granted an anti-suit injunction to prevent the Russian proceedings from continuing.

The Court of Appeal stated that the finding of vexatious or oppressive conduct was an evaluative assessment that must be made. Where such conduct existed, it was in the discretion of the court to decide whether an anti-suit injunction should or should not be granted. In the second discretionary stage, the court should consider factors such as the important matter of comity.[155] Cases of vexatious and unconscionable behaviour generally fell into two categories. In most cases the unconscionability came from the defendant's conduct in submitting to English jurisdiction as the forum where the parties' dispute would be resolved and then either seeking to extricate himself from the consequences of that submission, or oppressively seeking to prolong or multiply the litigation by commencing further proceedings abroad.[156] In other cases, the weakness of the proceedings in the other forum was a factor in declaring them vexatious. Such proceedings were considered hopeless or bound to fail.[157]

This case did not fall into either category. The proceedings in Russia were commenced before valid proceedings were taken in England, therefore they were not taken to frustrate proceedings in England.[158] JFC refused to submit to English jurisdiction and was entitled to do so having neither promised to litigate in England nor to engage in arbitration there. Although the proceedings in Russia were commenced without warning, this could not be said to be vexatious or oppressive practice.[159] While there were weaknesses in the Russian case, it could not be said to be doomed to fail.[160] Rix LJ held that the Commercial Court had gone too far in finding unconscionable conduct on the part of a foreign party who had not agreed to litigate or arbitrate in England and the application for the anti-suit injunction should have failed at this point.[161]

---

151 Ibid [33].
152 [1987] AC 871.
153 Ibid 896.
154 [2012] EWCA Civ 14.
155 Ibid [2].
156 Cases like this include: *Tonicstar Ltd v American Home Assurance Co* [2004] EWHC 1234 (Comm) [13]: *Glencore International AG v Exter Shipping Ltd* [2002] 2 All ER (Comm) 1.
157 E.g. *Shell International Petroleum Co v Coral Oil Co Ltd* [1999] 2 Lloyd's Rep 606; *Elektrim SA v Vivendi Holdings* [2009] 1 Lloyd's Rep 59 (CA).
158 *Star Reefers Pool Inc v JFC Group Co Ltd* [2012] EWCA Civ 14 [32].
159 Ibid [33].
160 Ibid [34].
161 Ibid [39].

In *Morris v Davies*,[162] the defendant's conduct in bringing proceedings in the Belgian courts was vexatious as they had submitted to English jurisdiction in relation to all issues. They had allowed substantial costs to mount up in pursuing the preliminary issue of the deceased's domicile.[163] In addition, the Belgian proceedings could not proceed without a determination by the English court of the defendant's domicile. Thus any potential advantages to the defendants from the Belgian proceedings would be unaffected if they were restrained from continuing them until the preliminary issue was determined.

4.7.3 Considerations of comity

An anti-suit injunction interferes with the processes of a foreign court. The doctrine of comity[164] means that, ordinarily, each court is left to determine the suitability of the litigation before it and should be wary of attempting to interfere with other courts' decisions. Although the anti-suit injunction is binding only on the litigant and not the foreign court, in some cases the English court will, in effect, review the legitimacy of the foreign court's jurisdiction. In *Re Maxwell*[165] Hoffman J stated that this is particularly the case where the English court considers the foreign proceedings to be unjust because the foreign court is asserting an excessive jurisdiction.[166]

Lord Denning MR warned in *Castanho v Brown and Root (UK) Ltd* that injunctions restraining foreign proceedings should only rarely be granted 'so as to avoid even the appearance of undue interference with another court'.[167]

In *Deutsche Bank AG v Highland Crusader Offshore Partner LP*,[168] the court held that the normal assumption must be that an English court has no superiority over a foreign court in deciding what justice between the parties requires. There must be a good reason why the decision to stop the foreign proceedings should be made by an English judge, rather than a foreign judge, and cases where justice requires the English court to intervene will be exceptional. However, there may be cases in which the judicial or legislative polices of England and the foreign court are so at variance that comity is overridden by a need to protect British interests or to prevent a violation of the principles of customary international law. The stronger the connection of the foreign court with the parties and the subject matter of the dispute, the stronger the argument against intervention.[169]

In *Star Reefers Pool Inc v JFC Group Co Ltd*[170] Rix LJ held that while the finding of vexatious conduct may lead the court to the conclusion that it would be right in the interests of justice to grant an anti-suit injunction despite considerations of comity, comity should always be considered.[171] In this case the anti-suit injunction was a needless interference with the Russian courts as it afforded no protection to the English proceedings, which were likely to be completed before the Russian proceedings.

4.7.4 Anti-suit injunctions to enforce a jurisdiction or arbitration clause

An exclusive jurisdiction clause in favour of the English courts creates a contractual right not to be sued elsewhere. The English court will ordinarily enforce the parties' exclusive jurisdiction agreement by granting an anti-suit injunction in the absence of a strong reason not to do so.

162 [2011] EWHC 1272 (Ch).
163 Ibid [36].
164 See Chapter 1.
165 *Re Maxwell Communications Corporation plc (No 2)* [1992] BCC 757.
166 Ibid 761.
167 [1980] 1 WLR 833, 856.
168 [2009] EWCA Civ 725 [56].
169 Ibid [50].
170 [2012] EWCA Civ 14.
171 Ibid [41].

In *Sohio Supply Co v Gatoil (USA) Inc*[172] an injunction was granted to restrain the defendants from continuing with the proceedings in Texas on the basis that the parties had an agreement to refer disputes exclusively to the English courts. Similarly, in *The Angelic Grace*[173] the Court of Appeal granted an injunction to prevent proceedings abroad brought in breach of an arbitration agreement in favour of England.

In *Donohue v Armco*,[174] Armco, a US-based conglomerate, agreed to sell three insurance companies, known as British National Insurance Group, to Donohue. The purchase agreements contained exclusive English jurisdiction clauses. Armco later alleged that it had been induced to enter into the agreements by fraud and it brought proceedings in New York against Donohue and several other parties. Donohue then brought proceedings against Armco in the English court in reliance on the exclusive jurisdiction clause and applied for an anti-suit injunction to prevent the action in New York continuing.

Lord Bingham stated that where there was an exclusive jurisdiction clause the English court would ordinarily exercise its discretion to secure compliance with the contractual bargain. However, in this case the ends of justice would be best served in this case by a single composite trial. This was only possible in New York, where proceedings had been commenced not only against Donohue but also against other defendants. On that ground he found strong reasons for not giving effect to the exclusive jurisdiction clause in favour of Donohue.[175]

In *Import Export Metro Ltd v Compania Sud Americana de Vapores SA*[176] Gross J stated that while a multiplicity of proceedings is, in general, undesirable and inconvenient, the weight given to this factor will turn on the facts of the case.[177]

In *Deutsche Bank AG v Highland Crusader Offshore Partners LP*[178] the court considered whether an anti-suit injunction should be granted where the parties were subject to a non-exclusive jurisdiction clause. Deutsche Bank was a major German bank and Highland was a major US hedge fund whose principal place of business was Dallas. The dispute concerned the purchase of a portfolio of securities. The parties were subject to a jurisdiction clause that all disputes should be brought in the English courts or in the courts of any other country of competent jurisdiction. Highland brought proceedings in the Texan courts for fraudulent misrepresentation. Deutsche Bank brought proceedings in England and applied for an anti-suit injunction to stop the Texan proceedings. Highland had submitted to the jurisdiction of the English courts.

The court held that by contracting for non-exclusive jurisdiction, parties had to have anticipated and accepted the possibility that proceedings could be brought in any competent forum and that parallel proceedings could be brought. It was not right to start from a general presumption that parallel proceedings in a non-selected forum were to be regarded as vexatious or oppressive.[179] In this case the anti-suit injunction was set aside. The case establishes that only foreign proceedings which are vexatious and oppressive for some reason that is independent of the mere presence of the non-exclusive clause should be restrained by injunction.

172 [1989] 1 Lloyd's Rep 588.
173 [1995] 1 Lloyd's Rep 87.
174 [2001] UKHL 64.
175 Ibid [34].
176 [2003] EWHC 11 (Comm).
177 Ibid 432. See also *Electronic Arts CV v CTO SpA* [2003] EWHC 1020 (Comm).
178 [2009] EWCA Civ 725.
179 Ibid [115].

4.7.5 The anti-suit injunction under Brussels I

As the Brussels I system is based on mutual trust, a court cannot restrain proceedings in another Member State or go ahead with parallel proceedings.

The English Court of Appeal initially took the view, in *Continental Bank v Aeokos Cia Naviera SA*,[180] that the court had power, by virtue of an exclusive jurisdiction clause in favour of the English courts, to grant an injunction restraining a group of borrowers and guarantors from bringing legal proceedings in another Contracting State, namely Greece. Even though the court first seised of the proceedings was the Greek court, the Court of Appeal stated that Art 17 of the Brussels Convention upholding jurisdiction agreements took precedence over the strict in time *lis pendens* rule.[181] Furthermore, there was nothing in the Brussels Convention which was inconsistent with a power vesting in the English courts, to grant an injunction, the objective of which was secure enforcement of an exclusive jurisdiction agreement.

In *Turner v Grovit*,[182] Turner sued Grovit in England for compensation for constructive dismissal. In turn Grovit sued Turner in Spain for damages for breach of his contract of employment. The Court of Appeal believed that Grovit's action was an attempt to oppress Turner, who was now unemployed. An anti-suit injunction was issued to restrain Grovit's proceedings in Spain. The House of Lords asked the ECJ for a preliminary ruling on whether the issue of an anti-suit injunction was consistent with the Brussels Convention. In 2004, the ECJ ruled that it was inconsistent, even where a party acted in bad faith with a view to frustrating existing proceedings. The ECJ held that the anti-suit injunction undermines the jurisdiction of another Member State and as such is incompatible with the scheme of the Convention.[183]

It would appear that anti-suit injunctions against actions taken in another Member State on the basis of Brussels I jurisdiction are not compatible with the regime. The exceptions to the *lis pendens* rule under Brussels I recast, where an exclusive jurisdiction agreement exists,[184] will prevent the situation in *Continental Bank v Aeokos Cia Naviera SA* from arising but not the situation in *Turner v Grovit*.

However, under Brussels I, anti-suit injunctions are still permissible against proceedings taking place in a third-country state. The fact that the English court has mandatory jurisdiction under Brussels I and cannot decline proceedings is sometimes a key reason for granting the anti-suit injunction. For example, in *Skype Technologies SA v Joltid Ltd & others*[185] Joltid took proceedings in the United States in spite of an exclusive jurisdiction clause in favour of the English courts. Skype sought an anti-suit injunction to prevent these proceedings taking place. The court held that in this case the jurisdiction agreement gave the English courts jurisdiction under Art 23 of Brussels I, which it could not decline to exercise. The anti-suit injunction was granted on the basis of the exclusive jurisdiction agreement. Lewison J made it very clear that the injunction was granted on the facts of the case and would not be automatically available where proceedings were taken in breach of an exclusive jurisdiction clause.

In *Samengo-Turner v J & H Marsh & McLennan (Services) Ltd and others*,[186] where the English courts had protective jurisdiction under Art 20 as the court of the employee's domicile, the courts held that the only way to protect the statutory rights of *Samengo-Turner* to be sued in the country of his domicile was to issue an anti-suit injunction against proceedings in New York. Here an anti-suit injunction was used to uphold the protections of Brussels I.

---

180 [1994] 1 Lloyd's Rep 505.
181 Explored in Chapter 3.
182 [2005] 1 AC 101.
183 A similar approach was taken in relation to an anti-suit injunction to uphold an arbitration agreement in C185/07 *Allianz SpA v West Tankers* [2009] 1 AC 1138. This case is discussed in Chapter 6.
184 Art 31(2) Brussels I recast. See Chapter 3.
185 [2009] EWHC 2783 (Ch).
186 [2007] EWCA Civ 723.

Exclusive jurisdiction agreement in favour of the English courts	Non-exclusive jurisdiction agreement in favour of the English courts	No jurisdiction agreement
• The English court will enforce the parties' exclusive jurisdiction agreement by granting an anti-suit injunction unless there is a strong reason not to do so.	• Proceedings in a foreign court must be **vexatious and oppressive.** • The English court must consider the principles of **comity.**	• England must be the **natural forum** for the proceedings. • Proceedings in a foreign court must be **vexatious and oppressive.** • The English court must consider the principles of **comity.**

Fig 4.3 Anti-suit injunctions.

4.8 Further reading

A Briggs, 'The Death of *Harrods. Forum non conveniens* and the European Court' [2005] 121 LQR 535.

J Fawcett, 'Trial in England and abroad; the underlying policy considerations' (1989) 9 OJLS 205.

CJS Knight, '*Owusu* and *Turner*: the shark in the water?' (2007) 66 *The Cambridge Law Journal*, 288–301.

L Merrett, 'Uncertainties in the first limb of the *Spiliada* test' (2005) 54 ICLQ 211–220.

E Peel, 'Exclusive jurisdiction agreements: purity and pragmatism in the conflict of laws' [1998] LMCLQ 182.

K Takahashi '*Forum non conveniens* discretion in third party proceedings' (2002) 51 ICLQ 127–134.

G Wilkes, 'Enforcing anti-suit injunctions against sovereign states' [2004] 53 ICLQ 512.

S Wood, '*Apple Corps Ltd v Apple Computer Inc*: Jurisdiction' (2005) 16 *Computers and Law* 21–23.

Chapter 5

Recognition and Enforcement of Judgments

Chapter Contents

Key Issues:

- The difference between recognition and enforcement of judgments
- Procedure for the recognition and enforcement of judgments from EU Member States under Brussels I
- Changes to exequatur procedure under Brussels I recast
- Procedure for the recognition and enforcement of judgments from other countries under the English traditional rules
- The obligations of the enforcing court to comply with public policy and human rights obligations

5.1 Introduction

This chapter will examine the circumstances in which an English court will recognise and enforce a foreign judgment.

The recognition and enforcement in England of judgments issued by the courts of EU Member States is governed by the provisions of Brussels I.[1] The Lugano Convention 2007[2] extends this regime to judgments from the courts of Iceland, Norway and Switzerland.

The recognition and enforcement in England of judgments from Scotland and Northern Ireland is governed by Scheds 6 and 7 of the Civil Jurisdiction and Judgments Act 1982 which provides for automatic recognition and enforcement of such judgments.[3] Judgments from the Isle of Man, the Channel Islands and Gibraltar are recognised and enforced according to the rules of Brussels I.[4]

English traditional rules apply to the recognition of judgments from other states. These rules are common law based but have been partially codified by the Foreign Judgments (Reciprocal Enforcement) Act 1933.

A key question in this chapter is to what extent the English courts should review the judgment by the foreign court (court of origin). Under EU law, the English courts must respect the rulings from other EU courts according to the principles of mutual trust and free movement of judgments. Grounds to review the judgment and refuse enforcement exist but are very limited. The jurisdiction of the court granting the judgment cannot generally be questioned.

Under the traditional rules, the English court will recognise the judgment as creating a vested right for the judgment creditor against the other party. The English court will not rehear the case but has greater powers to review the judgment to ensure that the court giving the judgment had competent jurisdiction to hear the case and that the judgment complies with English public policy and the principles of justice.

This chapter will first look at the Brussels I regime. The introduction of Brussels I recast[5] will make some changes to the process for recognition and enforcement of judgments from EU Member States. These changes are highlighted throughout.

---

1 Council Regulation (EC) No 44/2001 [2001] OJ L12/1.

2 Convention on jurisdiction and the enforcement of judgments in civil and commercial matters, signed in Lugano on 30 October 2007 [2007] OJ L339/3.

3 Recognition may only be refused where the judgment is irreconcilable with a previous judgment. Sched 6 (10) and Sched 7 (10).

4 S 39 Civil Jurisdiction and Judgments Act 1982.

5 Regulation (EU) No 1215/2012 of the European Parliament and of the Council [2012] OJ L351/1.

The second part of the chapter will look at the recognition and enforcement of foreign judgments under the English traditional rules.

5.2 The recognition and enforcement of judgments

The effect of recognition and enforcement of a judgment is the same regardless of whether the judgment is recognised under Brussels I or under the English traditional rules.

Recognition of a foreign judgment means that the English court will take note of the result of the judgment as *res judicata*. Once a just and fair ruling has been made by a foreign court the English court will take the matter as decided and it cannot be reopened.[6] Recognition of a foreign judgment will prevent new proceedings from being brought in England on the same cause of action unless some good reason why the judgment should not be recognised is shown.[7] This means that the successful party will not have to fight the case again but can apply for summary judgment to have a fresh proceeding by the other party dismissed.[8]

Recognition of a foreign judgment may also occur where the English courts hear proceedings on a different cause of action but an issue is raised that has already been decided in a foreign judgment. The court will take judicial notice of the foreign court's decisions on individual issues in the ruling, such as the determination of legal ownership, the status of a legal contract or the existence of negligence. The parties cannot later deny any matter of fact or law decided by the earlier judgment.[9]

The English courts considered the effects of recognition of a foreign judgment in *Naraji v Shelbourne*.[10] Here, the claimant was a professional footballer who claimed that his career had been destroyed at the age of 22 by medical negligence during an operation carried out to repair his knee after an injury. He issued proceedings in contract and tort in the English courts. Proceedings in tort had been previously brought in the court of Indiana. The defendant applied to have these proceedings struck out as groundless. The claimant withdrew his claim and it was dismissed by the Indiana courts. This precluded any more litigation in Indiana. The English courts found that this dismissal was a judgment and determinative of the rights of the parties.[11] The tort claim was barred on the basis of *res judicata*. However, the contract claim had not been addressed by the Indiana courts so this was not barred as a cause of action.[12]

The court next considered whether the judgment in the Indiana case precluded the claimant from alleging that he had received negligent medical care. The court held that it would not be fair to treat the dismissal as having determined the particular issue of whether the surgery had been carried out negligently as the particular issue had not been raised.[13] The English court later found that the procedure had been carried out in a way that was not proper or correct.[14] However, it had not been proved that but for the way the operation was carried out the claimant would have been able to return to a career as a professional footballer.[15]

6 This is also known as cause of action estoppel.
7 S 34 Civil Jurisdiction and Judgments Act 1982.
8 CPR 24.
9 This is also known as issue estoppel.
10 [2011] EWHC 3298 (QB).
11 Ibid [134].
12 Ibid [150].
13 Ibid [153].
14 Ibid [101].
15 Ibid [113]. See also *The Sennar (No 2)* [1985] 1 WLR 490; *House of Spring Garden Ltd v Waite* [1991] 1 AC 241; C456/11 *Gothaer Allgemeine Versicherung AG v Samskip GmbH* [2013] IL Pr. 7.; C442/03 P *& O European Ferries (Vizcaya) SA v Commission of the European Communities* [2006] ECR I-4845 [44]; and C442/03 P *Artegodan GmbH v European Commission* [2012] ECR I-0000 [87].

Enforcement of a foreign judgment in England means that the state can take action to make sure that the foreign judgment is obeyed. This may occur where the person who has won a monetary award in a foreign court (the judgment creditor) seeks assistance to ensure that the other party (the judgment debtor) pays the amount owed.

5.3 Recognition and enforcement of judgments under Brussels I

The rules governing recognition and enforcement of judgments under Brussels I are found in Chapter III of the regulation. A judgment given in a Member State shall be recognised in all other Member States without any special procedure.[16] A judgment given in a Member State that is enforceable in the state of origin shall be enforced in another Member State when it has either been declared enforceable there or has been registered for enforcement there.[17] A court may refuse to recognise or enforce a foreign judgment only on very limited grounds outlined in Arts 34 and 35.

This section will examine what kinds of judgments are given automatic recognition and enforcement under Brussels I. The bases for refusal of recognition and enforcement will be examined. Finally, procedures for recognition and enforcement of judgments will be outlined.

5.3.1 What sorts of judgments are recognisable and enforceable under Brussels I?

Article 32 defines a judgment as any judgment given by a court or tribunal of a Member State[18] as well as determination of costs by an officer of the court. All judgments must relate to a civil and commercial matter to be within the scope of Brussels I.[19]

5.3.1.1 Civil and commercial matters

In *Coursier v Fortis Bank*[20] the court held that a decision related to insolvency fell outside the scope of the Brussels Convention.

In *Realchemie Nederland BV v Bayer CropScience AG*[21] Bayer obtained an order from the German court prohibiting Realchemie from importing, possessing and marketing certain pesticides in Germany due to a patent infringement. An order was also made imposing a fine for breach of the initial order. The Dutch courts referred the question of whether an order for payment of a fine was within the scope of Brussels I to the ECJ. The ECJ held that the question should be determined by looking at the right this fine served to protect. In this case Bayer's right to exclusively exploit the invention protected by its patent was clearly a civil and commercial matter. Therefore the order imposing the fine was capable of being recognised and enforced in the Netherlands under Brussels I.

In *Gothaer Allgemeine Versicherung AG v Samskip GmbH*[22] the ECJ considered whether a judgment that an exclusive jurisdiction agreement was binding was enforceable under the Lugano Convention. In this case, an action for compensation was brought before the German courts for damage that had

---

16 Art 33.
17 Art 38.
18 C414/92 *Solo Kleinmotoren* [1994] ECR I-2237.
19 Outlined in Art 1.
20 C267/97 *Coursier v Fortis Bank* [1999] ECR 1- 2543.
21 C406/09 *Realchemie Nederland BV v Bayer CropScience AG* [2012] IL Pr 1.
22 C456/11 *Gothaer Allgemeine Versicherung AG v Samskip GmbH* [2013] IL Pr 7.

occurred to brewery equipment while being shipped from Belgium to Mexico. The delivery was subject to an exclusive jurisdiction agreement in favour of Iceland. Proceedings had initially been brought in Belgium as the place where the transporter was domiciled. The Belgian courts had declined to hear the case due to the exclusive jurisdiction clause in favour of the Icelandic courts. The German courts referred to the ECJ the question of whether they were bound by the decision of the Belgian courts to decline jurisdiction.

The ECJ warned that a restrictive approach to the concept of a 'judgment' would give rise to the creation of a category of judicial decisions which other Member States would not be obliged to recognise under Brussels I. This would undermine the principle of mutual trust.[23] Therefore the rules of automatic recognition under Brussels I cover a judgment where the court of origin declines jurisdiction on the basis of a jurisdiction clause. The ECJ held that the German courts were bound by the Belgian court's finding that a valid jurisdiction clause existed in favour of Iceland.[24]

5.3.1.2 Jurisdictional basis of judgment

The rules of recognition and enforcement in Brussels I apply not only to judgments where the EU State had jurisdiction under the rules of Brussels I but also to cases where the defendant was not an EU domiciliary and the EU State assumed jurisdiction under its own domestic rules under Art 4.

5.3.1.3 Recognition of judgments from third-country states

It is clear from the wording of Art 32 that the rules of Brussels I do not apply where a court is asked to recognise a judgment from a third-country state. However, a question arises where an EU Member State issues a judgment recognising a judgment from a third-country state according to national rules. This judgment of the Member State court is a judgment within the meaning of Art 32. Must this recognition of the foreign judgment be recognised in other Member States? This would mean that once recognised in one Member State, a foreign judgment would be automatically recognised in all Member States. In *Owens Bank v Bracco*[25] the ECJ held that the Brussels Convention does not apply to proceedings in Contracting States for the recognition and enforcement of a judgment from a non-Contracting State.[26]

5.3.1.4 Temporal scope

In *Wolf Naturprodukte v Sewar*[27] the ECJ held that in order for a judgment to be recognisable and enforceable under Brussels I, the regulation must have been binding in both the state of origin and the recognising state when the judgment was given. In this case, a judgment given in Austria in 2003 was not recognisable and enforceable in the Czech Republic under Brussels I because in 2003 the Czech Republic was not part of the EU and Brussels I was not binding there.

5.3.1.5 Provisional and protective measures

Judgments do not have to be final to be recognisable and enforceable under Brussels I. However, if the judgment is appealed in the state of origin, the recognising or enforcing state may stay proceedings under Art 37 to wait for the outcome of the appeal.[28]

Provisional and protective measures are *prima facie* enforceable as judgments.

23 Ibid [31].
24 Ibid [41].
25 C129/92 *Owens Bank v Bracco* [1994] ECR I-117.
26 Ibid [25], [37].
27 C514/10 *Wolf Naturprodukte GmbH v SEWAR spol s r o* [2012] IL Pr 37.
28 C43/77 *Industrial Diamond v Riva* [1977] ECR 2175.

In *Maersk v Firma M de Haan en W de Boer*[29] Maersk made a claim in Denmark against two ship owners for damage done by a trawler to an underwater oil and gas pipeline in the North Sea. The ship owners brought proceedings in the Netherlands to limit their liability under the International Convention relating to the Limitation of the Liability of Owners of Sea-Going Ships of 10 October 1957. Liability was fixed at a certain sum and a fund was created.

The ECJ confirmed that the rules of recognition and enforcement apply to provisional and interlocutory decisions.[30] The decision of the Dutch Court which provisionally fixed the amount to which the liability of a ship owner would be limited was recognised.

The ECJ examined whether provisional judgments given *ex parte* were recognisable and enforceable under the Brussels Convention in *Denilauler*.[31] Here, an *ex parte* provisional order was made by the French courts freezing Denilauler's assets in a German Bank. Denilauler appealed against the order. In the meantime, Couchet Frères applied to the German courts to have the order enforced and attached to the bank assets. This was granted. Denilauler appealed on the basis that it had not received notice of the *ex parte* proceedings to make the freezing order.

The ECJ noted that provisional or protective measures in the state of origin could be recognised and enforced under the Convention if they were made pursuant to adversarial proceedings. This was not the case where protective measures were ordered or authorised by a court without the defendant having been summoned to appear and were intended to be enforced without prior service on the defendant.[32]

Denilauler left the law in some confusion. It was not clear if provisional judgments made *ex parte* were enforceable 'judgments' within the meaning of Brussels I or whether such judgments were *prima facie* enforceable but the enforcing court could refuse to recognise or enforce them where no rights of defence had been given to the defendant.

In the Commission's 2010 proposal for Brussels I recast, it was made clear that provisional and protective measures granted by a court with jurisdiction under Brussels I were eligible for recognition and enforcement under the proposal even where the provisional judgment was made *ex parte*.[33] However, recognition could be refused on the basis that procedural safeguards had not been met.[34]

5.3.1.6 Provisional measures granted under Article 31

Article 31 of Brussels I allows provisional measures to be made in a court which does not have jurisdiction over the substance of the case. This might occur, for example, where a defendant had assets in a different state to where the main claim was heard. It is open to the claimant to seek a freezing order from the state where the assets are based in *ex parte* proceedings. This could be done instead of seeking to enforce a provisional ruling from the state with jurisdiction over the substance of the dispute.[35]

Whether a provisional measure granted where the court had jurisdiction under Art 31 was capable of being recognised and enforced in other Member States under Brussels I was examined in *Mietz v Intership Yachting Sneek BV*.[36] The ECJ noted that it was important that the Brussels Convention equivalent of Art 31 was not used to circumvent the normal jurisdictional rules of the regime.[37] It

29 C39/2002 *Maersk Olie & Gas A/S v Firma M de Haan en W de Boer* [2004] ECR I-9657.
30 Ibid [46].
31 C125/179 *Denilauler v SNC Couchet Frères* [1980] ECR 1553.
32 Ibid [17].
33 COM(2010) 748 final, 9–10.
34 See below.
35 See Chapter 3; C391/95 *Van Uden v Deco-Line* [1998] ECR I-709.
36 C99/96 *Mietz v Intership Yachting Sneek BV* [1999] ECR I-2277.
37 Ibid [47].

was held that where the court making the provisional order only had jurisdiction to do so under Art 31 the order would not be recognisable under the Brussels regime.[38]

Under Art 42(2)(b) of Brussels I recast, it is clear that in order for a provisional measure to be enforced, the court of origin must also have had jurisdiction over the substance of the dispute under the Brussels rules.

5.3.2 When recognition and enforcement can be refused

Recognition and enforcement of a judgment must be refused where any of the grounds stipulated in Arts 34 and 35 are present. These grounds are exclusive.[39] Under Art 34, recognition can be refused where the judgment is manifestly contrary to public policy, where the defendant's procedural rights have been infringed or where the judgment is irreconcilable with an earlier judgment.

Generally speaking, the recognising court cannot review whether the court of origin had a valid basis of jurisdiction to hear the case when the judgment was issued. However, Art 35 allows the recognising court to refuse recognition where the court of origin has infringed the exclusive rules of jurisdiction under Art 22 or the protective rules of jurisdiction governing consumer contracts and insurance contracts.[40] Jurisdiction can also be reviewed in very limited cases under Art 72.

The court is expressly prohibited from reviewing the substance of a judgment by Art 36. This means that a court cannot refuse to enforce or recognise a judgment where it believes that it has been wrongly decided.

The court reviewing the judgment can also refuse to recognise or enforce the judgment on the basis that it is not a 'judgment' within the meaning of Brussels I.[41]

5.3.2.1 Recognition is manifestly contrary to public policy

Recognition can be refused on the basis that recognition or enforcement of the judgment would be manifestly contrary to public policy in the recognising state.[42] This ground is interpreted very strictly. Although the content of public policy is up to each Member State, recognition can only be refused on this ground where it is contrary to public policy to the extent that recognition would infringe a fundamental principle of the legal order of the recognising state.

In *Krombach v Bamberski*[43] the German courts referred the question of whether the recognition of a French judgment could be refused on the basis of public policy to the ECJ. In this case Krombach was found guilty of involuntary manslaughter of a 14-year-old French girl. He did not attend the hearing but sent legal counsel to appear on his behalf. The French courts did not allow the counsel to appear, as Krombach himself had not attended. Krombach was sentenced to 15 years in prison and ordered to pay compensation to Bamberski, the girl's father. Bamberski sought to enforce the judgment in Germany. Krombach opposed enforcement as he had not been given an adequate chance to defend himself.

The ECJ stated that the content of public policy was up to the individual Member State but the Court was required to review the limits within which the Member State courts could rely on public policy to refuse to recognise a judgment.[44] In this case, it was open to the German courts to refuse

38 Ibid [54].
39 C139/10 *Prism Investments BV v van der Meer* [2012] IL Pr 13.
40 See Chapter 3.
41 See above.
42 Art 34(1).
43 C7/98 *Krombach v Bamberski* [2000] ECR I-1935.
44 Ibid [22]–[23].

to recognise the judgment on the basis that refusal to hear Krombach's counsel was manifestly contrary to his right to defend himself.

Many of the cases in which public policy has successfully been invoked to prevent recognition concern the rights of the defendant to be heard.

In *Gambazzi v Daimler Chrysler Canada Inc*[45] the English courts made a provisional freezing order and a disclosure order against Gambazzi, who was domiciled in Switzerland. When Gambazzi did not comply with the disclosure order after multiple reminders, the English courts held him to be in contempt of court and excluded him from the proceedings. In the final judgment, Gambazzi was ordered to pay damages to Daimler Chrysler. Daimler Chrysler sought enforcement of the judgment in Italy. Gambazzi appealed on the basis that enforcement of the judgment would be against public policy. The question was referred to the ECJ, who held that refusal to enforce based on the public policy exception could only be granted where recognition and enforcement would manifestly breach a fundamental principle or an essential rule of law in the enforcing state.[46] It was held that the exclusion of Gambazzi from the proceedings was a serious restriction on the rights of the defence but could be justified if it was a proportionate measure to ensure that proceedings were properly conducted. It was up to the national court to assess if the infringement of Gambazzi's defence rights was manifest and disproportionate.[47]

In *Pelligrini v Italy*[48] the European Court of Human Rights held that the Italian courts were under an obligation when recognising foreign judgments to satisfy themselves that the proceedings fulfilled the guarantees of Art 6 of the European Convention on Human Rights (ECHR).[49] Here the recognition of a ruling from the Vatican Ecclesiastical Courts violated Pelligrini's Art 6 right to a fair trial as she had not been given a proper opportunity to put arguments to the Vatican courts.

The effect of *Pelligrini* is that where recognition of the judgment is against the recognising state's obligations under the European Convention on Human Rights, the Member State may wish to refuse recognition on the basis of public policy. In *Maronier v Larmer*[50] the English courts refused to enforce the ruling of a Dutch court on the basis of public policy. The Court of Appeal held that there was a strong presumption that the procedures of other signatories to the European Convention on Human Rights were compliant with Art 6 but this was not irrebuttable. In this case, a judgment had been made against Larmer, without his knowledge, due to an error in procedure. This judgment could not be appealed in the Dutch courts as the period to lodge an appeal had passed.

When reviewing the Brussels I regulation in 2009, the Commission suggested that public policy should be removed as a basis on which to refuse recognition. All of the EU Member States were now signatories of the EU Charter of Fundamental Rights, and the defendant's procedural rights could be adequately protected by the terms of Brussels I. Challenges to recognition based on public policy were rarely successful. In the 2010 proposal, only judgments on defamation cases and collective actions could be refused recognition on the basis of public policy as Member States had very diverging approaches to these types of actions.

The abolition of the public policy ground was criticised by several commentators because of the substantial differences in public policy that remain between Member States.[51] Dickinson

---

45 C394/07 *Gambazzi v Daimler Chrysler Canada Inc* [2009] ECR I-2563.
46 Ibid [27].
47 See also *Apostolides v Orams* [2011] QB 519; C38/98 *Renault v Maxicar* [2000] ECR I-2973.
48 [2001] ECHR 480.
49 Ibid [40].
50 [2003] QB 620.
51 J Kramberger Škerl, 'European public policy (with an emphasis on exequatur proceedings)' (2011) 7 JPIL 461–490; A Dickinson, 'The Proposal for a Regulation of the European Parliament and of the Council on Jurisdiction and the Recognition and Enforcement of Judgments in Civil and Commercial Matters (Recast) ("Brussels I bis" Regulation)' Legal Studies Research Paper No. 11/58 September 2011, available online at: http://ssrn.com/abstract=1930712 (accessed 13 May 2013).

described the public policy exception as an 'essential safety valve'[52] and argued that if it remained as a ground for refusal there was no reason why exequatur (see below) could not be abolished for all types of civil and commercial judgments.

Under Brussels I recast, the public policy ground now remains as a ground for non-recognition of judgments that can be invoked by any interested party.[53]

5.3.2.2 Defendant's procedural rights have been infringed

Under Art 34(2), a judgment cannot be recognised where it has been given in default of appearance and the defendant was not served with the document that initiated proceedings in sufficient time to enable him to arrange a defence.

The meaning of 'the document that instituted proceedings' was considered in *Hengst Import*.[54] In this case an *ex parte* order for payment had been made by the Italian courts. A copy of the order was served on the debtor, who had a set period of time to oppose the order. The ECJ held that in *ex parte* proceedings such as these, the document which institutes proceedings is service of the *ex parte* order along with the claimant's initial application. This gives the defendant enough information to prepare a defence.[55]

In *Klomps v Michel*,[56] the court considered whether service of the document issuing proceedings had been effected in good time. An *ex parte* order for payment of debt was made against Klomps. Klomps was served with notice of this *ex parte* order at an address in Germany. He failed to submit an objection to the order and so an order was made in default of appearance. The order was enforced in the Netherlands. Klomps objected to the enforcement order, claiming that when the order for payment was made he was resident in the Netherlands and not in Germany. This meant that service was not effected in good time. The ECJ held that the relevant time period to be considered was the time between service of notice of the *ex parte* order and the date on which the default judgment was issued. The ECJ held that the question of whether Klomps had had enough time to prepare a defence was an objective matter to be considered by the court of enforcement. It did not matter, in this case, that the German courts had held that Klomps had been properly served with adequate notice.[57]

In *Maersk*[58] it was argued that the decision to limit the ship owner's liability should not be recognised. Maersk did not, at any time, make an appearance in the proceedings for the establishment of a liability limitation fund and was not served with notice of proceedings in advance of the order. Under Dutch law, this type of provisional order was made after a unilateral procedure by the ship owner, which was then followed by reasoned submissions by both parties. The ECJ held that the enforcing court must determine whether notification was effected in the proper form and in sufficient time to enable the defendant to arrange its defence effectively.[59] In this case the opportunity to make reasoned submissions before the order was made permanent could be considered as proper notification if, in the opinion of the enforcing court, notice was duly served in proper time.

If the defendant has an opportunity to commence proceedings to challenge the judgment in the state of origin and did not do so, the judgment can be recognised even where it was given in violation of the defendant's procedural rights.[60]

---

52 Dickinson, 'The Proposal for a Regulation of the European Parliament' op cit, 10.
53 Art 45(1)(a).
54 C474/93 *Hengst Import* [1995] ECR I-2113.
55 Ibid [21].
56 C166/80 *Klomps* [1981] ECR 1593.
57 See also C49/84 *Debacker v Bouwman* [1985] ECR 1779; *TSN Kunststoffrecycling GmbH v Jurgens* [2002] EWCA Civ 11.
58 C39/2002 *Maersk Olie & Gas A/S v Firma M de Haan en W de Boer* [2004] ECR I-9657.
59 Ibid [61].
60 Art 43(2).

In *Sonntag v Waidmann*[61] a teacher was found guilty of negligent homicide causing the death of a pupil by an Italian criminal court. The parents and brother of the dead child were joined to the proceedings as civil parties and were granted an order of compensation. They sought enforcement of the civil order in Germany. The question was whether the order could be refused recognition on the basis that the defendant had not been given sufficient notice of the civil proceedings against him. The defendant's counsel had raised no objection to the civil action when it was examined in court. The ECJ held that non-recognition of a judgment was only possible under Art 27(2) of the Brussels Convention where the defendant had not entered an appearance. Here the defendant had replied to both the civil and criminal claim through counsel.[62]

This ground for non-recognition remains under Brussels I recast.[63]

5.3.2.3 Judgment is irreconcilable with a previous judgment

The judgment will not be recognised or enforced if it is irreconcilable with a judgment given in a **dispute between the same parties** in the Member State in which recognition is sought.[64]

In *Hoffman v Krieg*[65] a German wife obtained an order from the German courts for maintenance against her husband. The husband had moved to the Netherlands and obtained a divorce from the Dutch courts. The German order for maintenance was incompatible with the Dutch divorce decree as under Dutch law all duties of maintenance ended upon divorce. Recognition of the German order for maintenance was refused on the basis that it was irreconcilable with a later order of the enforcing court.[66]

If the judgment is irreconcilable with an **earlier** judgment **involving the same cause of action and the same parties** given in another Member State or in a third-country state, it will not be recognised as long as the earlier judgment is recognised in the enforcing state.[67]

Recognition can only be refused where the judgment is irreconcilable with another 'judgment'. In *Solo Kleinmotoren GmbH v Boch*[68] the dispute between the parties was settled in a settlement approved by the German courts. Further action was taken in the Italian courts and Solo Kleinmotoren was ordered to pay damages to Boch. Boch sought to enforce this order in Germany. Kleinmotoren argued that recognition should be refused as the judgment was irreconcilable with the court-approved settlement. The ECJ held that the court-approved settlement was not a 'judgment given in a dispute between the same parties in the State in which recognition is sought' and so recognition could not be refused on this basis.

5.3.2.4 Reviewing jurisdiction of the court of origin

In general, the rule is that jurisdiction of the state of origin cannot be reviewed. Article 35 provides limited exceptions to this rule.[69] In these exceptional cases the reviewing state is bound by the findings of fact of state of origin. This limits the likelihood that the jurisdiction of the first court will be found to have been incorrect.[70]

Under Art 35(1) a court may refuse to recognise a judgment that violates the rules of exclusive jurisdiction under Art 22 of Brussels I. Thus a court could refuse to recognise a French judgment

---

61 C172/91 *Sonntag v Waidmann* [1993] ECR I-1963.

62 See also C283/05 *ASML Netherlands BV v Semiconductor Industry Services GmbH* [2006] ECR I 12041.

63 Art 45(1)(b).

64 Art 34(3).

65 C145/86 *Hoffman v Krieg* [1988] ECR 645.

66 See also C80/00 *Italian Leather v Weco Polstermobel GmbH & Co* [2002] ECR I-4995.

67 Art 34(4).

68 [1994] ECR I 2237.

69 The same exceptions are restated under Brussels I recast Art 45(1)(e) but are extended to cases where an employee is the defendant.

70 Art 35(2).

made about the ownership of land in Greece. A court may also refuse recognition where the judgment was made in violation of the protective rules of jurisdiction that apply to consumer contracts or insurance disputes.[71]

In *Mietz v Intership Yachting Sneek BV*,[72] Mr Mietz, domiciled in Germany, had agreed to buy a customised boat from a Dutch company. Payment was to be made in five instalments before the boat's delivery. Mr Mietz did not make all the payments and Intership obtained a provisional order from the Dutch courts for recovery of the monies owed. This order was enforced in the German courts and Mr Mietz appealed, claiming that this order was not enforceable under the Brussels Convention. Mr Mietz claimed that he was a consumer and could only be sued in the court of his own domicile, Germany. He had not raised these arguments in the Dutch courts. The ECJ held that the contract in this case was a contract that fell within the consumer protective regimes.

Article 35(3) expressly rules out a review of the jurisdiction of the court of origin on the basis of public policy. In *Krombach*[73] it was argued that the jurisdiction of the French courts which was based on the French nationality of the victim was contrary to public policy of the enforcing court. The ECJ confirmed that jurisdiction of the court of origin could only be reviewed in accordance with the grounds expressly laid out in the Brussels Convention. Public policy could not be used as an excuse to review the jurisdiction of the other court on other grounds.[74]

Recognition of a judgment can be refused on the basis that recognising the judgment would violate an agreement entered into by the recognising state under Art 59 of the Brussels Convention. Article 59 allowed EU Member States to enter into agreements with a third-country state for the reciprocal recognition of judgments. The UK entered into two such agreements with Canada[75] and Australia.[76] Under these agreements the UK has agreed not to recognise judgments from other Member States granted against Canadian or Australian domiciliaries if the EU Member State did not have jurisdiction under the EU regime but merely under national rules. This means, for example, that the UK will not recognise a judgment by the French courts for damages against a Canadian domiciliary where the jurisdiction of the French courts was based only on the fact that the claimant was a French national.[77] This ground is reiterated in Art 72 of Brussels I recast.

5.3.2.5 Review of jurisdiction under the Lugano Convention

Under the Lugano Convention, the recognition of a judgment can be refused where the state of origin assumed jurisdiction on a basis that was not within the Lugano rules and recognition or enforcement is sought against a person who is domiciled in a Lugano state – i.e. Iceland, Switzerland or Norway.[78] This prevents the recognition of judgments against Lugano state domiciliaries where the court of origin based jurisdiction on national rules.

5.3.3 Procedure for the recognition of judgments under Brussels I

A judgment that is eligible for recognition and enforcement under Brussels I will be recognised in all other Member States automatically[79] unless the grounds for refusal of recognition outlined in

71 See Chapter 3.
72 C99/96 *Mietz v Intership Yachting Sneek BV* [1999] ECR I-2277.
73 C7/98 *Krombach v Bamberski* [2000] ECR I-1935.
74 Ibid [31]–[32].
75 Reciprocal Enforcement of Foreign Judgments (Canada) Order SI 1987/468.
76 Reciprocal Enforcement of Foreign Judgments (Australia) Order 1994/1901.
77 See also C533/08 *TNT Express Nederland BV v AXA Versicherung AG* [2010] IL Pr 35.
78 Art 64(3) Lugano Convention.
79 Art 33(1).

Arts 34 and 35 exist.[80] There is no need for the parties to engage in any special procedure in the state of origin or the recognising state. The judgment becomes *res judicata* in the courts of all Member States. Where an issue is raised in proceedings in England that has already been decided by another Member State, the English court will have jurisdiction to investigate whether there is any reason to refuse the recognition of the judgment.[81]

In some circumstances, a court declaration that the foreign judgment is recognised may be desirable to clarify the rights and obligations of individuals. Any interested party may apply for such a declaration.[82] Article 53 requires the party seeking recognition to provide a copy of the judgment.[83] The requirements for this declaration are governed by Art 37 of Brussels I recast.

5.3.4 Procedure for enforcement of judgments under Brussels I

Once a judgment is made, it is automatically recognised in other EU Member States. Where a judgment is enforceable in one EU Member State it can be enforced in all other EU Member States.[84]

In *Coursier v Fortis Bank*[85] the ECJ considered the meaning of 'enforceable' in the state of origin. Mr and Mrs Coursier had failed to meet their obligations under a loan from Fortis Bank. Fortis Bank obtained a judgment order to pay from the French courts. Mr Coursier's business later went into court-supervised liquidation and Fortis Bank gave notice of claim. The liquidation was closed by order of the French courts as there were insufficient assets to pay all of Mr Coursier's creditors. Mr Coursier then obtained employment in Luxembourg. Fortis sought to enforce their order in Luxembourg as an attachment to Mr Coursier's salary. The Luxembourg court referred the matter of whether the French order was 'enforceable' to the ECJ. The ECJ held that the question of whether a judgment was formally enforceable in the state of origin should be distinguished from the question of whether the judgment could actually be enforced there.[86] The judgment was, in principle, enforceable in Luxembourg under the Brussels Convention.[87]

In order to enforce the judgment in a particular Member State, a declaration of enforceability must be obtained in the enforcing state.[88] In England, instead of obtaining a declaration, the foreign judgment is registered for enforcement.[89] This approval process of the foreign decision by the state of enforcement is known as exequatur.

The process for exequatur is governed by Arts 38 to 56 of Brussels I and by the national law of the enforcing state. There are three stages – registration of the judgment, serving notice on the judgment debtor and the possibility of appeal.

1) The person who seeks to have the judgment enforced (judgment creditor) will make an *ex parte* application to the English court to register the judgment.[90] This is done under s 4 of the Civil Jurisdiction and Judgments Act 1982. The judgment creditor is not required to inform the other party (judgment debtor) that he has applied to register the judgment and the judgment debtor cannot make submissions at this stage. The judgment creditor must produce a

---

80 These are examined below.
81 Art 33(3).
82 Art 33(2).
83 A translation must be provided if required. Art 55(2).
84 Art 38 (1).
85 C267/97 *Coursier v Fortis Bank* [1999] ECR 1 2543.
86 Ibid [24].
87 Ibid [31].
88 Art 38 (1).
89 Art 38(2).
90 Arts 39 and 40.

copy of the foreign judgment[91] **AND** a certificate from the court of origin that the judgment is enforceable there.[92] The judgment is immediately declared enforceable without any review.[93] At this stage the judgment creditor may apply for protective measures from the English courts such as a freezing order.[94]

2) The judgment creditor is made aware of the enforcement proceedings and is served with the declaration of enforceability and a copy of the original judgment.[95]
3) Either party[96] may appeal the registration of the foreign judgment within one month[97] of the service of the declaration of enforceability.[98] The English court may revoke the declaration of enforceability only where one of the grounds of Arts 34 and 35 is satisfied.

The judgment may be enforced where the judgment debtor does not appeal the declaration of enforceability or where the appeal is unsuccessful.[99] The judgment will have the same force and effect as if it was a judgment of the English court. In *Apostolides v Orams*[100] the ECJ held that the foreign judgment should not have a greater effect in the enforcing state than it did in the Member State of origin. Here the fact that the claimant would have difficulty having the order enforced in Northern Cyprus did not prevent the English court from declaring the claim enforceable.

Brussels I does not regulate the execution of enforcement, which is left to national law.[101] Article 54 of Brussels I recast allows foreign measures or orders in the judgment to be adapted to a measure that has equivalent effect and pursues similar aims and interest. This adaptation cannot result in effects going beyond those provided for in the state of origin. The nature of this adaptation can be appealed by either party.

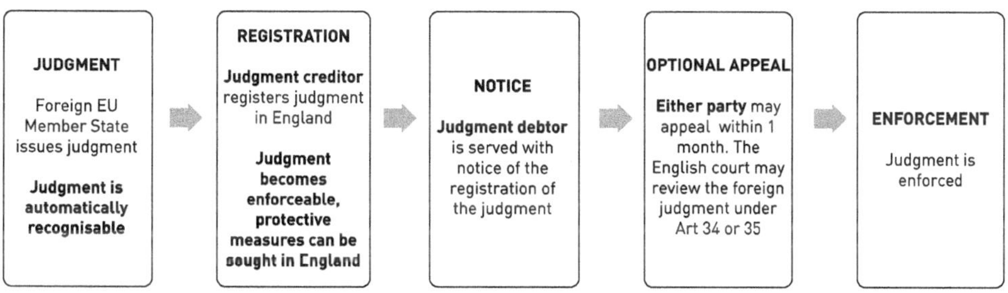

Fig 5.1 Procedure for exequatur under Brussels I.

5.3.5 The abolition of exequatur under Brussels I recast

While the recognition and enforcement procedures under Brussels I have been criticised by Hartley as failing to provide substantial review,[102] the Commission was of the view that the

---

91 Art 53(1).
92 Arts 54–55, the certificate is in Annex V of Brussels I.
93 Art 41.
94 Art 47(2).
95 Art 42.
96 C167/08 *Draka v Omnipol* [2009] ECR I-3477.
97 If the judgment debtor is domiciled in a different Member State, he has two months to appeal a declaration of enforceability in England. Art 3(5).
98 Art 43.
99 The review of the foreign judgment under Art 34 or 35 may be appealed on a point of law to a higher English court. Art 44.
100 C420/07 *Apostolides v Orams* [2009] ECR I-3571 [66].
101 C119/84 *Capelloni & Aquilini v Pelkmans* [1985] ECR 3147 [16]; C139/10 *Prism Investments v van de Meer* [2011] ECR I 000.
102 T Hartley, *International Commercial Litigation* (Cambridge University Press, 2009), 342.

enforcement procedures outlined above were unnecessary in most cases. Moreover, exequatur was an obstacle to the free circulation of judgments. The procedure meant unnecessary costs and delays for the parties involved and deterred companies and citizens from making full use of the internal market.

The main object of the revision of Brussels I was to abolish the exequatur procedure. It was felt that in an internal market without frontiers it should be possible to enforce rights abroad without the delay and expense of the exequatur stage. The Commission noted that most applications for enforceability were successful. Declarations of enforceability were rarely challenged and challenges were rarely successful.[103]

The House of Lords was supportive of proposals to abolish exequatur. It was, however, essential to forewarn a judgment debtor that steps are being taken to execute a judgment against him, in order to enable him to challenge enforcement of the judgment in the country where enforcement is intended.[104] Some safeguards were necessary.

In 2010, the Commission proposed abolition of the exequatur procedure for all civil and commercial judgments except for judgments in defamation cases and judgments given in collective compensatory proceedings.[105] Three safeguards would remain for the judgment debtor. First, he would be able to contest the judgment in the state of origin if he had not been properly informed about the proceedings in that state. Second, he could contest any other procedural defects by extraordinary procedure in the state of enforcement. Finally, he could stop the enforcement of the judgment where it was irreconcilable with another judgment. Non-recognition on the ground of public policy was to be abolished as the rights of the defendant were adequately protected by these remedies.[106]

The exequatur procedure was to remain in place for defamation cases and collective actions as Member States had widely diverging approaches to these types of actions and there were valid public policy concerns.[107]

In Brussels I recast exequatur has now been abolished for all types of actions. Judgments given in one Member State will be treated in another Member State as if they were given by the courts of that Member State.[108] The judgment creditor can proceed immediately with an application for protective measures in the state of enforcement.[109] In order to have the judgment enforced, the judgment creditor must provide the enforcing court with a copy of the foreign judgment and a certificate from the court of origin that the judgment is enforceable.[110]

Where the judgment creditor seeks to enforce a provisional measure,[111] he must provide the enforcing court with a copy of the judgment, and a certificate from the court of origin certifying that the measure is enforceable in the state of origin and that the court had jurisdiction over the substance of the dispute.[112] Where the provisional measure was made *ex parte*, the judgment creditor must also produce proof that the judgment debtor has been served with notice of the measure.[113]

---

103 COM (2009) 174 final, 4.
104 The European Union Committee of the House of Lords: Green Paper on the review of the Brussels Regulation Report with evidence, (2009) HL paper 148, [30].
105 COM (2010) 748 final [3.1].
106 Ibid [3.1].
107 See further Chapter 8.
108 Recital (26).
109 Art 40.
110 Art 42(1).
111 Art 42(2).
112 Found in Annex 1 to Brussels I recast.
113 Art 42(2)(b).

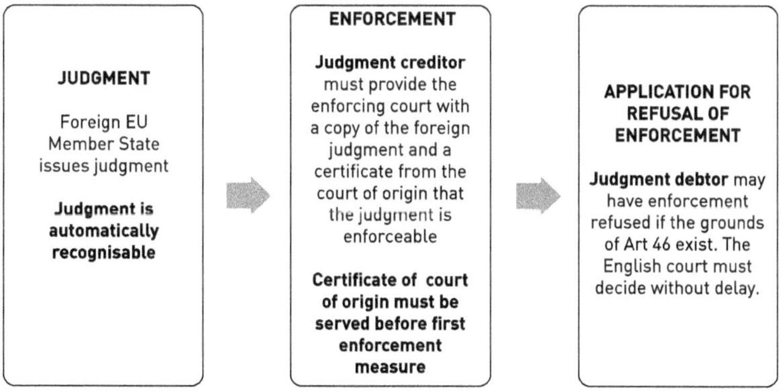

Fig 5.2 Enforcement under Brussels I recast.

The certificate of the court of origin must be served on the person against whom enforcement is sought prior to the first enforcement measure.[114] The person against whom enforcement is sought must also receive a copy of the judgment if he has not yet received this. The judgment can then be enforced.

The rights of the judgment debtor are protected by the right to make an application for refusal of enforcement on limited grounds outlined in Art 46. The court must make its decision without delay.[115] The decision can be appealed by either party.[116] During the challenge to enforcement the Member State can allow enforcement to proceed subject to a limitation or provision of security.[117]

5.4 Authentic instruments and court settlements

Under Brussels I, authentic instruments and court settlements are not automatically recognised in other Member States. Authentic instruments are private documents which have been authenticated by a public official and become legally binding.[118] Chapter IV of Brussels I allows authentic instruments and court settlements to be enforced in other Member States where they are enforceable in the state of origin. An application is made in the same fashion as for the enforcement of a judgment.[119] However, a declaration of enforceability can only be refused on one ground: where enforcement would be manifestly contrary to the public policy of the Member State where enforcement is sought.

Under Brussels I recast, authentic instruments and court settlements are now enforceable without exequatur.[120] An application for a refusal of enforcement can be made in the same way as for a judgment.[121] Enforcement can be refused only where enforcement is contrary to the public policy of the Member State.[122]

114 Art 43; Recital (32).
115 Art 48.
116 Art 50.
117 Recital (31).
118 C260/97 *Unibank v Christensen* [1999] ECR I -3715; J Fitchen, 'Authentic Instruments and European Private International Law in Civil and Commercial Matters: Is Now the Time to Break New Ground?' (2011) 7 JPIL 33–100.
119 Art 57(4).
120 Arts 58 and 59.
121 Arts 46–51.
122 Art 58(1).

5.5 Simplified enforcement procedures for uncontested claims

Where the judgment creditor is seeking to enforce an uncontested claim he has two options that make enforcement faster and more straightforward. He may choose to apply for a **European Enforcement Order**[123] or a **European Order for Payment**.[124]

The **European Enforcement Order** is available for claims for the payment of a specific sum of money[125] when the debtor has expressly agreed that the claim is due by admission in court proceedings or by settlement.[126] On application by the judgment creditor, the court of origin is authorised to issue a certificate that the judgment is a European Enforcement Order which can be enforced in all other Member States.[127] There is no need for a declaration of enforceability and no possibility of opposing enforcement. The certificate cannot be appealed but can be rectified in case of error.[128]

The court of origin must check that the judgment fulfils a number of conditions.[129] Enforcement may be refused by the enforcing state only if the judgment is irreconcilable with a judgment of the enforcing state that could not be raised as an objection in the court of origin.[130]

The **European Order for Payment**[131] introduces a type of summary procedure intended to speed up legal proceedings and reduce the costs of litigation. This procedure is outlined by rules 78.2 to 78.11 of the Civil Procedure Rules. The procedure applies to cross-border uncontested claims only.[132] Under the European Order for Payment procedure, the judgment creditor can apply to the enforcing court for an order calling the judgment debtor to either pay or oppose the claim. This order becomes enforceable unless the defendant opposes it within 30 days.[133] The only basis on which enforcement can be refused is where the claim is irreconcilable with a judgment from the enforcing state.[134]

5.6 Simplified enforcement procedures for small claims

The European Small Claims Procedure[135] applies to contested claims and uncontested claims up to the value of €2,000. It is designed for use for claimants without legal representation and the parties are not required to make any legal assessment of their claim.[136] Member States must ensure that parties can receive practical assistance in filling out the forms.[137] In England, the European Small Claims Procedure is laid out in rules 78.12 to 78.22 of the Civil Procedure Rules. The jurisdictional rules of Brussels I apply to determine whether the English courts can hear these claims.

---

123 Regulation 805/2004 of 21 April 2004 Creating a European Enforcement Order for uncontested claims [2004] OJ L143/15.
124 Regulation (EC) No 1896/2006 of the European Parliament and of the Council of 12 December 2006 creating a European order for payment procedure [2006] OJ L399/1.
125 Art 4(2) [2006] OJ L399/1.
126 Defined in Art 3.
127 Except Denmark, which has opted out of this measure.
128 Art 10; Regulation 805/2004.
129 Outlined in Art 6.
130 Art 21.
131 Regulation 1896/2006 [2006] OJ L399/1.
132 Arts 1–3.
133 Art 20.
134 Art 22.
135 Regulation (EC) No 861/2007 [2007] OJ L199/1.
136 Art 12.
137 Art 11.

The claimant must lodge a standard claim form in court with supporting documents. The claim form is dispatched to the defendant within 14 days. The defendant may submit a response within 14 days of receipt. Within 30 days of receipt of the defendant's response the court must give judgment or demand further evidence. The judgment can be reviewed in exceptional cases.[138]

A judgment delivered according to the European Small Claims Procedure will be recognised and enforced in other Member States without the need for an exequatur decision. There is no possibility of opposing recognition or enforcement unless it is irreconcilable with a previous judgment recognised in the enforcing state.[139]

5.7 The Mediation Settlement Enforcement Order

Alternative Dispute Resolution (ADR) is promoted by the Mediation Directive[140] as a way to settle civil and commercial disputes. The Directive obliges Member States to set up a mechanism to allow agreements reached in mediation to be made legally enforceable at the wishes of both parties.

The Mediation Directive has been implemented in English law by the Cross-Border Mediation (EU Directive) Regulations 2011[141] and by changes to the Civil Procedure Rules.[142] Where all the parties to a mediated settlement wish to have their agreement made legally enforceable, they may apply for a **Mediation Settlement Enforcement Order**.[143] This is only available where the mediation relates to a cross-border dispute relating to civil and commercial matters.

Once a Mediation Settlement Enforcement Order has been granted it is enforceable in other EU Member States as a judgment under Brussels I.

5.8 English rules for recognition and enforcement of judgments

The English traditional rules apply to judgments *in personam* from countries that are outside the EU and not bound by the Lugano Convention. The rules are common law based but have been codified by two pieces of legislation: the **Administration of Justice Act 1920** and the **Foreign Judgments (Reciprocal Enforcement) Act 1933**. These Acts were intended to provide a simpler procedure for the recognition and enforcement of foreign judgments from particular countries in the English courts.

Both the Administration of Justice Act 1920 and Foreign Judgments (Reciprocal Enforcement) Act 1933 are based on reciprocal agreements with other countries for the mutual recognition and enforcement of judgments. The rules become applicable to judgments from a particular country when that country is listed in Orders in Council.[144] The Administration of Justice Act 1920 applies to the recognition and enforcement of judgments from Commonwealth countries.[145] The Foreign Judgments (Reciprocal Enforcement) Act 1933 governs the recognition and enforcement of

138 Art 18.
139 Art 22.
140 Directive No 2008/52 on Certain Aspects of Mediation in Civil and Commercial Matters [2008] OJ L136/3.
141 SI 2011/1133.
142 Civil Procedure (Amendment) Rules 2011/88.
143 CPR 78.24.
144 S 14 1920 Act and s 1 1933 Act. E.g. Reciprocal Enforcement of Foreign Judgments (Canada) (Amendment) Order SI 1991/1724, which extends the 1933 Act to judgments from Newfoundland.
145 These countries were previously part of the British Empire.

judgments from a number of other countries. It was originally intended to replace the 1920 Act but both Acts remain in force.

If the judgment comes from a country that is not covered by either of these two Acts or by the European regime then the recognition and enforcement of the judgment will be regulated by the English common law rules. There is no need for there to be reciprocity in the foreign country for the common law rules to apply.

5.8.1 Procedure for enforcement and recognition

The foreign judgment itself creates the vested right or legal obligation to be enforced in England.[146] Foreign judgments are recognised by the English courts unless some cause of reason exists why they should not be recognised. This means that the claimant does not have to have the whole dispute retried in England but instead can sue to enforce the foreign judgment as if it was a debt. The judgment creditor can apply for summary judgment under Part 24 of the CPR. The burden lies on the judgment debtor to prove to the court that a reason exists that negates his obligation to the judgment creditor or excuses him from performing the obligation.

A fresh set of proceedings on the same cause of action cannot be brought in England.[147] If the judgment debtor makes an attempt to issue proceedings on the same cause of action, the other party can apply for summary judgment.[148] Summary judgment allows the court to dismiss the claim without a trial.

Where the 1920 and 1933 Acts apply, the judgment creditor may apply to register the foreign judgment.[149] The debtor is informed and has a specified time to apply to set the registration aside. Setting registration aside is based on the same grounds as those which allow the court to refuse recognition of a judgment in an action for enforcement.

Section 9(1) of the 1920 Act allows a person who has obtained a judgment in any part of the Commonwealth to apply within 12 months to the High Court to have that judgment registered. Registration is discretionary. In addition, the court must refuse to register the judgment were the common law grounds for recognition and enforcement have been proved. These are listed in s 9(2).

Section 2 of the 1933 Act allows a successful litigant to apply to the High Court for the registration of a foreign judgment within six years. No discretion is granted to the High Court under the 1933 Act. It must order the judgment to be registered unless one of the grounds for non-recognition listed in s 4 is proved.

5.8.2 What types of judgments can be enforced?

In order to be registered under the English traditional rules, the foreign judgment **must be final and conclusive**[150] and be for a **fixed and definite sum of money**.[151] Injunctions and decrees of specific performance will not be enforced. The judgment must also be a decision on the merits which determines facts and applies the law and expresses a conclusion.[152]

146 *Societe Cooperative Sidmetal v Titan International Ltd* [1966] 1 QB 828, 836–839. See also Chapter 1.
147 S 34 Civil Jurisdiction and Judgments Act 1982; *Republic of India v Indian Steamship Co Ltd* [1998] AC 878; [1998] IL Pr 511.
148 CPR 24.2.
149 Part 74(1) CPR. This procedure is optional under s 9(5) of the 1920 Act but is mandatory for judgments covered by the 1933 Act (s 3); *Yukon Consolidated Gold Corp Ltd v Clark* [1938] 2 KB 241; [1938] 1 All ER 366.
150 *Nouvion v Freeman* (1889) 15 App Cas 1; s 12(1) of the 1920 Act; s 1(2) of the 1933 Act.
151 *Beatty v Beatty* [1924] 1 KB 807; s 12(1) of the 1920 Act; s 1(2) of the 1933 Act.
152 *The Sennar (No 2)* [1985] 1 WLR 490, 499.

In general, if a judgment is final but subject to appeal, it can be enforced[153] as it is possible to set aside the judgment later if the appeal is successful.[154] Provisional awards cannot be enforced under the English traditional rules.

A judgment that **indirectly enforces another country's penal or tax laws** will not be enforceable.[155] It is up to the English court to decide if a claim is a public penalty.[156]

In *Lewis v Eliades (No 2)*[157] the boxer, Lennox Lewis, obtained judgment for over $7 million damages from the New York against his managers and promoters. The claim was based on several heads of damages which included breach of fiduciary duty and fraud. It also included $396,082 of basic damages for racketeering, contrary to the Racketeer Influenced and Corrupt Organisations Act (RICO). The RICO Act allowed Lewis to treble his damages by application to the New York Courts and this application was pending when Lewis sought enforcement of the judgment in England. Judgments for multiple damages are not enforceable in England under s 5 of the Protection of Trading Interests Act 1980. The judgment debtors claimed that the entire judgment was unenforceable in England.

The court held that the Protection of Trading Interests Act did not prevent the enforcement of the award that was based on ordinary compensatory damages.[158] The court mentioned that the RICO damages might also be unenforceable at common law as a foreign judgment for a penalty.[159]

5.8.3 The jurisdiction of the foreign court

Foreign judgments are enforceable in England as long as the court of origin had competent jurisdiction to issue the judgment.[160] This competence is determined by **English law**. The rules applied are not the same as those applied to determine whether the English court has jurisdiction to hear a dispute. A narrower set of rules is used. The foreign court will only have competent jurisdiction (1) where there is a **strong connection between the judgment debtor and the foreign court** that created a duty for the defendant to obey the judgment or (2) where the **judgment debtor submitted to the jurisdiction of the foreign court**. No other type of jurisdiction is considered to be competent for recognition and enforcement purposes under the traditional legal rules.

5.8.3.2 Connection between the judgment debtor and the court

Both statutes require the judgment debtor to have been resident in the foreign country in order for the foreign court to have jurisdiction.[161] The foreign court will have jurisdiction where the judgment debtor had an office or place of business in that country under the 1920 Act.[162] Under the 1933 Act, the foreign court will have jurisdiction over a claim related to a business transaction carried out in that foreign country, if the judgment debtor had an office or a place of business in that country.[163]

153 *Colt Industries Inc v Sarlie (No 2)* [1966] 1 WLR 1287.

154 S 9(2)(e) of the 1920 Act precludes the court from registering a judgment if the judgment debtor can prove that an appeal is pending.

155 *Government of India v Taylour* [1955] AC 461; *United States of America v Inkley* [1989] QB 255.

156 *SA Consortium General Textiles v Sun and Sand Agencies Ltd* [1978] QB 279, 309; *United States Securities and Exchange Commission v Manterfield* [2010] 1 WLR 172.

157 [2004] 1 WLR 692; [2003] EWCA Civ 1758.

158 Ibid [52]. See further E Kellman 'Enforcement of judgments and blocking statutes: *Lewis v Eliades*' (2004) 53 ICLQ 1025–1030.

159 Ibid [50].

160 *Adams v Cape Industries plc* [1990] Ch 433; s 4(1)(a)(ii) 1933 Act; s 9(2)(a) 1920 Act.

161 S 9(2)(b) 1920 Act; s 4(2)(a)(iv) 1933 Act.

162 S 9(2)(c) 1920 Act.; *Sfeir v National Insurance Company of New Zealand Ltd* [1964] 1 Lloyd's Rep 330.

163 S 4(2)(a)(v) 1933 Act.

Under the common law rules, a foreign judgment will be recognised where the judgment debtor had a duty to observe the terms of the foreign judgment.[164] Traditionally this was the case where the judgment debtor is a subject or citizen[165] of the foreign country in which the judgment was obtained or where he was resident in the foreign country when the action began.[166] Lord Diplock expressed doubt over whether a court had valid competent jurisdiction based on mere nationality in *Blohn v Desser*.[167] This is supported by the comments of Lord Collins in *Rubin v Eurofinance SA*,[168] who did not consider nationality as a basis for competent jurisdiction.

Mere presence in the foreign country was not originally considered to create an obligation on the defendant to observe a foreign judgment.[169] However, in *Adams v Cape Industries*[170] the court stated that the voluntary presence of an individual in a foreign country, whether permanent or temporary, was sufficient to give the courts of that country territorial jurisdiction over him under English rules of private international law.[171] This was approved in *Rubin v Eurofinance SA*.[172]

Where the judgment debtor is a body corporate, the foreign court will have jurisdiction where the foreign country is the body corporate's **principal place of business**[173] or if the company **carried out business in the foreign country**.[174] This is the same as the basis for serving an English claim form.[175]

In *Sfeir v National Insurance Co of New Zealand Ltd*[176] the court considered a case where a New Zealand company was allegedly carrying out business in Ghana through an appointed agent. The New Zealand company was not resident in Ghana when the action began. Mocatta J declined to enforce the judgment from the Ghana courts, holding that although the defendants had business carried out by their agent in Ghana, this business was not that of the defendants and so the company could not be said to have carried out business in Ghana.

In *Adams v Cap Industries*[177] the Court of Appeal applied the agency principles to a situation where the overseas corporation carried out business through its subsidiary in the USA. It was held that a subsidiary normally acted for itself and not for the overseas parent corporation and had no power to bind the parent corporation contractually. Therefore the parent company and the subsidiary were to be treated as separate legal entities.

5.8.3.2 Submission

Where a person submits to the jurisdiction of a foreign court, he or she cannot later contend that the foreign court did not have jurisdiction when an action is taken to enforce that judgment in England.[178]

In *Emanuel and Others v Symon*[179] it was held that the foreign court had competent jurisdiction by submission where (1) the person against whom the judgment is being enforced selected the court

---

164 *Societe Cooperative Sidmetal v Titan International Ltd*, [1966] 1 QB 828, 836.
165 Lord Diplock expressed doubt over the continuing validity of this basis of jurisdiction in *Blohn v Desser* [1962] 2 QB 116, 123.
166 *Emanuel and Others v Symon* [1908] 1 KB 302, 309. *Report of Foreign Judgments (Reciprocal Enforcement) Committee* (HMSO 1932) Cmd 4213, 8–9.
167 [1962] 2 QB 116, 123.
168 [2012] UKSC 46 [10].
169 Ibid.
170 [1990] Ch 433, [1990] 2 WLR 657.
171 Ibid 736.
172 [2012] UKSC 46 [10].
173 S 4(2)(a)(iv) 1933 Act.
174 S 9(2)(b) 1920 Act; s 4(1)(a)(ii) 1933 Act.
175 See Chapter 4.
176 [1964] 1 Lloyd's Rep 330.
177 [1990] Ch 433.
178 See Chapter 4.
179 [1908] 1 KB 302, 309.

as the claimant in the original proceedings. The foreign court will also have competent jurisdiction where (2) the judgment debtor voluntarily appeared to contest the case on its merits or (3) if he contracted to submit himself to the foreign forum.

These three bases of submission are also outlined in the two statutes.[180] Where the judgment debtor has taken no part in the foreign proceedings, it is clear that he has not submitted to the jurisdiction of the foreign court. However, the position is less clear when the judgment debtor has objected to the jurisdiction of the foreign court and, while maintaining that objection, has taken part in the proceedings. The question of when the defendant has taken such steps as to constitute submission to the foreign court is clarified in s 33 of the Civil Jurisdiction and Judgment Act 1982.

The question of whether there has been submission is governed by English law.[181] However, the English court must have due regard to the procedural rules of the foreign court.[182]

In *Chief Harry Akande v Balfour Beatty Construction Ltd*[183] the defendant sought to have registration under s 20 of the 1920 Act set aside, on the grounds that it did not submit to the Nigerian jurisdiction within the meaning of s 33 of the Civil Jurisdiction and Judgment Act 1982. In this case the defendant was served outside the jurisdiction. He entered conditional appearance to the claim and sought to challenge the jurisdiction of the Nigeria courts. The court held that the judgment debtor had not submitted to the jurisdiction of the Nigerian court. He had not taken any steps that would be necessary or useful to him only if jurisdiction of the foreign court had been accepted.[184]

In *Rubin v Eurofinance SA*[185] the defendants were members of a Lloyd's syndicate which had received payments from an Australian reinsurance company shortly before it went into liquidation. The liquidator brought proceedings in New South Wales to recover the payments made to the syndicate on the basis that the company had been insolvent when they were made. The Court of New South Wales set the payments aside and asked the English court to order the defendants to pay the sum specified in the order.

The judgment debtors had been served out of the jurisdiction. They did not accept service or enter an appearance in the Australian court, but their solicitors commented on the evidence and these comments were put before the Australian judge. They also participated in creditors' meetings in Australia in relation to some unsettled claims which they had against the company. The Supreme Court held that the English court could enforce the judgment under the Foreign Judgments (Reciprocal Enforcement) Act 1933. While the judgment debtors had not taken any steps that would amount to submission under Australian law, Lord Collins considered the syndicate's participation in the liquidation by way of proof and receipt of dividends was submission to the Australian insolvency proceedings. This meant that the syndicate should be taken to have submitted to the jurisdiction of the Australian court responsible for the supervision of that proceeding.[186]

Where the judgment debtor submits to the jurisdiction of the court he will be considered to have submitted for the purposes of any related counterclaims. In *Murthy v Sivajothi*[187] the defendant had voluntarily submitted to the jurisdiction of the Florida courts in respect of a mortgage foreclosure. The claimants had been joined as co-defendants. They submitted counterclaims against the

180 S 9(2)(b) 1920 Act; s 4(2)(a)(i)–(iii) 1933 Act.
181 *Rubin v Eurofinance SA* [2012] UKSC 46 [61].
182 *Akai Pty Ltd v People's Insurance Co Ltd* [1998] 1 Lloyd's Rep 90, 97.
183 [1998] IL Pr 110.
184 Ibid [29].
185 [2012] UKSC 46.
186 Ibid [167].
187 [1999] IL Pr 320.

defendant and received default judgments. The defendant challenged the enforcement of these counterclaims in England on the basis that he had only submitted to jurisdiction in respect of the foreclosure. Evans LJ, delivering the judgment of the Court of Appeal, stated that the claimant must be considered to have submitted to the jurisdiction of the courts in respect of related counterclaims as long as such claims were properly brought against him.[188]

5.8.4 Where enforcement of foreign judgments will be refused

The English courts will not generally examine the merits of a foreign judgment even where it is alleged that the foreign court decided the case incorrectly or applied English law incorrectly.[189] The English court will refuse to register or enforce a judgment of a court with competent jurisdictions in four circumstances. These grounds can be gleaned from the common law cases and are outlined in the 1920 Act and the 1933 Act.[190]

1. The judgment debtor was not properly served with notice of the proceedings.
2. The judgment was obtained by fraud.
3. The judgment is irreconcilable with English public policy or natural justice.
4. The judgment is irreconcilable with a prior judgment on the same cause of action.

These defences to recognition and enforcement may be raised in answer to an application for enforcement or as part of an application to set aside registration of judgment. They are examined in turn.

5.8.4.1 Defendant had inadequate notice of proceedings

A default judgment cannot be registered or enforced where the judgment debtor was not properly served in the original proceedings in the foreign court or did not have adequate time to defend the proceedings.[191] This is very similar to the ground for non-recognition under Brussels I.

As the defendant's right to a fair trial is guaranteed under Art 6 of the European Convention on Human Rights, where there are major procedural rights infringements, recognition and enforcement may also be refused on a public policy or natural justice basis.[192]

5.8.4.2 Fraud

In general, the judgment debtor will not be permitted to reopen issues of either fact or law which have been decided against him by the foreign court. But this is subject to the special defence that the foreign judgment was obtained by fraud.[193]

The burden is on the **judgment debtor** to raise the issue of fraud and to prove it on the balance of probabilities.[194] Fraud may have been committed by the judgment creditor or by corruption in the foreign court itself.[195]

An issue of fraud raised in the original trial can be reheard by the English court.[196] It is not necessary for the judgment debtor to produce new evidence of the fraud that was not considered

188 Ibid 329–330.
189 *Godard v Gray* (1870–71) LR 6 QB 139.
190 S 9(2) 1920 Act; s 4(1) 1933 Act.
191 S 9(2)(c) 1920 Act; s 4(1)(a)(iii) 1933 Act.
192 See below.
193 S 9(s)(d) 1920 Act; s 4(1)(a)(iv) 1933 Act.
194 *Owens Bank v Bracco* [1992] 2 AC 443, 489.
195 *Price v Dewhurst* (1837) 8 Simons 279, 59 ER 111
196 *Abuloff v Oppenheimer & Co* (1882) 10 QBD 295; *House of Spring Gardens v Waite* [1990] 2 All ER 990; *Owens Bank v Bracco* [1992] AC 443.

by the court of origin. In *Owens Bank v Bracco*,[197] Owens Bank sought repayment of a loan. The existence of the loan was supported by documents signed by Bracco. Bracco challenged the loan, stating that the contracts were forged; the bank had taken other contracts with his signature on them and written the new contract on them. This argument had been rejected by a court in St Vincent. An application for registration of the judgment was brought under the Administration of Justice Act 1920. Bracco raised the issue again and was successful in having recognition refused.

Lord Bridge recognised that there might be a very strong case to be made in favour of according to overseas judgments the same finality as the courts accord to English judgments, which cannot be reopened on the basis of fraud unless there is new evidence. However, the question for reform was one for the legislature.[198] Hartley argues that the rule is legitimate as the fraudulent party may have chosen the first court precisely because it would be unsympathetic to the allegations of fraud.[199]

5.8.4.3 Public policy and natural justice

Enforcement of foreign judgments must be refused where enforcement of the judgment is contrary to English public policy or natural justice.[200]

For example, in *Adams v Cape Industries* a settlement that had been given legal force as a consent order prevented judicial assessment of damages for asbestos victims. The Court of Appeal held that the judgment violated the principles of natural justice and would not be enforced on a public policy basis.[201]

Where procedural guarantees have not been followed by the court of origin and enforcement of the judgment infringes the defendant's procedural rights under Art 6 of the ECHR, enforcement of the judgment will be refused on the basis of English public policy. The English courts cannot expose an individual to a denial of justice by the enforcement of such a judgment.[202]

In *United States v Montgomery (No 2)*[203] the court considered the enforcement of a confiscation order by the USA. In this case, shares in a Panama company had been transferred from a husband to his wife shortly before the husband was convicted for fraud on the US government. The USA courts made an order against the wife for discovery of the value of the shares. The wife did not comply as she had moved to England. The US courts then made an order for confiscation of the shares. The wife appealed, but this appeal was not permitted as the US courts are not required to hear appeals from fugitives from justice under US fugitive disentitlement doctrine. The US government applied to register the confiscation order in the English courts. The judge held that even though such a judgment would be contrary to Art 6 of the ECHR if made in a Convention country, it was not against public policy for the English courts to register such a judgment. The House of Lords affirmed this decision. The US fugitive disentitlement doctrine was not an arbitrary deprivation of a party's right to a hearing, but was a means of securing proper obedience to the orders of the court.[204] It was not a flagrant denial of the defendant's Art 6 rights or a fundamental breach of the requirements of Art 6.[205]

---

197 [1992] 2 AC 443.
198 Ibid 489.
199 Hartley, *International Commercial Litigation*, 363.
200 S 9(2)(f) 1920 Act; s 4(1)(a)(v) 1933 Act.
201 See also *Jacobson v Frachon* (1927) 138 LT Rep 386.
202 See *Pelligrini v Italy* [2001] ECHR 480 and *Maronier v Larmer* [2003] QB 620.
203 [2004] 1 WLR 2241.
204 Ibid 2253.
205 See further A Briggs, 'Foreign judgments and human rights' (2005) 121 LQR 185–189.

5.8.4.4 Judgment is irreconcilable with a previous judgment

A foreign judgment will not be recognised if it is inconsistent with an earlier English judgment or an earlier foreign judgment that is recognised in England.[206]

Brussels I

Applies to judgments from EU Member States:

1. The judgment relates to a civil and commercial matter.
2. If the judgment is provisional, the court of origin must have jurisdiction over the substance of the matter.

Recognition and enforcement may be refused where:

1. It is manifestly contrary to public policy.
2. Defendant has not been given adequate notice to prepare a defence and judgment was given in default of appearance.
3. Judgment is **irreconcilable** with a previous judgment.
4. The court of origin violated the rules of **exclusive jurisdiction** under Art 22 of Brussels I or the jurisdictional rules relating to **consumer contracts** or **insurance disputes.**
5. Recognition would violate an **agreement entered into by the recognising state** under Art 59 of the Brussels Convention.

English Traditional Rules

Apply to judgments from non-EU or Lugano States that:

1. are **final and conclusive**
   AND
2. for a fixed sum of money
   AND
3. are made by a foreign court with **competent jurisdiction**
   AND
4. do not indirectly enforce another country's **penal or tax laws.**

Recognition and enforcement may be refused where:

1. It is contrary to public policy or natural justice.
2. Defendant has not been given adequate notice to prepare a defence and judgment was given in default of appearance.
3. Judgment is **irreconcilable** with a previous judgment.
4. Judgment is **based on fraud.**

Fig 5.3 The grounds for non-recognition of foreign judgments.

206 S 4(1)(b) 1933 Act.

In *Showlag v Mansour*[207] the legal representatives of a deceased individual discovered that two of his deposits in English banks had been transferred to an account in Switzerland. They believed this money to have been stolen. The holder of the Swiss account claimed that the deceased had given him the money. The money had now been dispersed to a number of different jurisdictions including Egypt and Jersey. The English courts found that the money had been stolen. The Egyptian courts found that the money had been a gift. The representatives commenced proceedings in Jersey. The Jersey courts held that they were bound to recognise the English judgment as *res judicata*. The Privy Council held that where there were two competing foreign judgments, each pronounced by a court of competent jurisdiction and not open to impeachment on any ground, the earlier of them in time must be recognised and given effect to the exclusion of the later.[208]

5.9 Further reading

A Briggs, 'Which foreign judgments should we recognise today?' (1987) 36 ICLQ 240–259.
A Briggs 'Foreign judgments: more surprises' (1992) 108 LQR 549–533.
A Chong, 'Transnational public policy in civil and commercial matters' (2012) 128 LQR 88–113.
A Dickinson, 'The Proposal for a Regulation of the European Parliament and of the Council on Jurisdiction and the Recognition and Enforcement of Judgments in Civil and Commercial Matters (Recast) ("Brussels I *bis*" Regulation)', *Legal Studies Research Paper No. 11/58* September 2011, available at: http://ssrn.com/abstract=1930712 (accessed 13 May 2013).
JJ Fawcett, 'The impact of Article 6(1) of the ECHR on private international law' (2007) 56 ICLQ 1–47.
J Fitchen, 'Authentic instruments and European private international law in civil and commercial matters: is now the time to break new ground?' (2011) 7 JPIL 33–100.
J Kramberger Škerl, 'European public policy (with an emphasis on exequatur proceedings)' (2011) 7 JPIL 461–490.
P Mariani, 'Recognition and enforcement of judgments in carriage of goods by road matters in the European Union' (2012) 8 JPIL 17–33.
HP Meidianis 'Public policy and ordre public in the private international law of the EU: traditional positions and modern trends' (2005) 30 *European Law Review* 95–110.
C Montgomery, 'Keep calm and don't submit: the Supreme Court has its say on recognition of foreign insolvency proceedings' (2013) *Insolvency Intelligence* 29–32.
RF Oppong, 'Mere presence and international competence in private international law' (2007) 3 JPIL 321–333.
S Pitel, 'A modern approach to enforcing judgments' [2004] LMCLQ 288.
A Scott, 'Exclusionary principles and the Judgments Regulation' (2007) 3 JPIL 309–320.

207 [1995] 1 AC 431.
208 Ibid 440.

Chapter 6

Arbitration

Chapter Contents

Key Issues:

- Introduction to arbitration and the role of national courts
- Enforcing arbitration agreements
- Recognition and enforcement of arbitral awards under the New York Convention
- Applicable law in arbitration proceedings

6.1 Introduction

This chapter will look at some of the conflict of law issues that arise in international arbitration.

The Arbitration Act 1996 applies to both domestic and international arbitration carried out in England and Wales. This Act incorporates certain provisions of the UNCITRAL Model Law on International Commercial Arbitration and gives effect to the Convention on the Recognition and Enforcement of Foreign Arbitral Awards 1958 (New York Convention).

The New York Convention is the main international instrument determining the recognition and enforcement of foreign arbitral awards in all Convention States. This Convention has been ratified by 148 countries, including all EU Member States.[1] The New York Convention requires national courts to uphold arbitration agreements by declining jurisdiction to hear legal proceedings in favour of arbitration when appropriate. As the New York Convention is an intergovernmental agreement, there is no overarching review body to ensure that its provisions are consistently interpreted by all Convention States. The United Nations Commission on International Trade Law (UNCITRAL) has provided some guidance on how the Convention should be interpreted[2] but national court decisions remain inconsistent.

This chapter will begin with a general introduction to arbitration and the role of national courts in supporting arbitration before going on to examine the conflict of laws issues encountered by the English courts when supporting international arbitration and the choice-of-law issues faced by arbitral tribunals situated in England.

6.2 Introduction to arbitration

Arbitration is a method of dispute resolution chosen by the parties. It is a privatised legal process. Instead of going to court, the parties agree to submit their disagreement to a private arbitrator or an arbitral institution such as the London Court of International Arbitration (LCIA). The assigned arbitrator will listen to the arguments of the parties and come to a decision on the dispute. The decision of the arbitrator is binding on the parties by virtue of their private agreement.

Arbitration is often preferred to legal proceedings in national courts for its neutrality. Parties can deliberately choose a neutral venue and a neutral state law or non-state law such as the *lex mercatoria* to govern their dispute. This practice is popular in the international commercial context, where the application of national law with its particular 'parochial quirks'[3] may be

1 For an up-to-date list see: www.uncitral.org/uncitral/en/uncitral_texts/arbitration/NYConvention_status.html (accessed 13 May 2013).

2 UNICITRAL, 'Recommendation regarding the interpretation of article II (2) and article VII (1) of the Convention on the Recognition and Enforcement of Foreign Arbitral Awards (New York, 1958)' available at www.uncitral.org/uncitral/uncitral_texts/arbitration/2006recommendation.html (accessed 13 May 2013).

3 N Blackaby et al, *Redfern & Hunter on International Arbitration* (5th ed, OUP 2009), [1.252].

unsuitable. The issues to be resolved could relate to business arrangements between multinational corporations that cross borders and which are not particularly linked to the legal system of one country.

Arbitration is also very flexible, as the rules of procedure can be adapted to suit the dispute. English law requires only that an arbitral tribunal acts fairly and gives each party the right to be heard.[4] This can make arbitration more desirable than court proceedings for reasons of speed and reduced cost.

The arbitration agreement is the source of the powers of the arbitral tribunal. It outlines what issues the arbitration tribunal will consider and the powers of the arbitration tribunal. The arbitral tribunal may exercise any authority conferred on it by the parties within the limits of national law of the place of arbitration. As the arbitration tribunal can only consider the matters that the parties put before it, and its ruling is only binding on the parties to the dispute, the tribunal is not always required to consider matters of public interest or the effect of the award on third parties. For this reason, some countries limit the availability of arbitration for disputes in which there are strong public interest concerns. In England there are no express limits on arbitration in the Arbitration Act 1996 but criminal matters are not considered to be arbitrable.[5]

6.3 Role of national courts in supporting arbitration

Arbitration operates outside any court structure and is subject to only limited supervision by the courts. Some tension exists between the use of arbitration to achieve transnational neutral justice and the necessity for the involvement of state courts.[6] Only national courts possess coercive powers which can be used to rescue or enforce arbitration if the parties do not abide by their agreements. In addition, national courts have a role in supporting arbitration where there are gaps in the parties' arbitration agreement.

An English court may enforce an arbitration agreement by staying legal proceedings where a valid arbitration agreement exists.[7] The English court may also be asked to intervene in arbitration to grant interim relief,[8] or to assist in setting the arbitration in motion.[9]

In most cases, once the arbitration tribunal proceedings have started, there is no future role for the court. The arbitral tribunal itself has the power to determine whether or not the arbitration agreement on which the tribunal's jurisdiction is based is valid and whether the issue in dispute is within the scope of the arbitration agreement.[10] The arbitral tribunal may determine its own procedural rules, as long as it acts fairly.[11] The arbitration tribunal also has the power to determine the appropriate substantive rules by which to resolve the dispute.[12] The choice of law will usually be outlined in the arbitration agreement. The parties may choose a national law, a non-national set of principles such as the UNIDROIT Principles of International Commercial Contracts, or the parties may choose to dispense with the law and allow the arbitrator to come up with a solution based on

---

4 S 33(1)(a) Arbitration Act 1996.

5 This limit is imposed by common law rules: s 81(a) Arbitration Act 1996. Arbitration is available for family matters excluding child welfare issues and issues over recognition of a foreign marriage or divorce. A scheme was launched by the Institute of Family Law Arbitrators Limited in 2012. See further: http://ifla.org.uk/cms/wp-content/uploads/2012/02/Rules-Final-22.02.12.pdf (accessed 13 May 2013).

6 *Coppée-Lavalin SA v Ken-Ren Chemicals and Fertilizers Ltd* [1994] 2 Lloyd's Rep 109, 116.

7 S 9 Arbitration Act 1996.

8 S 42 Arbitration Act 1996.

9 S 18 Arbitration Act 1996.

10 S 30 Arbitration Act 1996; see discussion in *Broda Agro Trade (Cyprus) Ltd v Alfred C Toepfer International GmbH* [2010] EWCA Civ 1100 [39]; *Christopher Brown Ltd v Genossenschaft Oesterreichischer Waldbesitzer Holzwirtschaftsbetriebe GessmbH* [1954] 1 QB 8.

11 Ss 33–34 Arbitration Act 1996.

12 S 46 Arbitration Act 1996.

what seems fair and equitable.[13] The conflict of laws issues faced by the arbitral tribunal during this process are discussed in more detail below.

Where arbitration proceedings take place in England, the arbitral tribunal may seek assistance from the English court by means of orders to preserve evidence, protect assets and maintain the status quo pending the outcome of the arbitration.[14]

Where one of the parties challenges the jurisdiction of the arbitration tribunal, this is initially dealt with by the arbitration tribunal but may be referred to the English courts for resolution.[15]

Once the arbitration tribunal has made an award, the parties should voluntarily[16] carry out the award as a binding decision on their dispute. If the parties do not carry out their obligations under the award, the arbitral tribunal has no powers of enforcement. In order to enforce the award, legal proceedings must be taken. These can be taken either in England as the seat of arbitration or in another country where the party refusing to comply with the award has assets. An application can be made to an English court to enforce[17] or set aside an arbitral award.[18]

In order for any particular international arbitration to proceed smoothly, the involvement of several different national courts may be required. For example, a German company and a Dutch company who have entered into a business venture together might agree to submit any future disputes to arbitration at the LCIA as a neutral venue. When a dispute arises, both parties are bound by the arbitration agreement to submit to arbitration proceedings in London. However, one party might try to take legal proceedings in another country such as Spain. The Spanish courts will be required to consider the validity of the arbitration agreement. If they find the agreement to be valid, they should decline jurisdiction in favour of the LCIA in England. The arbitration proceedings in England might require support from the English courts to make orders to preserve evidence. Finally, when the arbitral award is made, the winning party will seek to enforce the award in the country where the other party has financial assets. Therefore the Dutch courts or the German courts may be required to consider enforcement of the arbitral award. In this scenario, at least three different national courts will be involved in supporting one arbitration proceedings in London.

6.4 Conflict of laws issues in international arbitration

International arbitration proceedings may be subject to several different systems of law. This raises several conflict of law issues for the different supporting courts.

The **validity of the arbitration agreement** will be considered by a court which is asked to stay legal proceedings in favour of arbitration. The question may arise a second time when a court is asked to enforce a foreign arbitral award. Such an award will only be enforceable where the original arbitration agreement is valid.[19] This raises questions of which **applicable law** is appropriate to determine the validity of the arbitration agreement.

A second issue arises relating to the powers of the national court to **decline jurisdiction** over legal proceedings in favour of an arbitration tribunal. The New York Convention requires

13 Also know as arbitration *ex aequo et bono*.

14 Ss 42–44 Arbitration Act 1996.

15 Ss 31 and S32 Arbitration Act 1996; *Trafigura Beheer BV v Yieh Phui (China) Technomaterial Co Ltd* [2009] EWHC 2054 (Comm).

16 This is usually the case; see research by Queen Mary School of International Arbitration, *International Arbitration: Corporate Attitudes and Practices* 2008, available online at www.arbitrationonline.org/docs/IAstudy_2008.pdf (accessed 13 May 2013)

17 S 66 Arbitration Act 1996.

18 Ss 67–69 Arbitration Act 1996.

19 Art V(1)(a) New York Convention 1958.

Convention States to uphold arbitration agreements by declining jurisdiction and referring the parties to arbitration if seised of a matter that the parties have agreed to submit to arbitration.[20] As we have seen in Chapter 3, Brussels I governs the jurisdiction of EU courts in civil and commercial matters. The Regulation excludes arbitration from its scope, leaving the matter to be regulated entirely by the New York Convention to which all Member States are signatories. However, the scope of the exclusion has been a topic of some controversy and the approach of the CJEU to this matter has affected the efficiency of international arbitration within the EU. This problem has been addressed in the reforms to Brussels I.

Conflict of law issues also arise when a court is asked to **recognise or enforce a foreign arbitral award** under the New York Convention. Recognition and enforcement can be refused where the arbitral agreement was not valid or where the dispute submitted to arbitration was not within the scope of the arbitration agreement. Recognition and enforcement can also be refused where the procedural rights of the parties to arbitration were not respected, where the subject matter of the arbitration is non-arbitral under the law of the recognising state or where the recognition of the award would be contrary to public policy.[21]

The **arbitral tribunal** itself may need to consider conflict of law issues when determining the procedural law of the tribunal (*lex arbitri* or curial law) or the substantive law to be applied to the dispute. These issues may be determined by the arbitration agreement itself or be left to the determination of the arbitral tribunal. Where the arbitral tribunal has to determine questions of applicable law it is bound by the domestic law of the place of arbitration.

Each of these four issues will be discussed in turn.

6.4.1 Validity of arbitration agreements

Parties may agree to submit a dispute to arbitration in a number of different ways. The arbitration agreement may take the form of an arbitration clause in a contract, or the parties may make a separate agreement once a dispute arises, to refer their grievance to an arbitration tribunal.

Where a national court is asked to decline jurisdiction in favour of arbitration or to enforce an arbitral award, the court will consider the validity of the arbitration agreement itself. The New York Convention lays down some minimum requirements but it is up to the court examining the agreement to determine the law governing the validity of the arbitration agreement according to **national choice-of-law rules**. Arbitration agreements are expressly excluded from the Rome I Regulation by Art 1(2)(e).[22]

6.4.1.1 Formal validity

The New York Convention requires an arbitration agreement to be in writing.[23] The agreement may take the form of an arbitral clause in a contract, a signed agreement or an exchange of letters or telegrams.[24] It could also include an exchange of emails.[25]

No specific wording is required, but the agreement must make it clear that the parties have agreed to refer a current or future dispute to arbitration.[26]

20 Art II(3) New York Convention 1958.
21 Art V New York Convention 1958.
22 See Chapter 7.
23 Art II(1) New York Convention 1958; s 6 Arbitration Act 1996.
24 Art II(2) New York Convention 1958.
25 UNCITRAL, 'Recommendation Regarding the Interpretation of Art II, paragraph 2 and Art VII paragraph 1 of the Convention on the Recognition and Enforcement of Foreign Arbitral Awards' available online at www.uncitral.org/pdf/english/texts/arbitration/NY-conv/A2E.pdf (accessed 13 May 2013).
26 *David Wilson Homes Limited v Survey Services Limited* [2001] EWCA Civ 34.

6.4.2.2 Material validity

Under the New York Convention, the agreement must relate to differences that arise between the parties in respect of a defined legal relationship. The subject matter of the dispute must be one that a court declining jurisdiction considered to be capable of settlement by arbitration.[27]

A foreign arbitral award will not be recognised for enforcement under the New York Convention where the arbitration agreement is not considered to be valid by the enforcing court.[28] This could occur where the parties lacked capacity to make the agreement or where the agreement is not valid under law applicable to the agreement or under the law of the country where the award was made.[29]

6.4.2.3 Applicable law in the English courts

Where the English courts are asked to consider the validity or interpretation of an arbitration agreement they will apply the law chosen by the parties. For example, in *Tamil Nadu Electricity Board v ST-CMS Electric Company Private Limited*[30] a clause in the parties' contract specifically stated that the effect and interpretation of the arbitration agreement is to be governed 'by the laws of England and by the New York Convention'. A choice may also be implied from the behaviour of the parties.

Where the parties have not chosen an applicable law, the English courts will apply the 'proper law'[31] of the arbitration agreement, which is the law of the country to which the arbitration agreement is most closely connected. In *International Tank and Pipe SAK v Kuwait Aviation Fuelling Co KSC*[32] the parties contracted to construct a fuelling depot at Kuwait International Airport. The arbitration clause provided that disputes would be decided by the engineer. However, a party dissatisfied with the engineer's decision had 90 days in which to require the dispute to be referred to arbitration, failing which the engineer's decision became final and binding. The contractors sought payment for some asphalting which it claimed was extra to the agreed price. The engineer decided against the contractors.

The Court of Appeal had to consider which national law governed the validity and interpretation of the arbitration clause. The arbitration proceedings themselves were subject to procedural rules of the International Chamber of Commerce. The contract for building the depot was subject to English law. The court held that English law was the proper law to govern the validity and interpretation of the arbitration clause.

Normally, the proper law of an arbitration clause in a contract will be the law applicable to the contract of which it forms part, but this is not always the case. For example, in *Black-Clawson International Ltd v Papierwerke Waldhof-Aschaffenburg AG*[33] a contract for the manufacture and supply of a paper-making machine contained an arbitration clause in favour of arbitration in Zurich. While the contract itself was governed by English law, the Commercial Court held that the validity of the arbitration clause itself should be governed by Swiss Law.[34]

Under s 7 of the Arbitration Act 1996, an arbitration clause in a contract shall not be regarded as invalid, where the contract itself is invalid. The arbitration agreement is treated as a distinct agreement.

Under Art V (a) of the New York Convention, recognition and enforcement of an award can be refused where agreement to arbitrate is invalid due to lack of capacity of the parties or because it is

27 Art II (1) New York Convention.
28 Art V(1)(a) New York Convention 1958.
29 Art V (1)(b).
30 [2007] EWHC 1713.
31 See Chapter 7.
32 [1975] QB 224.
33 [1981] 3 Lloyd's Reports 446.
34 See also the comments in *Abuja International Hotels Ltd v Meridien SAS* [2012] EWHC 87 (Comm).

not valid according to the law chosen by the parties. Where no choice of law was made, recognition and enforcement can be refused where the agreement is invalid by the law of the country where the award was made.[35]

6.4.2 Declining jurisdiction in favour of arbitration

Article II(3) of the New York Convention requires a contracting state to refer a matter to arbitration when seised on an action that is the subject of a valid arbitration agreement. This referral is not done on the court's own motion, but at the request of one of the parties. The power of the English courts to stay legal proceedings in favour of arbitration is found in s 9 of the Arbitration Act 1996.

6.4.2.1 The effect of Brussels I

Section 1(2)(d) of Brussels I excludes arbitration agreements from its scope. However, the interpretation of this exclusion has been a matter of dispute.

The recognition and enforcement of arbitral awards was originally excluded from the Brussels Convention[36] because the Council of Europe had prepared a European Convention with a uniform law on arbitration which would facilitate the recognition and enforcement of arbitral awards to a greater extent than the New York Convention.[37] Brussels I does not, therefore, apply to determine jurisdiction for the recognition and enforcement of arbitration awards.[38]

Article 71 of Brussels I states that the regulation will not affect any Conventions to which the Member States are parties and which govern jurisdiction. This suggests that requirements placed on national courts by the New York Convention to decline jurisdiction in favour of arbitration should take precedence over the mandatory rules of jurisdiction under Brussels I. In other words, Brussels I should not apply to determine the jurisdiction of courts in relation to disputes that are the subject of binding arbitration agreements.

Because national courts apply national rules when deciding whether or not an arbitration agreement is valid,[39] different EU Member State courts may issue different decisions in relation to the same arbitration agreement. For example, the English court may uphold an arbitration agreement and decline to hear legal proceedings relating to a contractual dispute. An Italian court seised of the same matter might decide that the arbitration clause is invalid and rule on the substance of the matter as the court of the domicile of the defendant.

The general rule of Brussels I prohibits Member States from reviewing the jurisdiction of a court in another Member State.[40] In the decisions in *Overseas Union Insurance Ltd v New Hampshire Insurance Co*[41] and *Turner v Grovit*[42] the ECJ ruled that a court second seised of a dispute must wait for the court first seised to decline jurisdiction even where it is clear that the court first seised does not have jurisdiction under Brussels I to hear the dispute. In effect, the court second seised must trust the first court to apply the rules of Brussels I correctly and decline jurisdiction in a speedy manner.

The question arose whether the English courts could take measures to commence arbitration in England where the Italian courts were seised of the substance of the dispute, had jurisdiction

35 See s 103(2)(a)–(b) Arbitration Act 1996.

36 Convention on jurisdiction and the enforcement of judgments in civil and commercial matters (consolidated version) [2008] OJ C27/1.

37 However, this Convention was not a success and was only implemented in Belgium.

38 Report on the Convention on jurisdiction and the enforcement of judgments in civil and commercial matters 1969 5.3. 1979. OJ C59/13.

39 See above.

40 See Chapter 3.

41 C351/89 *Overseas Union Insurance Ltd v New Hampshire Insurance Co* [1992] QB 434 [24].

42 C159/02 *Turner v Grovit* [2005] 1 AC 101 [26].

over the substance of the dispute under the rules of Brussels I and were still considering the validity of the arbitration agreement. In such a scenario, is the English court bound by the *lis pendens* rules of Brussels I or does the situation fall within the arbitration exception in Brussels I?

In *Marc Rich & Co AG v Societa Italiana Impianti SpA*,[43] Societa Italiana took proceedings for a declaration of no liability for breach of contract in Italy. Marc Rich, relying on a disputed arbitration clause, commenced arbitration proceedings in London and applied to the High Court to have an arbitrator appointed. On appeal, the Court of Appeal referred the question of the scope of the arbitration exception to the ECJ. Were the English courts permitted to rule on a matter related to a cause of action that was the subject of legal proceedings in the Italian courts? It was possible in this case for the English courts and the Italian courts to come to conflicting conclusions on the validity of the arbitration agreement.

The Court held that the principal subject matter of the proceedings before the English courts was the appointment of an arbitrator. The Brussels Convention did not apply to this question. The question of whether the arbitration agreement was valid was a preliminary issue that would determine the jurisdiction of the Italian courts. The ECJ held that the appointment of an arbitrator remained outside the scope of the Brussels Convention even where the validity of an arbitration agreement was a preliminary issue in that litigation. If the Convention did not apply to the principal subject matter of a dispute, then it did not apply to the preliminary issue before the courts even if that issue would, if raised by itself, fall under the scope of the Convention. It was up to the rules of English law to determine whether the English court had jurisdiction to deal with the preliminary matter.

The scope of the arbitration exclusion was examined again in *Van Uden*.[44] This case involved a contract that contained a clause for arbitration in the Netherlands. Van Uden commenced arbitration proceedings in the Netherlands when Deco-Line failed to make payment. Deco-Line delayed in appointing an arbitrator. Van Uden sought a supportive action from the Dutch courts to require Deco-Line to make an interim payment while it was waiting for arbitration to commence. Deco-Line objected, stating that the Dutch courts had no jurisdiction to make such a ruling following the requirements of the Brussels Convention, which granted jurisdiction to the German courts, as the court of the defendant's domicile, to hear such matters.

Here the subject matter of the claim was not directly related to setting up the arbitration proceedings but related to the obligations of the underlying contract. The Dutch courts referred the question to the ECJ of whether it had jurisdiction under the Brussels Convention to make such a preliminary ruling.

In this case, the UK argued for a broad interpretation of the arbitration exclusion. It argued that the proceedings for interim payment could not be governed by the provisions of the Convention but must instead be determined by national law since the parties had agreed, under the terms of the agreement, to submit their disputes to arbitration.[45]

The ECJ held that where the parties had validly excluded the jurisdiction of the courts to hear a contractual dispute and had referred the dispute to arbitration, Member State courts had no jurisdiction as to the substance of the case under the jurisdictional rules of the Brussels Convention.[46] Ordinarily the jurisdiction of the Dutch courts to determine a matter relating to the substance of a dispute which had been referred to arbitration was governed by national rules. However, the Brussels Convention allowed a court to make provisional measures even where a court of another

43 C190/89 *Marc Rich & Co AG v Societa Italiana Impianti SpA* [1991] IL Pr 524.
44 C391/95 *Van Uden Maritime BV v Kommanditgesellschaft in Firma Deco-Line* [1999] 2 WLR 1181.
45 Ibid AG [38].
46 Ibid [24].

Contracting State had jurisdiction over the substance of the dispute.[47] Therefore, the Dutch courts had jurisdiction under the Brussels Convention to issue provisional measures.

These cases left it open to the English courts to take measures to commence arbitration or support arbitration in England where a valid arbitration agreement existed, even where another Member State court was seised of the substance of the dispute. The English understanding was that the arbitrational exception excluded any decisions relating to a dispute that was subject to a valid arbitration agreement from Brussels I.

6.4.2.2 Anti-suit injunctions

In *Turner v Grovit*[48] the ECJ ruled that the English court could not use an anti-suit injunction to prevent pending proceedings another Member State court even where that court appeared to have no valid jurisdiction under Brussels I. The English courts limited the effect of *Turner v Grovit* to proceedings within the scope of the Brussels Convention or Brussels I. The English courts continued to issue anti-suit injunctions to prevent proceedings pending in another Member State court where the parties had submitted the dispute to arbitration in England.

In *Navigation Maritime Bulgare v Rustal Trading Ltd*,[49] cargo owners and insurers issued proceedings in France in violation of an arbitration clause in favour of London. They contended, *inter alia*, that the Brussels Convention gave jurisdiction to the court of their domicile (France) to hear the matter and that the English courts were precluded by the Brussels Convention from issuing an injunction to restrain the proceedings. The English court found that an injunction to restrain proceedings in breach of a binding arbitration agreement fell within the 'arbitration exception' because the principal focus of those proceedings was arbitration.

This interpretation of the arbitration exception was also used in *Through Transport Mutual Insurance Association (Eurasia) Ltd v New India Assurance Co Ltd (No 1)*,[50] a case determined under Brussels I.[51]

The ECJ put a stop to this use of anti-suit injunctions in *West Tankers Inc v Allianz SpA*.[52] In this case, a charter party contained a clause that any disputes were to be resolved by arbitration in London. The vessel damaged a jetty in Italy owned by the charterer. The defendant insurers began proceedings in Italy against the claimant. The claimant disputed the proceedings on the ground of the arbitration agreement. In parallel proceedings, the claimant sought a declaration from the English courts that the arbitration would go ahead in London and an order to discontinue the Italian action. The High Court granted the orders.

In the House of Lords, Lord Hoffman was of the opinion that arbitration should be left untroubled by the effects of EU regulation of private international law. He felt that the practical reality of arbitration required the court supervising arbitration in its jurisdiction to be able to issue an anti-suit injunction. Following *Van Uden* and *Marc Rich*, the House of Lords felt that proceedings to protect the contractual right to have a dispute determined by arbitration fell outside Brussels I.[53] The argument that any attempts to interfere with another court's jurisdiction over the substance of the dispute was incompatible with Brussels I was 'divorced from reality'.[54] However, as the scope of the arbitration exception was not clear, the House of Lords sought a preliminary ruling from the ECJ.

The ECJ held that it was incompatible with Brussels I for a court of a Member State to make an order to restrain a person from commencing or continuing proceedings before the courts of

---

47 Ibid [28].
48 C159/02 *Turner v Grovit* [2005] 1 AC 101.
49 [2000] EWHC 222 (Comm).
50 [2004] EWCA Civ 1598.
51 *Through Transport Mutual Insurance Association (Eurasia) Ltd v New India Assurance Co Ltd* [2005] 1 Lloyd's Rep 67.
52 C185/07 *West Tankers Inc v Allianz SpA* [2009] 1 AC 1138.
53 Ibid [14].
54 Ibid [15]–[16].

another Member State even on the basis that such proceedings would be contrary to an arbitration agreement.

The court looked at the English proceedings which led to the granting of the anti-suit injunction to see if they fell within Brussels I. In making this determination, the court followed *Van Uden* and looked at the nature of the rights which the proceedings served to protect.[55] The court held that the English proceedings to protect the arbitration did not fall within the ambit of Brussels I.[56] The court then looked at the proceedings before the Italian courts. In *West Tankers* the main dispute was a tort claim which fell into Brussels I. Therefore the Italian courts also had jurisdiction under Brussels I to hear the incidental issue of whether the arbitration agreement was valid.[57] The English anti-suit injunction had the effect of interfering with the rights of the Italian court to determine its own jurisdiction under Brussels I. This rendered the anti-suit injunction incompatible with Brussels I.[58] To hold otherwise would prevent a party who legitimately believed the arbitration agreement to be void from taking legal proceedings in the appropriate jurisdiction under Brussels I.[59]

The effect of *West Tankers* was that the English courts could not issue an anti-suit injunction against proceedings in other Member States to protect arbitration in England. They were required to wait and trust the Italian courts to refer the matter to arbitration in London under the New York Convention.

The arbitration proceedings that were the subject of dispute in *West Tankers* went ahead in England in spite of the pending proceedings in Italy. The arbitrator held that the claimant was under no liability to the charterers' insurers in respect of the collision. The legal proceedings were still pending in Italy. In 2012, the English Court of Appeal enforced the award of the arbitrator, giving it the force of an English declaratory judgment.[60] This meant that if the Italian courts came to a differing decision, two conflicting judgments on the merits of the dispute would exist. The English judgment would take precedence for recognition and enforcement in other Member States as the first in time under Brussels I.[61] In addition, EU Member States would be required to enforce the arbitral award of the English courts under the New York Convention.

The ECJ ruling in *West Tankers* was criticised[62] as obstructive to the efficient use of arbitration to resolve commercial disagreements and for opening up the possibility of conflicting judgments from EU Member States in relation to the same cause of action. The effect of the ECJ ruling in *West Tankers* on the arbitration exception has now been reversed by the terms of Brussels I recast, which will come into force in January 2015.

6.4.2.3 The arbitration exception under Brussels I recast

The scope of the exclusion of Art 1(2)(d) was reviewed during the preparations for Brussels I recast.

The 2007 Heidelberg Report[63] outlined three potential solutions to the practical problems relating to the enforcement of arbitration agreements caused by Brussels I. One option was to abolish the arbitration exception and include judgments recognising the validity of arbitration agreements within the scope of Brussels.[64] A second option was to give the arbitral tribunal exclusive

55 Ibid. [22].
56 Ibid [23].
57 Ibid [27].
58 Ibid [29]–[33]
59 Ibid [31].
60 *West Tankers Inc v Allianz SpA and another* [2012] EWCA Civ 27.
61 See Chapter 5.
62 R Fentiman, 'Arbitration and Anti-suit Injunctions in Europe' (2009) 68 *Cambridge Law Journal* 278; G Van Calster, 'Kerpow! The United Kingdom courts, West Tankers, and the arbitration "exception" in the Brussels I Regulation,' (2013) 21 *European Review of Private Law* 205–220.
63 Hess, Pfeiffer and Schlosser, *Report on the Application Study of Regulation Brussels I in the Member States* (Study JLS/C4/2005/03), September 2007.
64 Ibid [122].

jurisdiction under Art 22 to hear matters subject to an arbitration agreement.[65] The third proposed solution was to amend the arbitration exception to state exactly when an arbitration agreement was valid and when the courts should decline jurisdiction.[66]

In light of the *West Tankers* decision, in 2009 the Commission proposed that court proceedings on the validity of arbitration agreements should be recognised under Brussels I and that the effectiveness of arbitration agreements should be strengthened.[67] In 2010, it was proposed that a court seised of a dispute that was the subject of an arbitration agreement would be obliged to stay proceedings if court proceedings relating to the arbitration agreement had been commenced in the Member State of the seat of the proposed arbitration or if an arbitration tribunal had been seised in that state.[68] The court would stay proceedings until the existence of the agreement had been determined by the tribunal or Member State court. If a valid agreement was in existence, the court first seised would decline jurisdiction.[69]

In the end, this proposed amendment was rejected. It was felt that arbitration was satisfactorily dealt with by the New York Convention and that a rule giving exclusive jurisdiction to courts of the seat of the arbitration was not desirable.[70] It was suggested that *West Tankers* should be reversed and the various national procedural devices developed to protect arbitration such, as anti-suit injunctions, should continue to be available under the national law of the Member States. The effect of court decisions on the validity of arbitration was to be left to the individual Member States.

The arbitration exception appears in much the same terms under Brussels I recast as it did under Brussels I.[71] However, recital 12 makes it clear that Brussels I recast will not prevent Member States, when seised of an action that is the subject of an arbitration agreement, from referring the parties to arbitration or from examining the validity of the arbitration agreement in accordance with national law.

Any ruling by a Member State on the validity of an arbitration agreement is not automatically recognisable and enforceable under the Regulation, regardless of whether the validity of the arbitration agreement is the principal issue in the ruling or merely an incidental question. This allows national courts to form their own views on the validity of an arbitration agreement. For example, if the German courts have determined the agreement to be invalid, this does not prevent the English courts from later upholding the agreement.

Where a Member State has found the arbitration agreement to be invalid and gone on to make a ruling on the merits of the dispute, this judgment is automatically recognisable and enforceable under the Regulation. So where an Italian court finds an arbitration agreement to be invalid and rules on the underlying contractual dispute, this judgment is recognisable and enforceable. However, the recognition of this judgment could be refused where the recognising state has upheld the arbitration agreement and there is a conflicting arbitral award or judgment on the merits. Recital 12 expressly states that the New York Convention takes precedence over the Regulation and this is reinforced by Art 73(2). This allows a Member State to enforce a foreign arbitral award under the New York Convention, even where it conflicts with a judgment from another Member State, if the enforcing state finds that the underlying arbitration agreement was indeed valid.

65 Ibid [124].

66 Ibid [126].

67 Report from the Commission to the European Parliament, the Council and the European Economic and Social Committee COM (2009) 174 final, 9.

68 Proposal for a Regulation of the European Parliament and of the Council on jurisdiction and the recognition of judgments in civil and commercial matters (recast) COM (2010) 748 final [3.1.4].

69 See further L Radicati Di Brozolo, 'Arbitration and the Draft Revised Brussels I Regulation: Seeds of Home Country Control and of Harmonisation' (2011) 7 JPIL 423–460.

70 Committee of Legal Affairs, Report on the Implementation and Review of Council Regulation (EC) No 44/2001 on jurisdiction and the recognition and enforcement of judgments in civil and commercial matters A7-0219/2010.

71 Art 1(2)(d).

Finally, Recital 12 makes it clear that the regulation does not apply to court actions ancillary to the establishment of the arbitration tribunal or to any judgment relating to the annulment, review or recognition and enforcement of an arbitral award.

6.4.3 Recognition and enforcement of arbitral awards

Arbitral awards can be enforced by the courts of the seat of arbitration under national law or by the court of another country under the New York Convention. This section will consider (1) the enforcement of arbitration awards in England where England is the seat of arbitration and (2) the enforcement of foreign arbitral awards in England under the New York Convention.

6.4.3.1 Enforcement where England is the seat of arbitration

Where arbitration takes place in England, the arbitral award can be enforced by leave of the English courts under s 66 of the Arbitration Act 1996. Where leave is granted, s 66 allows an arbitral award to be enforced as if it were an order of court. Leave to enforce an award will not be granted where the person against whom the award is enforced shows that the tribunal lacked substantive jurisdiction to make the award.[72] In addition, the court may exercise its discretion not to enforce the award.

In *Soleimany v Soleimany*[73] the dispute related to the division or proceeds of the sale of Persian carpets which had been illegally exported out of Iran to be sold. The parties submitted the dispute for arbitration under Jewish law. The Beth Din acknowledged the illegality of the contract but assessed the shares of each party and made an award. Enforcement of the award in the English courts was sought under the Arbitration Act 1950. The defendant applied to set aside the order on the basis that the illegality rendered the claim unenforceable in an English court and that it would be contrary to public policy for an award founded on an illegal agreement or transaction to be enforced as a judgment of the High Court. The court held that the award was not enforceable on the basis of public policy.

Kohn v Wagschal[74] concerned a dispute over the intentions of a deceased individual in executing share transfers just before he died. The deceased's daughters claimed that their father had intended to make them a gift of these share transfers. The matter was submitted to arbitration under Jewish law at the London Beth Din. The Beth Din award concluded that the father had not intended to gift the shares. Instead, the object of the execution of the share transfers was to evade inheritance tax by persuading the Revenue that the shares were not part of the deceased's estate at his death.[75]

The son applied for leave to enforce the award under s 66 of the Arbitration Act 1996. It was argued that the court should not apply its leave to enforce the award due to the finding of illegality by the Beth Din. The court held that the award could be enforced as the finding of the arbitral tribunal that the share transfers had not been gifted to the sisters had the effect of reinstating them as part of the deceased's estate and rendering them subject to inheritance tax.

A party to an arbitral proceeding may apply to the English courts to challenge an arbitral award where the arbitral tribunal lacked jurisdiction[76] or where there had been a serious irregularity affecting the tribunal, the proceedings or the award.[77] The party is under a duty to appeal the matters to the arbitral tribunal first and must exhaust any available arbitral process of review before

72 Art 66(3); *African Fertilizers and Chemicals NIG Ltd v BD Shipsnavo GmbH & Co Reederei KG* [2011] EWHC 2452.
73 [1999] QB 785.
74 [2007] EWCA Civ 1022.
75 See also *R v V* [2008] EWHC 1531 (Comm).
76 S 67 Arbitration Act 1996.
77 S 68 Arbitration Act 1996.

approaching the courts.[78] The arbitral award debtor may lose the right to raise objections which were not previously raised during the arbitration proceedings unless he can show that at the time he took part in, or continued to take part in the proceedings, he did not know and could not with reasonable diligence have discovered the grounds for the objection.[79]

In *Kazakhstan v Istil Group Inc*[80] Metalsrussia made three contracts for the purchase of rolled steel from two Kazakh companies. All the contracts contained arbitration agreements in favour of the LCIA. The arbitral tribunal decided that it had jurisdiction over the dispute in January 2003. Metalsrussia then ceased to exist and was succeeded by Istil, which was substituted as a claimant. The arbitral tribunal found in favour of Istil and ordered the Republic of Kazakhstan to pay $6 million. Kazakhstan challenged the award under s 67 of the 1996 Act, claiming that the tribunal lacked substantive jurisdiction as no valid contract existed between the parties. The first instance judge held in Kazakhstan's favour, set aside the award and refused leave for appeal under s 67(4) of the Arbitration Act 1996.

In *Abuja International Hotels Ltd v Meridien SAS*[81] an International Chamber of Commerce (ICC) award was challenged on the basis that the arbitrators had exceeded their jurisdiction or alternatively because they had failed to deal with a fundamental issue and so the award was subject to a serious irregularity. In this case, Abuja owned a hotel in Nigeria which was marketed and managed by Meridien in return for certain fees. Abuja had violated the management agreement by depriving the hotel of funds so that staff and suppliers could not be paid and by sacking several employees. Meridien terminated the management agreement and began arbitration proceedings against Abuja.

The court held that the arbitral tribunal had substantive jurisdiction, as a valid arbitration agreement existed between the parties. In order to challenge the award for 'serious irregularity', the applicant was required to show that the irregularity was serious and fell within the list of categories outlined in s 68(2). In addition, the applicant must show that the irregularity claimed had caused substantial injustice.[82] In this case, the court found that no unfairness or breach of natural justice had been made out and the appeal was dismissed.

An award may also be appealed under s 69 of the Arbitration Act on agreement of all the parties to the arbitration or by leave of court where the arbitration tribunal has made a mistake on a point of law.[83] The threshold to be reached before leave will be granted from the court to appeal on a point of law is a very high one.[84] The question of law in dispute must have been put squarely before the arbitrator and the determination of the question must substantially affect the rights of the parties. Awards may not be appealed where the arbitrator's determination of fact is questioned.

In *House of Fraser Ltd v Scottish Widows Plc*,[85] an award relating to the determination of a commercial rent was appealed on a point of law. In this case, the applicant raised issues of law which were not considered in his submissions to the arbitrator or in the award itself. The court upheld the award on the basis that if any error of law had in fact occurred, it was not related to a question which the tribunal was asked to determine, nor did it substantially affect the rights of the parties. In addition, the weight attached to each piece of evidence before the arbitrator was a matter within the sole remit of the arbitrator and could not be appealed as an error of law.[86]

The option of appeal on a point of law will not be available where the parties have excluded appeal on this ground in clear words under the arbitration agreement. An expression that

78 S 70(2) Arbitration Act 1996.
79 S 73 Arbitration Act 1996.
80 [2006] EWHC 448 (Comm).
81 [2012] EWHC 87 (Comm).
82 Ibid [48]–[51].
83 *Pace Shipping Co Ltd v Churchgate Nigeria Ltd* [2009] EWHC 1975 (Comm).
84 S 69(3) Arbitration Act 1996.
85 [2011] EWHC 2800.
86 Ibid [36].

arbitration is to be 'final conclusive and binding' will not be enough to exclude appeal on a point of law.[87]

In *Lesotho Highlands Development Authority v Impregilo SpA*,[88] the arbitrators had made an error of law by selecting the wrong exchange rates in an award for extra costs incurred when constructing a dam in Lesotho. The parties had excluded the right of appeal for error of law under s 69 of the Arbitration Act 1996. The court held that a mere error of law could not amount to a serious irregularity under s 68 of the Arbitration Act 1996[89] as the requirement of substantial injustice had not been met.[90]

6.4.3.2 Enforcement under the New York Convention

Where the arbitral award is made by an arbitration tribunal situated outside the UK, recognition and enforcement of the arbitral award is regulated by the New York Convention, which is given effect by ss 100–104 of the Arbitration Act 1996. English law limits the recognition and enforcement under the New York Convention to arbitral awards made in the territory of other Contracting States to the New York Convention.[91] Under the New York Convention itself, recognition and enforcement can also be limited to arbitral awards which are considered commercial under the law of the recognising state, but England has not taken up this reservation.[92]

Article III of the New York Convention requires Contracting States to recognise arbitral awards as binding and to enforce them under substantially the same conditions as apply to the recognition and enforcement of domestic arbitral awards. In English law, a New York Convention award is recognised as binding on the parties to the arbitration and may be relied on by the parties in any legal proceedings in England and Wales.[93] A New York Convention award is enforceable in exactly the same way as a domestic arbitral award. With leave of court it may be enforced in the same manner as a judgment.[94]

Under the New York Convention, both the original award and the original arbitration agreement must be presented to the court of enforcement for scrutiny.[95]

The New York Convention requires arbitration awards to be recognised and enforced except in exceptional cases.[96] Recognition and enforcement of a New York Convention award may only be refused where the **party against whom it is to be enforced** can prove one of five substantive grounds to the enforcing court.[97]

Recognition or enforcement may be refused where:

1. The agreement to arbitrate is invalid due to lack of capacity of the parties or because it is not valid according to the law chosen by the parties. Where no choice of law was made, recognition and enforcement can be refused where the agreement is invalid by the law of the country where the award was made.
2. No proper notice of commencement of arbitration was given to the person against whom the award is enforced, or that party was otherwise unable to present his case.

87 *Shell Egypt West Manzala GmbH v Dana Gas Egypt Ltd (formerly Centurion Petroleum Corp)* [2010] 1 Lloyd's Rep 109.
88 [2005] UKHL 43.
89 Ibid [26].
90 Ibid [35].
91 S 100 Arbitration Act 1996.
92 Art I (3).
93 S 101(1) Arbitration Act 1996.
94 S 101(2) Arbitration Act 1996.
95 Art IV S 102 Arbitration Act 1996.
96 S 103(1) Arbitration Act 1996.
97 Art V(1) New York Convention; s 103(2) Arbitration Act 1996.

3. The award determines a matter that was outside the scope of the arbitration agreement. Where an award contains decisions on matters not submitted to arbitration but also determines matters which were validly submitted to arbitration, the award may be recognised or enforced to the extent that it contains decisions on matters submitted to arbitration which can be separated from those on matters not so submitted.[98]
4. The composition of the arbitral tribunal was not as agreed by the parties or was not in accordance with the law of the place where the arbitration agreement was made.
5. The award is not yet binding or has been set aside under the law of the country where it was made. In this situation, the English court may, if it considers it proper, adjourn the decision on the recognition or enforcement of the award.[99]

In *Dallah Real Estate & Tourism Holding Co v Pakistan*[100] the court considered whether an arbitral award made by an arbitral tribunal sitting in France should be refused recognition on the basis that the award was invalid under French law. In this case the government of Pakistan claimed that it was not a party to the arbitration agreement and so was not bound by the arbitral award. The arbitration agreement had been agreed between Dallah Real Estate and a trust set up by the Pakistan Ministry of Religious Affairs. This trust ceased to exist in 1996. The arbitral tribunal declared that the Ministry of Religious Affairs was bound by the agreement as the trust was set up as an emanation of the Ministry of Religious Affairs. The Court of Appeal refused to enforce the award as the government of Pakistan had not been a party to the agreement containing an arbitration clause. It could not be considered to have the necessary intention of being bound by the agreement under French law. This meant that the agreement was invalid by the law of the place where the award was made.

In *Dowans Holding SA v Tanzania Electric Supply Co Ltd*[101] the court considered whether recognition of an arbitral award from an ICC Tribunal should be set aside or adjourned where the award had been appealed to the court of the seat of arbitration: the High Court of Tanzania. In this case, the Tanzanian court was to reconsider the award on its merits to see if there had been error on the face of the award. The English court held that the award was binding on the parties within the meaning of the New York Convention.[102] However, the appeal before the Tanzanian courts had a more than fanciful chance of success. The English court adjourned permission to enforce the award.

Even where the award has been set aside in the home jurisdiction, the English court may enforce the award, although this power should be exercised sparingly.[103]

In addition, **the court can refuse to recognise or enforce the award on its own motion** where the subject matter of the award is not capable of settlement by arbitration in the law of the enforcing court or where recognition or enforcement of the award would be contrary to public policy of the enforcing state.[104]

Foreign arbitral awards may not be refused recognition on the basis that the arbitral tribunal made an error on point of law unless to do so would violate national public policy.

6.4.4 Applicable law issues in international arbitration proceedings

Although the legitimacy of arbitration relies on the private agreement of the parties, and arbitration is often conducted without any reference to national law, arbitration tribunals do not exist in a

98 S 103(4) Arbitration Act 1996.
99 S 103(5) Arbitration Act 1996; Art VI New York Convention.
100 [2010] UKSC 46.
101 [2011] EWHC 1957 (Comm).
102 Ibid [27].
103 *Dallah Real Estate & Tourism Holding Co v Pakistan* [2010] UKSC 46 [67]–[68].
104 Art V (2) New York Convention; s 103(3)–(4) Arbitration Act 1996.

legal vacuum. This section will consider the law that is applied by arbitral tribunals sitting in England and Wales.

The arbitral tribunal is governed by **rules of procedure**, which may be adopted by the parties but are also subject to the control of the national law of the place of arbitration. A question arises as to what extent the law of the seat of arbitration should be permitted to affect the procedure of the arbitral tribunal.

In addition, the arbitral tribunal must apply a law to determine the **substantive issues in dispute**. This applicable law is, more often than not, the law chosen by the parties. The first question arises where the parties have not chosen an applicable law: to what extent is the arbitral tribunal bound by the conflicts of law provisions of the country that is the seat of arbitration? The second question that will be addressed is whether the arbitration tribunal is bound to apply mandatory provisions of the law of the seat of arbitration.

6.4.4.1 Choice of law determining procedural issues

The parties to arbitration may choose to outline their own rules of procedure or they may choose to conduct the arbitration according to the established rules of an arbitral institution. For example, the LCIA in London has its own established procedural rules. Rules of procedure, whether agreed by the parties or set by the arbitral tribunal, are subject to the national law of the seat of arbitration. National law will be used to fill the gaps in the parties' agreement in order to enable the arbitration to run smoothly. National law will also ensure that procedural due process is observed.

In England, the Arbitration Act 1996 gives a great deal of freedom to the parties to determine the procedure for their arbitration but also lays down default rules of procedure where the parties have not agreed on what should happen. For example, s 15 of the Arbitration Act 1996 allows the parties to choose how many arbitrators are to be appointed, but where no agreement has been reached the tribunal is required to have one arbitrator.

6.4.4.2 Procedural fairness

The Arbitration Act 1996 also lays down minimum standards of procedure[105] to which the arbitral tribunal must adhere. For example, under s 33, the tribunal must act fairly and impartially as between the parties, giving each party a reasonable opportunity to put his case to the tribunal and to deal with the case of the opponent. The procedures of the tribunal must be suitable for the particular case and provide a fair means for the resolution of the matters falling to be determined.

Section 33 is a mandatory provision which cannot be excluded by agreement of the parties.[106] While it is theoretically possible for the parties to choose a foreign law[107] to regulate the procedure of an arbitral tribunal, this will not allow the parties to avoid the mandatory provisions of s 33. Failure to comply with s 33 may lead to a refusal by the English courts to recognise and enforce the award due to serious irregularity.[108]

In *ED&F Man Sugar Ltd v Belmont Shipping Ltd*[109] the arbitration tribunal made its award on the documents alone, including written submissions by the parties, and recorded that neither party had requested an oral hearing. One of the parties to the dispute argued that the tribunal had not adhered to its duty under s 33 to act fairly between the parties by not alerting him to a potential argument

105 Ss 33–41 Arbitration Act 1996.
106 S 4 Arbitration Act 1996.
107 *Naviera Amazonica Peruana SA* v *Compania Internacional de Seguros del Peru* [1988] 1 Lloyd's Rep 116; *Union of India* v *McDonnell Douglas Inc* [1993] 2 Lloyd's Rep 46.
108 See above.
109 [2011] EWHC 2992 (Comm).

that he could have raised. This argument did not relate to a point in issue and so the tribunal was not obliged to bring it to the attention of the parties.[110]

In *Pacol Ltd v Joint Stock Company Rossakhar*[111] the English court refused to recognise an arbitral award where the arbitrator had made the award based on issues which were not introduced by the parties. This meant that the party against whom the award was enforced had had no opportunity to make submissions or adduce evidence on the issues that had formed the basis of the award.

If the arbitration procedure does not comply with the minimum requirements of the national law of the seat of arbitration, the arbitral award may later be refused recognition in another country under the New York Convention.[112]

6.4.4.3 Delocalisation

Where arbitration is international in nature and has no natural link to the seat of arbitration which has been chosen as a neutral venue, the legitimacy of refusing to enforce an arbitral award on the basis of non-compliance with the mandatory procedural rules of the seat of arbitration has been queried. It has been suggested that the introduction of universal rules of procedure for arbitration would allow arbitral proceedings to be conducted in the same way and held to the same standards of procedural fairness regardless of the seat of arbitration. This would make it impossible for an arbitral award to be denied recognition on the basis that the arbitral tribunal had not complied with the mandatory rules of the place of arbitration. However, such universal consensus seems unrealistic.[113]

Another suggested solution is to detach the arbitration from the national law of the seat. This would mean that the arbitration is subject only to the rules agreed by the parties and the tribunal. This is known as the theory of delocalisation.[114] Under this theory the courts of the seat of arbitration would have no control over the procedure of the arbitral tribunal. It would be up to the courts of the place of enforcement of the arbitral award to ensure that due process was observed. Arguably, these courts have a more legitimate basis to control the procedure of the arbitration as the court of the place of the assets of the person against whom the arbitral award is enforced. The venue for arbitration may have been chosen specifically because it has no link to either party.

While many commentators have argued in favour of delocalisation it is only possible where the law of the seat of arbitration allows no judicial control over the procedure of arbitration.[115]

Under the common law, the law governing the procedure of the arbitration tribunal determined which choice-of-law rules should guide the arbitral tribunal. This meant that if England was the seat of arbitration, an arbitral tribunal was bound by the same choice-of-law rules to determine the substance of a dispute as the English court.[116] Mann[117] argued that the national law of the seat of arbitration was binding on the arbitration tribunal. While most domestic legal orders permit the parties to use the law of another state as applicable law, this is done in respect for the theory of party autonomy, not because the arbitral tribunal does not have to apply the laws of the seat of arbitration. The central tenet of this theory is that the arbitrator must obey the national rules of private international law of the seat of arbitration if the parties have not chosen applicable law. He does not merely use the rules as convenient legal principles. Proponents of delocalisation of the arbitral

110 See also *Bandwidth Shipping Corp v Intaari* [2007] EWCA Civ 998.
111 [1999] 2 All ER (Comm) 778 QBD.
112 Art V(1)(d) New York Convention.
113 The editors of *Redfern* note that this is as illusory as universal peace: Blackaby et al, *Redfern & Hunter on International Arbitration* (5th ed, OUP 2009) [3.72].
114 J Paulsson, 'Arbitration in Three Dimensions' (2011) 60 ICLQ 291–323.
115 Blackaby et al, *Redfern & Hunter on International Arbitration* [3.79].
116 *Czarnikow v Roth, Schmidt & Co* [1922] 2 KB 478; *Nationale des Coopératives Agricoles de Céréales v Robert Catterall & Co Ltd* [1959] 2 QB 44.
117 FA Mann, 'The UNCITRAL Model Law: *Lex facit arbitrium*' (1986) 2 *Arbitration International* 241–261.

tribunal are in favour of freeing arbitrators from national rules relating to choice of law as well as freedom from national mandatory rules relating to procedure.[118]

6.4.5 Choice of law determining substantive issues

The arbitral tribunal will determine the substantive issue in dispute according to rules chosen by the parties. In many cases, the tribunal will not have to ground its decision in a national system of law at all. Instead, it will merely establish the facts in dispute and apply the provisions of the parties' contractual agreement. The contractual agreement itself will make clear the duties of each party and the consequences of failure to perform. In exceptional cases, where there is dispute over a principle of law the tribunal must decide the applicable law to govern the dispute.

Under s 46 of the Arbitration Act 1996, arbitration tribunals in England must decide the substance of a dispute according to the rules chosen by the parties. The parties may choose English law as the law of the seat of arbitration, or they may choose a foreign national law to govern the dispute. The parties may even choose religious law to govern their dispute[119] or a set of non-national principles such as the *lex mercatoria* or UNIDROIT principles. The parties may even opt for the arbitral tribunal to determine the dispute by general principles of fairness. Section 46 allows the parties a much wider choice of applicable law than Rome I, which limits choice of law to systems of national law or to non-national rules that are incorporated into the terms of the contract.[120]

Where the parties have expressly chosen to submit to arbitration proceedings in England but have not specified an applicable law, the arbitral tribunal may consider that English law applies to the substance of the dispute as the law implicitly chosen by the parties.[121]

6.4.6 Where no choice of law is made

Where no choice of law is made by the parties, s 46(3) of the Arbitration Act 1996 allows the tribunal to apply the law determined by whatever conflict-of-laws rules it considers to be applicable.

Arbitral tribunals situated in England are not bound under English law to apply English choice-of-law rules. Hill argues that this means that the tribunal is not obliged to apply the principles which the English court would apply, though it is, of course, free to do so if it thinks that English choice-of-law rules are applicable.[122] Although arbitral tribunals may find it useful to refer to Rome I when determining what law to apply to determine a contractual dispute, the Arbitration Act 1996 does not require them to do so.[123]

A question arises as to whether arbitral tribunals are required to apply EU regulations on private international law as a mandatory rule of EU law. This is examined below.

Generally speaking, the decisions of arbitral tribunals on applicable law are not subject to judicial review. Section 69 of the Arbitration Act 1996 would allow such a decision to be appealed to the court as a point of law. However, as previously examined, appeals on points of law are limited to questions of law that were directly put to the arbitral tribunal that substantially affect the interests of the parties.[124]

118 Paulsson, 'Arbitration in Three Dimensions'; M Blessing, 'Choice of Substantive Law in International Arbitration' (1997) 14 *Journal of International Arbitration* 39.
119 *Kohn v Wagschal* [2007] EWCA Civ 1022; *Musawi v RE International (UK) Ltd* [2007] EWHC 2981 (Ch).
120 See Chapter 7.
121 *Egon Oldendorff v Liberia Corporation* [1996] 1 Lloyd's Rep 380; *Sonatrach Petroleum v Ferrell International* [2002] 1 All ER (Comm) 627
122 J Hill, 'Some private international law aspects of the Arbitration Act 1996' (1997) 46 ICLQ 300.
123 F Marrella, 'The New (Rome I) European Regulation on the Law Applicable to Contractual Obligations; What had changed?' (2008) 19 *ICC Bulletin* 87, 107.
124 J Hill, 'Some private international law aspects of the Arbitration Act 1996' (1997) 46 ICLQ 274–308. 304.

6.4.7 Are mandatory rules of the seat of arbitration binding on arbitral tribunals?

Unlike national courts, arbitral tribunals are not guardians of public interests but are empowered to resolve the private dispute of the parties. Their powers of adjudication stem from the agreement of the parties and they consider only the issues put to them by the parties. This raises the question of whether arbitral tribunals are required to apply the mandatory rules of the seat of arbitration, such as rules of EU competition law or issues of ECHR human rights law, where these mandatory rules are relevant to the dispute involving the parties. Although s 46 is silent on the question of mandatory rules of substantive law, this does not necessarily mean that the arbitral tribunal is free to have regard only to the law chosen by the parties.[125]

Where the parties choose the law of a nation state, the arbitrator should apply the mandatory rules that form part of the chosen law. So, for example, if English law is chosen, the Human Rights Act 1998 will require the tribunal to comply with the European Convention of Human Rights. If the chosen law is the national law of an EU Member State, EU law is applied as part of the national law of a Member State.

The tribunal may be given a broad discretion by the parties to apply whatever rules and principles it considers appropriate. Section 46(3) of the Arbitration Act 1996 allows the tribunal to use whatever choice-of-law rules it considers appropriate where the parties fail to make a choice of applicable law. In these cases, the tribunal is given the power to apply mandatory rules if it considers them to be appropriate. The Arbitration Act 1996 does not expressly require the arbitration tribunal to apply mandatory national or EU rules beyond what is required to ensure procedural fairness.

While arbitration occurs regularly in EU Member States, the CJEU does not have direct control over the substantive law applied by arbitral tribunals but instead requires national courts to police arbitral awards in order to ensure that fundamental values of EU law are respected.[126]

In *Van Schijndel*[127] the ECJ held that where a national court had an obligation or discretion to raise points of law of their own motion based on binding domestic rules not raised by the parties, so that obligation or discretion also existed where binding or directly effective EU rules were concerned. However, where the legal system allows the court to be passive and merely address the issues as outlined by the parties this can be justified by the principle that, in a civil suit, it is for the parties to take the initiative, the court being able to act of its own motion only in exceptional cases where the public interest requires its intervention.[128] This seems to allow arbitral tribunals to ignore the application of mandatory rules where they are not expressly raised by the parties.

In *Eco Swiss*,[129] Eco Swiss had been given exclusive rights to sell watches and clocks bearing the words 'Benetton by Bulova'. A Dutch Arbitration Tribunal found Benetton liable for wrongfully terminating this exclusive licensing agreement. When Eco Swiss sought to enforce the arbitral award, Benetton claimed that the agreement had violated EU anti-competition laws and was invalid. This issue had not been raised in the arbitration proceedings themselves.

In this case, AG Saggio states that arbitrators are bound by EU law when they are invited to rule on a dispute in accordance with the national law of a Member State. This is due to the fact that relevant provisions of Community law are an integral part of the national legal order in question.[130]

125 Ibid 304–305.

126 C102/81 *Nordsee Deutsche Hochseefischerei GmbH v Reedrei Mond Hochseefischere Nordstein AC* [1982] ECR 1095; C125/04 *Denuit and Cordenier v Transorient — Mosaïque Voyages and Culture SA* [2005] 1 CMLR 48.

127 C430/93 and C431/93 *Van Schijndel v Stichting Pensioenfonds voor Fysiotherapeuten* [1995] ECR I-4705.

128 Ibid [21].

129 C126/97 *Eco Swiss China Time Ltd v Benetton International NV* [1999] ECR I-3055.

130 Ibid AG [21].

The ECJ held that although it was in the interest of efficient arbitration proceedings that review of arbitration awards should be limited in scope,[131] where national rules allow a reviewing court to refuse to enforce an arbitration on the basis that it violates national public policy, enforcement must also be refused where it would violate fundamental principles of EU law.[132] Where a foreign award violated fundamental principles of EU law this should be considered to be non-recognisable under the public policy exception of the New York Convention.[133]

The ECJ held that the Dutch domestic procedures for recognition and enforcement of arbitral awards which restricted the possibility of applying for annulment were permissible as they did not render it excessively difficult or virtually impossible for an individual to exercise rights conferred on him by EU law and were justified by the basic principles of the national judicial system, such as the principle of legal certainty.

The EU case law suggests that arbitrators are required to raise questions of Community law when the national legal order requires them to do so. The editors of *Redfern* argue that *Eco Swiss* also provides a powerful incentive for the arbitration tribunals to raise and apply issues of European competition law themselves if they are concerned about the enforceability of their awards in the EU.[134]

6.4.7.1 Is Rome I applicable to choice of law in arbitration proceedings as a mandatory rule of EU law?

It is clear that the 1996 Arbitration Act does not require arbitrators to abide by the rules of Rome I when deciding what applicable law will determine the substance of a contractual dispute. While arbitration agreements are expressly excluded by Art 1(2)(e) of Rome I, the extent of this exclusion is unclear.

It has been argued that Rome I is designed to complement Brussels I, which excludes arbitration from its scope and so Rome I does not apply to arbitrators.[135] The recitals of Rome I make no references to arbitral tribunals and instead refer only to national courts. This stance permits arbitrators to merely refer to the Regulation as one of the various methods for determining the most suitable applicable law in the absence of party choice.[136]

However, Yuksel argues that such freedom may potentially be incompatible with EU law[137] and a broader application of Rome I should be taken.[138] If it is accepted that Rome I is binding on the choice of law issues relating to the substantive dispute before an arbitral tribunal, the choice-of-law rules of Rome I would take precedence over national law and reduce the choice of law allowed by s 46 of the Arbitration Act 1996.[139] *Eco Swiss* would then require national courts to refuse to recognise arbitral awards where the applicable law applied by the arbitral tribunal under s 46 deprived an individual of a fundamental EU right. Until this point on the scope of Rome I is determined by the ECJ it will remain open to debate whether arbitrators are required to apply the choice-of-law rules under Rome I to substantive contractual disputes.

131 Ibid [34].
132 Ibid [37].
133 Ibid [39]. See further Y Brulard and Y Quintin, 'European Community Law and Arbitration: National Versus Community Public Policy' (2001) 18 *Journal of International Arbitration* 533, 536.
134 Blackaby et al, *Redfern & Hunter on International Arbitration*, [3.135].
135 B Yuksel, 'The relevance of the Rome I regulation to International Commercial Arbitration in the European Union,' [2010] 7 JPIL, 149–178, 157. In *Syska v Vivendi* [2008] EWHC 2155 (Comm) [99] the English court stated *obiter* that the Rome Convention did not apply to arbitration.
136 *Syska v Vivendi* [2008] EWHC 2155 (Comm) [99].
137 Yuksel, 'The relevance of the Rome I regulation to international Commercial Arbitration in the European Union'.
138 Ibid 165.
139 Ibid 169.

6.5 Further reading

D Altaras, 'Arbitration in England and Wales and the European Convention on Human Rights: should arbitrators be frightened?' (2007) 73 *Arbitration* 262–268.

R Fentiman, 'Arbitration in Europe: immunity or regulation?' (2011) 1 *International Journal of Procedural Law* 151.

J Hill, 'Some private international law aspects of the Arbitration Act 1996' (1997) 46 ICLQ 274–308.

Lord Justice Saville, 'The 1996 DAC Report on the English Arbitration Bill' (1997) 13 *Arbitration International*, 275–316.

R Thomas, 'Proper law of arbitration agreements' [1984] LMCLQ 304.

B Yuksel, 'The relevance of the Rome I regulation to international commercial arbitration in the European Union' [2010] 7 JPIL 149–178.

Chapter 7

Choice of Law in Contract

Chapter Contents

Key Issues:

- The development of choice-of-law rules in contract
- The differences between an international Convention and an EU regulation
- General applicable law rules under Rome I
- Specific contracts under Rome I

7.1 Introduction

Once an English court has established jurisdiction to rule on a dispute, it will then determine what system of law should apply to the dispute itself. A contract can be connected to a number of different legal systems. For example, a contract between a French company and a German company could be made in Belgium for delivery of goods to China. The court will have to decide what system of law should govern any dispute related to the contract. This is called the **applicable law** or *lex causae*.

The rules used to determine the applicable law differ, depending on the subject matter of the dispute. The choice-of-law rules for some issues such as tort,[1] contract,[2] maintenance[3] and insolvency[4] are now determined by EU legislation. Other matters are still determined by the common law rules, for example the applicable law for marriage.[5] The decision of whether a matter falls into the category of tort, contract, marriage, divorce etc. is called **classification** or **characterisation**. This decision is made by the forum where the dispute is heard.[6] This chapter will examine the choice-of-law rules used to determine the applicable law in contractual disputes.

Traditionally, the English courts used a common law doctrine called **the proper law of contract** to determine applicable law where a dispute involved a contract with foreign connections. This doctrine applied the law chosen by the parties.[7] In most international contracts, the parties will have decided what system of law should apply to their contract. This will be written into the contract in a choice-of-law clause. Where the parties had not made a choice of law, the proper law of contract gave considerable discretion to the English courts to choose the most suitable applicable law.[8] A choice could be implied on behalf of the parties.[9] Where no choice could be implied the court chose the system of law with the closest and most real connection to the contract.[10] The doctrine of the proper law of contract is now largely obsolete and relevant only to the issue of capacity to contract.

On 1 April 1991, the proper law of contract was replaced[11] by a European Convention which created uniform choice-of-law rules for all signatories – the Rome Convention.[12]

---

1 Council Regulation (EC) No 864/2007of the European Parliament and of the Council of 11 July 2007 on the law applicable to non-contractual obligations (Rome II) [2007] OJ L199/40.

2 Council Regulation (EC) No 593/2008 of the European Parliament and of the Council of 17 June2008 on the law applicable to contractual obligations (Rome I) [2008] OJ L177/6.

3 Council Regulation (EC) No 4/2009 of 18 December 2008 on jurisdiction, applicable law, recognition and enforcement of decisions and cooperation in matters relating to maintenance obligations [2009] OJ L7/1.

4 Council Regulation (EC) No 1346/2000 of 29 May 2000 on insolvency proceedings [2000] OJ L160/1.

5 Law Commission, *Choice of Law Rules in Marriage* (Law Com CP No 165, 1987).

6 *Raiffeisen Zentralbank Österreich AG v Five Star General Trading LLC* [2001] QB 825, 841-842; C6/01 *Anomar and Others* [2003] ECR I-8621, [37], C-20/87 *Gauchard* [1987] ECR 4879, [7].

7 *Vita Foods Products Inc v Unus Shipping Co* [1939] AC 277.

8 *The Azzunzione* [1954] P 150.

9 *Amin Rasheed Shipping Corporation Appellants v Kuwait Insurance Co* [1984] AC 50.

10 *Bonython v Commonwealth of Australia* [1951] AC 201.

11 FA Mann, 'The proper law of contract: an obituary' (1991) 107 LQR 353–355.

12 Convention 80/934/EEC on the law applicable to contractual obligations [1980] OJ L266, 6. This was implemented in England by the Contracts (Applicable Law) Act 1990.

On 17 June 2008, the Rome Convention was replaced by an EU Regulation – Rome I.[13] The English courts now apply the Rome I Regulation in conflict of law cases involving contracts concluded as from 17 December 2009.[14]

Many of the provisions of the Rome I Regulation are identical to those of the Rome Convention. This means that case law on the interpretation of the Rome Convention continues to be useful in interpreting the provisions of Rome I. The Giuliano-Lagarde Report, written to accompany the publication of the Rome Convention,[15] also functions as an interpretative aid. Rome I is designed to be consistent with Brussels I and Rome II[16] and so the case law on Brussels I is referred to throughout this chapter.

This chapter will provide a brief overview of the regime under the Rome Convention and explain the events that led to the transition from the Rome Convention to the Rome I Regulation. The key differences between the Rome Regulation and the Rome Convention will be highlighted. The Rome I Regulation will then be examined using case law on the Rome Convention and Brussels Regulation to aid in interpretation.

7.2 The Rome Convention 1980

An international Convention to harmonise choice-of-law rules for contract cases was first proposed in 1967.[17] Such a measure would make the law governing contractual disputes more certain. The parties would be able to anticipate what law would apply to any potential contractual dispute when drawing up the contracts. This would combat 'forum shopping' in contractual disputes. Forum shopping occurs when one party chooses to take an action in a state that will apply legal rules that favour their side of the dispute. The Convention was intended to ensure that the same law would be applied to a particular contract, regardless of where the action was brought. For example, if a dispute arose between a French national and a German national, the same law would be used to resolve the dispute regardless of whether the case was brought in Germany or in France.

The Rome Convention was published in the Official Journal in 1980 and opened for signing on 19 June 1980. At that point in time, the EEC competence in civil and judicial matters was intergovernmental in nature.[18] The Rome Convention was only binding on states that signed and ratified the Convention. The UK signed the Rome Convention in 1981, and the Contracts (Applicable Law) Act 1990 implemented the Convention. The Convention came into force after being ratified by seven Member States on 1 April 1991.[19] The Rome Convention applied to any contracts made after 1 April 1991.[20]

The Rome Convention applied to all contract cases where a choice was made between the laws of different countries.[21] Like the common law, the Rome Convention applied the law chosen by the parties.[22] Where the contract was connected to one country only, the parties could not avoid the mandatory rules of that country by choosing foreign law.[23]

13 Council Regulation (EC) No 593/2008 of the European Parliament and of the Council of 17 June 2008 on the law applicable to contractual obligations (Rome I) [2008] OJ L177/6.

14 Art 28 Rome I, Corrigendum to Regulation (EC) No 593/2008 of the European Parliament and of the Council of 17 June 2008 on the law applicable to contractual obligations (Rome I) OJ [2009] OJ L 309/87.

15 Council, 'Report on the Convention on the law applicable to contractual obligations' [1980] OJ C282, 1/50 (The Giuliano-Lagarde Report).

16 Recital (7), Rome I.

17 The Giuliano-Lagarde Report, 4.

18 Unlike the Brussels Convention 1968, the Rome Convention was not specifically entered into pursuant to Art 220 of the EEC Treaty but it did further similar goals.

19 Art 12 Rome Convention.

20 Art 17 Rome Convention.

21 Art 1 Rome Convention.

22 Art 3 Rome Convention.

23 Art 3(3) Rome Convention.

Where no choice of law was made, the Convention applied the law of the country which was most closely connected to the contract.[24] A system of presumptions was laid down in Art 4 to determine the country of closest connection. Where a contract related to a right in immovable property, it was presumed to be most closely connected to the country where the immovable property was located.[25] For a contract of carriage, the closest connected law was presumed to be that where the carrier had his principal place of business, if this was also the place of loading or discharge or the principal place of business of the consignor.[26] In other cases, the contract was presumed to be most closely connected to the habitual residence or principal place of business of the party who had to effect 'performance which is characteristic' of the contract.[27] Characteristic performance is the performance for which payment is due[28] such as delivery of goods, provision of a service, insurance etc.[29] The use of presumptions was designed to make the court's determination of the law with the closest connection more certain and predictable.

Under the Rome Convention, special rules applied to consumer contracts[30] and employment contracts[31] in order to protect the weaker party to a contract. It was presumed by Art 5 that the consumer was best protected by the application of the law of his habitual residence. Article 5 protected the consumer from entering into a choice-of-law agreement which deprived the consumer of the protection of the mandatory rules of his habitual residence.[32] No such agreement was valid where the consumer had been induced into entering a contract by specific invitation, or by advertising in the country of his habitual residence, if the order was received in the consumer's country of habitual residence or if the seller had arranged for the consumer to travel to another country to buy goods. Where no choice of agreement was made, the applicable law was that of the consumer's habitual residence.[33]

For individual contracts of employment, Art 6(2) applied the law of the place where an employee habitually carried out his employment. Where the employee did not habitually work in any one country, the law of the country of the place of business that engaged him applied. Article 6(1) held that employees could not be deprived of the protection given to them by Art 6(2) by a choice-of-law agreement.

The Rome Convention was intergovernmental in nature and individually ratified by Contracting States. Unlike EU regulations, which are binding in their entirety, the Rome Convention allowed Contracting States to lodge reservations to certain articles.[34] The UK reserved the right not to apply Art 7(1), which applied the mandatory rules of all countries closely connected to a contract.[35] The UK considered this provision to be too vague and inconsistent. There were fears that Art 7(1) would oblige the court to take a large number of different and contradictory laws into account, which would make the court's job difficult and delay proceedings. In the UK, the application of mandatory rules was limited to the mandatory rules of the forum.[36] Mandatory rules also applied in cases where the parties to a purely domestic contract had agreed to apply foreign law, merely to evade the application of domestic law.[37]

---

24 Art 4(1) Rome Convention.
25 Art 4(3) Rome Convention.
26 Art 4(4) Rome Convention.
27 Art 4(2) Rome Convention.
28 The Giuliano-Lagarde Report, 20.
29 The Giuliano-Lagarde Report, 20–21.
30 Art 5 Rome Convention.
31 Art 6 Rome Convention.
32 Art 5(2) Rome Convention.
33 Art 5(4) Rome Convention.
34 Art 22 Rome Convention.
35 S 2 Contracts (Applicable Law Act) 1990.
36 Art 7(2) Rome Convention.
37 Art 3(3) Rome Convention.

The UK also declined to apply Art 10(e) of the Rome Convention to the consequences of nullity.[38] In English law the consequences of nullity of contract are governed by the law of restitution and not by the law of contract.[39]

The interpretation of the Rome Convention was initially left up to the courts of the individual signatory states: the ECJ had no jurisdiction to interpret the Convention. Article 18 of the Convention stated that states should have regard to the international character of the Convention and the desirability of achieving uniformity in its interpretation and application.

On 19 December 1988, two protocols were drawn up to allow the Convention to be interpreted by the ECJ.[40] To come into force, the protocols had to be ratified by all Contracting States. The commencement of the Brussels Protocol only became possible when it was ratified by Belgium on 5 May 2004. The Brussels Protocol was ratified by the UK on 29 January 1991 but it did not come into force in the UK until 2005.[41] The first ruling of the ECJ on the interpretation of the Rome Convention took place in 2009.[42]

As new Member States joined the EU, they also adopted the Rome Convention. Originally the addition of new signatories to the Convention required a specific protocol to be drawn up and approved by all Member States who were already signatories to the Convention. This was a lengthy and complicated procedure and meant that the Rome Convention came into force at different times in different Member States.[43] When Bulgaria and Romania joined the EU[44] it was no longer necessary to negotiate and conclude specific protocols for accession to these Conventions. Instead, Bulgaria and Romania adopted the Convention by decision of the Council[45] according to the procedure under Art 34 of the TEU (now repealed).

The Rome Convention rules were applied to conflicts of law issues within the UK.[46]

7.3 From Convention to Regulation

In January 2003, the European Commission published a Green Paper on the conversion of the Rome Convention into a Community instrument and its modernisation.[47] After the entry into force of the Treaty of Amsterdam,[48] the European Community was expressly empowered to take measures in the field of judicial co-operation in civil law cases to ensure an area of freedom, security and justice.[49] Denmark, Ireland and England negotiated a protocol to limit the application of measures relating to this new area of freedom, justice and security. Denmark does not take part in measures

38 S 2 Contracts (Applicable Law Act) 1990.

39 The Giuliano-Lagarde Report, 33; *Fibrosa Spolka Akcyjna v Fairbairn Lawson Combe Barbour Ltd* [1943] AC 32, 61

40 Protocol 89/128/EEC [1989] OJ L48/1; Protocol 89/129/EEC [1989] OJ L48/17.

41 The Contracts (Applicable Law) Act 1990 (Commencement No 2) Order 2004(SI 2004/3448). The Brussels Protocol is given effect in the UK by s 3 of the Contracts (Applicable Law) Act 1990. This requires the English courts to take judicial notice of the rulings of the ECJ and also allows the Giuliano-Lagarde report to be considered in ascertaining the meaning or effect of any provision of the Rome Convention.

42 C-133/08 *Intercontainer Interfrigo SC (ICF) v Balkenende Oosthuizen BV and MIC Operations BV* [2009] ECR I-9687.

43 Greece acceded to the Rome Convention in 1984, OJ L146/ 1. This was ratified by the UK in the Contracts (Applicable Law) Act 1990. Spain and Portugal acceded in 1992 OJ L333/1. This was ratified by the UK Contracts (Applicable Law) Act 1990 (Amendment) Order 1994/1900. Austria, Finland and Sweden acceded in 1996, [1997] OJ C15/10; [1997] OJ C191/11. This has been ratified by the UK Contracts (Applicable Law) Act 1990 (Amendment) Order 2000/1825. A Convention was signed on the accession of 27 new Member States to the EU in 14 April 2005; this has yet to be ratified by the UK or to come into force among the Member States.

44 [2005] OJ L157/203.

45 Council Decision 2007/856/EC [2007] OJ L347/1.

46 S 2(3) Contracts (Applicable Law) Act 1990. This was not required by the Rome Convention Art 19(2).

47 COM (2002) 654 final.

48 Treaty of Amsterdam Amending the Treaty on European Union, the Treaties establishing the European Communities and Related Acts [1997] OJ C340.

49 Art 65 of the Treaty Establishing the European Community (EC Treaty) [1997] OJ C340/03. This power is now found in Art 81 of the TFEU.

relating to judicial co-operation in civil law cases and these are not binding in Denmark.[50] Ireland and England can choose whether to opt in to such measures.[51]

In December 2005, the Commission presented a proposal for the new regulation.[52] The presumptions of Art 4 were to be replaced by fixed rules to make applicable law as precise and foreseeable as possible. Consumer protection was to be enhanced by the application of the law of the consumer's habitual residence and the elimination of choice-of-law agreements in consumer contracts.

In May 2006, the UK Government decided not to opt in to Rome I. A number of concerns were expressed. The proposal allowed for the application of mandatory rules of all countries connected to the contract. The UK had opted out of a similar provision of the Rome Convention.[53] The vast majority of cross-border financial transactions within the European Union were conducted in the UK.[54] The Financial Markets Law Committee felt that the adoption of Rome I with its application of mandatory rules would cause uncertainty in the financial markets.[55] The UK was also concerned that no impact assessment had been carried out.[56] It was felt that the elimination of choice-of-law agreements in consumer contracts placed an undue burden on businesses to research the entire law of contract in every country in which goods and services were to be supplied to consumers. The UK argued to restore the partial autonomy enjoyed by consumers under the Rome Convention.

Opting out of the Regulation meant that the UK would not be legally bound when the Council of Ministers adopted Rome I. The UK continued to participate fully in the negotiations, although they did not have the capacity to vote in the Council. The Council and the European Parliament agreed the text in December 2007.[57] A number of changes were made to Rome I which addressed the UK's major concerns.

In 2008, the Ministry of Justice went to consultation on whether the UK should opt into the 'new and improved' Rome I.[58] A UK decision to remain outside the Regulation would have resulted in the creation of two systems – one for the UK and Denmark under the Rome Convention and another for the rest of the European Union. It was felt that the articles of greatest concern to the UK had been removed or revised and overall the Regulation represented an improvement on the Convention.[59]

On 21 July 2008, the United Kingdom informed the European Commission and Council of the UK's intention to participate in the Rome I Regulation. The European Commission adopted a decision to extend the application of the Rome I Regulation to the United Kingdom on 22 December 2008.[60]

7.4 Rome I

The general object of Rome I is to create legal certainty in the European judicial area.[61] The Regulation uses fixed rules which are highly foreseeable, but retains a degree of flexibility by giving

50 Protocol No 5 1997 annexed by the Treaty of Amsterdam to the EC Treaty.

51 Protocol No 4 1997 annexed by the Treaty of Amsterdam to the EC Treaty. Both protocols are maintained by Protocol No 1 annexed to the Treaty of Lisbon [2007] C306/165.

52 COM (2005) 650 final.

53 Art 7(1).

54 Ministry for Justice, 'Rome I – Should the UK opt in?' (CP05/08, 2008) 8.

55 See A Dickinson, 'Third-country mandatory rules in the law applicable to contractual obligations; so long, farewell, auf wiedersehen, adieu?' (2007) 3 JPIL 53–88; M Hellner, 'Third Country Overriding Mandatory Rules in the Rome I Regulation: Old Wine in New Bottles?' (2009) 5 JPIL, 447–470.

56 Ministry for Justice 'Rome I – Should the UK opt in?' (CP05/08, 2008) 14.

57 Ibid 7.

58 Ibid.

59 Ibid 5–6.

60 Commission Decision of 22 December 2008 on the request from the United Kingdom to accept Regulation (EC) No 593/2008 of the European Parliament and the Council on the law applicable to contractual obligations (Rome I) [2009] OJ L10/22.

61 Recital (16).

the courts the power to depart from rules where the contract is, on the facts, more closely connected with another system of law. High importance is given to the parties' freedom to choose applicable law, which is referred to as the cornerstone of the conflict of laws system.[62] Consumers, employees, passengers and policyholders are protected by choice-of-law rules that are more favourable to their interests than those generally applied under the Regulation.[63]

The Rome I Regulation is directly applicable in all EU Member States[64] as a matter of EU law. Member States have no power to make reservations. The ECJ has competence to rule on the interpretation of the Regulation under Art 267 TFEU. The Rome I Regulation replaces the Rome Convention for contracts concluded as from 17 December 2009.

The Regulation is very similar to the Rome Convention:

1. Applicable law can be chosen by the parties (Art 3).
2. Where no choice is made, clear rules apply to determining the applicable law (Art 4).
3. Special rules apply to contracts involving weaker parties with little bargaining power (Arts 5–9).
4. Article 2 requires the court to apply the law of a non-Member State if such a law is chosen by applying the rules of Rome I.
5. Habitual residence for the purposes of Rome I is determined from the time of conclusion of the contract (Art 19).

Rome I was adopted in the UK by the Law Applicable to Contractual Obligations (England and Wales and Northern Ireland) Regulations[65] amending the Contracts (Applicable Law) Act 1990.

7.4.1 Intra UK conflicts

Article 22 of Rome I leaves the decision of which choice-of-law rules to apply to conflict of laws issues between internal jurisdictions to the individual Member States. As a result, disputes that are connected to two or more of the jurisdictions of England and Wales, Scotland, and Northern Ireland can be subject to whatever choice-of-law rules the UK deems most appropriate. Regulation 5 of the Law Applicable to Contractual Obligations (England and Wales and Northern Ireland) Regulations 2009[66] extends the rules of Rome I to cases involving conflicts between the laws of different parts of the United Kingdom. The one exception to this general extension of Rome I concerns insurance contracts, which are provided for in the Financial Services and Markets Act 2000 (Law Applicable to Contracts of Insurance) Regulations 2001.[67]

7.4.2 Scope

Rome I applies to conflict of laws cases, involving contractual obligations in civil and commercial matters.[68] The dispute must involve a choice between the laws of different countries; Rome I is not applicable to purely domestic contracts. 'Civil and commercial matters' should be interpreted consistently with Brussels I case law.[69]

---

62 Recital (11).
63 Recital (21).
64 Except Denmark, recital (46).
65 SI 2009/3064.
66 Ibid.
67 SI 2001/2635.
68 Art 1(1).
69 See Chapter 3.

The phrase 'contractual obligations' is not defined in the Regulation. The domestic laws of the Member States differ as to what type of obligations are characterised as contractual. For example, while Italian law classifies an agreement unsupported by consideration as a contract, English domestic law requires consideration to exist before an agreement can be recognised as a contract. The Giuliano-Lagarde Report provides that gifts and promises not supported by consideration are encompassed by 'contractual obligations' for the purposes of the Convention.[70] An autonomous EU meaning of 'contractual obligations' is being developed. This meaning must be consistent with the meaning given to 'non-contractual obligations' under Rome II. Even under the common law, English courts did not strictly stick to the domestic definition of a contract in international contract cases.[71]

Rome I applies to any contractual case heard by a Member State court. Article 2 provides that the law specified by the Regulation must be applied even if it is not the law of a Member State. In *Iran Continental Oil*[72] an English court applying the Convention found that the law of Texas governed the contract under dispute. Rome I also allows for the application of non-state law where the principles are incorporated into the terms of the contract.[73]

The Regulation does not apply to matters involving revenue, customs or administrative matters. The Regulation excludes a number of matters from its scope and these are outlined in Art 1(2). Many of these exclusions are the subject of other EU regulations:

(a) questions involving the status of legal capacity of natural persons, subject to Art 13;
(b) obligations arising out of family relationships and maintenance obligations;
(c) contractual obligations relating to rights in property arising out of matrimonial relationships and wills and succession;
(d) obligations arising under negotiable instruments, such as a cheque or a bill of exchange;
(e) arbitration and jurisdiction agreements.[74] (note that a substantive contract that contains an arbitration or jurisdiction clause is covered by Rome I);
(f) questions governed by the law of companies such as the creation, legal capacity, internal organisation or winding up of companies and the personal liability of officers and members as such for the obligations of the company or body;[75]
(g) the question of whether an agent is able to bind a principal;
(h) the constitution of trusts and the relationship between settlers, trustees and beneficiaries;
(i) obligations arising out of dealings prior to the conclusion of a contract;[76]
(j) evidence and procedure; and
(k) certain life assurance contracts.[77]

7.4.3 Choice of law by the parties (Art 3)

Article 3 states that contracts are governed by the law chosen by the parties. A choice of law by the parties can be made in express terms in a choice-of-law clause. Alternatively, this choice can be

---

70 The Giuliano-Lagarde Report, 10
71 *Re Bonacina*' [1912] 2 Ch 394.
72 [2002] EWCA Civ 1024.
73 Recital (13).
74 The validity of jurisdiction clauses is covered by the provisions of Brussels I. The Green Paper sought opinions as to whether arbitration should be included in Rome I. It was excluded in the final proposal: COM (2005) 650 final, 5. The validity of arbitration clauses is governed by the New York Convention on the Recognition and Enforcement of Foreign Arbitral Awards 1958.
75 See *Base Metal Trading Ltd v Shamurin* [2004] EWCA Civ 1316.
76 These are governed by the provisions of Rome II.
77 Most insurance contracts are covered by Rome I.

demonstrated from the terms of the contract or the circumstances of the case. The Giuliano-Lagarde Report provides examples of relevant factors to be taken into account such as: a choice of jurisdiction or arbitration clause; previous dealings of the parties; a reference to a particular system of law in the contract such as reference to the French Civil Code; and the use of a standard form etc.[78]

In *Oldendorff v Liberia Corporation*,[79] a Rome Convention case, a contract was made between a Japanese company and a German company without any express choice-of-law provision. The contract provided for arbitration in London and was in a well-known form of English charter party which contained standard clauses used in English law. Clarke J held that although the parties had not expressly agreed whether English or Japanese law applied, the claimant had demonstrated with reasonable certainty that the parties had intended English law to apply.[80]

A court cannot make a choice for the parties. If there is no evidence to suggest, with 'reasonable certainty', that the parties have chosen an applicable law, Art 4 will apply.[81] In *Land Rover Exports Ltd v Samcrete Egypt Engineers and Contractors SAE*,[82] Samcrete had deleted the English jurisdiction and choice-of-law clause in the terms put forward by Land Rover. The parties had not made a choice and it was clear from the circumstances that there was no common intention that English law governed the contract.

There has been some difference of judicial opinion as to the strictness of the reasonable certainty test. In *American Motorists Insurance Co v Cellstar Corp*[83] the claimant denied that any choice of law had been made. In the High Court, Steel J held that the focus on Texas as the place where the insurance policy was negotiated and issued, as between the assured, who employed a Texas broker, and an insurer situated in Texas, went beyond demonstrating a close connection with Texas. It was only consistent with a choice of Texan law.[84] This was confirmed by the Court of Appeal.[85]

In *FR Lurssen Werft GmbH & Co KG v Halle*[86] the parties had entered into two shipbuilding contracts to build motor yachts. These contained no choice of national law but provided that in the case of dispute the matter would be settled under the rules of arbitration of the London Maritime Arbitrators Association. The parties subsequently entered into a commission contract relating to the sale of the yachts. This contained no choice-of-law clause or mention of arbitration. The claimant was a German shipbuilding company, while the defendant was an American citizen resident in the state of Florida. The dispute related to the commission contract. The English courts would have no jurisdiction over the case if no implied choice of law in favour of England existed. Aikens LJ held that the commission contract was part of a series of contracts which included the two shipbuilding contracts. There was nothing in the commission contract or the surrounding circumstances to suggest that the parties had departed from their choice of English law demonstrated by the shipbuilding contracts.[87] English law governed the contract.

Under Art 3 of Rome I the parties are free to designate any system of national law; it does not have to be the law of a Member State.[88] Parties can also choose a non-state body of law where the rules of law are incorporated into the contract.[89] It is not enough to include a choice-of-law clause referring to a non-state body of law, such as the UNIDROIT Principles of International

---

78 The Giuliano-Lagarde Report, 17.
79 [1996] 1 Lloyd's Reports 380.
80 Ibid 390.
81 *ISS Machinery Services Ltd v Aeolian Shipping SA* [2004] 2 Lloyd's Rep 641, 645; The Giuliano-Lagarde Report, 17.
82 [2001] EWCA Civ 2019.
83 [2002] EWHC 421 (Comm).
84 Ibid [16].
85 (2003) Times, 1 April.
86 [2010] EWCA Civ 587.
87 Ibid [21].
88 Art 2.
89 Recital (13).

Commercial Contracts or the *lex mercatoria*.[90] The principles themselves must be part of the text of the contract.

The parties have the freedom to choose different laws for different parts of the contract.[91] This is called 'dѐcepage' and allows the contract to be severed between the different legal systems. One law could be chosen to govern the interpretation of the contract and a different law to govern its discharge. The choice must be logically consistent. If the choices cannot be reconciled, Art 4 should be applied.[92]

The parties can change the applicable law by agreement as long as this change does not affect the rights of third parties.[93] This provision enables the parties to have maximum freedom as to when a choice of law can be made. A choice of law can be made either at the time of contracting or before or after the conclusion of the contract.[94]

There are some geographical limitations on the parties' freedom to choose applicable law. Where all aspects of the contract are located in one country, the choice of foreign law will not affect the application of national law which cannot be derogated from by agreement.[95] This prevents parties to a domestic contract trying to avoid the application of national rules by choosing foreign law. For example, contracts for prostitution are void under English law. Two English parties cannot avoid the application of this rule by choosing the law of another country to apply to their contract for prostitution services in England.

In the same fashion, Art 3(4) prevents evasion of EU law for contracts that are solely connected to EU Member States. Where all elements of the contract are situated within Member States, the parties cannot avoid provisions of EU law which cannot be derogated from by agreement, such as competition law. When an EU forum court comes to consider an anti-competitive agreement based in the EU but governed by foreign law, it will only apply the aspects of that foreign law that are compatible with EU competition law.

If a choice-of-law clause exists but there is a question over the validity of consent to the choice of law, the matter is determined by Arts 10, 11 and 13 of Rome I.[96]

7.4.4 Applicable law in the absence of choice (Art 4)

Where no choice has been made by the parties, Art 4 will determine the applicable law. This is much simpler in structure than the presumptions of the Rome Convention. Under Art 4(1) specific rules apply to different types of contract:

(a) **A contract for the sale of goods** is governed by the law of the seller's habitual residence.
(b) **A contract for provision of services** is governed by the law of the service provider's habitual residence.
(c) **A contract relating to a right in immovable property** is governed by the law of the country where the property is located. This does not include contracts for the construction or repair of immovable property.[97] In such contracts, the subject matter is not a right over the property, but a supply of services.

---

90 This option was part of the initial proposal but ultimately dropped: COM (2005) 650 final 5.
91 Art 3(1).
92 The Giuliano-Lagarde Report, 17.
93 Art 3(2).
94 See *ISS Machinery Services v Aeolian Shipping SA* [2004] 2 Lloyd's Reports 641, 645.
95 Art 3(3)
96 See below.
97 The Giuliano-Lagarde Report, 10.

(d) **A private tenancy for six months or less** is governed by the law of the country where the landlord has his habitual residence, if the tenant is also habitually resident there. This allows an English landlord to extend a holiday let of his villa in Spain to another English resident under English law.
(e) **A franchise agreement** is governed by the law of the franchisee's habitual residence.
(f) **A distribution contract** is governed by the law of the distributor's habitual residence.
(g) **A contract for the sale of goods by auction** is governed by the law of place of auction.
(h) **A contract concluded within a multilateral financial trading system**[98] (such as the NASDAQ) is governed by the law of that system.

Where these rules are inconclusive, either because the type of contract is not covered or the particular contract is covered by more than one rule,[99] the choice of law is made under Art 4(2). The contract is governed by the law of the country where the person required to effect the **characteristic performance** of the contract has his habitual residence.[100]

7.4.4.1 Characteristic performance

Characteristic performance is undefined under the Regulation but is explained in the Giuliano-Lagarde Report as being the performance for which the payment is due, such as the delivery of goods, the provision of a service or the granting of the right to make use of an item of property. This will usually form the centre of the gravity and function of the contractual obligation.[101] This law will be familiar to the supplier of characteristic performance and he can legitimately rely on its application.[102]

In many instances, identifying the characteristic performance is not difficult. In some cases where there are reciprocal obligations of performance on both sides, this can prove more difficult to ascertain. In the Northern Ireland decision of *Governor & Company of the Bank of Ireland v State Bank of India*[103] the court had to deal with a series of related contractual obligations. Bank of India, which had no place of business in Northern Ireland, issued a credit note to a company based in India ('the buyer'), which was conducting business in Northern Ireland, in favour of a company based in the United Kingdom ('the seller'). The letter of credit was to facilitate payment for goods shipped and sold by the seller to the buyer. The seller had requested Bank of Ireland to act as the confirming bank. It was a pre-condition of the payment for the goods and the letter of credit that the seller presented specific documentation to Bank of Ireland. These were presented and approved but Bank of India later rejected the documents, claiming discrepancies, and refused to reimburse Bank of Ireland for the sums that had been paid to the seller.

There were two performance obligations in the contract between the issuing bank and the confirming bank. On one side, Bank of Ireland was obliged to furnish the appropriate documents. On the other side, Bank of India was obliged to make the payment on receipt of the documents.

The court held that the characteristic performance was reimbursement on receipt of the appropriate documents. India was the place of business of the party obliged to make characteristic performance and so the contract was most closely connected to India.[104]

98 As defined by Art 4(1) point 17 of Directive 2004/39/EC.
99 C133/08 *Intercontainer Interfrigo SC (ICF) v Balkenende Oosthuizen BV and MIC Operations BV* [2009] ECR I-9687.
100 Art 4(1).
101 The Giuliano-Lagarde Report, 20.
102 C133/08 *Intercontainer Interfrigo SC (ICF) v Balkenende Oosthuizen BV and MIC Operations BV* [2009] ECR I-9687. Opinion of AG Bot [45].
103 [2011] NIQB 22.
104 Ibid [25].

7.4.4.2 Country most closely connected with the contract

If the habitual residence of the person effecting characteristic performance cannot be determined, Art 4(4) states that the contract will be governed by the law of the country with which it is most closely connected. This general escape clause allows the courts to apply the law of the country more closely connected to the contract than the country designated by the rules of Art 4(1) and 4(2). These provisions create a degree of flexibility for situations where the strict application of the rules of Art 4 would produce inappropriate results. If the escape clause is used too readily it would make it difficult for the parties to foresee what law might apply to their contractual obligation. When the use of this clause was reviewed by the Green Paper on Rome I, it was found that the English courts have been willing to displace the presumptions of the Rome Convention where another system of law is more closely connected.[105] In contrast, the Dutch courts have only ruled out the designated law where it was obviously unsuited to the case.[106]

In *Definitely Maybe (Touring) Ltd*[107] the defendant company contracted for live performances by the group Oasis. One member of the group did not participate; accordingly, the defendant refused to pay in full and was sued. The court had to determine if English law governed the contract so that the English courts would have jurisdiction. Morison J referred to the two approaches to displacing the presumptions of Art 4.[108] English law would have governed as the habitual residence of the person giving characteristic performance. The only real connections to England were that the claimant and the group were located there. There were significant connections to Germany; the performances were in Germany and payment was to be made in German currency. Accordingly, Morison J decided Art 4(2) was displaced, holding that it had been clearly established that the contract was more closely connected to Germany.[109]

In *Ennstone Building Products Ltd v Stanger Ltd*[110] the Court of Appeal refused to use the escape clause. In this case, stone testing was carried out from Stanger's Scottish Office but Stanger's principal place of business was in England. It was held that English law applied under the presumptions of the Rome Convention. There was not sufficient linkage with Scotland to rebut the presumption. Although it had been anticipated that the Scottish office would carry out the testing, there was no contractual requirement to that effect.[111]

In *Intercontainer v Balkenende Oosthuizen*,[112] the ECJ held that the escape clause should only be applied where it is evident from the circumstances in their totality that the connecting criteria indicated do not have any genuine connecting value, **or** it is clear from those circumstances that there is a stronger connection with some other country.[113]

7.5 Special regimes for specific contracts

Rome I contains special rules for four different types of contract: contracts of carriage; consumer contracts; contracts of insurance; and individual employment contracts.

These types of contracts are governed by rules that are protective to the weaker party. Consumer contracts and contracts of individual employment were also subject to special rules under the Rome Convention. Contracts for carriage of passengers and insurance contracts with consumers are

105 This is also the approach of The Giuliano-Lagarde Report, 22.
106 Com (2002) 654 final, 25–26.
107 *Definitely Maybe (Touring) Ltd v Marek Lieberberg Konzertagentur GmbH* [2001] 2 All ER (Comm) 1.
108 Ibid [9].
109 Ibid [17]. Followed in *Kenburn Waste Management Ltd v Bergmann* [2002] EWCA Civ 98.
110 [2002] EWCA Civ 916.
111 See also *Commercial Marine Piling Ltd v Pierse Contracting Ltd* [2009] EWHC 2241 (TCC).
112 C133/08 *Intercontainer Interfrigo SC (ICF) v Balkenende Oosthuizen BV and MIC Operations BV* [2009] ECR I-9687.
113 Ibid [57].

treated separately from consumer contracts under Rome I due to the complex nature of insurance contracts and contracts of carriage.[114] Such contracts are also subject to protective measures to ensure an adequate level of protection for passengers and policyholders.

7.5.1 Contracts of carriage (Art 5)

Contracts of carriage are divided into two types – contracts for the carriage of goods and contracts for the carriage of passengers.

Parties are free to choose the law applicable to a contract of carriage of goods in accordance with Art 3. Where no choice of law is made, the law applicable is that of the country of habitual residence of the carrier, as long as that place is connected to the contract as the place of delivery or the habitual residence of the consignor.[115] Where this is not the case, the law of the place of delivery shall apply.[116]

In *Intercontainer v Balkenende*,[117] the ECJ considered the meaning of a 'contract of carriage'. This case involved a dispute between Intercontainer, a company established in Belgium, and Balkenende and MIC Operations, companies established in the Netherlands. Intercontainer and MIC had entered a charter party agreement, which is a contract where the owner of a transport vessel enters into a contract for use of the vessel. Intercontainer provided trains and services necessary to transport cargo; MIC had leased these services to Balkenende.

Intercontainer took legal action against MIC in the Netherlands for non-payment of invoices. Intercontainer's debt claims were time-barred under Dutch law. The question of the application of the Rome Convention to charter parties was referred to the ECJ. The ECJ confirmed that charter parties are equated with contracts of carriage where the main purpose of the contract is not merely to make available a means of transport, but the actual carriage of goods.[118]

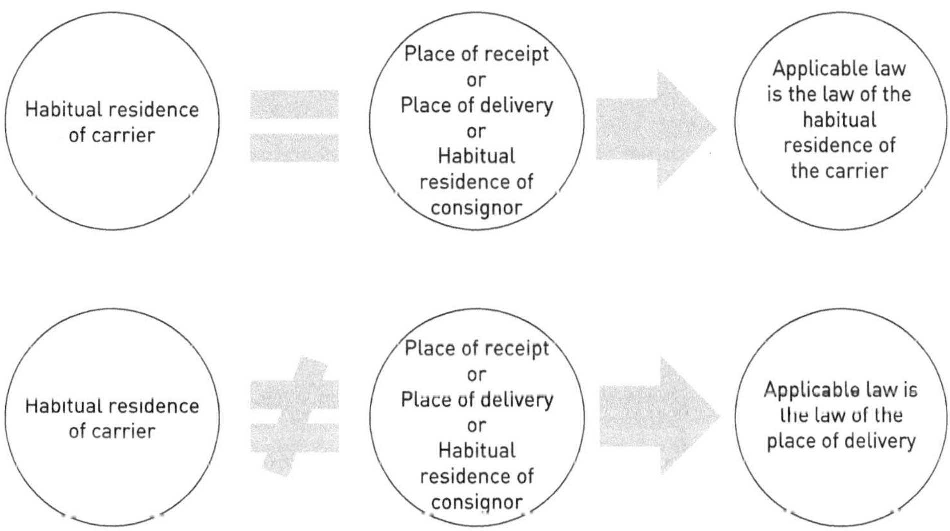

Fig 7.1 The law applicable to contracts for the carriage of goods.

114 Recital (32).
115 Art 5(1).
116 Art 5(2).
117 C133/08 *Intercontainer Interfrigo SC (ICF) v Balkenende Oosthuizen BV and MIC Operations BV* [2009] ECR I-9687.
118 Ibid [37]

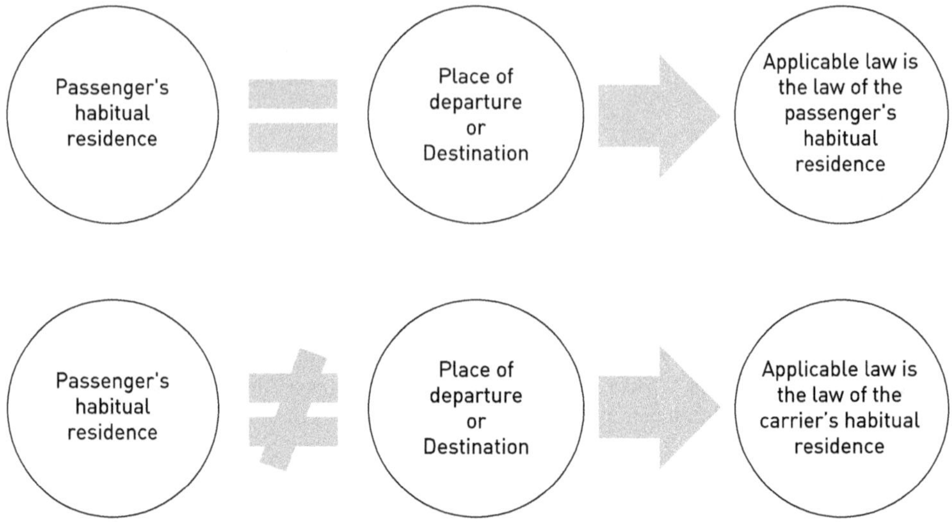

Fig 7.2 The law applicable to contracts for the carriage of passengers.

The applicable law for contracts for the carriage of passengers is limited to countries connected with the contract of carriage.[119] Parties can choose from a selection of four possible laws: the law of the place where the passenger has his habitual residence; the law of the place where the carrier has his habitual residence; the law of the place of departure; or the law of the destination.[120]

Where no choice of law is made, contracts of carriage of passengers are governed by the law of the country where the passenger has his habitual residence, as long as this is also the place of departure or the place of destination. Otherwise the law of the country where the carrier is habitually resident will apply.[121]

The court has the ability to apply law that is manifestly more closely connected to the contract for both contracts for the carriage of passengers and contracts for the carriage of goods.[122]

7.5.2 Consumer contracts (Art 6)

Article 6 is protective of consumer interests. In the absence of choice, the law of the consumer's habitual residence is applied. This is presumed to be the law most protective of consumer interests. Choice-of-law clauses in consumer contracts cannot deprive the consumer of the protection afforded to him by the law of his habitual residence.

In order to fall within the protective regime the contract must satisfy three conditions:

1. it must be concluded between a consumer and a professional;
2. the professional must have directed his activities towards the consumer's habitual residence; **and**
3. the contract must fall into the scope of such activities.

Article 27 of Rome I requires the Commission to submit a report on the evaluation of Art 6 and the coherence of Community law in the field of consumer protection by June 2013.

---

119 Art 5(2).
120 In the case of the carrier, this includes the place of central administration.
121 Art 5(2).
122 Art 5(3).

7.5.2.1 Meaning of consumer

Article 6(1) defines a consumer contract as 'a contract concluded by a natural person for a purpose which can be regarded as being outside his trade or profession with another person acting in the exercise of his trade or profession'. These definitions of a consumer and a professional are commonly used in EU law[123] and are identical to those of Art 15 of Brussels I.[124]

In *Gruber v BayWa AG*[125] a farmer bought roofing tiles to tile the roof of a farm building. The farm building in question was used both for farming and for private purposes. The court held that a contract concluded for mixed purposes does not merit the protection accorded to consumer contracts unless the professional purpose is so limited as to be negligible.[126] It is up to the court seised to make this determination on the facts.

7.5.2.2 'Directed activity'

Article 6(1) protects the consumer from the application of foreign law where the professional has pursued professional activities in the consumer's habitual residence or has directed his activities to that country.[127] Where a consumer has entered into a contract while present in another Member State, this will not be covered by Art 6 unless the professional induced the consumer to go abroad for the purposes of entering into a contract or has otherwise directed activities towards that consumer's Member State. As many consumers now enter into contracts online, the question of whether e-commerce constitutes directed activity has received much attention.[128]

Recital 24 of Rome I states that the mere fact that a website is accessible in a Member State is not sufficient to conclude that activity had been directed towards that Member State. Providing an email address on the website where the seller can be contacted, or a geographical address, or a telephone number without an international code does not constitute 'directed activity' either, as professionals are required to post such information to comply with the Directive on electronic commerce, even where their activities are limited to trade within their own country.[129]

The Grand Chamber of the ECJ considered the issue of 'directed activity' in e-commerce in the joined cases of *Pammer v Reederei* and *Hotel Alpenhof v Heller*.[130] Although this case concerned matters of jurisdiction, the definition of directed activity will be relevant to issues of applicable law.

Pammer v Reederei concerned a dispute between Pammer, who resided in Austria, and Reederei, a company established in Germany. Pammer had booked a voyage by freighter with Reederei from Trieste to the Far East. The voyage was advertised on a website run by an intermediary company also based in Germany. This website described the voyage on its website, showing a fitness room, an outdoor swimming pool, a saloon, and video and television access on the vessel. Pammer initially contacted the intermediary company by email to obtain further information and subsequently booked the voyage by post. When Pammer arrived onboard he felt that the ship did not live up to the description on the internet, refused to embark and demanded his money back. He took action in the Austrian court. Reederei argued that it did not pursue any commercial activity in Austria and challenged the jurisdiction of the Austrian court.

123 See for example Directive 85/577, Art 2, Directive 94/47, Art 2, Directive 97/7, Art 2(2) etc.

124 See C269/95 *Benincasa v Dentalkit Srl* [1997] E.C.R. I-3767; see Chapter 3

125 C464/01 *Gruber v BayWa AG* [2005] ECR I-439, [2006] QB 204.

126 Ibid [54].

127 This requirement is also found in Art 15(1)(c) of Brussels I.

128 L Gillies, 'Choice of law rules for electronic consumer contracts: Replacement of the Rome Convention with the Rome I Regulation' (2007) 3 JPIL 89–112. Z Tang, 'Parties' choice of law in e-consumer contracts' (2007) 3 JPIL 113–136.

129 Directive 2000/31/EC of the European Parliament and of the Council of 8 June 2000 on certain legal aspects of information society services, in particular electronic commerce, in the Internal Market [2000] OJ L178/1, Art 5(1)(c); C298/07 *Bundesverband der Verbraucherzentralen und Verbraucherverbände* [2008] ECR I-784 [40].

130 Joined Cases C585/08 and C144/09, *Peter Pammer v Reederei Karl Schlüter GmbH & Co KG* and *Hotel Alpenhof GesmbH v Oliver Heller* [2010] OJ C55/4.

In *Hotel Alpenhof v Heller*, a dispute arose between Hotel Alpenhof, a company running a hotel based in Austria, and Heller, who resided in Germany. Heller had booked the hotel over the internet. The reservation and confirmation were made by email. When he arrived, Heller found fault with the rooms and left without paying his bill. Hotel Alpenhof brought an action for payment before the Austrian courts. Heller argued that, as a consumer, he could only be sued in the court of his domicile.[131]

The ECJ considered whether the existence of a website could constitute 'directed activity' within the meaning of Brussels I. The court held that intention on the part of the trader to target one or more other Member States is required, and this must be evidenced in each case.[132] It must be shown that the trader envisaged doing business with consumers domiciled in the Member State of the consumer's domicile in the sense that it was minded to conclude a contract with those consumers.[133]

The court held that a finding that an activity is 'directed to' other Member States does not depend solely on the existence of particular evidence and instead a broad test could be used.[134] National courts must decide on a case-by-case basis whether evidence exists that a particular trader's activity is directed to other Member States by looking at particular websites as a whole.

The court gave a long list of matter which could constitute evidence that the trader's activity is directed to the Member State of the consumer's domicile if included on a website: offering services or goods to Member States mentioned by name, the international nature of the activity, mention of itineraries from other Member States for going to the place where the trader is established, use of a language or a currency other than the language or currency generally used in the Member State in which the trader is established (and the possibility of making and confirming the reservation in that other language exists), mention of telephone numbers with an international code, use of a top-level domain name other than that of the Member State in which the trader is established, and mention of an international clientele composed of customers domiciled in various Member States. Evidence that the website owner had paid money to search engines to prioritise access to the site by consumers in other Member States could also demonstrate such an intention, even where the website was run by an intermediary.[135]

In *Hotel Alpenhof*, the fact that the keys were handed over to the consumer and the payment was made in the Member State where the trader was established did not prevent protective provisions from applying if the reservation was made and confirmed at a distance, so that the consumer became contractually bound at a distance.[136] In *Pammer*, the fact that the website was run by an intermediary company did not preclude the trader from being regarded as directing its activity to other Member States, including that of the consumer's domicile, since that company was acting for and on behalf of the trader. It is for the relevant national court to ascertain whether the trader was or should have been aware of the international dimension of the intermediary company's activity and how the intermediary company and the trader were linked.[137]

In *Mühlleitner v Yusufi*[138] an Austrian woman negotiated a contract to buy a car through a German website. The German company was aware that she was Austrian. Ms Mühlleitner travelled to Germany to sign the contract. The car was defective and when the German company refused to repair it, Ms Mühlleitner brought proceedings in the Austrian courts as a consumer. The German company protested that it had not directed activities to Austria and that the ruling in *Pammer v Reederei*

131 Art 16(2) Brussels I.
132 Joined Cases C-585/08 and C-144/09, *Peter Pammer v Reederei Karl Schlüter GmbH & Co KG* and *Hotel Alpenhof GesmbH v Oliver Heller* [2010] OJ C55/4 [75].
133 Ibid [76].
134 Ibid [83].
135 Ibid [81].
136 Ibid [87].
137 Ibid [89].
138 C190/11, *Mühlleitner v Yusufi* [2012] IL Pr 46.

and *Hotel Alpenhof v Heller* only applied to distance contracts. In this case the contract had been made in person. The ECJ held that 'directed activity' could exist where the contract was concluded in person. It was not limited to distance contracts.

7.5.2.3 Contract within the scope of directed activities

In order to qualify for the protections of Art 6, a contract must be concluded as a result of the activities the professional has directed towards the Member State. Several cases under Brussels I have examined the question of whether a unilateral offer of a prize, accepted by a consumer, is a contract within the scope of directed activities.

In *Gabriel v Schlank*[139] the ECJ held that where a company informed a consumer that they had won a prize which could be claimed by placing an order with that company and the consumer then ordered goods from the company, there could be no doubt that the vendor and the consumer were in a contractual relationship. By ordering the goods, the consumer had accepted the offer sent to him by the vendor, including all the conditions attaching to that offer. Any action for payment of the prize was a contract falling within the scope of directed activities.

In *Renate Ilsinger v Martin Dreschers*,[140] Ilsinger, an Austrian national domiciled in Austria, received an envelope from the mail-order company Schlank & Schick GmbH, established in Germany. The envelope stated that she had won a prize of €20,000. Ilsinger would obtain the prize 'if she had the identification number which authorised her to obtain the prize' and returned her prize claim certificate to Schlank & Schick within seven days. The ECJ considered whether the claim for payment of the prize was a consumer contract concluded between Ilsinger and Schlank & Schick.[141]

The court held that the right of action by which consumers may bring legal proceedings against suppliers for payment of prizes ostensibly won is a right connected with a consumer contract if the recipient of the communication has actually placed an order for goods. It was immaterial whether the prize was made conditional upon ordering goods or not.

Where the consumer had not actually ordered goods, it was up to the national court to determine whether a contractual obligation for payment of the prize exists. The court held the legal classification under national law of a claim for payment of a promised prize is not relevant and instead the courts should refer to an EU meaning of contract.[142] If such a contractual obligation exists, it falls within the scope of directed activities and is considered to be a consumer contract.[143] This means that if a contractual obligation is found to exist, the law designated by Art 6 would determine whether an obligation to pay out the prize existed.

7.5.2.4 Consumer contracts specifically excluded from Article 6

Article 6(4) excludes several types of consumer contract from its protective regime. Contracts for the supply of services, where the services are supplied to a consumer who is in a country other than his habitual residence, fall outside Art 6.

All contracts of carriage fall outside Art 6 except package holiday deals.[144] For a service to qualify as a package holiday, it must be sold at an inclusive price, combine transport and accommodation and cover a period of more than 24 hours.[145]

---

139 C96/00 *Gabriel v Schlank & Schick GmbH* [2002] ECR I-6367; see also Case C-27/02 *Engler v Janus Versand GmbH* [2005] ECR I-481; C234/04 *Kapferer* [2006] ECR I-2585.
140 C180/06 *Renate Ilsinger v Martin Dreschers* [2009] ECR I-03961.
141 Ibid [35].
142 Ibid [54].
143 Ibid [63].
144 Within the meaning of Council Directive 90/314/EC of 13 June 1990.
145 C400/00 *Club-Tour* [2002] ECR I-4051, [13]; Joined Cases C585/08 and C144/09, *Peter Pammer v Reederei Karl Schlüter GmbH & Co KG and Hotel Alpenhof GesmbH v Oliver Heller* [2010] OJ C55/4.

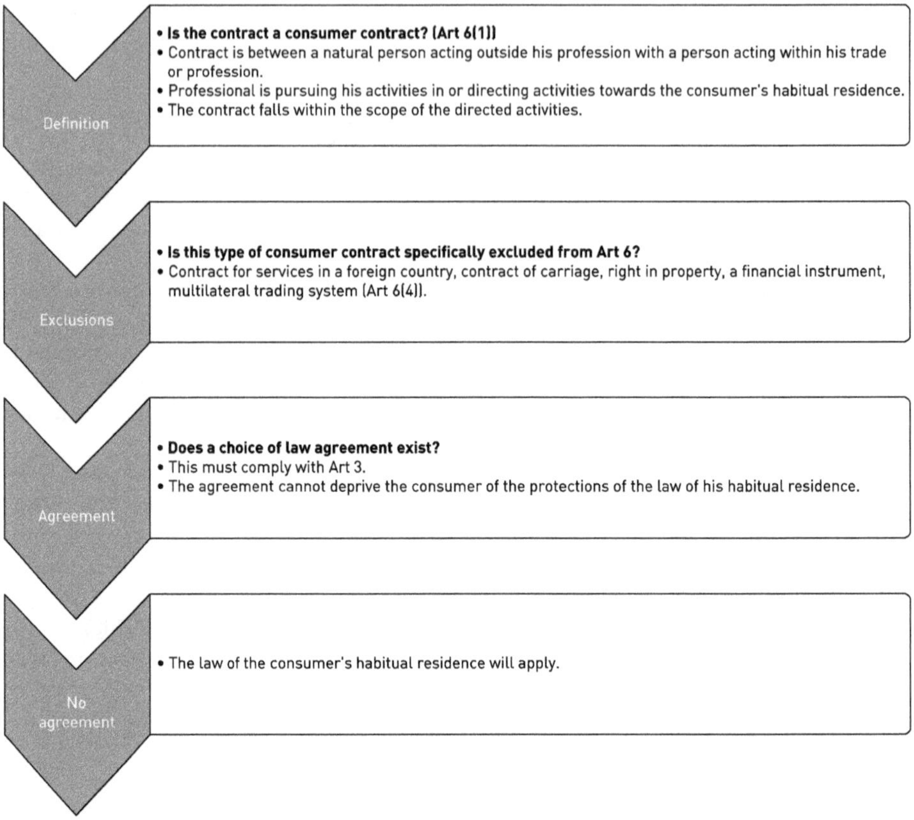

Fig 7.3 The law applicable to consumer contracts.

Contracts relating to rights in property are excluded, apart from contracts relating to timeshare properties.[146] Obligations relating to financial instruments and multilateral trading systems are also excluded from Art 6. To include them would change the nature of financial instruments that were issued to consumers. This would prevent efficient financial trading.[147]

7.5.3 Insurance contracts (Art 7)

Article 7 of Rome I lays out the rules applicable to insurance contracts. It was decided to include insurance contracts in Rome I because the previous regime, made up of numerous directives[148] and the Rome Convention, was considered to be overly complicated. Responses to the Green Paper argued that clearer and more uniform rules were needed to govern choice-of-law questions relating to insurance contracts in order to ensure transparency in EU law.

In spite of the desire to bring clarity, the rules of Rome I in relation to insurance contracts are quite complicated. Some provisions are directly copied from the previous insurance directives. The

146 Within the meaning of Directive 94/47/EC.

147 Recital (28).

148 See the First Non-Life Directive 72/239/EEC, the Consolidated Life Assurance Directive 2002/83/EC, and the Second Non-Life Insurance Directive 88/357/EEC as amended by the Third Non-Life Insurance Directive 92/49/EEC.

choice-of-law rules differ depending on the type of insurance, the type of risk covered and where the risk is located. Five categories can be identified:

(1) a contract for reinsurance;
(2) a contract covering a large risk, such as a ship or aircraft;[149]
(3) a contract covering all other risks (mass risk), where the risk is located outside an EU Member State;
(4) a contract covering all other risks (mass risk), where the risk is located within an EU Member State; and
(5) a contract for compulsory insurance.

Article 7 is implemented in English law by the Financial Services and Markets Act 2000 Regulations.[150] These regulations also extend the Rome I choice-of-law rules in insurance contracts to intra-UK conflicts.[151]

Contracts for reinsurance are excluded from Art 7 and are covered by the general rules of Arts 3 and 4.

Article 7 applies to **insurance contracts covering large risks** whether or not the risk covered is situated in a Member State. Large-risk insurance contracts are governed by the law chosen by the parties under Art 3 of Rome I. Where no law is chosen, Art 7(2) applies the law of the country where the insurer has his habitual residence. Where the contract is more closely connected to another country the courts can apply the law of that country.

Article 7 only applies to **contracts covering mass risks** if the risk is situated within an EU Member State. In order to locate the risk, Art 7(6) refers to the provisions of Directive 2002/83/EC[152] in the case of life assurance and Directive 88/357/EEC for all other mass risk contracts.[153]

Where mass risk is located outside of the Member States, the choice of law is governed by the general rules of Arts 3 and 4 of Rome I. Where a mass risk contract covers both risks situated in Member States and risks situated outside a Member State, Art 7 applies only to the risk located in the Member States.[154]

The parties' freedom to choose the law applicable to mass risk contracts where the risk covered is in the territory of a Member State is limited by Art 7(3). The parties have the option of choosing the law of the Member State where the risk is located or the law of the country where the policy holder has his habitual residence.[155] Where the **policyholder is a professional** and the insurance contract covers risks located in different Member States, the law of any of the Member States concerned can be chosen in addition to the law of the policyholder's habitual residence.[156]

The domestic law of individual Member States can provide for a greater choice of law. Where English law is the designated law, Regulation 4 of the Financial Services and Markets Act 2000 (Law Applicable to Contracts of Insurance) Regulations[157] allows the parties to choose the law of any country so long as the choice complies with Art 3, Art 6 and Arts 9 to 22 of Rome I.

Article 7 gives further options to the parties in two cases: for life assurance, the parties are given the additional choice of the law of the Member State of which the policyholder is a national.[158]

149 Art 7(2). A large risk is defined by Art 5(d) of First Council Directive 73/239/EEC.
150 SI 2009/3075.
151 Regulation 3, SI 2009/3075.
152 Art 1(1)(g) The Consolidated Life Assurance Directive.
153 Art 2(d) The Second Non-Life Directive.
154 Recital (33).
155 Art 7(3)(a) and (b).
156 Art 7(3)(e).
157 SI 2009/3075.
158 Art 7(3)(c).

Where the insurance contract is limited to events occurring in a state other than the state in which the risk is located, the law of the state where the events occur may be chosen.[159]

Where a **consumer** takes out a contract of insurance, this is governed solely by the provisions of Art 7; Art 6 is excluded.[160] Recital (32) makes it clear that the provisions of Art 7 are considered to provide an adequate level of protection to policyholders. However, the options of Art 7 provide a greater choice of law for consumers in insurance contracts than is permitted under Art 6, for other consumer contracts. This has been criticised by commentators as undermining consumer protection in insurance contract cases.[161] The UK regulations expressly limit choice of law in the case of consumers to those options permitted by Art 6, but this is not required by the Regulation itself.

Where the parties have not chosen the law applicable for a mass risk contract, the law of the Member State in which the risk is situated will apply.[162]

If a Member State imposes compulsory insurance, such as the requirement for car insurance, Art 7(4) will apply. It has been argued that Art 7(4) leaves so much room for the Member States to maintain their own rules and policies that it does not contribute to uniformity or legal certainty.[163] The Member State imposing an obligation to take out insurance can provide that such contracts will be governed by domestic law.[164] An insurance contract will only satisfy the state obligation to take out insurance if it complies with the requirements laid down by that state.[165] Where there is a contradiction between the law of the Member State where the risk is situated and the law of the Member State imposing the obligation to take out insurance, the law of the Member State imposing the obligation will prevail.[166]

The Commission is required to carry out a study on the law applicable to insurance contracts by June 2013.[167]

7.5.4 Individual contracts of employment (Art 8)

Rome I requires employees to be protected as weaker parties to contracts, by conflict-of-law rules that are more favourable to their interests.[168]

The meaning of 'individual contracts of employment' was examined in *Samengo-Turner v Marsh & McLennan*.[169] The Court of Appeal held that a claimant's bonus agreement was part of his contract of employment as it was not possible to ascertain the terms of employment without looking at both the employment contract and the bonus agreement.[170]

Article 8(2) provides that in the absence of choice, an individual contract of employment will be governed by the law of the country in which, or from which, the employee habitually carries out his work. In *Rutten v Cross Medical Ltd*[171] an employee carried out his work in the Netherlands, the UK, Belgium, Germany and the USA. He used an office in the Netherlands as a base from which he organised his working activities. The ECJ ruled that the habitual place of work referred to the place where the employee had established the effective centre of his activities and from which he performed the essential part of his duties.

---

159 Art 7(3)(d).
160 Recital (33).
161 X Kramer, 'The New European Conflict of Law Rules on Insurance Contracts in Rome I: A Complex Compromise' (2008) 6 *ICFAI Journal of Insurance Law*, 23–42.
162 Art 7(3)(a).
163 X Kramer, 'The New European Conflict of Law Rules on Insurance Contracts in Rome I: A Complex Compromise' (2008) 6 *ICFAI Journal of Insurance Law*, 40.
164 Art 7(4)(b).
165 Art 7(4)(a).
166 Art 7(4)(a)
167 Art 27.
168 Recital (23).
169 *Samengo-Turner and others v J & H Marsh & McLennan (Services) Ltd and others* [2007] EWCA Civ 723.
170 Ibid [30]. See also *Duarte v Black and Decker* [2007] EWHC 272 [53].
171 [1997] ECR I-57.

Where an employee is temporarily deployed to another country, the law governing the contract does not change.[172] Work carried out in another country is considered temporary if the employee is to resume working in his country of origin afterwards.[173] Where it is unclear where the employee habitually carries out his work, or the employee habitually carries out his work in more than one country, the law of the place of business through which the employee was engaged will apply.[174]

Where it is clear from the circumstances that the contract is more closely connected with a country other than that indicated by Arts 8(2) and (3) the court shall apply the closer connected law.[175]

In *Jan Voogsgeerd v Navimer SA*[176] the meaning of 'the place of business through which the employee was engaged' was clarified. The court held that this referred to the place in which the employment contract was concluded and the employment relationship began.[177] When applying this provision, no account should be taken of where the employee was currently undertaking his duties.

The place of business must have a degree of permanency.[178] A purely transitory presence in a state for the purpose of engaging employees cannot be regarded as constituting a place of business which connects the contract to that state.[179] There is also a requirement that the place of business in question has been actively involved in the conclusion of the employment contract on the instructions of the employer, for example by taking part in contractual negotiations with the employee.[180]

Article 8(1) ensures that employees are not deprived of legal protection, which cannot be derogated from by contract. This could include maternity leave rights, redundancy protection and minimum periods of notice by choice-of-law agreements. Choice-of-law agreements can be made for individual contracts of employment in accordance with Art 3. However, they cannot deprive the employee of the protection he would be entitled to under Art 8. Such agreements cannot exclude the protection of the law of the country in which he habitually works or the law of the place of business through with the employee was engaged (whichever is applicable).

In *Koelzsch*[181] the ECJ established that the place of habitual employment should be given a broad interpretation. In this case, Koelzsch, who was domiciled in Germany, was employed as a lorry driver by Gasa. The contract of employment was made in Luxembourg, governed by Luxembourg law and conferred exclusive jurisdiction on the Luxembourg courts. Gasa was a subsidiary of a company established under Danish law. It transported flowers from Denmark to other European countries. The lorries used were registered in Luxembourg, but stationed in Germany.

Koelzsch was elected to a works council (a shop-floor organisation representing workers) after Gasa announced a reduction in transport activities from Germany. In March 2001, Koelzsch's contract of employment was terminated. Under German law, a member of a works council could not be dismissed without a compelling reason during a term of office. These provisions gave employees a higher degree of protection than equivalent provisions of Luxembourg law.

Koelzsch brought an action against Gasa claiming that his contract of employment could not exclude the mandatory provisions of German law, as the law that would have governed his contract in the absence of choice. The Luxembourg court referred the question of which law would apply in the absence of choice to the ECJ under the Brussels Protocol.

Luxembourg argued that this contract should be governed by the seat of 'the place of business through which he was engaged', as in the transport sector employees by definition do not habitu-

172 Art 8(2); Recital (36).
173 Recital (36).
174 Art 8(3).
175 Art 8(4).
176 C384/10 *Jan Voogsgeerd v Navimer SA* (2011) (15 December 2011).
177 Ibid opinion of AG Trstenjak [64].
178 Ibid [54].
179 Ibid [55].
180 Ibid opinion of AG Trstenjak [70].
181 C29/10 *Heiko Koelzsch v Etat du Grand-Duche de Luxembourg* [2011] All ER (D) 165 (Mar).

ally carry out their work in a single country. The ECJ held that, as far as possible, the employee must receive the protection of the state where he carries out his working activities as it is there that the business and political environment most affects employment activities.[182]

The criterion of the country in which the work is habitually carried out must be understood as referring to the place in which or from which the employee actually carries out his working activities and, in the absence of a centre of activities, to the place where he carries out the majority of his activities.[183] In this case the court specifically noted that this definition was compatible with the new Art 8 Rome I.[184]

When assessing the nature of work in the international transport sector, the court must consider the state from which the employee carries out his transport tasks, receives instructions concerning his tasks and organises his work, and the place where his work tools are situated. The places where the transport is principally carried out, where the goods are unloaded and the place to which the employee returns after completion of his tasks are also relevant.[185]

In *Jan Voogsgeerd v Navimer SA*[186] a Dutch national worked for a company established in Luxembourg. A choice-of-law clause in the employment agreement specified that the law of Luxembourg would apply to the contract. Mr Voogsgeerd worked as an engineer aboard ships based in the North Sea. His work required him to go to Antwerp in Belgium, to be present as the ships were loaded and to take instructions from his employer.

Voogsgeerd brought a claim for compensation for the alleged wrongful termination of his employment relationship. The claim was actionable under Belgian law but not under the law of Luxembourg as the three-month limitation period had expired. Voogsgeerd claimed that the three-month limitation period was incompatible with the mandatory rules of Belgian law which would have applied in this case had there been no agreement.

The ECJ held that the place where a person habitually carries out his work is more closely connected with the employment contract and should be interpreted broadly as the clear centre of activity of the employment.[187] The place of business was a back-up consideration which

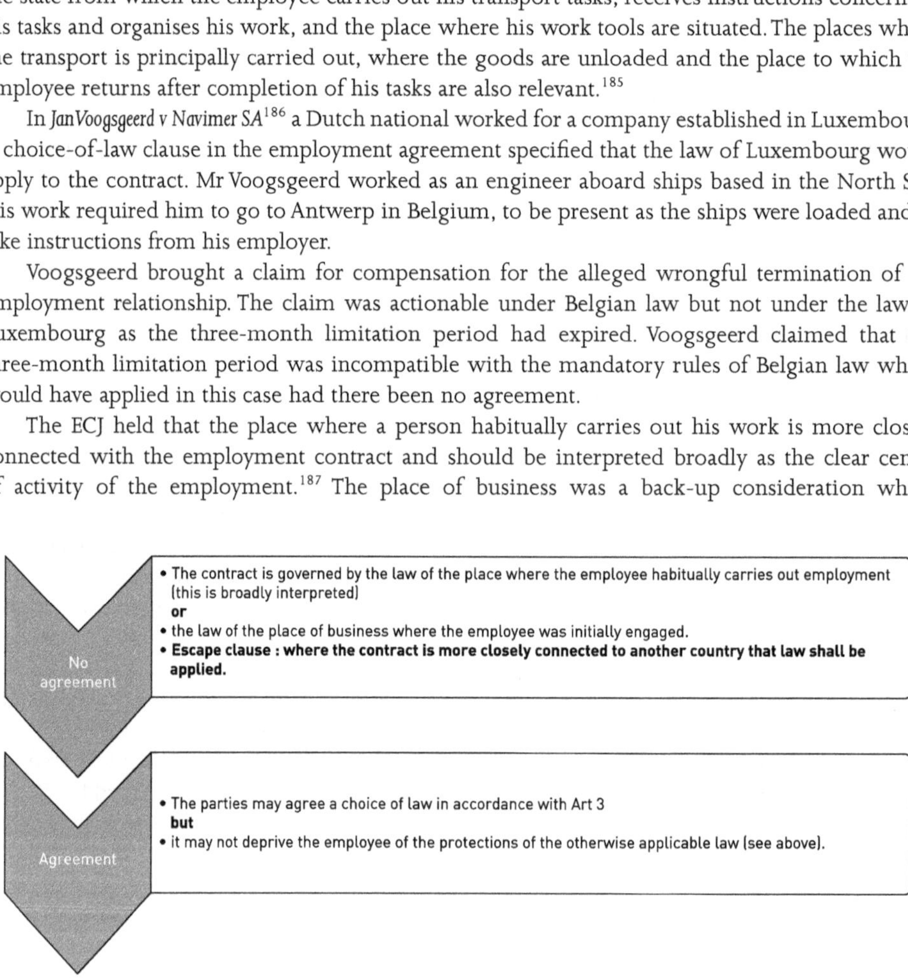

Fig 7.4 The law applicable to individual contracts of employment.

182 Ibid [41].
183 Ibid [45].
184 Ibid [46].
185 Ibid [49].
186 C384/10 *Jan Voogsgeerd v Navimer SA* (2011) (15 December 2011).
187 C384/10 *Jan Voogsgeerd v Navimer SA* (2011) (15 December 2011), opinion of AG Trstenjak [67].

should only be used on the rare occasion[188] where the habitual place of employment could not be ascertained.

If an employee carried out work in more than one state the court should determine the state with which the work has the most significant connection.[189] When the court establishes that the employee must always report to the same place where he receives instructions, that court must regard the employee as habitually carrying out his work in that place.[190]

7.6 The influence of the law of the forum and the place of performance

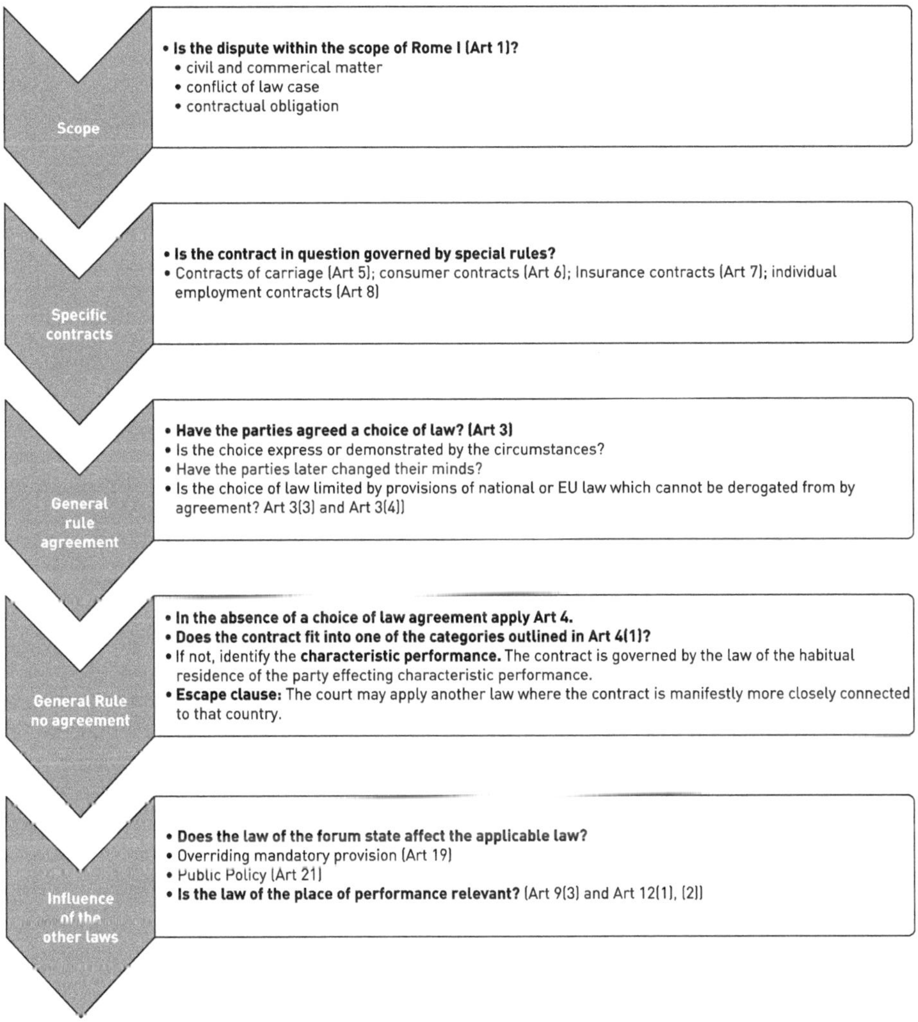

Fig 7.5 Finding the applicable law under the rules of Rome I.

188 Ibid opinion of AG Trstenjak [69].
189 Ibid [36].
190 Ibid [44].

Article 9 of Rome I allows the court to give effect to the 'overriding mandatory provisions' of the law of the forum in exceptional circumstances.[191] Article 21 allows the forum court to refuse to apply provisions of foreign law which are manifestly incompatible with the law of the forum.

Article 9(3) gives limited effect to the overriding mandatory provisions of the law of the country where the contract is to be performed. If the performance is illegal by the law of the place of performance this rule may be given effect.

Similarly, in Art 12(2) the law of the country where the performance is made is considered for issues relating to the manner of performance or the steps to be taken in the event of defective performance. The Giuliano-Lagarde Report provides some examples of such matters, such as the manner in which goods are to be examined and the steps to be taken in case of refusal to accept delivery.[192] Article 12(2) gives discretion to the court to decide whether this law has any relevance to the manner in which the contract should be performed.

7.7 Scope of applicable law

Once the court has used Rome I to determine applicable law, it must then check to see if the issue before the court is within the scope of the law chosen. The law designated by Rome I is applicable to issues surrounding formation, performance and discharge of contracts.

7.7.1 Formation of contract

The applicable law designated by Rome I applies to determine whether a valid contract exists at all.[193]

A contract is formed by the consent of the parties.[194] The applicable law will determine whether the consent given is valid. In exceptional circumstances, a party may rely on the law of his habitual residence to establish that he has not consented to the formation of a contract.[195] This provision is designed to protect a party who, for example, did not reply to an offer. While silence may amount to acceptance in some countries, it may not be so under the law of the country where the offeree has his habitual residence. To avoid any unfairness, Art 10(2) allows that party to plead the law of his habitual residence to deny the existence of the contract.

Although capacity to contract is expressly excluded from the scope of Rome I,[196] Art 12 of Rome I applies to the issue of capacity where two parties are in the same country when they conclude a contract. In such a scenario, the contract will be valid if both parties have capacity under the law of that country. A contracting party can only rely on his incapacity under a different law if the other party was aware of the incapacity or should have been aware of the incapacity.

Where the parties are in different countries when they contract, the issue of capacity is determined by domestic conflict of law rules. In England, this issue is determined by common law rules. It is not very clear what law applies to determine capacity to contract in English law. Some cases point to the law of an individual's domicile;[197] others point to the proper law of

191 Recital (37).
192 The Giuliano-Lagarde Report, 33.
193 Art 10.
194 Case C180/06 *Renate Ilsinger v Martin Dreschers* [2009] ECR I-03961 [46].
195 Art 10(2).
196 Art 1(2)(a).
197 In the sense of his common law domicile or personal law.

contract.[198] It has also been suggested that a contract should be upheld if a party has capacity under *either* the law of his common law domicile or by the proper law of contract.[199]

Article 11 determines the applicable law to the question of formal validity. In some jurisdictions, certain contracts must be made in writing, witnessed or drawn up by a qualified person etc.[200] Without such formalities the contract is not valid. For example, in *Golden Ocean Group Ltd v Salgaocar Mining Industries PVT Ltd and another*[201] the High Court decided that a series of emails satisfied the formal requirement of s 4 of the Statute of Frauds 1677 that a guarantee be in writing.

For consumer contracts, the form of the contract is determined by the law of the consumer's habitual residence.[202] For non-consumer contracts the choice-of-law rules are very flexible and ensure that the contract will generally be upheld. If the contract is concluded by two people who are in the same country, the contract will be valid if it complies with the formalities of place where the contract was concluded **or** the applicable law as determined by Rome I.[203]

Where the parties are in different countries at the time the contract is concluded, the contract must satisfy the formal requirements of the applicable law under Rome I, **or** the law of the place where either party is present at the time of conclusion, **or** the law of the habitual residence of either party.[204]

Contracts concerning rights in immovable property are subject to the formalities of the law of the place where the property is located if these requirements cannot be derogated from by agreement and are imposed irrespective of the place of contract or the law governing the contract.[205]

Article 11(3) designates the applicable law to determine if unilateral acts are formally valid. Such acts include a notice of termination or a declaration of recission.[206] Again, the law is very flexible. Such an act is formally valid if it satisfies the requirements of the applicable law under Rome I, the law of the country were the act was done or the law of the habitual residence of the person performing the act.

7.7.2 Performance and discharge of contract

Most issues relating to performance and discharge of contract are determined by the applicable law under Rome I. Article 12 specifies that the applicable law shall govern questions of interpretation and performance.

The applicable law also governs the powers of the court where the contract is breached. This includes the determination of the consequences of breach and the assessment of damages.[207] These issues are subject to the limits of the powers of the forum court. These powers are determined by domestic procedural law. The applicable law will apply to the prescription and limitation of actions and the ways in which contractual obligations can be extinguished.[208]

Finally, the applicable law will determine the consequences of nullity of contract.[209] This provision marks a departure from English law. Under English law the consequences of nullity are

198 *Baindail v Baindail* [1946] P 122, 128 (CA)
199 Dicey, Morris and Collins, *The Conflict of Laws* (14th ed, Sweet and Maxwell), Rule 209 [32-216]. *Cooper v Cooper* (1888) 13 App Cas 88, 108.
200 The Giuliano-Lagarde Report, 29.
201 [2011] EWHC 56 (Comm).
202 Art 11(4).
203 Art 11(1).
204 Art 11(2).
205 Art 11(5).
206 The Giuliano-Lagarde Report, 29.
207 Art 12(1)(c).
208 Art 12(1)(d).
209 Art 12(1)(e).

considered to be a matter for the law of restitution and not a matter for the law of contract. The UK opted out of a similar provision of the Rome Convention. Under Rome I the law applicable to the consequence of nullity will be the law that would have been applicable to the contract, if it had been valid.

7.8 Further reading

R Brand, 'The Rome I Regulation Rules on party autonomy for choice of law: A U.S. perspective' (December 1, 2011) *University of Pittsburgh Legal Studies Research Paper Series No 2011-29*. Available at SSRN: http://ssrn.com/abstract=1973162 (accessed 15 May 2013).

F Ferrari and S Leible (eds), *Rome I Regulation* (Sellier, 2009).

F Garcimartin Alferez, 'The Rome I Regulation: exceptions to the rule on consumer contracts and financial instruments' (2009) 5 JPIL 85–103.

J Hill, *Cross-border Consumer Contracts* (OUP, 2008).

X Kramer, 'The New European Conflict of Law Rules on Insurance Contracts in Rome I: A complex compromise' (2008) 6 *ICFAI Journal of Insurance Law*, 23–42.

L Merrett, 'Choice of Law in insurance contracts Under the Rome I Regulation' (2009) 5 JPIL 49–67.

L Merrett, *Employment Contracts in Private International Law* (OUP, 2011).

S Symeonides, 'Party autonomy in Rome I and I? from a comparative perspective' in K Boele-Woelki, T Einhorn, D Girsberger and S Symeonides (eds) *Convergence and Divergence in Private International Law – Liber Amicorium*, (Eleven International Publishing, 2010) 513–550. Available at SSRN: http://ssrn.com/abstract=1697372 (accessed 15 May 2013).

Z Tang, 'Private international law in consumer contracts: A European perspective' (2010) 6 JPIL 225–248.

Chapter 8

Tort

Chapter Contents

Key Issues:

- Historic development of the choice of law rules for tort
- Choice-of-law rules under Rome II
- Assessment of damages in tort cases
- Conflict of laws in defamation cases

8.1 Introduction

The choice-of-law rules for tort have traditionally focused on the geographical location of specific elements of the tort, such as where the tort was committed or where the victim was injured. While the breakdown of a contract is anticipated and choice-of-law rules are routinely inserted by the parties, tort injuries are unexpected and the parties are unlikely to give advance thought to any choice-of-law rules that might govern.

English choice-of-law rules in tort remained undeveloped until the second half of the nineteenth century, when the development of modern transportation allowed more people to travel internationally and allowed products to be marketed all over the world. In the famous English tort case of *Donoghue v Stevenson*,[1] a Scottish woman sued a local company after drinking a bottle of their ginger beer which contained the remains of a snail. Her Scottish friend had purchased the beer. It is easy to imagine an updated version of the scenario containing many cross-border issues. The two friends could be English tourists. The ginger beer could be manufactured by a US company in Africa and bottled in Germany. If an action is brought in England on the basis of this updated scenario, what law would the English courts apply? Which law is appropriate to govern the dispute?

The appropriate connecting factor in tort has been an area of much controversy. The domestic law governing liability for tort, and the availability of defences and remedies available to the victim, can differ from jurisdiction to jurisdiction. To apply the law of the forum in which the action is brought could be unjust where the defendant is held liable for actions which constituted a tort in the forum but not in the place where they were committed. It would also encourage claimants to take legal action in countries where the law is more generous to claimants.

Applying the law of the place where the tort happened might generally give effect to the natural expectations of the parties. It would seem logical that if you commit a tort in Rome, you must make compensation according to Roman law. But, as seen from the example above, the place where the tort happened can be difficult to ascertain. Many different types of tort exist, and it is necessary to look at how liability is constructed before assessing the geographical links of each part of the tort. The English tort of negligence requires a negligent breach of duty and damage. In the above updated example, the damage occurred in Scotland. It is unclear if the breach of duty occurred in the USA, where the health and safety protocols of the company were made, or in Africa or Germany where the introduction of the snail may have occurred.

The English choice-of-law rules for tort have gone through two major changes in the last 20 years. On 1 May 1996 Part III of the **Private International Law (Miscellaneous Provisions) Act 1995** (PILA) repealed the traditional common law rules for choice of law in tort. Today, the common law rules are only applicable to the tort of defamation.

An EU regulation on the law applicable to non-contractual obligations (Rome II)[2] was adopted on 11 July 2007 and applies to all torts occurring after 11 January 2009. This regulation was

1 [1932] AC 562.
2 Regulation (EC) No 864/2007 [2007] OJ L299/40.

implemented in the UK by the Law Applicable to Non-Contractual Obligations (England and Wales and Northern Ireland) Regulations 2008[3] and replaces PILA. Today there is a harmonised EU approach to the choice of law in non-contractual obligations including tort.

This chapter will give a short overview of the main principles of each regime before going on to focus on the provisions of Rome II. The assessment of damages in tort cases and the common law rules as they apply to defamation will then be examined in further detail.

8.2 Overview of the three legal regimes

8.2.1 The common law rules

At common law, the courts treated tort actions differently depending on whether they were caused by conduct carried out in England (a **domestic tort**) or carried out overseas (a **foreign tort**).

If the tort was based on conduct carried out in England, the English courts treated the tort in the same fashion as any other domestic tort: the English courts heard the action and applied English law. There was no discretion for the court to apply a foreign law even if the people involved had strong links to another legal system. In *Szalatnay-Stacho v Fink*,[4] the defendant was an official of the Czechoslovakian government who was in exile in England. He sent some documents to the Czechoslovakian President, who was also in England. The documents contained serious unfounded allegations about the claimant, who was the Czechoslovakian acting minister in Egypt. The claimant brought an action for defamation. The Court of Appeal held that, as the documents had been published in England, the tort was committed in England and therefore English law applied.

The ability of the English courts to hear actions where the wrongful conduct was carried out abroad was limited both by rules of jurisdiction and the common law rules governing choice of law. Where a tort was caused by conduct committed outside England, the **rule of double actionability**[5] allowed the case to be heard only where the alleged wrong gave rise to liability both in England and in the place where the action was committed. This rule was designed to avoid the unfair situation where a defendant could be held liable for an action that was not wrongful in the place in which it occurred. It also ensured that the English courts did not impose liability for an action that was not considered tortious by English law. In *Boys v Chaplin*[6] two English residents were involved in a motor scooter accident in Malta. An action was brought in England for negligence. A similar action was possible under Maltese law so the case satisfied the double actionablity rule.

Once the requirement of double actionability was satisfied, the courts could decide what rule of law to apply to the dispute. Effectively, the law applied was a combination of the law of both jurisdictions. The alleged wrongdoer would not be liable if he had a defence in either English law or the law of the country where the conduct took place.[7]

In *Boys v Chaplin*, Maltese law was indicated as the law of the place of injury. English law allowed recovery of damages for pain and suffering but Maltese law did not. In this case, both parties were resident in England and only temporarily present in Malta. Lord Wilberforce held that English law was manifestly more closely connected to the tort.[8] It is generally accepted that *Boys v Chaplin* created an exception to the rule in *Phillips v Eyre*[9] that a combination of the two connected laws should be applied. Lord Wilberforce held that in particular circumstances a court could use its discretion to apply English law alone. It was not clear from *Boys v Chaplin* in what circumstances this exception applied.

3 SI 2008/2986.
4 *Szalatnay-Stacho v Fink* [1947] KB 1.
5 *Phillips v Eyre* (1870–71) LR 6 QB 1.
6 [1971] AC 356 (UKHL).
7 *Phillips v Eyre* (1870–71) LR 6 QB 1.
8 *Boys v Chaplin* [1971] AC 356 (UKHL) [392].
9 (1870–71) LR 6 QB 1.

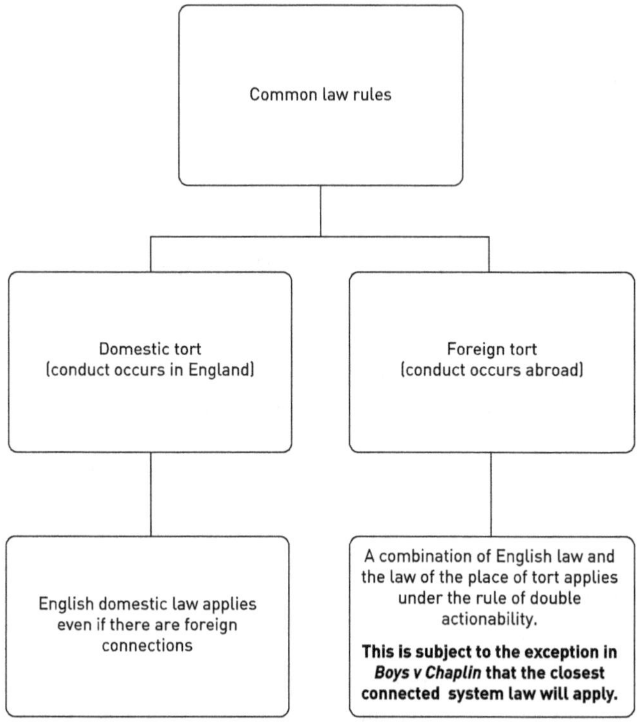

Fig 8.1 Applicable law under the common law rules.

This exception to applicable law under the rule of double actionability was extended in *Red Sea Insurance Co Ltd v Bouygues SA*.[10] In this case, the law of the place of injury alone was applied. This extended flexibility of the common law rules rendered the regime very uncertain.

The common law regime focused on the geographical location of the tort. No importance was given to the autonomy of the parties to form agreements as to what law might be appropriate.

The place of wrongful conduct was crucial. If the conduct occurred in the UK, it was treated as a domestic tort and English standards applied. If the conduct happened in a foreign country, a combination of English law and the law of that foreign country applied, subject to judicial discretion. The rules assumed that torts were confined to a single country. There was little consideration of what might happen if different elements of the torts occurred in different countries. This failure to consider transnational torts has caused problems in modern cases involving defamation which are still governed by the common law rules.[11]

8.3 The Private International Law (Miscellaneous Provisions) Act 1995 (PILA)

Part III of this Act made provision for choice of law in tort and implemented the changes proposed by the Law Commission Report in 1990.[12] The general rule under this Act applied the law of the place

10 [1995] 1 AC 190.
11 See below.
12 Law Commission, *Private International Law: Choice of Law in Tort and Delict* (Law Com No 193, 1990).

where the tort occurred unless another legal system had the 'closest and the most real connection' to the dispute. It was argued by the Law Commission that this rule promoted uniformity, prevented forum shopping and accorded to the expectations of the parties.

Section 10 of PILA abolished the rule of double actionability, allowing the English courts to hear any tort claim if jurisdiction could be established. Section 13 excluded defamation claims from Part III of PILA and such claims are regulated by the common law rules.

PILA abolished the common law distinction between foreign torts and domestic torts. Instead, a distinction is made in PILA between **single country torts**, where all elements of the tort occur in one country, and **transnational torts**, where elements occur in different countries. Under s 11, the applicable law for all torts is the law of the country in which all the elements constituting the tort arise. So for a single country tort, committed completely in France with no foreign elements, French law would apply[13] unless displaced by s 12.

Guidelines for determining the law applicable to transnational torts are found in s 11(2). In the case of a tort involving personal injury, the law of the country where the individual was located when he sustained the injury is applied.[14] In the case of a tort involving damage to property, the law of the country where the property was when it was damaged is applied.[15] If a transnational tort does not result in personal injury or property damage, the law of the country in which the most significant element of the tort occurred is applied.[16] This required the court to identify all the elements constituting the tort and establish where each element occurred. Then a value judgment was made to determine whether one element, or several elements taken together, outweighs the significance of elements to be found in any other country. This is done on a case-by-case basis.[17]

The guidelines in s 11 are subject to a general discretion under s 12 where the court can apply a different law if it would be substantially more appropriate in the circumstances. This discretion applies both to single country torts and transnational torts. The factors that may be taken into account when attempting to invoke the exception include those relating to the parties, to any of the events which constitute the tort in question, or to any of the circumstances or consequences of those events. In *Edmunds v Simmonds*,[18] a case which involved a car accident in Spain, the rule of s 11, designating the law of Spain the applicable law, was displaced by s 12 in favour of English law. Both parties were ordinarily resident in England and the judge also took into consideration that the cost of care and loss of earnings arose in England.

It was initially unclear whether PILA applied to domestic torts, i.e. torts where all elements occurred within the England. The Law Commission consultation paper suggested that foreign law should be, in theory, applicable to torts which had occurred in the UK if a closer and more real connection to another legal system existed.[19] Yet in the Law Commission Report it was recommended that domestic torts be excluded from the scope of PILA.[20] The terms of PILA itself were unclear. Section 11(1) suggested that a domestic tort be treated like any other single country tort; this was confirmed by s 9(6). However, s 14(2) appeared to preserve the common law rule that for torts occurring in England, English law would apply regardless of foreign connections.

In *Roerig v Valiant Trawlers*,[21] the Court of Appeal held that the s 12 exception applied equally to domestic torts and foreign single country torts. In this case, a Dutchman was killed aboard an

13 S 11(1)
14 S 11(2)(a).
15 S 11(2)(b).
16 S 11(2)(c).
17 See also *Morin v Bonhams & Brooks Ltd* [2003] EWCA Civ 1802; *Trafigura Beheer BV v Kookmin Bank Co* [2006] EWHC 1450 (Comm); and *Fiona Trust & Holding Corp v Privalov* [2010] EWHC 3199 (Comm).
18 [2001] 1 WLR 1003.
19 Law Commission, *Private International Law: Choice of Law in Tort and Delict* (Law Com WP No 87, 1984) [5.92].
20 Law Commission, *Private International Law: Choice of Law in Tort and Delict* (Law Com No 193, 1990) [3.16]–[3.19].
21 [2002] EWCA Civ 21.

English trawler. As all elements of this tort occurred in England, English law applied. The court considered whether Dutch law would be more appropriate in the circumstances under s 12. After weighing up all the factors the court held that the nationality of the victim was not enough to make it substantially more appropriate for Dutch law to apply.

In *VTB Capital Plc v Nutritek International Corp and Ors*,[22] the claimant brought an action against a company, owned and operated in Russia, for fraudulent misrepresentation. This tort was comprised of several components – the statement of misrepresentation, reliance on the statement and resulting loss. Here, the statements were made and received in Russia, the statements were relied on both in

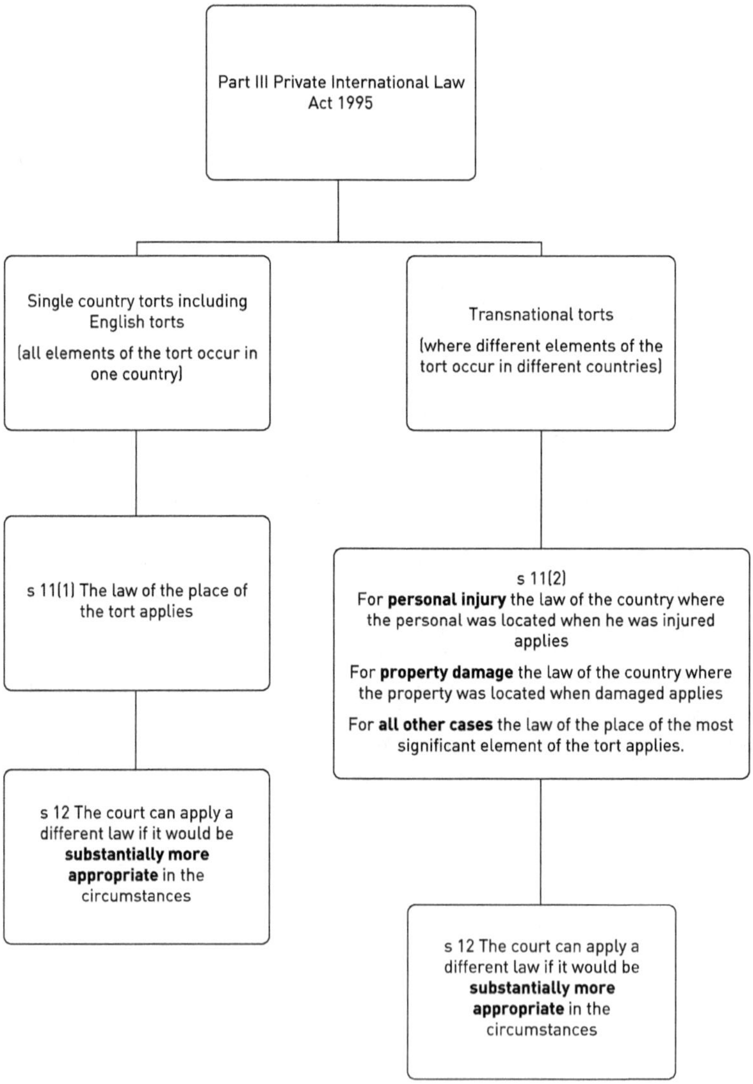

Fig 8.2 Applicable law under PILA.

22 [2011] EWHC 3107 (Ch).

Russia and England and the loss was suffered in England. On the facts, the court held that the most significant elements of the tort had occurred in Russia as this was where the statements were made and primary reliance occurred. In addition the loss made in England had to be accounted for in Russia.

Although PILA does not expressly allow choice-of-law agreements to determine the applicable law for tort disputes, s 12 has allowed existing contracts to be taken into account when the court was using its discretion to determine if a different law would be more appropriate.[23] This could also allow an express agreement between the parties on the law governing the tort to be applied.[24]

In *Trafigura v Kookmin*[25] the existence of a choice-of-law agreement governing a contract between the parties meant that it was appropriate for the tort issue to be determined by the same regime. The contract was central to the dispute in this case. In *VTB Capital Plc v Nutritek International Corp*,[26] even though a facility agreement governed by English law existed between the parties, it had been entered into on foot of the fraudulent misrepresentation that was the issue in the case. The existence of the facility agreement did not render it more appropriate for the tort issue to be governed by English law.

PILA remains in force but s 15a means that its rules now only apply to the determination of issues relating to tort that do not fall under the Rome II Regulation. This would apply to any torts which are not civil and commercial matters. Such torts might include intra-family torts.

8.4 Rome II

8.4.1 Background to Rome II

Rome II[27] was adopted following a long and controversial legislative process. The Commission presented the initial proposal on 22 July 2003.[28] The House of Lords European Union Committee raised serious concerns in relation to this proposal. [29] The Regulation was considered unnecessary for the completion of the internal market and was considered to be outside the legislative powers of the EU as they stood before the Treaty of Lisbon. The Committee was also critical of the European approach to choice-of-law rules in tort which involved many specialised rules. Up until this point English law had operated a general rule applicable to all torts.

Several amendments were made to the original proposal[30] including the exclusion of matters relating to defamation. The United Kingdom and Ireland have adopted the Regulation. Denmark is excluded from Rome II.[31] Rome II was adopted in England by the Law Applicable to Non-Contractual Obligations (England and Wales and Northern Ireland) Regulations 2008.[32]

Brussels I, Rome I and Rome II create an integrated system of uniform private international law rules throughout the EU when it comes to civil and commercial matters. The CJEU will have a key role to play in interpreting the three regulations in a consistent and coherent fashion.

---

23 *Morin v Bonhams & Brooks Ltd* [2003] EWCA Civ 1802; *Trafigura Beheer BVV Kookmin Bank Co* [2006] EWHC 1450 (Comm) [23].

24 *VTB Capital Plc v Nutritek International Corp and Ors* [2011] EWHC 3107 (Ch).

25 [2006] EWHC 1450 (Comm) [102]–[104].

26 [2011] EWHC 3107 (Ch) [143].

27 Regulation (EC) No 864/2007 [2007] OJ L299/40.

28 Commission, 'Proposal for a Regulation of the European Parliament and the Council on the Law applicable to non-contractual obligations', COM (2003) 427 final.

29 European Union Committee, *The Rome II Regulation*, (HL 2003-4, 66), www.publications.parliament.uk/pa/ld200304/ldselect/ldeucom/66/66.pdf (accessed 15 May 2013).

30 Commission, 'Proposal for a Regulation of the European Parliament and the Council on the Law applicable to non-contractual obligations', COM (2006) 0083 final; common position (EC) No 22/2006 adopted by the Council on 25 September 2006 with a view to adopting Rome II [2006] OJ C289E/68.

31 Art 1(4).

32 SI 2008/2986.

8.4.2 Scope of Rome II

The scope of Rome II is wider than PILA 1995. It applies to all situations involving a conflict of laws in relation to non-contractual obligations in civil and commercial matters.[33] The limitation of the regulation to conflict-of-laws cases excludes purely domestic torts with no foreign elements, such as a personal injury case between an English motorist and an English victim occurring in England. As a result of English legislation, the rules of the Regulation are applicable to non-contractual cases involving conflicts between the laws of the different parts of the UK.[34] For example, if elements of a tort have occurred in both Northern Ireland and England, Rome II will apply to determine which law should govern the dispute.

'Civil and commercial matters' should be interpreted in the same way as for Brussels I and Rome I.[35] The idea of a non-contractual obligation differs from state to state and so the term 'non-contractual obligation' has an autonomous meaning within EU law.[36] This meaning should be consistent with the meaning given to non-contractual obligations for the purposes of Brussels I.[37] Revenue, customs and state liability for acts of state authority are excluded from the Regulation. Article 1(2) also specifically excludes a number of matters from the scope of the regulation, including non-contractual obligations arising out of family matters, matrimonial property, wills, succession and defamation and privacy proceedings.

A reference from the High Court of England and Wales to the ECJ has clarified the temporal scope of Rome II. In *Homawoo v GMF Assurances SA*,[38] an English domiciliary was injured in a car accident which occurred in France on 29 August 2007. It was unclear if the choice of law question in *Homawoo* should be determined by Rome II or PILA. This would have a significant effect on the damages awarded.

Article 32 of Rome II states that the Regulation shall apply from 11 January 2009. Article 31 states that Rome II applies to events giving rise to damage which occur after its *entry into force*. According to Art 297 TFEU, regulations come into force 20 days after their publication in the *Official Journal* if no other date for entry into force is specified in the regulation. Rome II was published in the *Official Journal* on 31 July 2007.

In *Bacon v Nacional Suiza CIA Seguros Y Reseguros*,[39] an English pedestrian brought proceedings against the insurers of a Spanish motorist in relation to an accident suffered in Spain which rendered him paraplegic. Tomlinson J held that Rome II applied to accidents occurring after its *entry into force*, i.e. accidents occurring after 20 August 2007. It was suggested that Art 32 simply meant that the courts would only begin using the Regulation in cases that appeared before them after 11 January 2009.[40]

The ECJ[41] has now ruled that Rome II applies only to cases where damage occurred after 11 January 2009. An examination of the preparatory documents for the Regulation showed legislative intention that 'entry into force' in Art 31 and 'date of application' in Art 32 should refer to the same date.

8.4.3 Applicable law

Rome II has four key features:

---

33 Art 1(1).
34 The Law Applicable to Non-Contractual Obligations (England and Wales and Northern Ireland) Regulations 2008, SI 2008/2986.
35 See Chapter 3 and Chapter 7.
36 Recital (11).
37 See Chapter 3; C189/87 *Kalfelis v Schroder, Munchmeyer, Hengst and Co* [1988] ECR 1 5565 [18].
38 [2010] EWHC 1941.
39 [2010] EWHC 2017 (QB).
40 See also A Dickinson, *The Rome II Regulation* (OUP, 2008) [3.315].
41 C412/10 *Homawoo v GMF Assurances SA* [2012] IL Pr 2.

1. Article 14 expressly allows the parties to choose the law applicable to their dispute in certain circumstances.
2. The general rule under Art 4 applies the law of the **place of damage**.
3. There are special rules (Arts 5–13) to determine the applicable law for specified non-contractual obligations including product liability, unfair competition and environmental torts.
4. Article 3 requires the court to apply the law of a non-Member State if such a law is chosen by applying the rules of Rome II. For example, an English court might have to apply the law of Japan under Rome II if that is where the damage occurred.

8.4.4 Choice of law by the parties (Art 14)

Rome II expressly allows the parties to choose the law applicable to their dispute under Art 14. This is a revolutionary development for choice-of-law rules in tort which accords importance to party autonomy. There are some limitations. In order to ensure legal certainty, Art 14 requires the choice to be expressed or to be clearly ascertained from the circumstances of the case. The choice of law cannot prejudice the rights of third parties. This is reinforced by Art 6(4), which precludes a choice-of-law agreement where the tort arises out of an act of unfair competition, and Art 8(3), where the tort arises out of an infringement of intellectual property.

Choice-of-law agreements cannot be used to avoid mandatory rules of national or EU law. Here a distinction is made between transnational torts and single country torts. Where all elements of the tort occur in a single country, the parties cannot choose the law of another country merely to avoid a mandatory rule of national law.[42] Where the tort is transnational and elements occur in more than one EU Member State, the parties can choose the law of any Member State. If the law of a non-Member State is chosen, the parties cannot avoid EU rules that are of mandatory application within the EU.[43]

Limitations are placed on when choice-of-law agreements can be made. Choice of law can have a significant effect on the amount of damages that can be awarded to a claimant. If an agreement on the law applicable is made before any damage occurs, this can be seen as a form of risk limitation. If all the parties to the choice of law agreement are pursuing a commercial activity and have freely negotiated the agreement, it can be entered into before any damage occurs.[44] This means that two parties, with equal bargaining power, who are going into business together can agree that the same law will apply to any future contractual and tortious disputes that may occur.

For all other parties, a choice-of-law agreement can be made only **after** damage has occurred.[45] This allows the claimant to decide whether he wishes to make a choice-of-law agreement on all the facts. This ensures that weaker parties understand the real effects that a choice-of-law agreement will have on their situation.

8.4.5 The general rule in absence of choice (Art 4)

Article 4 states the general rule for choice of law. It applies where there is no valid agreement as to choice of law and the dispute does not fall into the specified categories of Arts 5–13. The general rule of Rome II designates the law of the place where the damage occurs.[46] This mirrors the provisions of Art 5(3) of Brussels I. The applicable law is that of the place where a personal injury was sustained or where property was damaged. The indirect results of the damage, such as financial loss caused by the reduced ability of an injured person to work in their home country, are not

42 Art 14(2).
43 Art 14(3).
44 Art 14(1)(b).
45 Art 14(1).
46 Art 4(1).

considered for the purpose of choosing the applicable law.[47] The law of the place of direct damage was thought to strike an appropriate balance between the interests of the defendant and those of the claimant.[48] Article 4(1) was applied by the English courts in *Jacobs v Motor Insurers Bureau*.[49]

An exception to the general rule is made where both parties have their habitual residence in the same country.[50] If this is the case, the law of the common habitual residence will apply. Thus if two English motorists have a collision while on holiday in Malta, English law will apply.

Article 4(3) creates an 'escape clause' allowing the court to apply the law of a different country if it is clear from all the circumstances of the case that the tort is manifestly more closely connected to the law of that country.

8.4.6 Special rules for particular torts (Arts 5–9)

Specific rules exist under Rome II for establishing the law applicable to particular torts. It was considered that there were special considerations to be made in each of these cases when balancing the interests of the claimant and the defendant.[51] This meant that the general rule would be inappropriate.

8.4.6.1 Product liability (Art 5)

The question of choice of law to designate liability for manufactured products is not as simple as weighing up the interests of the claimant and the particular defendant. The health of the general consumer must be protected while facilitating trade and encouraging innovation. It was important to give foreseeability to manufacturers and distributors as to where they might be held liable for their products. Therefore a checklist system is set up by Art 5 which takes into account where products are marketed.[52]

If both the claimant and the defendant have their habitual residence in the same country, the law of that country will apply.[53] For example, if an Irish tourist is injured by a defective product in Portugal but makes a claim against an Irish manufacturer, Irish law will apply.

If the parties to the dispute do not have the same habitual residence the rules of Art 5(1) apply.

- If the product was marketed in **the habitual residence of the claimant** when the damage occurred, the law of the claimant's habitual residence will apply.[54] For example, if an Irish tourist is injured by a defective product acquired in Portugal while on holidays in Portugal, Irish law will apply if the product was also marketed in Ireland at that time.
- **Failing this**, the law of the country where the product was acquired applies if the **product was marketed in that country**.[55] So Portuguese law will be applicable to the above dispute if the defective product was acquired and marketed in Portugal.
- Failing this, the law of the country where **the damage occurred** will apply, but only if the product was marketed in that country.[56] This would cover the situation where the product was acquired in a country where the product was not marketed but caused injury in a different country where the product was marketed.

---

47 See Chapter 3.
48 Recital (16).
49 [2010] EWCA Civ 1208.
50 Art 4(2).
51 Recital (19).
52 Recital (20).
53 Art 5(1).
54 Art 5(1)(a).
55 Art 5(1)(b).
56 Art 5(1)(c).

An exception to the hierarchy of rules laid down by Art 5(1) applies if the defendant could not have foreseen the marketing of the product in the country designated by the above rules. In this case, the law applicable to the dispute will be the law of the habitual residence of the defendant. This allows a balance to be achieved between the interests of small manufacturers and of consumers.

Article 5(2) allows the court to apply the law of any country manifestly more closely connected to the dispute.

8.4.6.2 Unfair competition (Art 6)

This article seeks to protect competitors, consumers and the general public from the consequences of unfair competition. In English law there is no specific tort of unfair competition but it is likely to include many economic torts. The scope of Art 6 will require clarification from the CJEU. Article 6 designates the law of the country where the damage arises but clarifies what this means in unfair competition scenarios.

- If the act of the unfair competition only affects one specific competitor, the general rule of Art 4 will apply.[57]
- If the act of unfair competition affects the general consumer, the law of the country where these collective interests are based applies.[58] For example, if damage occurred as a result of misleading advertising, the law of the country where the misleading advertising affects the collective interests of consumers would apply.
- If the tort arises out of a restriction of competition, then the law of the country where the market is affected will apply.[59] If the markets of several countries are affected, the claimant can choose to base his claim of the law of the forum where legal action is taken if this is one of the affected countries.[60]

It is not possible to make a choice-of-law agreement to depart from the law designated by Art 6.[61] This is because disputes involving unfair competition affect third parties and collective interests.

8.4.6.3 Environmental damage (Art 7)

Article 7 applies to torts causing an adverse change in a natural resource or damage to ecosystems. There is a strong public interest in protecting the environment. This is expressed in EU law through the 'polluter pays' principle found in Art 191 TFEU. The result is that Art 7 promotes the interests of the claimant who has suffered environmental damage over the interests of the defendant. The claimant can choose the law of the place of damage or the law of the country where the event giving rise to the damage occurred. For example, if a factory in Serbia pollutes the Danube, which causes damage to farmland in Bulgaria, the claimant can choose the law of either Serbia or Bulgaria. This ensures that the law least favourable to the defendant and most protective to the environment is applied. This could include rules of strict liability.

8.4.6.4 Intellectual property rights (Art 8)

In cases relating to infringement of intellectual property rights, the applicable law is that of the country where the right infringed is protected.[62] If the infringement relates to an intellectual

57 Art 6(2).
58 Art 6(1).
59 Art (6)(3)(a).
60 Art (6)(3)(b).
61 Art 6(4).
62 Art 8(1).

property right protected throughout the EU, such as a Community trademark, the law applicable is the law of the place of infringement.[63]

No choice-of-law agreement derogating from the rules of Art 8 is permitted.

8.4.6.5 Industrial action (Art 9)

If the tort involves a question of liability for damages caused by industrial action, the applicable law will be the law of the place where the industrial action is carried out.[64] This rule acknowledges that the right to take industrial action is treated differently in each Member State. The balance achieved between the rights of workers and employers in each Member State is best supported by the application of the internal rules of the Member State in which the industrial action occurs.[65]

8.4.7 Choice-of-law rules for other specific non-contractual obligations

Articles 10 to 13 of Rome II contain special choice-of-law rules for specified non-contractual obligations. Article 10 covers unjust enrichment. Articles 11 and 12 refer to types of obligations which are not part of English law. Article 11 covers *negotiorum gestio*, a type of liability arising out of acts carried out on behalf of another person without proper authority. Article 12 covers *culpa in contrahendo*, a form of liability which occurs during the breakdown of contractual negotiations.

The choice-of-law rules for these specified non-contractual obligations follow a very similar pattern. The law applicable is the law governing any pre-existing legal relationship between the parties that is connected to the dispute.[66] If no such relationship exists, the law applicable is that of the common habitual residence of the claimant and defendant.[67] Failing this, the law applicable is the law of the country where the unjust enrichment or unauthorised action took place.[68] In the case of *culpa in contrahendo*, the law applicable is the place of the damage.[69]

A general escape clause which allows the court to apply the law of a country manifestly more closely connected exists for each of the specified non-contractual obligations.[70]

8.4.8 The influence of the law of the forum

Rome II often requires the courts to apply foreign law. However, the law of the forum is not ignored by the Regulation. Under Art 16 the application of foreign law cannot displace the application of mandatory rules of the forum. Under Art 26 the courts can refuse to apply foreign law to the dispute if to do so would be manifestly incompatible with the law of the forum. An example would include awarding punitive damages of an excessive nature.[71]

Both deviations from the application of foreign law can only be used in exceptional circumstances.

---

63 Art 8(2).
64 Art 9.
65 Recital (27).
66 Art 10(1), Art 11(1) and Art 12(1).
67 Art 10(2), Art 11(2) and Art 12(1)(b).
68 Art 10(3) and Art 11(3).
69 Art 12(2)(b).
70 Art 10(4), Art 11(4) and Art 12(2)(c).
71 Recital (32).

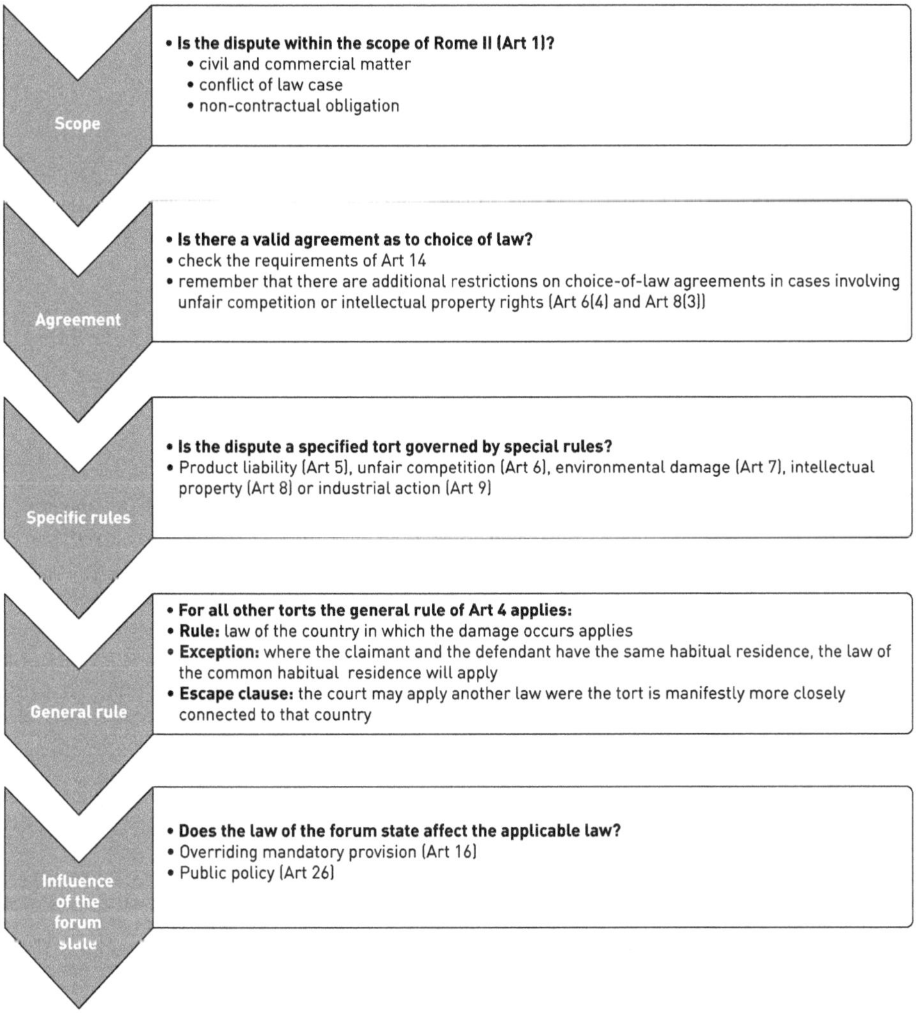

Fig 8.3 Applicable law under Rome II.

8.5 Scope of applicable law

Once the court has used Rome II to determine applicable law, it must then check to see if the issue before the court is within the scope of the law chosen.

The scope of the applicable law will govern whether the defendant is actually liable.[72] This includes possible defences or limitations on liability.[73] It also governs the question of whether the defendant can be held liable for the acts of another person.[74]

72 Art 15(a).
73 Art 15(b).
74 Art 15(g).

Article 15 extends the choice-of-law rules to matters which were previously considered by the English courts to be part of procedural law. Under English law, procedural matters are governed by the law of the forum. However, under Rome II the applicable law governs prescription and limitation of obligations.[75] It will also govern the possible remedies that can be given by the court.[76] This includes the claimant's right to compensation for personal injury.[77] Most controversially, the applicable law governs the assessment of damages.[78] This is a radical departure from the previous English position.

The question of whether assessment of damages is a matter for the law of the forum or the applicable law has been central to the English cases on the temporal scope of Rome II.

8.5.1 Assessment of damages

Under the common law and PILA, the assessment of damages was a matter for the forum. Under Rome II, the assessment of damages is a matter for the applicable law. The most appropriate law to govern the assessment of damages has been the subject of debate for many years. If the law of the place of damage is used, the defendant is required to make compensation under the rules of the place where the injury took place. If the claimant is merely visiting the country where the injury took place and returns home with a significant personal injury, medical treatment and the cost of living with the injury may be much higher than in the country where the injury occurred.

The issue of assessment of damages was vital in *Boys v Chaplin*, where an English motorist was severely injured in a crash in Malta. Under English law, damages for pain and suffering were recoverable; under Maltese law they were not. The House of Lords held unanimously that *lex fori* applied the quantum of damages but that the availability of a particular head of damages was a substantive issue to be determined by the applicable law.[79] In this case, English law was both the law of the forum and the applicable law. Lord Pearson argued that the boundary between procedural and substantive law was unclear when it came to the existence of a right of recovery.[80] He also noted the difficulty the court faced in this case. For an English court to award an Englishman much-reduced damages seemed unfair, yet to consider the right to recover a particular head of damage as a procedural rule encouraged forum shopping.[81]

The Law Commission Report in 1990 preserved the common law position on damages. It confirmed that the availability of a particular head of damage was a matter for substantive law and governed by the applicable law. However, the quantification of damages was a matter for *lex fori*.[82] Under PILA, the distinction between matters of substance and procedure is preserved by s 14(3)(b). This approach was followed in *Edmunds v Simmonds*.[83]

Legal authorities relating to the boundary between substance and procedure in assessment of damages were reviewed in the famous case of *Harding v Wealands*.[84] Here the claimant, an English national, was badly injured in a road accident as a passenger in a car driven by the defendant, an Australian national, in New South Wales, Australia. The law of New South Wales[85] imposed a cap on recovery of damages. English law contained no such restriction. Section 11 of PILA designated the law of New South Wales as the applicable law. The issue in the case was whether the existence of a cap on damages was a substantive issue or a matter of procedural law.

75 Art 15(h).
76 Art 15(d).
77 Art 15(f).
78 Art 15(c).
79 *Boys v Chaplin* [1971] AC 356 (UKHL) 379.
80 *Ibid* 395.
81 *Ibid* 401.
82 Law Commission, *Private International Law: Choice of law in Tort and Delict* (Law Com No 193, 1990) [3.38].
83 [2001] 1 WLR 1003.
84 [2006] UKHL 32.
85 The Motor Accidents Compensation Act 1999.

The Court of Appeal favoured a narrow interpretation of procedural law and found that the restriction on damages in NSW law was a substantive matter.[86] The House of Lords reversed this position and held that restrictions on recovery of damages were a matter of procedural law. Lord Hoffman held that the general approach of PILA was to preserve the dichotomy between substantive law and procedural law as understood by the common law.[87] *Harding v Wealands* confirmed that the position under the common law and PILA was to treat the availability of a head of damages as a matter of substantive law to be determined by the applicable law. In contrast, restrictions on recovery of damages and quantum of damages were matters for procedural law and determined by the law of the forum.

Under Rome II, the existence, nature and assessment of a remedy are matters determined by the applicable law.[88] This is a clear departure from the English position. The question of compensation for victims of traffic accidents which occurred while the victim was visiting another country was a highly disputed matter during the drafting of Rome II. It was suggested by the EU Parliament that the rules of a victim's habitual residence should determine the type of claim and the quantum of damages.[89] It was considered unfair to award damages on the scale of the country where the incident happened rather than the country of the victim's habitual residence. The Council disagreed. The approach would make the question of liability subject to one law and the assessment of damages subject to another law. This was incompatible with the existing approach in most Member States and would create uncertainty.[90]

As a compromise, Recital (33) of Rome II provides that when calculating personal injury damages for traffic accidents, the court must consider all relevant factual circumstances of the victim, including the actual costs of aftercare. This means that national rules can be taken into account as facts when assessing compensation.[91] In addition, the Commission was obliged to provide a preparatory study on the compensation of cross-border victims by the end of 2008.[92] This report was published in 2009.[93] It highlights important differences in levels of compensation in the EU. In addition, not all types of losses are recognised in every Member State, and cross-border victims show a lack of understanding of the limitation periods relevant to their claim. The Commission launched a consultation paper on this issue in 2009.[94]

In 2011 the Commission announced plans to ensure effective action on the rights of road accident victims. Harmonising the rules on limitation periods for legal actions across Europe has been proposed to allow victims to benefit from the limitation period of their home country. A consultation on the limitation periods for compensation claims for traffic accidents was launched in 2012.[95]

---

86 Following the Australian case of *John Pfeiffer Pty Ltd v Rogerson* (2000) 203 CLR 503 and Law Commission, *Private International Law: Choice of Law in Tort and Delict* (Law Com No 193, 1990) [3.39].
87 *Harding v Wealands* [2006] UKHL 32 [66].
88 Arts 21 and 22.
89 Committee on Legal Affairs, 'On the proposal for a regulation of the European Parliament and of the Council on the law applicable to non-contractual obligations ("Rome II")' A6-0211/2005.
90 Council, 'Common Position adopted by the Council with a view to the adoption of a Regulation of the European Parliament and of the Council on the law applicable to non-contractual obligations ("Rome II")' 9751/06 ADD 1.
91 S Symeonides, 'Rome II and Tort Conflicts: A Missed Opportunity', (2008) 56 *American Journal of Comparative Law*, 173–222, 183.
92 Art 30.
93 Demolin, Brulard, Barthelemy – Hoche, 'Compensation of victims of cross-border traffic accidents in the EU' (2009), http://ec.europa.eu/internal_market/insurance/docs/motor/20090129report_en.pdf (accessed 15 May 2013).
94 Commission, 'Consultation Paper on the Compensation of victims of Cross-Border Road Traffic Accidents in the European Union' (2009), http://ec.europa.eu/internal_market/consultations/docs/2009/cross-border-accidents/rome2study_en.pdf; Commission, 'Feedback Statement: Consultation Paper on the Compensation of victims of Cross-Border Road Traffic Accidents in the European Union' (2009), http://ec.europa.eu/internal_market/consultations/docs/2009/cross-border-accidents/feedback.pdf (both accessed 15 May 2013).
95 See http://ec.europa.eu/justice/civil/commercial/car-accident/index_en.htm (accessed 15 May 2013).

8.6 Defamation

In the original draft of Rome II, defamation and torts involving a violation of privacy were included.[96] It was generally agreed that Art 4(1) was not appropriate to ensure the balance between freedom of speech and protection of privacy and that a special rule should be formulated to deal with such cases. In the end, no agreement could be reached as to what would be an appropriate rule.[97] Defamation and invasion of privacy torts were excluded from the scope of Rome II. Article 30 of Rome II commissioned a study to look into the issue with a view to future EU regulation. This was published in 2009.[98]

In deciding which law should govern international defamation torts, a balance must be achieved between freedom of expression and the protection of individual reputation. These interests are valued differently in the domestic law of different countries. For example, in the United States, freedom of expression is highly valued at a constitutional level, and restrictions on the media are very unpopular. In contrast, England is considered to have a claimant-friendly approach to defamation.[99]

In transnational cases it is even more difficult to find an appropriate balance between the competing rights. It is difficult to justify the application of English law to a foreign publisher who works in a country where freedom of speech is prioritised. However, the English courts have an interest in protecting the reputation of English domiciliaries from defamatory statements made by foreign publishers.

The English tort of defamation is a common law tort, although some aspects are governed by the Defamation Act 1996 and the Defamation Act 2013 (which received Royal Assent in April 2013 and is due to come into force in 2013). At common law, the tort of defamation was committed when a statement was published which was likely to damage the reputation of an individual in the eyes of right-thinking members of society.[100] At common law, damage was presumed from the existence of the defamatory statement.[101] The Defamation Act 2013 introduces a requirement for the claimant to show that the publication has caused or is likely to cause serious harm to the reputation of the claimant.[102] The publication can be verbal (slander) or written (libel). In contrast to other jurisdictions, there is no need to show that publication is malicious. It is a defence to the tort to show that the statement is true.[103] Statutory defences of honest opinion[104] and public interest[105] can also be used.

The Human Rights Act 1998 now requires English courts to interpret national law in a manner compatible with the European Convention on Human Rights. In *Tolstoy Miloslavsky v United Kingdom*[106] the applicant to the ECtHR claimed successfully that the award of £1.5 million awarded against him by a jury for defamation was excessive and constituted a breach of Art 10 of the ECHR as being an undue restraint on freedom of speech.[107] Some reforms to the assessment of damages by juries were made by the Defamation Act 1996 and under the Defamation Act 2013 trial by jury will take place only in exceptional circumstances.[108]

---

96 Commission, 'Proposal for a Regulation of the European Parliament and the Council on the Law applicable to non-contractual obligations', COM (2003) 427 final.
97 Council, 'Common Position adopted by the Council with a view to the adoption of a Regulation of the European Parliament and of the Council on the law applicable to non-contractual obligations ("Rome II")' 9751/06 ADD 1.
98 MainStrat, 'Comparative study on the situation in the 27 Member States as regards the law applicable to non-contractual obligations arising out of violations of privacy and rights relating to personality' (2009, JLS/2007/C4/028).
99 T Hartley, '"Libel tourism" and Conflict of Laws' (2010) 59 ICLQ 25–38, 26.
100 *Skuse v Granada Television Ltd* [1996] EMLR 278, 286.
101 *Shevill v Presse Alliance* [1996] AC 959; *Jameel v Dow Jones* [2005] QB 946 [39].
102 S 1 Defamation Act 2013.
103 S 2 Defamation Act 2013.
104 S 3 Defamation Act 2013.
105 S 4 Defamation Act 2013.
106 (1995) 20 EHRR 442.
107 For a similar but unsuccessful challenge see *Jameel v Dow Jones* [2005] QB 946.
108 S 11 Defamation Act 2013.

English libel laws are attractive to individuals who have no recourse under their domestic system. High costs are associated with legal action for defamation in England. This means that the threat of legal action in London can effectively censor authors and journalists. This inhibits the right to free speech and can have a 'chilling effect' on international publication.[109] The English law pre-dating the Defamation Act 2013 was criticised as allowing actions to be brought in England where there was very little link to the jurisdiction. This problem is referred to as libel tourism.

8.6.1 Jurisdiction and the single publication rule

Under Brussels I, an action for defamation can be brought in England if that is where the defendant is domiciled[110] or where the harmful event occurred.[111] In *Shevill v Presse Alliance SA*[112] a claimant domiciled in England brought a libel action against a French newspaper in England. The newspaper had a wide circulation in France but only 230 copies of the paper had been sold in England. The ECJ held that in international libel cases the claimant can bring proceedings under Art 5(3) in the place where the material was distributed or in the place where the publisher is established. If the claim is brought in the place where the publisher is established, the court can award damages for all harm caused. Where the claim is brought in a place where material was distributed, the court can award damages only for harm caused in the forum state. This second approach allows the claimant to bring a separate action in each jurisdiction where they claim to have suffered damage.

In *eDate Advertising GmbH v X*[113] the ECJ was asked to interpret 'the place where the harmful event occurred or may occur' where a breach of personality rights occurred by means of content placed online on an internet website. In this hearing the ECJ heard two joined cases. In the first one, a report had been posted on eDate's website which stated that X and his brother, who were appealing a conviction for X in a German court, intended to prove that the prosecution witnesses had lied. X sought to have the report taken down. The jurisdiction of the German courts was questioned.

In the second case, the French actor Olivier Martinez had taken proceedings in the French courts complaining that a story entitled 'Kylie Minogue is back with Olivier Martinez', posted on www.sundaymirror.co.uk interfered with his private life and infringed his right to use of his own image.

The ECJ noted that a person who placed material on the internet rendered it instantly accessible by an unlimited number of internet users throughout the world.[114] This meant that the test in *Shevill* was less useful, as damage could be suffered on a worldwide basis. In such cases it was appropriate for the person suffering an infringement of a personality right to bring an action in one forum in respect of all of the damage caused. The impact of the material posted on the internet was best assessed by the court of the place where the alleged victim has his centre of interests.[115] This place would generally be the habitual residence of the alleged victim or the place where he pursues his professional activities. This place should be predictable for the publisher and allows the applicant to identify the court in which he may sue and the defendant reasonably to foresee before which court he may be sued.[116]

eDate has modified the *Shevill* test in cases where defamatory material has been placed on the internet. In such cases the claimant may bring proceedings in respect of all the damage caused, either before the courts of the Member State in which the publisher of that content is established or before the courts of the Member State in which the centre of the claimant's interests is based. It

109 Ministry of Justice, 'Draft Defamation Bill Consultation' (2011 CP3/11) [79]–[92].
110 Art 2 Brussels I.
111 Art 5(3) Brussels I.
112 [1995] ECR I-415.
113 C509/9 *eDate Advertising GmbH v X* [2012] QB 654.
114 Ibid [45].
115 Ibid [48].
116 Ibid [50].

is also open to the claimant to bring separate actions before the courts of each Member State in the territory of which content placed online is or has been accessible. Where separate actions are taken, the courts have jurisdiction only in respect of the damage caused in the territory of the Member State of the court seised.

If the defendant is not domiciled in the EU, English law will apply to establishing jurisdiction for defamation actions. The Defamation Act 2013 will make a number of changes to jurisdiction in cases of defamation. Under English law, a claim form can be served on a defendant who is not domiciled in a Member State during a temporary presence in England[117] or by service outside the jurisdiction.[118] For tort actions, service outside the jurisdiction is only permitted if injury occurred in England or if injury was sustained from an action occurring in England.[119] As damage was presumed in defamation cases, prior to the coming into force of the Defamation Act 2013, the preconditions could generally be satisfied by publication in England.[120] Such cases were generally limited to claims for damage caused by publication in England. Section 9 of the Defamation Act 2013 now limits the jurisdiction of the English court to disputes where England and Wales is clearly the most appropriate place in which to bring an action.

Prior to the Defamation Act 2013, English law treated every publication as giving rise to a separate action.[121] For example, in *Berezovsky v Michaels*,[122] *Forbes* magazine published an article claiming that two prominent Russian businessmen, B and G, were involved in leading organised crime in Russia. The magazine sold 785,000 copies in the USA and Canada, 1,900 copies in England and 13 copies in Russia. The claimants successfully obtained leave to serve claims outside the jurisdiction. The claim was limited to damages resulting from the publication in England. It was held that publication in England of an internationally distributed statement constituted a separate tort that was actionable in England.[123]

In *King v Lewis*[124] the dispute was based on texts published on websites based in California which alleged that King had made anti-Semitic remarks. These sites had been accessed from England. The court accepted that text on the internet is published in England if it is accessed or downloaded there. This was confirmed in *Richardson v Schwarzenegger*.[125]

At first glance, the old English rules of jurisdiction seemed to invite libel tourism. The English interpretation of publication allowed a foreign claimant to bring an action against a foreign publisher in England if he could show that defamatory material published on the internet had been accessed in England. There was no need for the claimant to show that he had a reputation in England or that he had suffered actual damage. However, the defendant could apply to have service set aside where the tort lacked any substance, where the continuation of the claim amounted to abuse of process or where England was *forum non conveniens*. These controls prevented cases being brought in England where there was no real connection to the jurisdiction.

In *Kroch v Rossell et Compagnie Société*[126] a foreign gentleman took action in England against two newspaper publishers based in Belgium and France. The stories complained of were published exclusively in Belgium and France. A limited number of copies of the newspapers were distributed in England. Mr Koch was unknown in England. Jurisdiction was refused on the basis that no substantial tort had occurred in England.[127]

---

117 S IV Part 6.36 of the CPR.
118 S IV Part 6.36 of the CPR in accordance with Practice Direction 6B rule 3(1)(9). See Chapter 4.
119 Practice Direction 6B rule 3(1)(9).
120 Ibid.
121 *Duke of Brunswick v Harmer* (1849) 14 QB 185.
122 [2000] 1 WLR 1004.
123 Ibid 1012.
124 [2004] EWCA Civ 1329.
125 [2004] All ER (D) 432 [19].
126 *Kroch v Rossell et Compagnie Société* [1937] 1 All ER 725.
127 Ibid 730; *Tamiz v Google Inc* [2013] EWCA Civ 68.

In *Jameel (Yousef) v Dow Jones*,[128] a foreign claimant issued proceedings against an American publisher in England for an article that had been posted on an American website. Only five subscribers had accessed the article in England. The court acknowledged that the presumption in English law that the publication of a defamatory article has caused damage allowed cases to be brought where there was minimal circulation in England and no actual damage to the claimant's reputation. Such cases were rare, and the appropriate action in such a case is to strike out the action for abuse of process.[129] Where publication within the jurisdiction was minimal and damage to the claimant's reputation was insignificant, it was disproportionate and an abuse of process for the claimant to proceed with his claim. The court referred to the obligation imposed by the Human Rights Act 1998 to interpret the law governing jurisdiction in a manner that balanced the right to free speech and the protection of individual reputation.[130]

In *Berezovsky v Michaels* the defendants applied to have jurisdiction set aside on the basis that England was *forum non conveniens*.[131] The *Spiliada* test[132] was applied to determine whether proceedings should be stayed on the basis of *forum non conveniens*. *Forum non conveniens* was rejected as the claimants had significant connections with England. Actions in Russia and America could not redress the damage done to the claimants' reputations in England. The House of Lords confirmed that *prima facie* the jurisdiction where the tort was committed was the most appropriate place to bring an action under English rules of jurisdiction.[133]

If claims for damages were limited to damage caused by publication in England this meant that England would always be presumed to be the best forum. However, in *King v Lewis* it was confirmed that the weaker the claimant's link to England and the greater the publication outside England the weaker this presumption became.[134]

If jurisdiction in England was based on Art 5(3) of Brussels I it was not possible to challenge jurisdiction on the basis that England is not the most appropriate forum.[135]

Section 8 of the Defamation Act 2013 introduces a single publication rule into English law for the first time. This means that multiple publications of the same defamatory statement will be treated as one cause of action. This provides greater protection to publishers.

8.6.2 Applicable law

Under the common law rules of choice of law in tort, if a tort is committed in England, English law alone applies. If the tort occurs abroad, the double actionability rule means that the law applicable is a combination of the *lex fori* and the law of place of the tort.[136] For the tort of defamation, the location of the tort is the place of publication. Therefore most cases involving international dissemination will be treated as domestic English torts, as publication will be deemed to have occurred in England in order to establish jurisdiction. Only where publication occurs abroad will the common law rule of double actionability apply.

In *Bata v Bata*[137] the Court of Appeal held that where a defamatory letter had been written in Switzerland but published in England, the tort was committed in England. Hence the tort was treated as a domestic English tort.

128 *Jameel (Yousef) v Dow Jones* [2005] QB 946.
129 Ibid [40].
130 Ibid [55].
131 See further Chapter 4.
132 *Spiliada Martime Corpn v Cansulex Ltd* [1987] AC 460.
133 [2000] 1 WLR 1004, 1015.
134 *King v Lewis* [2004] EWCA Civ 1329, 27.
135 *Jameel v Dow Jones* [2005] QB 946 [40].
136 See above.
137 [1984] WN 366.

In *Church of Scientology of California v Commissioner of Police of the Metropolis (No 1)*[138] the English Metropolitan Police made an allegedly defamatory report to the West German federal police. The Court of Appeal confirmed that this was a foreign tort to which the rule of double actionability applied. In such a case there will be no liability where there is a defence under English law or under the law of the place of publication. It was suggested by the Court of Appeal that the exception in *Boys v Chaplin* which allowed the application of English law alone might apply in the circumstances as the claimants had a closer relationship to the *lex fori*.

8.6.3 Proposed reforms to deal with libel tourism

Both the EU rules of jurisdiction and the English rules of jurisdiction limit the possibility of foreign claimants using English courts to pursue defamation claims against foreign defendants.

At EU level, the MainStrat study[139] outlined the options for an EU choice-of-law regime for defamation torts. It argued that choosing the law of the place of damage was an appropriate balance between the rights of the press and the rights of the victim.[140] It was usually the place of residence of the victim, and it would be easy for the press to identify potential victims of defamation in the countries in which they published material. In contrast, choosing the place of establishment of the publisher significantly favoured the publisher over the victim.[141] Whereas a publisher has control over where material is published, the victim cannot predict in which country the publisher who makes the statement will be established. The report also recommended harmonisation of substantive law to ensure a minimal level of protection for individual privacy.[142]

In May 2012, the European Parliament requested the Commission to propose additions to Rome II to regulate choice of law for claims relating to violations of privacy and rights relating to personality.[143] It was suggested that the applicable law for such matters should include the law of the **country in which the most significant element of the damage occurred** or was likely to occur. If this was not reasonably foreseeable, the law of the habitual residence of the defendant would apply.

A special rule is proposed where the damage was caused by publication of printed matter or by broadcast. In such a case, **the country to which the publication or broadcast was principally directed** should be considered to be the country in which the most significant element of the damage occurred. If it is not clear where the publication or broadcast was principally directed, **the country in which editorial control is exercised** is considered to be the country in which the most significant element of the damage occurred.

The Commission was also requested to generate a proposal for the creation of a centre for the voluntary settlement of cross-border disputes arising out of violations of privacy and rights relating to personality by way of alternative dispute resolution

---

138 (1976) 120 SJ 690.

139 MainStrat, 'Comparative study on the situation in the 27 Member States as regards the law applicable to non-contractual obligations arising out of violations of privacy and rights relating to personality' (2009, JLS/2007/C4/028), available at http://ec.europa.eu/justice/civil/files/study_privacy_en.pdf (accessed 24 May 2013).

140 Ibid 145.

141 Ibid 145.

142 European Parliament, 'Working Document on the amendment of Regulation (EC) No 864/2007 on the law applicable to non-contractual obligations (Rome II)' (2011), available at www.europarl.europa.eu/meetdocs/2009_2014/documents/juri/dv/836/836983/836983_en.pdf (accessed 15 May 2013).

143 European Parliament resolution of 10 May 2012 with recommendations to the Commission on the amendment of Regulation (EC) No 864/2007 on the law applicable to non-contractual obligations (Rome II) (2009/2170(INI)).

8.7 Further reading

J Ahern and W Binchy (eds), *The Rome II Regulation on the Law Applicable to Non-Contractual Relations* (Martinus Nijhoff, 2009).

P Beaumont and Z Tang, 'Classification of delictual damages: *Harding v Wealands* and the Rome II Regulation' (2008) 12 *Edinburgh Law Review* 131–137.

A Briggs, 'What did *Boys v Chaplin* decide?' (1984) 12 *Anglo American Law Review*, 237.

A Briggs, 'When in Rome choose as the Romans choose' (2009) 125 *Law Quarterly Review* 191.

A Dickinson, *The Rome II Regulation* (OUP, 2008).

L Gillies, 'Jurisdiction for cross-border breach of personality and defamation: *eDate Advertising* and *Martinez*' (2012) 61 ICLQ 1007–1016.

E Guinshard and S Lamont-Black, 'Environmental Law: the Black Sheep in Rome II's Drive for Legal Certainty?' (2009) 11 *Environmental Law Review* 161–172.

T Hartley, ' "Libel tourism" and Conflict of Laws', (2010) 59 ICLQ 25–38.

P Huber (ed), *Rome II Regulation: Pocket Commentary* (Sellier, 2011).

E Lein, 'The New Rome I/Rome II/ Brussels I Synergy', in Šarcevic et al (eds) *Yearbook of Private International Law 2008* (Sellier: 2009) 177–198.

J Oster, 'Rethinking *Shevill*: Conceptualising the EU private international law of internet torts against personality rights' (2012) 26 *International Review of Law Computers & Technology* 113–128.

A Reed and TP Kennedy, 'International torts and *Shevill*: the ghost of forum shopping yet to come' [1996] LMCLQ 108.

S Symeonides, 'Rome II and tort conflicts: A missed opportunity' (2008) 56 *American Journal of Comparative Law* 173–222.

Chapter 9

Property

Chapter Contents

Key Issues:

- The difference between property rights and personal obligations
- Jurisdictional restrictions on actions relating to foreign rights in immovable property
- Applicable law for property transfers
- Jurisdiction and applicable law relating to wills
- Applicable law for property passed by succession
- The EU Succession Regulation

9.1 Introduction

This chapter will examine the conflict of law issues that arise in disputes relating to the transfer of property rights. Property rights can be transferred between living people by means of direct property transfer or by a gift, contractual transaction or assignment. Property rights are transferred on death by a will or through intestate succession.

The conflict-of-law rules relating to property rights divide cases into two classifications: cases relating to rights in **immovable property**, such as land or real property, and cases relating **movable property**. Movable property includes personal property, goods and intangible property rights such as securities, choses in action and intellectual property rights.

The application of the conflict-of-law rules relating to the transfer of property rights is complex because property issues are often connected to other matters with their own separate conflicts-of-law rules, such as when a property interest is transferred by contract. The conflict-of-law rules relating to property will apply where the validity of a property right transfer is in question. The conflict-of-law rules relating to contract will apply where the dispute centres on the personal obligations between the parties to each other, such as whether damages are payable for a breach of a contractual obligation to transfer ownership or whether an obligation to pay exists under a lease.

The first part of this chapter will consider the rules of jurisdiction and applicable law that apply when the English courts are asked to hear a dispute regarding the transfer of the property rights between two living individuals.

The second half of the chapter examines the jurisdictional and applicable law rules that apply when property is transferred through succession.

9.2 The distinction between movable and immovable property

It is well settled that the applicable law to determine whether a piece of property is movable or immovable is the law of the *situs* (the place where the property is).

In *Re Berchtold*[1] Berchtold had died domiciled in Hungary. He left a will in English form dealing with his immovable property in England. He put all his freehold estate, which was situated in England, in trust to English trustees. This trust was for sale and conversion with the power to

1 [1923] 1 Ch 192; *Re Hoyles* [1911] 1 Ch 179.

postpone such sale and conversion for as long as they thought fit. The will provided that the proceeds of the sale and the rents and profits for the part of the estate which remained unsold were to be held in trust for his son subject to an annuity to the testator's wife for life. The question arose whether the proceeds of sale and the rents and profits were interests in movable or immovable property.

Russell J held that where an interest in the proceeds of sale of English freeholds was subject to a trust and the property was for sale but not yet sold, this was an interest in immovable property in accordance with English law, the *lex situs*.

9.3 Jurisdictional issues relating to immovable property

Disputes relating to rights in immovable property are subject to the exclusive jurisdiction of the court where the immovable property is situated – the court of a *situs*. This is the case both under Brussels I[2] and the Lugano Convention[3] and under the traditional English rules of jurisdiction.[4]

9.3.1 Brussels I rules

Article 22(1) grants exclusive jurisdiction for proceedings having as their object rights *in rem* in immovable property or tenancies in immovable property to the courts of the Member State where the immovable property is situated. This means that the English courts have no jurisdiction to hear cases relating to rights *in rem* or to tenancies in immovable property where the property is situated in another Member State.

The ECJ has interpreted matters relating to **rights *in rem*** to include cases relating to ownership and possession of immovable property. Contract issues such as actions for rescission of a contract for sale of immovable property are not included.[5] Instead these cases are classified as matters relating to personal obligations between the parties.

However, the ECJ has interpreted the exclusive jurisdiction to determine **matters relating to tenancies** to extend well beyond the determination of property matters such as whether a valid tenancy exists. The ECJ has held that the courts of the *situs* also have exclusive jurisdiction to determine matters relating to the personal obligations that a tenancy imposes on a landlord and the tenant.[6]

An exception to the rule in Art 22(1) exists where a short tenancy is concluded for private use for a maximum of six months and **the landlord and tenant are domiciled in the same country**. In such a case, the Member State in which the defendant is domiciled will also have jurisdiction to hear the case. So, for example, where an English landlord leased a holiday villa in Spain to an English holidaymaker, both the English courts and the Spanish courts would have jurisdiction to hear a dispute over the tenancy.

Under the modified regulation in Sched 4 of the Civil Judgments and Jurisdiction Act,[7] where the immovable property is situated in Scotland or Northern Ireland the court of that jurisdiction will have exclusive jurisdiction to hear the dispute.

---

2 Council Regulation (EC) No 44/2001 [2001] OJ L12/1.

3 See Chapter 3.

4 See Chapter 4.

5 C518/99 *Gaillard v Chekili* [2001] IL Pr 474; C115/88 *Riechert v Dresdner Bank* [1990] ECR I-27; C343/04 *Land Oberosterreich v CEZ* [2006] ECR I-4557.

6 C241/83 *Rosler v Rottwinkel* [1986] QB 33; *Jareet and Others v Barclays Bank plc* [1997] 3 WLR 654; C8/98 *Dansommer A/S v Gotz* [2000] ECR I-393.

7 Sched 4 Rule 11(a)(i).

Article 22(1) does not grant exclusive jurisdiction to non-Member State countries where immovable property is situated outside the European Union. If there are no EU domiciliaries involved in such a dispute, jurisdiction will be determined by the national rules of the court hearing the dispute. As examined in Chapter 3, it is unclear whether Brussels I allows a court with jurisdiction under the general rules of Brussels I[8] to decline jurisdiction over a dispute relating to property issues in favour of the court of the *situs*, for example, if a Spanish claimant issues proceedings in England against an English domiciliary and the nature of the dispute is a tenancy in property situated in Morocco.

The English courts have indicated that in such cases they will stay proceedings in favour of the third-country state.[9] It is unclear if this is compatible with Brussels I. This practice is compatible with Brussels I recast if there are pending proceedings in the third-country state and the provisions of Arts 33 and 34 are satisfied.[10]

If a case where property rights are in dispute is not a 'civil or commercial' case, the case will fall outside the scope of Brussels I. So a dispute about matrimonial property rights is not governed by the rules of Brussels I.[11]

9.3.2 English traditional rules: the rule in *Mocambique*

The jurisdiction of the English courts to hear disputes relating to property rights where the **immovable property is situated in a country that is not part of the EU or EFTA** is governed by the traditional rules of English law.

Under the common law, English courts have no jurisdiction to hear cases relating to title or rights of possession in real property that is outside the jurisdiction.[12] The court of the *situs* is considered to be the only court with competent jurisdiction to determine title to the property or the right to possession of the property. This common law rule was restated by the House of Lords in *British South Africa v Companhia de Mocambique*.[13] It is considered to be a breach of international comity to try issues of foreign land and also problematic, as the court would not be able to enforce any orders that were made.[14]

In *British South Africa v Companhia de Mocambique*,[15] the House of Lords held that this common law rule prevented the English courts from hearing disputes for the recovery of damages for trespass or other torts to such immovable property. The tort of trespass to land requires the claimant to show that there has been an unjustified interference with the possession of land. This means that a court might have to determine property interests as a preliminary issue if this is challenged by the parties.

This ruling prevented the courts from hearing disputes connected to foreign immovable property, even where the action had nothing to do with ownership or use of land but concerned the recovery of damage for trespass to foreign land.[16] The bar on hearing cases involving trespass to foreign land was limited in *Re Polly Peck International plc*.[17] Here, the claimant owned properties in Northern Cyprus. After the Turkish invasion of North Cyprus these properties were appropriated by law by the Turkish Cypriot Authorities. The claimants alleged that since the appropriation, Polly

8 Perhaps as the domicile of the defendant, Art 2.
9 *Ferrexpo AG v Gilson Investments Ltd* [2012] EWHC 721 (Comm).
10 See below.
11 See Chapter 11.
12 *British South Africa v Companhia de Mocambique* [1893] AC 602 backed up by s 30 of the Civil Jurisdiction and Judgments Act 1982.
13 [1893] AC 602.
14 See *R Griggs Group Ltd v Evans (No 2)* [2004] EWHC 1088 (Ch) [72]–[78].
15 [1893] AC 602.
16 *St Pierre v South American Stores ltd* [1936] 1 KB 382; *Hesperides Hotels Ltd v Aegean Turkish Holiday Ltd* [1978] AC 508.
17 [1997] 1 LS Gaz R 23.

Peck, a company in administration, had trespassed on their property by actively encouraging Polly Peck's subsidiaries to occupy it without authority. Whether or not Polly Peck had trespassed was dependent on whether the Turkish Cypriot law appropriating the property was recognised. The defendant objected to the jurisdiction of the English courts, claiming that case was 'principally concerned with a question of the title, or the right to possession of the properties' rather than the tort of trespass.

The court held that although it was necessary to show that the claimants had a right of possession, in order to prove the tort of trespass this was not the only substantial question to be answered. This case raised a number of other serious issues such as whether Polly Peck itself had committed an act of trespass and whether the actions of its subsidiaries could impose liability on Polly Peck. Therefore the English courts had jurisdiction to hear the case. Rattee J stated that the purpose of s 30(1) of the 1982 Act was to preserve the *Mocambique* rule for cases where the real issue in the proceedings was the question of title to, or the right to possession of, foreign land and all other questions were merely incidental.

Today, s 30 of the Civil Jurisdiction and Justice Act 1982 permits the English courts to hear cases for torts affecting immovable property even where the property is outside the UK, unless the proceedings are principally concerned with a question of the title to, or the right to possession of, that property.

9.3.2.1 Exceptions to the *Mocambique* rule

While English courts may not generally determine a question of title or right of possession in foreign immovable property, the common law permits the courts to hear proceedings based on (1) **personal obligations between the parties** in relation to foreign law and also (2) cases based on the **administration of trusts of estates** of foreign land.

9.3.2.2 Personal obligations between the parties

Where the claim is based on a personal obligation based on contract or an equitable obligation between the parties, the English courts could have *in personam* jurisdiction according to the traditional rules.[18] However, the result of a ruling might affect the ownership or rights in possession of foreign property, something the English courts have no jurisdiction to determine. For example, if the claimant issues proceedings for a breach of contract for sale of land and the English court determines that the contract has indeed been breached, the court has *in personam* jurisdiction over a properly served defendant to compel him to give effect to his obligation under the contract. This will affect the ownership of the foreign land. Lord Esher noted that this power of the English courts seemed to allow the court to indirectly rule on the ownership of foreign property, something it would not dare to do directly.[19]

This long-standing exception[20] was examined in *Penn v Lord Baltimore*.[21] In this case, a contract was made in England between the claimant and the defendant to settle the boundaries of the provinces of Pennsylvania and Maryland. The parties had submitted to the jurisdiction of the English court. Lord Hardwicke granted specific performance of the contract, which had been executed in England under seal. This created a personal obligation between the parties which could be granted specific performance by the Court of Equity. The obligation could not be enforced directly *in rem* as a charge against the land, but could be enforced against the defendant by process for contempt of court.[22]

18 See Chapter 4.
19 *British South Africa v Companhia de Mocambique* [1892] 2 QB 358, 404–405.
20 *Arglasse v Muschamp* (1682) 1 Vern 76.
21 (1750) 1 Ves Sen 444; 27 ER 1132.
22 Ibid 1139.

In *Deschamps v Miller*,[23] Parker J explained that a personal obligation may arise out of contract or implied contract or out of a fiduciary relationship or because one of the parties had committed fraud or engaged in other conduct which is unconscionable. In such a case, equity will intervene to remedy the unconscionable behaviour and jurisdiction does not depend on the location of the immovable property that is the subject of the obligation. The English courts may assume jurisdiction *in personam* in cases of trusts, applications for specific performance of contract, foreclosure, or redemption of mortgages or in the case of land obtained by the defendant by fraud or other such unconscionable conduct.

In *Massey v Glover*[24] the court had jurisdiction under equitable jurisdiction to order a South African domiciliary to co-operate by carrying out actions to procure the sale of an estate in South Africa. The defendant applied for a stay of proceedings on the basis of *forum non conveniens*[25] but the court held that England was the most appropriate forum as all relevant witnesses were in England and all the relevant dealings between the parties had taken place in England.

The English courts will not grant specific performance if the specific performance cannot be effected because the law of *situs* does not permit or did not enable the defendant to do what the English court has ordered. In such cases it would be useless and unjust to direct the defendant to do the act.[26]

In *R Griggs Group Ltd v Evans (No 2)*[27] the court held that specific performance could be permitted where the defendant had sold the property to a third-party purchaser with notice of the prior obligation between the claimant and the defendant.[28]

9.3.2.3 Administration of an estate of a deceased person or a trust

Where the English court is asked to determine the administration of the estate of a deceased person through intestacy or through a will, the court will have jurisdiction to determine a dispute over title to foreign land that forms part of the estate. This may require the determination of property interests or rights *in rem*. This will also be the case where the court is asked to administer a trust. It is essential that the trust or estate consists of movables or immovables in England as well as the immovable property outside England.

The reason for this exception is unclear, as the court is not enforcing any personal obligation but is instead determining questions of title to foreign immovable property.

9.3.2.4 Extension of the rule in *Mocambique* to intellectual property rights

Cases which involve disputes over property rights in movable property are governed by the ordinary rules of jurisdiction under Brussels I and the traditional English rules of jurisdiction. However, the rule in *Mocambique* has been extended to cases involving intellectual property rights.

In *Tyburn Productions Ltd v Conan Doyle*[29] the court was asked to determine whether any intellectual property rights existed in the United States that would be asserted to prevent a film about Sherlock Holmes from being distributed in that country. Vinelott J extended the rule in *Mocambique* to intellectual property rights, holding that the question of whether US intellectual property rights existed was not justiciable in England.

Some intellectual property rights must be registered or deposited. Under the Brussels Convention and Brussels I, exclusive jurisdiction is given to the courts of the place in which such a

23 [1908] 1 Ch 856.
24 [2006] EWHC 2323 (Ch).
25 See Chapter 4.
26 *Re Courtney* [1835–42] All ER Rep 415.
27 [2004] EWHC 1088 (Ch).
28 Ibid [111].
29 [1991] Ch 75.

right is registered or deposited for any proceedings concerned with either *the registration or the validity* of the intellectual property right.

In *Pearce v Ove Arup Partnership*[30] the claimant brought a claim for breach of Dutch copyrights and UK copyrights, alleging that the defendant had used his drawing when designing a public building in Rotterdam. The defendant argued that the claim should be struck out as, following *Mocambique*, torts on foreign intellectual property rights could not be heard by the English courts. The court held that limitations placed on the English courts to hear claims for foreign trespass to land had now been lifted by s 30 of the Civil Jurisdiction and Justice Act 1982. In addition, there was no case law to suggest that the English court did not have jurisdiction to hear a case relating to an *infringement* of a foreign intellectual property right.[31]

The extension of the *Mocambique* rule to intellectual property rights was overruled by the Supreme Court in *Lucasfilm Ltd v Ainsworth*.[32] This case involved a dispute about whether the sale of *Star Wars* stormtrooper helmets in England infringed foreign copyright. The Supreme Court held that Brussels I only assigned exclusive jurisdiction to the state where intellectual property rights were registered, in cases concerning the registration or validity of those intellectual property rights. Brussels I plainly envisaged that litigation for infringement of foreign intellectual property rights should be possible as the modern trend was to allow such litigation.[33]

The Supreme Court confirmed that all that now remains of the *Mocambique* rule is that the English courts had no jurisdiction in proceedings for infringement of rights in a foreign land where the proceedings are 'principally concerned with a question of the title, or the right to possession, of that property'.[34] While the rationality for the *Mocambique* rule could be applied to patents, it was very difficult to see how it could apply to copyright.[35] The Supreme Court concluded that *Tyburn Productions Ltd v Conan Doyle* had been wrongly decided.

9.4 Applicable law

The law applicable to property aspects of disputes relating both to movable and immovable property rights is the law of the *situs*.

Where the movable property has been passed **by succession**, the validity of transfer is determined by the law of the deceased's domicile at the time of death.[36]

9.4.1 Applicable law to transfers of immovable property

There are relatively few English cases on the validity of foreign immovable property rights as most of these cases are non-justicable under the *Mocambique* rule.

The general rule is that the *lex situs* determines the question of both formal and essential validity of property transfers. The rationale behind the rule is that uniformity with the *lex situs* is crucial. In reality, a piece of land can only be dealt with in a manner permitted by the law of the country in which it is situated. This rule has been criticised as being too broad in the succession context and this criticism is discussed below.

30 [2000] Ch 403.
31 See further *R Griggs Group Ltd v Evans (No 2)* [2004] EWHC 1088 (Ch).
32 [2011] UKSC 39.
33 Ibid [108].
34 Ibid [105].
35 Ibid [106].
36 See below.

9.4.1.1 Formal validity

For a transfer of foreign immovable property to be considered valid by the English courts, the transfer must comply with the formalities required by the domestic law of the *situs*. This would include requirements that the transfer be under deed or that it is registered.

In *Adams v Clutterbuck*[37] a conveyance for the right of shooting over land in Scotland was made in England between two domiciled Englishmen. English law required such instruments to be made under seal. Scots law did not. It was held that the instrument was valid because it was valid under the *lex situs*.

9.4.1.2 Essential validity

The essential validity of a transfer of immovable property is also governed by the *lex situs*. This will determine whether gifts to charities are valid,[38] whether an estate can actually be legally created, and whether a transfer complies with the rules on perpetuities and accumulations.[39]

Separate rules govern the validity of the will or contracts to transfer immovable property. In both cases a distinction must be made between the applicable law to determine the validity of the will[40] or contract and applicable law determining whether that will or contract has effected a valid property transfer.

9.4.1.3 Validity of a contract to transfer property

Where an interest in immovable property is transferred by contract, questions relating to the validity of the contract will be determined by Rome I. Questions relating to the validity of the property transfer will be governed by the *lex situs*. For example, A contracts with B to sell to B a plot in a foreign country. The contract creates obligations between the parties under the contract, the result of which is to transfer interest in immovable property.

Article 9(3) of Rome I allows for the mandatory provisions of the law of the country where the obligations arising out of the contract are to be performed to be given effect where they render performance of the contract to be unlawful. When a court is considering enforcement of a contract for a transfer of rights *in rem*, the enforcing court may have to consider if a transfer of property will be lawful in the *lex situs*.

In *Bank of Africa v Cohen*[41] the Court of Appeal laid down a rule that the capacity of a person to enter into a contract relating to immovables is governed by the *lex situs*.[42] In this case, a married woman, domiciled in England, made a contract with an English bank whereby she agreed to mortgage her land in South Africa as security for loans to her husband. She gave her documents of title to the bank. The bank was unable to register its interest in the plots of land in South Africa, and the property remained registered in Mrs Cohen's name. The bank sought specific performance of the agreement to transfer the property or alternatively damages. The defendant raised the defence that, by South African law at that time, married women had no capacity to give security for their husband's debts and so the agreement to transfer the property interests was void.

This case involved a contract relating to ownership of immovable property. Mrs Cohen had no capacity to transfer property under the *lex situs* and so the property transfer was invalid.

Specific performance of the contract could not be ordered as it was not possible for the land to be transferred. The court considered whether the bank could sue on the contractual obligation for breach of promise. The court held that there could be no right to damages for not performing a

---

37 (1883) 10 QBD 403.
38 *Duncan v Lawson* (1889) 41 Ch D 394.
39 *Freke v Carbery* (1873) LR 16 Eq 461.
40 See below.
41 [1909] 2 Ch 129.
42 Rather than the *lex domicilii* which is more usually the case. See Chapter 7.

promise to do an act when in reality such a promise could not be made because the promisor could not make it.[43]

The Court of Appeal upheld the defence on the basis that Mrs Cohen's capacity to enter into the contract was governed by the *lex situs* and accordingly the contract was void.

9.4.1.4 *Renvoi*

The doctrine of *renvoi* is applicable to cases involving immovable property.[44] This means that when the court applies the law of the *situs* they will apply both the domestic law of that country and also its conflict-of-laws rules. This may refer the dispute to the law of a third country. The reason for applying the doctrine of *renvoi* to disputes involving immovable property is that there are strong policy considerations in favour of deciding the dispute in the same way as it would have been decided by the courts of the *situs*. It is particularly common in succession cases and is examined in the next section.

9.5 Transfers of movables

The *lex situs* applies to determine the validity of a transfer of movable property between two living individuals. Establishing the *situs* of a movable can be more difficult than establishing the *situs* for immovable property.

Movable property can be subdivided into two categories: tangible movables and intangible movables.

9.5.1 Tangible movables

Tangible movables are items such as goods, personal property and other physical things. Ownership of tangible movables can be transferred by gifting them, by handing them over or through a contract of sale. There is no need for separate formal transfer. Most disputes between parties to a sale of goods relate to the rights and liabilities of the parties under the contract and are determined by the applicable law to the contract.[45]

If there is a question of ownership to be determined, such as whether the seller had title of the goods sold or whether the transaction worked to transfer title, the *lex situs* of the movable property at the time of the purported transfer of property rights will apply. This is not necessarily the same law as the law that determines whether the contract of sale was valid. Unlike immovable property, tangible movables can be transferred from country to country. Some questions arise as to the *lex situs* when goods are sold while in transit.

The basic rule is that the *lex situs* at the time of the disposition of the property determines the validity of any property transfer. If the movable property was validly transferred according to its *lex situs* at the time of the disposition then that transfer would be recognised in England. This rule has been justified on the basis that a purchaser ought to satisfy himself that he has obtained good title by the law prevailing in the place of purchase. An owner who wishes to ensure he is not deprived of his property by a foreign law can do his best to keep that property in his own country.[46]

In *Cammell v Sewell*[47] a cargo of timber was shipped from Russia to Hull in England on a Prussian ship. The vessel was seriously damaged off the Norwegian coast, so the master of the ship sold the

---

43 *Bank of Africa v Cohen* [1909] 2 Ch 129, 144.
44 See Chapter 1.
45 See Chapter 7.
46 *Macmillan Inc v Bishopsgate Investment Trust plc (No 3)* [1996] 1 WLR 387, 400.
47 (1860) 5 H & N 728.

damaged timber without obtaining the owner's consent. The goods were subsequently brought to England and sold to the defendants. On an action by the original owners challenging the defendant's ownership, the English courts held that the transfer of title was valid in Norway. The timber was in Norway when the transfer happened. This meant that the transfer would be recognised in England and so the claim failed.

In *Winkworth v Christie Manson and Woods*[48] works of art were stolen from the claimant's house in England and taken to Italy, where they were sold to the second defendant. Subsequently, the works were sent back to England to be auctioned by the first defendant. By Italian law, the second defendant had obtained good title when he bought the paintings in Italy. The English court held that, as the *lex situs* at the time of the disposition, Italian law, recognised the transfer as valid, the second defendant had obtained good title. The application of Italian law was justified on the grounds that the transaction had occurred in Italy and nothing had occurred in England afterwards to deprive the holder of this title. The claim failed.

In *Glencore International AG v Metro Trading International Inc* (No 2)[49] the title to a consignment of oil held in storage in the United Arab Emirates was in question. Glencore had deposited the oil with a storage company which had become insolvent. Glencore alleged that the storage company had sold the oil on to third parties and claimed against the third parties in conversion. The sale of the oil to the third parties was valid under the law of the UAE. The issue before the court was whether title was governed by English law, which was the law applicable to the contract of storage, or the law of the United Arab Emirates, as the *lex situs* of the oil. Moore-Bick J held that there was strong support for the adoption of a *lex situs* rule in all cases which complied with the practical considerations of trade and commerce.[50]

9.5.2 Intangible movables

An intangible movable is an interest which is not directly related to a physical object such as shares, patents, copyrights, contractual debts, bank accounts, bonds, negotiable instruments[51] and other choses in action.[52] Mortgages and leases are considered by English classification rules to be immovable property.

9.5.2.1 *Situs* of intangible movables

Most intangible movables have no physical existence although some, like negotiable instruments or registered intellectual property rights, are notionally embedded into a document or an instrument such as a share certificate. It is therefore difficult to ascertain the *situs* of intangible movables. The courts have developed a series of artificial rules to determine *situs*.

For example, in *Macmillan Inc v Bishopsgate Investment Trust plc* (No 3)[53] the court held that the *situs* of shares in a company was the place of incorporation of that company. In *Libyan Arab Foreign Bank v Bankers Trust Co*[54] the court held that the *situs* of a bank account was the country in which the account was based.

The approach of English conflicts of law is to treat an intangible movable as a tangible movable as much as possible by giving it an artificial *situs*. This approach has been criticised by commentators

48 [1980] 1 All ER 1121.
49 [2001] CLC 1732, [2001] 1 All ER (Comm) 103.
50 Ibid [32]. See also *Air Foyle Ltd v Center Capital Ltd* [2002] EWHC 2535 (Comm).
51 A negotiable instrument is a document guaranteeing the payment of a specific amount of money, either on demand or at a set time.
52 A chose in action is a property right that can only be enforced through legal action.
53 [1996] 1 WLR 387.
54 [1989] QB 728.

such as Goode and Hartley,[55] who suggest that a direct rule such as the debtor's residence or place of business would be more appropriate.

9.5.2.2 Transfer by assignment

Intangible movables are not transferred in the same way as tangible movables as they cannot be physically delivered. Instead they are assigned. When it comes to disputes about intangible property there may be questions over whether the transaction worked to transfer title.

Intangible property rights can be transferred by assignment. Most intangible property rights relate to an obligation: a debt that must be paid or a payment that will be made on a future contingency. This obligation is owed by a debtor to the creditor. For example, the balance of a bank account is a monetary obligation that the bank, as a debtor, owes to the account holder who is the creditor. The bank account is a chose in action. If the bank does not pay on request, the account holder can sue on the debt.

An assignment allows the creditor to transfer the benefit of the obligation to a third party called an assignee. If a bank account debt is transferred, the assignee is given the benefit of the claim against the bank under the contract between the account holder and the bank. The holder of the bank account is known as the assignor. Assignments can be used to make an outright transfer or merely to create a security interest in the claim.

A distinction must be drawn between the validity of the transaction by which the intangible interest was created in the first place (the contract between the bank and the customer), the validity of the transaction by which the right was assigned (the contract between the assignor and the assignee) and the question of whether the property transfer is effective. Many of these questions are now determined by the rules of Rome I.[56]

The obligations between the original debtor and creditor are governed by the law that created the obligation. This is usually a contract and so the applicable law is determined by Rome I. However, the initial obligation or claim may also have been created by tort or equity.

Article 14(1) of Rome I provides that the mutual rights and obligations of the assignor and assignee under a voluntary assignment or contractual subrogation are governed by the law applicable to the contract between the assignor and assignee.

The law governing some of the property aspects of the assignment is now governed by the rules of Rome I. Article 14(2) designates that the applicable law to determine whether or not the initial obligation was assignable will be the law governing the assigned claim. Where the original claim was a contract, this will be the law applicable to that contract. Under Art 14(2) the law governing the assigned claim also determines the relationship between the assignee and the debtor, the conditions under which the assignment or subrogation can be invoked and whether the debtor's obligations have been discharged.

In *Raiffeisen Zentralbank Ostterreich v Five Star Trading*[57] there had been a collision at sea which had sunk a ship and destroyed cargo owned by AFS. The owners of the colliding ship had insured their ship against collisions under a policy underwritten by a French company and governed by English law. The benefit of the insurance claim had been assigned by the shipowners to RZO as security for a loan.

AFS obtained provisional attachment orders in France against the owners of the ship which had caused the collision in respect of any insurance proceeds. The key question for the court was whether the insurance policy taken out by the owners of the ship and underwritten by a French

---

55 R Goode and E McKendrick, *Goode on Commercial Law* (4th Ed, Penguin, 2010) 1240; T Hartley, *International Commercial Litigation* (Cambridge University Press, 2009) 720–742.

56 Council Regulation (EC) 593/2008 [2008] L177/6.

57 [2001] EWCA Civ 68.

insurance company had been validly assigned to RZO. If so, the attachment order obtained by AFS could not be enforced.

The court at first instance held that a valid assignment of the insurance policy had been made, even though French formalities had not been complied with. The court characterised the dispute as a contractual dispute.

AFS submitted that the issue was a proprietary one rather than a contractual one since it related to whether the assignment of the insurance policy was valid against third parties. This would need to be resolved by the *lex situs* of the insurance policy, which would be France. Under French law, the assignment was formally invalid, as no bailiff authorisation had been obtained. This would mean that the attachment order would take precedence over the purported assignment.

Lord Mance held that Art 12(2) of the Rome Convention determined the applicable law for the dispute. The law applicable to the original contract of insurance governed the issue of assignment, the relationship between assignee and debtor together with the conditions under which the assignment could be invoked as against the debtor. The assignment was valid as an equitable assignment under English law.

9.5.2.3 The effectiveness of an assignment against a third party and the priority of successive assignments

Rome I does not designate the law governing the effectiveness of an assignment as against a third part or the priority of successive assignments. At the time of drafting the Regulation, agreement could not be secured on these issues. At the moment, national rules on conflict of laws apply to determine the effectiveness of an assignment against a third party and the priority of claims.

In English law, the question of priority of claims is determined by the law of the *situs* of the intangible movable. In *Macmillan Inc v Bishopsgate Investment Trust plc* (No 3),[58] Macmillan had transferred shares in Berlitz to Bishopsgate as security for private loans made to him by the three defendants. These shares were to be held in trust by Bishopsgate. The shares were later transferred into a central depository system in New York and subsequently used as security for loans to finance the Maxwell group of companies. This was done without the claimant's knowledge. Macmillan took an action against eight companies seeking return of the shares in Berlitz or compensation. He claimed that he was still beneficially entitled to the shares and this was binding on the eight companies, who merely held the shares on trust for Macmillan. The issue for the court was whether the defendants obtained good title to the shares by being purchasers for value in good faith without notice.

At first instance, the court held that the issue of priority should be determined by the place where the transfers to the Maxwell group of companies had happened, which was New York. The shares were considered negotiable instruments under New York law. This meant that property transfer was validly effected by delivery alone. The eight companies had taken delivery of the shares through the depository system and had no prior notice of Macmillan's claim on the shares. Under English law the requirements for notice were stricter. The application of New York law meant that Macmillan could not recover. Macmillian appealed.

The Court of Appeal held that the issue as to who has title to shares in a company should be decided by the law of the *situs*. For shares, this is the place where the company is incorporated. The court applied New York law as the law of the place of incorporation of Berlitz.

Article 27(2) of Rome I called for a report on the question of the effectiveness of an assignment or subrogation of a claim against third parties and the priority of the assigned or subrogated claim over a right of another person to be completed by June 2010. In 2011, the British

58 [1996] 1 WLR 387.

Institution of International and Comparative Law completed a study that will form the basis of this report.[59] The study called for a harmonised conflict of laws rule for all proprietary aspects of assignments and proposed a number of options.[60]

9.5.2.4 Involuntary assignments of intangible movables

Rome I does not determine applicable law for involuntary assignments of intangible property such as where a court attaches an order to a debt. The English courts have refused to enforce an involuntary assignment where it could not be carried out under the law of the situs.

In *Societe Eram Shipping Co Ltd v Compagnie Internationale de Navigation*[61] the judgment creditor sought to enforce a judgment obtained in a French court and registered in England against judgment debtors who were resident in Hong Kong. Execution of the order was sought against the judgment debtor's bank account held in Hong Kong, but there was a registered branch of the bank in London. The judgment creditor had obtained a third-party debt order from the English court against the bank. This was being appealed.

The court held that the credit balance was situated in Hong Kong and governed by local law. Hong Kong law did not recognise such an order made in England against a debt situated in Hong Kong.

The English court had never before made a third-party debt order against a foreign debt.[62] The court held that a third-party debt order was a proprietary remedy which operates by way of attachment against the property of the judgment debtor – in this case the balance of the bank account.[63] The court held that it was not open to the English court to make such an order where the order would not be carried out under the law that governed the balance of the bank account. The court had no jurisdiction to do so, or if it did it should use its discretion to refuse to make the order.[64]

9.6 Transfer of property rights through succession

Where property is transferred on the death of an individual, this will occur either by the application of a will or through the rules of intestacy.

A valid will determines who is entitled to the deceased's property. It does not itself transfer the property. In England, on death, the property vests in the personal representatives of the deceased, who hold the property in trust. Where the deceased has left a will, the executor of the estate, who is named in the will, must get a **grant of probate** to enable him to transfer the property according to the testator's wishes. Where the deceased has died intestate, his personal representatives will apply to the English court for **letters of administration**. The authority will be granted according to English rules.[65] The English grant vests authority only for property in England. If the deceased has property outside England the personal representative may have to take further steps to recover property abroad. Once the authority has been granted, the personal representative clears the debts of the estate and then transfers the property according to the will or the rules of intestacy.

59 BIICL, 'Study on the question of effectiveness of an assignment or subrogation of a claim against third parties and the priority of the assigned or subrogated claim over a right of another person', available at http://ec.europa.eu/justice/civil/files/report_assignment_en.pdf (accessed 15 May 2013).

60 Ibid 46–47.

61 [2003] UKHL 30.

62 See *Deutsche Sahchtbau und Tiefbohrgesellschaft mbH v Ras Al-Khaimah National Oil Co* [1990] 1 AC 295.

63 *Societe Eram Shipping Co Ltd v Compagnie Internationale de Navigation* [2003] UKHL 30 [24].

64 Ibid [25].

65 Where the deceased died domiciled in another country, the English court may grant authority to the representative who has been appointed by the court of the deceased's domicile: Non-Contentious Probate Rules SI 1987/2024 r 30.

9.6.1 Jurisdiction

Once a person has obtained an English grant of probate or administration, the English courts may determine a number of issues related to the will or intestacy. The English High Court will have jurisdiction to determine whether the will is a valid testamentary disposition, what is the construction and effect of the will, and who is entitled to succeed to the property and generally to determine any question with regard to the succession. This means that the court has jurisdiction to determine title of movables and immovables wherever situated and is an exception to the *Mocambique* rule.[66]

The English court will respect the rulings of foreign courts in relation to movables of their domiciliaries situated in England[67] but will not give any effect to foreign rulings relating to immovable property in England.

The English courts will also respect rulings of foreign courts in relation to movables situated in that country regardless of where the deceased was domiciled.[68]

9.6.2 Applicable law to testamentary succession

Testamentary succession to **movable property** is governed by the law of the domicile of the deceased. The law of the domicile will determine whether the gift is essentially valid. Some issues are determined by the domicile of the deceased at the time of his death, while other issues are determined by the domicile of the deceased at the time the will was executed.

Testamentary succession to **immovable property** is governed by the law of the *situs*. This means that the essential validity of a gift of immovables will be governed by the *lex situs*.

9.6.2.1 Validity of wills

Under English domestic law, a will must satisfy certain formalities before it has effect. For example, it must be signed in the presence of two witnesses. However, the English courts will also treat a will as properly executed if it conforms to the formal requirements of any connected foreign law.

Under s 1 of the Wills Act 1963[69] a will is treated as properly executed if it conforms to the domestic law of the place in which it was executed or the law of the testator's domicile either at the time of execution of the will or time of death, or the law of the testator's nationality, or the law of the state of the testator's habitual residence.

The capacity of a testator to make a will is determined by the law of his or her domicile at the time the will was executed.[70]

In English law, a will may be voluntarily revoked either by making a fresh will or by destroying a will with the intention of revoking it. The issue of whether the will has been revoked by the subsequent marriage of the testator was held by the Court of Appeal in *Re Martin*[71] to be determined by the law of the testator's domicile at the time of the marriage.

9.6.2.2 What does the will mean?

Issues relating to the construction and meaning of a will are determined by the law intended by the testator. For movable property this is presumed to be the law of the domicile of the testator at the time of making the will[72] unless a contrary intention can be shown. This is justified on the ground

---

66 See above.
67 *Re Trufort* (1887) 36 ChD 600, 611.
68 *Al-Bassam v Al-Bassam* [2004] EWCA Civ 857 [26]–[27].
69 Which implements the International Convention on the Formal Validity of Wills 1961.
70 *In the Estate of Fuld (No 3)* [1968] P 675.
71 [1900] P 211.
72 S 4 of the Wills Act 1963 provides that the construction of a will shall not be altered by reason of any change in domicile of the testator after the execution of the will.

that it is reasonable to assume that, when the testator made the will, he or she had the law of his or her own domicile in contemplation.

For example, in *Re Cunnington*[73] the testator left the residue of his estate to be divided between ten residuary legatees. If any of these ten legatees were to die during the testator's lifetime, the will provided that the share in the residue would pass to the issue of the legatee. Two of the legatees died during the testator's lifetime but they left no issue. The testator, a French domiciliary, died in France but the will was proved in England, the residue of the estate was in England and all the legatees were English. Under French law, the shares of the two deceased legatees would be distributed between the remaining eight. Under English law, the shares of the deceased legatees would lapse into intestacy. Eve J held that French law should apply unless there was a clear intention to the contrary, and here no contrary intention could be found.

In *Re Price*[74] the testatrix had stipulated that her will was to be 'considered in England the same as in France'. The court held that the will had been written with reference to the law of England as well as the law of France. The testatrix had contemplated that English law would apply, albeit she was domiciled in France. The court applied the English rules of construction to the will.[75]

In *Re Duke of Wellington*,[76] the deceased made a Spanish will by which he had bequeathed his lands in Spain and all associated chattels and rents to the person who became the next Duke of Wellington and Ciudad Rodrigo. He also had an English will by which he had bequeathed his personal property in England and the residue of his property in Spain to the Duke of Wellington. As it happened, the title of Duke of Wellington went to one individual and the title of Duke of Ciudad Rodrigo to another.

The court held that the succession of the movable property under the Spanish will was governed by English law as the law of the domicile. The succession of the immovable property was governed by Spanish law as the *lex situs*. The court used the doctrine of *renvoi* to apply English law to the succession of the immovable property, as Spanish law would apply the law of the nationality of the deceased, and adhered to the principle of unity of estate. The court applied English law to the question of interpretation and granted all of the property to the Duke of Wellington.

A will governing immovable property cannot be constructed under the law of the testator's domicile if such an action would be illegal by the law of the *situs*.[77] For example, in *Philipson-Stow v IRC*,[78] even though the testator declared that his will was to be governed by English law, English estate duty could not be levied against his shares in South African land.

9.6.2.3 Validity of gifts under the will

The material validity of a gift of **movables** is determined by the law of the testator's domicile at the time of death. This will determine whether the testator is required to leave a certain share of his estate to his dependents. For example, in *Re Groos*[79] a Dutch woman with English domicile made a will in the Netherlands to the effect that her husband would inherit her movable property except for the legitimate portion to which her children were entitled. By Dutch law the legitimate portion was three-quarters of the estate. Under English law it was nothing. The English court applied the English law as the law of the testatrix's domicile at the time of death.

In *Al-Bassam v Al-Bassam*[80] a wealthy national from Saudi Arabia died while living in London. His wife sought a declaration that he died domiciled in England, in which case she would be entitled

73 [1924] 1 Ch 68.
74 [1900] 1 Ch 442.
75 See also *Dellar v Zivy* [2007] EWHC 2266 (Ch), [2007] IL Pr 868.
76 [1947] Ch 506.
77 *Re Miller* [1914] 1 Ch 511.
78 [1961] AC 727.
79 [1915] 1 Ch 572.
80 [2004] EWCA Civ 857.

to the whole estate. If the deceased had died domiciled in Saudi Arabia or Iraq, as claimed by the son, the wife would be entitled to only one-third of the estate.

For gifts of **immovable property**, the material validity of the gift is determined by the *lex situs*. In *Re Ross*[81] the testatrix, a British subject, died domiciled in Italy. Her wills in respect of her English and Italian estates excluded her son from the list of beneficiaries. This was permitted under English domestic law but was contrary to Italian domestic law, which required her to leave one-half of her property to her son.

The son brought an action in the English court contesting the validity of the wills. The English court referred the essential validity of these wills to Italian law in relation to both immovable property as the *lex situs* and the movables as the law of her domicile. Expert evidence showed that an Italian court would have applied the law of the testatrix's nationality, and accordingly the will was held to be valid through the doctrine of *renvoi*.

9.6.3 Applicable law to intestate succession

Different applicable laws also apply to the distribution of immovable property and immovable property under the law of intestate succession.

All **movable property** is distributed in accordance with the **law of the domicile** of the deceased at the time of his or her death. This law will determine such questions as the rights of a surviving spouse, the proportions to be given to other relatives, and so forth. If, however, no relatives or next of kin exist, then movables situated in England would pass to the Crown unless they are claimed by somebody in the state of domicile as the ultimate heir by claim of succession.

In *Re Barnett's Trusts*[82] the deceased died domiciled in Austria, but left property in England. He was heirless, and the Austrian State claimed the property in England as *bona vacantia*. The English court rejected the claim on the ground that it was classified as an issue of administration of the estate rather than a rule of succession, and accordingly the property went to the Crown. However, in *Re Maldonado*[83] similar facts were involved but the foreign state claimed the property in England as the *ultimus heres*. Here, the English court held that the claim was one of succession and accordingly the foreign state was entitled to the property.

The rule that **immovable property** is distributed by the **law of the situs** has been subject to much criticism, as most other countries have one system of intestate succession for all kinds of property.[84] Morris has argued that the rule should be abandoned and where a person dies intestate, all property should be distributed according to the intestacy laws of the deceased's domicile.[85]

In *Re Collens*[86] the deceased died intestate domiciled in Trinidad and Tobago. Most of his estate consisted of property in Trinidad and Tobago and Barbados. He had a small amount of property in the UK, some of which was immovable. He was survived by two ex-wives and seven children. Under the law of the intestate's domicile, a widow was entitled to one-third of the estate absolutely. The children took the rest of the estate equally. There was litigation between the first wife and the second wife in Trinidad as to who was the 'widow'. This ended in a settlement and the first wife took $1 million in satisfaction of her intestacy rights. The first wife then applied to the English courts for her statutory share in the deceased's immovable property in England. The court was reluctant to grant her this as, altogether, it gave her more than a third of the entire estate; however, they were bound to apply the *lex situs* of the immovable property.

81 [1930] 1 Ch 377.
82 [1902] 1 Ch 847.
83 [1954] P 223.
84 Collins et al, *Dicey, Morris & Collins on the Conflict of Laws* (15th Ed, Sweet and Maxwell, 2009), comment 27-018.
85 JHC Morris, 'Intestate Succession to Land in the Conflict of Laws' (1969) 85 LQR 339–371.
86 [1986] 1 All ER 611.

9.7 Cross-border succession and the EU Succession Regulation

Cross-border succession is potentially very complex in English law. The English court will apply the law of a person's domicile to the movable property. Questions can arise when determining a deceased's domicile.[87] As the domicile of origin is very adherent, it is possible for an individual to live abroad for many years but maintain an English domicile. On death they may have a great deal of immovable and movable property situated outside England. In this situation, succession will be governed by two different national laws. The movable property will be subject to English law while immovable property will be governed by the law of *situs*.

This means that English domiciliaries who own property abroad need to be aware of the succession laws of the country where the property is situated and may have to make a separate will for the foreign property. Where succession is governed by different laws, complicated issues relating to inheritance tax can arise.

The European Union has now regulated the conflict-of-laws issues related to succession in the Succession Regulation.[88] The UK, Ireland and Denmark did not take part in the regulation and are not bound by it. This Regulation entered into force on 17 August 2012 and will apply fully from 17 August 2015 in all other Member States.

The UK chose not to take part in the Regulation. The Succession Regulation does make it easier for the testator to predict what law will apply to his foreign property upon death. The House of Lords Committee acknowledged that simplification of the law on cross-border successions, if it could be achieved, would be likely to bring real practical benefits. However, it was felt that the Commission failed to show evidence of the number of cross-border successions and the extent to which complexities and expenses involved in cross-border succession impaired the mobility and exercise of free movement rights within the EU.[89] The potential benefits of the scheme were outweighed by the risk that the Regulation would inadvertently make cases even more complex.[90] Of particular concern was the potential for property transferred during the testator's lifetime to be clawed back to satisfy mandatory succession rights under foreign laws.[91]

The general jurisdictional rule of the Succession Regulation is that the court of the state where the deceased had his habitual residence at the time of death will have jurisdiction to rule on succession matters relating to the entire estate. This includes all property, whether movable or immovable, wherever situated.[92]

The Regulation allows a testator a limited choice of laws to apply to his entire estate both movable and immovable wherever situated.[93] Where no choice of law is made, the law of the country where the deceased had his habitual residence at the time of death will apply.[94]

Decisions relating to succession will be automatically recognisable and enforceable in other EU Member States which have not opted out of the Succession Regulation. The Regulation also creates a new European Certificate of Succession[95] which will allow the deceased's personal representative's

---

87 See Chapter 2.

88 Regulation (EU) No 650/2012 of the European Parliament and of the Council of 4 July 2012 on jurisdiction, applicable law, recognition and enforcement of decisions and acceptance and enforcement of authentic instruments in matters of succession and on the creation of a European Certificate of Succession [2012] OJ L201/107.

89 European Union Committee, *The EU's Regulation on Succession: Report with Evidence* (HL Paper 75 2009–10) available online at http://www.publications.parliament.uk/pa/ld200910/ldselect/ldeucom/75/75.pdf (accessed 15 May 2013) [45].

90 Ibid [45]

91 Ibid [98].

92 Art 4

93 Art 22.

94 Art 21.

95 Art 62

power to execute the will and dispose of assets to be recognised in all EU Member States which are parties to the Succession Regulation.

9.8 Further reading

JM Carruthers, *The Transfer of Property in the Conflict of Laws* (OUP, 2005).
European Union Committee, *The EU's Regulation on Succession: Report with Evidence* (HL Paper 75 2009–10) available at www.publications.parliament.uk/pa/ld200910/ldselect/ldeucom/75/75.pdf (accessed 15 May 2013).
R Frimston, 'Legislative comment: The European Union Succession Regulation (EU) No 650/2012' (2012) 6 *Private Client Business* 213–216.
P Gardiner, '*Lucasfilm Ltd v Ainsworth*: Focus on the justiciability of foreign copyright infringement claims' (2012) 23 *Entertainment Law Review* 23–24.
RM Goode, 'Ownership and obligation in commercial transactions' (1987) 103 LQR 433.
A Hansebout, 'The international dimension of the attachment of debts' [2010] *Dispute Resolution International* 219–228.
T Hartley, 'Choice of law regarding the voluntary assignment of contractual obligations under the Rome I Regulation' (2011) 60 ICLQ 29–56.
M Moshinsky, 'The assignment of debts in the conflict of laws' (1992) 108 LQR 591.
S Nott, 'Title to illegally exported items of historic or artistic worth' (1984) 33 ICLQ 203.
M Ooi, *Shares and Other Securities in the Conflict of Laws* (OUP, 2003).
PJ Rogerson, 'The *situs* of debts in the conflict of laws – illogical, unnecessary and misleading', [1990] *Cambridge Law Journal* 441–460.

Chapter 10

Marriage and Civil Partnership

Chapter Contents

Key Issues:

- The definition of marriage in English domestic law
- The **applicable law** for determining the essential validity of a marriage with foreign elements
- The **applicable law** for determining the formal validity of a marriage with foreign elements
- The legal consequences where a marriage is found to be invalid under foreign law
- The legal recognition of foreign same sex partnerships/ marriages

10.1 Introduction

Marriage is an ancient social and religious institution that creates rights and obligations between the spouses and also changes their personal status in the eyes of the state. Where a marriage is legally recognised, the state will uphold certain mutual rights and obligations between the parties that can be enforced in a court of law, for example, the obligation to provide financial support for one's spouse. Legally recognised marriages also work as a convenient method of social categorisation. The status of marriage can create inheritance rights and immigration rights. Certain states accord taxation benefits to married couples in order to promote marriage and family. While all countries have a legally recognised institution of marriage, the nature of the institution and its consequences may differ from country to country. The right to marry is protected by the European Convention on Human Rights (ECHR).[1] So far this right has been limited to a marriage between a man and woman.[2]

In different countries, different legal restrictions are placed on the categories of people who are permitted to marry or considered in law to have the capacity to get married. For example, in England, same-sex couples are currently precluded from marrying[3] but may enter into a legally recognised civil partnership which is nearly identical to marriage in terms of legal effect.

Each state regulates the formalities required for a couple to get married. These formalities differ from country to country. For example, in some countries a legally recognised marriage may be entered into only by civil procedures. In other countries only religious institutions of marriage may exist and these are considered to be legally binding in that country.

The nature of the commitment of marriage can differ from country to country. In some countries polygamous marriage is permitted; in others a spouse can only enter into a marital relationship that is intended to be monogamous.

English domestic law controls the categories of individuals who are permitted to enter into a marriage in England. It also determines the formalities required in order to enter into marriage where the wedding takes place in England. Under English law, spouses owe each other a financial duty of support, and spouses cannot end the marriage legally without complying with English divorce law. Spouses are granted tax exemptions in respect of inheritance tax and capital gains tax. A spouse of a British citizen can naturalise by complying with different requirements to an unmarried person and the spouse of a person settled in the UK is given entry clearance.

---

1 Art 12 ECHR.

2 *Schalk and Kopf v Austria* (App No 301414/04) [2010] ECHR 995.

3 The Marriage (Same Sex Couples) Bill 2012–13 to 2013–14 is currently before Parliament.

The English courts will have to consider whether a marriage with foreign elements should be given the same effect as a domestic marriage in English law in a number of situations that raise conflict of laws issues. Throughout this chapter the term **foreign marriage** is used to describe a marriage that has either taken place in a foreign country or a marriage where one or both of the parties to the marriage is a foreign domiciliary.

The foreign marriage may be of a type that is unknown to the English domestic law such as a polygamous marriage. One of the parties to the marriage may have been precluded from marrying according to a **connected foreign law**. For example, the English courts may have to consider the validity of marriage between two Texan first cousins, a class of relatives that are prohibited from marrying in many states in the USA although not in the UK. Alternatively, the spouses may be precluded from marrying under English law. For example, the spouses may be a same-sex couple who have married under Dutch law.

When considering whether such marriages are legally valid for English purposes, the English courts must decide what system of **applicable law** to apply to this determination. For example, when deciding whether to attach a financial duty to support to a marriage between American spouses from Texas who are first cousins, should the court consider the marriage valid because it complies with English law or invalid because it does not comply with the law of Texas?

The rules determining whether a marriage with foreign elements will be recognised in England have developed from the common law. As such, the case law is not entirely consistent but general rules and principles can be identified. Policy plays a large role in the case law as the English courts have tended to uphold the status of long-standing marriages where there are children. The English courts have also tried to prevent the creation of **limping statuses** where a couple is considered married in one country but not in other countries. There is no EU regulation of the recognition of marriage. Rome III, the EU regulation that determines applicable law for divorces in Member States who have adopted enhanced recognition,[4] expressly leaves the determination of what is and what is not a valid marriage up to the national law of the Member States.

This chapter will consider what **applicable law** is used by the English courts when deciding if marriages with foreign elements should be given full legal recognition in England. The chapter will also consider the legal consequences where such 'marriages' are denied recognition. Finally, the chapter will examine the conflict-of-law issues connected to the institution of civil partnership.

10.2 When does the question of validity arise?

The English courts may have to determine the validity of a foreign marriage in many different circumstances. The question of the validity of a marriage can be put to the court as the main issue in an application for a declaration as to marital status[5] or an application for nullity. An application for nullity asks the court to rule that the marriage was never validly created in the first place due to a problem relating to capacity or the legal formalities.

Alternatively, the validity of a marriage may arise as a question for determination in an application for judicial separation, divorce, financial relief, an inheritance dispute, immigration or in a criminal prosecution for bigamy. In all these cases the existence of a valid marriage is crucial to the cause of action.

4 See Chapter 11.

5 S 55 Family Law Act 1986.

10.3 The definition of marriage in English domestic law

There is no statutory definition of marriage in the UK. The nature and consequences of marriage have differed throughout English history. For example, before 1970, spouses were legally required to live together and conjugal duties were enforceable.[6] Today many such matters are left up to spouses. The best way of understanding the nature of marriage in English law today is to look at the rules governing the formation of marriage and the grounds which render a marriage a nullity in English law.

10.3.1 Formalities

The formalities for entering into marriage are found the Marriage Act 1949. English law allows spouses to marry through certain religious rites or through a civil ceremony. The Marriage Act 1949 lays out rules governing the necessary preliminaries, the nature of the ceremony itself and the necessity for registration for each type of marriage.[7] The Marriage Act 1949 is due to be replaced with more modern legislation which will provide for the same formalities for each of the different types of marriage permitted by English law, as the rules are currently extremely complex.[8] Part 1 of the Marriage Act 1949 sets out several prohibitions on classes of people who can marry. Parties may not marry who are closely related by blood or a legal relationship.[9] Parties under 16 may not marry and those under 18 may require the permission of their parent or guardian.[10]

Where the requirements of the Marriage Act 1949 are not complied with, the marriage may still be valid. No statutory consequences are outlined in the Marriage Act for failure to comply with many of the stated formalities such as the requirement for parental consent if one of the parties is under 18. A marriage that takes place at the wrong time will be valid in spite of non-compliance. A marriage will be **void** if the parties 'knowingly and wilfully' disregard specified requirements.[11] If the couple marry in a ceremony outside the forms of marriage outlined in the Marriage Act 1949 the marriage may be considered to be a **non-marriage** with no legal effect whatsoever.[12]

10.3.2 Essential validity

Sections 11 and 12 of the Matrimonial Cause Act 1973 outline the grounds upon which the courts may find a marriage to be invalid or a nullity under domestic English law. While a divorce decree dissolves a marriage that was validly created, a nullity decree or declaration of nullity establishes that the marriage was not validly created in the first place.

The grounds for nullity are drawn from ecclesiastical law and are divided into two different categories – **void** and **voidable**. Void marriages are fundamentally flawed in a way that is publically acknowledged to be fundamental to the English understanding of marriage. Therefore any interested person may take proceedings to have such a marriage declared void. Voidable marriages are also flawed but this is an issue between the parties. Only the parties to the marriage may take proceedings for a decree of nullity in respect of a voidable marriage.

Under s 11(a)(i) a marriage will be found void if the parties are within the prohibited degrees of relationship.[13] The prohibited degrees of relationship are outlined in the Marriage (Prohibited

6 This was abolished by s 20 of the Matrimonial Proceedings and Property Act 1970.
7 R Probert, *Cretney and Probert's Family Law* (7th Ed, Sweet & Maxwell, 2009), [2-002]–[2-012].
8 *Registration Modernisation: A Position and Consultation Paper on the Delivery of the Local Registration Service in England and Wales* (Nov 2005).
9 S 1 Marriage Act 1949.
10 S 3 Marriage Act 1949.
11 S 25; *Gereis v Yagoub* [1997] 1 FLR 854.
12 *Gandhi v Patel* [2001] 1 FLR 603.
13 This is reinforced by s 1 of the Marriage Act 1949.

Degrees of Relationship) Act 1986.[14] The class of relatives prohibited from marrying has gradually diminished over the years.[15] Today marriage is prohibited between a person and his or her parent, child, grandparent, sibling, uncle or aunt or nephew and niece. A marriage between an individual and his/her stepchild is permitted in certain circumstances.[16]

A marriage will be void if either party was under the age of 16 at the time of the marriage.[17] A marriage will also be void if either party was already in an existing marriage or civil partnership when the marriage was entered into.[18]

Under s 11(c) a marriage will be void if parties are of the same sex. Section 11 of the Gender Recognition Act 2004 allows a transsexual person who has been granted a gender recognition certificate to marry in their reassigned sex.[19]

Section 11(d) states that a marriage contracted overseas which was polygamous will be void if either party was domiciled in England and Wales. A marriage contracted in England and Wales that is polygamous will be non-existent.[20] The extent to which English law will recognise a foreign polygamous marriage is examined below.

Section 12 outlines the grounds on which a marriage is voidable. A marriage is voidable where the marriage has not been consummated either through incapacity[21] or through wilful refusal.[22] A marriage can also be annulled where, previous to the marriage, one party obtained a gender recognition certificate and the other party was unaware of that fact or where one of the spouses seeks a legal reassignment of gender while married.[23] Marriages are also voidable on the grounds that at the time of the marriage one of the spouses was suffering from a venereal disease[24] or where the wife was pregnant by another man.[25] These rules indicate that there is an expectation in English law that spouses will have a sexual relationship with a view to having children together. However, whether this is a matter important enough to render the marriage void is left to the spouses themselves to decide.

Section 12(c) and (d) of the Matrimonial Causes Act 1973 renders a marriage voidable where either party did not validly consent. Consent will be invalid where it is given by a person who is considered incapable of consenting to marriage under English law, such as a person with diminished understanding or a mental disorder. The courts have considered a person's capacity to marry on a case-by-case basis but the level of understanding required is not particularly high.[26]

Consent will also be invalid where it has been obtained by fear or undue pressure. In *Hirani v Hirani*[27] the Court of Appeal held that the test of whether consent had been given as a result of threats or pressure is a subjective one.[28] The UK has also taken steps to ensure that forced marriage can be prevented from happening.[29]

A marriage will be voidable where the consent given is based on a mistake about the identity of the other spouse or the nature of the ceremony.[30]

A petitioner will not be entitled to a decree of nullity based on a s 12 ground, if proceedings were not instituted within the requisite time period, if the petitioner was aware of the defect before

14 As amended by the Marriage Act 1949 (Remedial) Order 2007/438.
15 *B and L v UK* [2006] 1 FLR 35.
16 *Smith v Clerical Medical and General Life Assurance Society and Others* [1993] 1 FLR 47.
17 S 11(a)(ii), see also s 2 Marriage Act 1949.
18 S 11(b).
19 *Bellinger v Bellinger* [2003] UKHL 21.
20 *Gandhi v Patel* [2001] 1 FLR 603.
21 S 12(a); *Singh v Singh* [1971] P 226.
22 S 12(b); *Potter v Potter* (1975) 5 Fam Law 161.
23 S 12(g) and (h).
24 S 12(e).
25 S 12(f).
26 *Sheffield CC v E* [2004] EWHC 2808 (Fam); *Re SK* [2008] EWCA Civ 198; *City of Westminster v C* [2008] EWCA Civ 198.
27 [1982] 4 FLR 232.
28 *NS v MI* [2006] EWHC 1646 (Fam).
29 The Forced Marriage (Civil Protection) Act 2007.
30 *Mehta v Mehta* [1945] 2 All ER 690.

he entered into the marriage or if he conducted himself in a way that led the respondent to believe that he would not seek an annulment.[31]

Different consequences attach to a declaration that a marriage is void *ab initio* on the basis of s 11 and a decree stating that a marriage is void under s 12.

From looking at the formalities and grounds for nullity it is clear that the definition of marriage in English law is limited to opposite-sex couples over 16 who are not blood relations. Marriage is intended to be monogamous. Marriages that are from the inception polygamous or bigamous, because one of the parties is already married or in a civil partnership, will not be valid. Adultery will not invalidate a marriage; it is merely a basis for divorce. The marriage must be entered into by a public ceremony and comply with state-imposed formalities. The parties should give consent to the marriage that is based on a proper understanding and not undermined by fear or pressure. There is an expectation that the marriage will lead to a sexual relationship. The marriage subsists until it is brought to an end by state formalities for divorce.

10.3.3 Consequences of invalidity in English law

Where the court annuls a voidable marriage, the marriage is treated as having existed up until the date of the court annulment.

Void marriages have no legal existence and do not have be declared void by the English courts. For the sake of clarity, parties may ask the courts to make a declaration of nullity. Where such a declaration is made the marriage will be treated as never having existed.

The court has the discretionary power to make financial orders against either party after a decree of nullity or declaration of nullity.[32]

Where a marriage is found to be non-existent, it will have no legal consequences at all, and the 'spouses' have no ability to apply for financial relief under the Matrimonial Causes Act 1973.[33]

Non-existent marriage	Void marriage	Voidable marriage
The test is derived from case law. The court must be satisfied that the ceremony has not effected any form of marriage	Section 11 of the Matrimonial Causes Act 1973	Section 12 of the Matrimonial Causes Act 1973
Has no legal existence from the very beginning	Void from the beginning; there is no need to obtain a declaration of nullity	Valid until annulled by the court
Can be pronounced after the death of both parties	Can be pronounced void after the death of either or both parties	Can only be annulled in the lifetime of the parties
No bars to a declaration of non-existence	No bars to a declaration of nullity	Decree of nullity can be barred in certain circumstances
No opportunity for financial relief	Gives rise to a opportunity for financial relief	Gives rise to a opportunity for financial relief

Fig 10.1 Consequences of invalidity in English law.

31 S 13 MCA 1973.
32 *Whiston v Whiston* [1995] 2 FLR 268; *Rampal v Rampal* [2001] EWCA 989.
33 *Gereis v Yagoub* [1997] 1 FLR 854; *Gandhi v Patel* [2001] 1 FLR 603; *A-M v A-M* [2001] 2 FLR 6.

10.4 Applying this definition to foreign marriages

For centuries, the English courts have recognised that many foreign marriages are very similar to the English understanding of marriage, and so there is no reason why they should not be given full legal effect in England. Other marriages are so different to the English idea of marriage that to give them the same effect as English marriage is considered to undermine English morals or create unfairness. The courts must consider which **applicable law** is appropriate to determine the validity of a marriage where one of the spouses is foreign or where the marriage was celebrated in another country. Must such a marriage be valid according to the requirements of English law in order to be given legal effect, or is it enough that they are valid according to a foreign law?

In *Hyde v Hyde and Woodmansee*[34] the English courts laid down a bare minimum definition of marriage against which foreign marriages could be measured. In this case, a husband applied for a divorce on the grounds of adultery. The husband was an English domiciliary who had emigrated to Utah after being raised in the Mormon faith. He married his American wife in a Mormon ceremony in Salt Lake City in 1853. In 1856, the husband went abroad as a missionary to the Sandwich Islands. While there he renounced his faith and preached against Mormonism and in particular the practice of polygamy.[35] As a consequence he was excommunicated by the Mormon Church, and his wife was declared free to marry again. Although the petitioner urged his wife to come and join him in England she remained in Utah and married again according to the Mormon faith.

Lord Penzance had to determine if the English courts could grant a divorce in this case. He held that the Utah marriage was not a marriage within the meaning of the Matrimonial Court of England. This meant that it was inappropriate to grant a divorce under English law. Lord Penzance acknowledged that the law of England could recognise some foreign marriages contracted under a different understanding of the nature and obligations of marriage but, being Christian law, it could not recognise a polygamous marriage:

> Different incidents of minor importance attach to that contract of marriage in different countries in Christendom but in all countries in Christendom the parties to that contract agree to cohabit with each other alone. It is inconsistent with marriage as understood in Christendom, that the husband should have more than one wife.[36]

Lord Penzance held that marriage must satisfy some fundamental requirements in order to be recognised in England. He decided that the key elements of this identity were 'the voluntary union, for life, of one man and one woman to the exclusion of all others'. In reaching this conclusion, he relied on *Warrender v Warrender*,[37] where Lord Brougham had held that marriage is the same thing throughout the Christian world but it is a different status entirely among 'infidel nations'.

Hyde was denied his divorce. The actual status of Hyde's marriage after the decision was unclear. He had been denied a divorce, so it would appear that the marriage was still valid in English law. Poulter suggests that the open-endedness of the decision made it likely that a limping marriage was formed, where Hyde was married in the UK but not in Utah.[38] It is also possible that Hyde's marriage was a **non-marriage**, meaning that it was of no consequence to the English legal system.

Following this case, any foreign marriage that was too far removed from the *Hyde v Hyde* understanding of the essence of marriage in Christendom could not be recognised as a marriage by the English courts.

---

34 [1861–73] All ER 175.
35 S Poulter, '*Hyde v Hyde*: A Reappraisal' (1976) 25 *International and Comparative Law Quarterly* 475, 476.
36 *Hyde v Hyde and Woodmansee* [1861–1873] All ER 175, (1866) 1 P&D LR 130.
37 *Warrender v Warrender* (1835) 2 Cl & F 531; *Ardaseer Cursetjee v Perozeboye* (1856) 10 Moo PC 375,420.
38 Poulter, '*Hyde v Hyde*: A Reappraisal' (1976) 25 *International and Comparative Law Quarterly* 489–490.

In *Re Bethell*[39] the son of a former Lord Chancellor married the daughter of an African Chief in a tribal ceremony in South Africa, where he had been sent by his father after running up considerable gambling debts.[40] The son died in an encounter with the Boers in 1884, and the question for the court was whether his daughter, born after his death, could succeed to estates in Yorkshire which had been left to 'Christopher Bethell for life and the remainder to any Children he might have'.

Stirling J held that as the Barolong tribe permitted polygamous marriage, the marriage in question did not fit the definition of marriage according to the laws of England. In this case the child was not entitled to inherit although the marriage had, in fact, been monogamous.

Poulter argues that *Re Bethell* misinterpreted *Hyde* to hold that no potentially polygamous marriage could be recognised for any purposes in the UK.[41] Probert argues that invoking *Hyde* to deny this marriage any recognition 'may not have been necessary as a matter of precedent, but it was certainly expedient as a matter of policy'.[42]

10.4.1 Problems with using *Hyde* as a strict legal definition

As a bare minimum definition of marriage, *Hyde v Hyde* is deeply flawed. Not every relationship that satisfies the definition will have legal effect as a marriage. There is no requirement in the definition for the parties to have a legal ceremony; they could be mere cohabitants.[43]

Many domestic English marriages that do not comply with *Hyde v Hyde* are fully valid in law, such as a marriage in which there is adultery or where the parties later divorce. The requirement that a marriage be for life was out of date even in 1866. In this regard, the definition reflects an aspirational ideal of legal marriage, not the minimum required to gain legal recognition.

The *Hyde* definition is expressly limited to Christian marriage, and so is unsuited to the needs of a modern English pluralist society. Today, when the *Hyde* definition is cited in cases, the Christian element is often dropped. This uses the *dictum* out of context and hides the specificity of this view of marriage to a particular place and time.

From the outset, the courts recognised that the *Hyde* criteria should not be applied literally to all cases where the recognition of a foreign marriage was in question. For example, the idea that Christianity was essential for a marriage to be recognised was disregarded in *Brinkley v Attorney General*.[44] In *Nachimson v Nachimson*,[45] the court upheld the validity of a Russian marriage entered into at a time when divorce was available by mutual consent, thus eroding the importance of the idea that marriage had to be a lifetime commitment.

Today, most validly formed foreign marriages are recognised in English law. English law will recognise marriages that could not be legally entered into in England and are far removed from the *Hyde* definition.

10.5 Applicable law when determining the validity of foreign marriages

The Matrimonial Causes Act 1973 does not specify which applicable law the courts should apply when determining if a foreign marriage is void or voidable. Section 14 leaves it open to the English

39 *Re Bethell* (1888) 38 Ch D 220 (EWCA).
40 Poulter, '*Hyde v Hyde*: A Reappraisal' (1976) 25 *International and Comparative Law Quarterly* 492.
41 Ibid 493.
42 R Probert, '*Hyde v Hyde*: Defining or Defending Marriage?' (2007) 19 (3) *Child and Family Law Quarterly* 322.
43 Ibid.
44 (1890) 15 PD 76.
45 [1930] 1 P 217.

courts to consider matters outside the scope of ss 11 and 12 that may affect the validity of a marriage where the marriage is governed by foreign law.[46] This means that impediment under foreign law may be taken into account. Additionally, it is open to the English courts to consider such a foreign marriage to be valid even where the application of ss 11 and 12 would render it invalid.[47] This gives the English courts the discretion to uphold a foreign marriage which is valid under foreign law but not under English law. However, the English courts cannot consider a marriage governed by foreign law to be valid where one of the parties was in a subsisting civil partnership at the time of the marriage.[48]

When assessing the validity of a foreign marriage the courts may look to English law or foreign law. A large collection of common law rules have been created to determine which law should be applied. These rules are drawn from case law and are neither comprehensive nor entirely consistent.

When determining whether a foreign marriage should be recognised in English law, the court will look at three issues:

- Did both spouses have capacity to marry under the law of their premarital domicile?
- Was the marriage validity created under the required formalities of the law of the place where the marriage was celebrated?
- Should the relationship be given the same effect in England as domestic marriage?

10.6 Essential validity of foreign marriages

The court must establish that both parties to the foreign marriage had the capacity to enter into a marriage. When looking at whether both parties had capacity it is important to apply the appropriate law. For many years, the courts considered whether the parties had capacity under several different laws connected with the marriage, including the law of the spouses' domicile, the law of the place where the marriage was formed and the law of the spouses' matrimonial home.[49] In older cases, when couples were not as internationally mobile as they are today, many of these factors pointed to the same legal system. Several theories emerged on what should be the determining applicable law, most supported to some extent in case law. All of these options were considered in the Law Commission Consultation Paper in 1985[50] and the Law Commission Report in 1987.[51]

One option was simply for the English court to apply **lex fori**. This would hold the marriage to be valid unless invalid under English law. There was clear authority in English case law that where a marriage was carried out in England between one person domiciled in England and one person domiciled abroad, the applicable law to determine validity was English law.[52] The Law Commission considered these cases to be exceptional and held that a rule applying *lex fori* was not desirable.[53] *Lex fori* would be quite difficult for the parties to the marriage in predicting whether their marriage would be valid in England if they had married abroad or had connections to other countries. It would also promote forum shopping by the party who wished to have the marriage declared invalid.[54]

46 S 14(1)(a).
47 S 14(1)(b).
48 S 14(1)(c).
49 *Brook v Brook* (1861) 9 HL Cas 196.
50 Law Commission & Scottish Law Commission, 'Private International Law: Choice of Law Rules in Marriage' (Cons Memo 64, 1985).
51 Law Commision & Scottish Law Commission, 'Private International Law Choice of Law Rules In Marriage' (LC 164, 1987).
52 *Sottomayer v De Burros (No 2)* (1879) 5 PD 94; *Vervaeke v Smith* [1981] Fam 77, 122.
53 Consultation Paper [3.6].
54 Consultation Paper [3.19].

The Law Commission also considered whether the law of the place of the marriage, **lex loci**, should be applied. This would be clear, certain and simple. It promoted the idea that foreign marriages which were validly entered into should be upheld.[55] This choice of law might also be expected by the parties. However, the application of the *lex loci* would enable the parties to evade the restrictions of the law of their domicile.[56]

Applying the **law of the matrimonial home** was considered desirable in policy terms as the validity of a marriage is most relevant to the community of the country where the parties live together as husband and wife. There was also some authority for this approach.[57] The Commission felt that it could be difficult to predict the future matrimonial home of a married couple and it was undesirable that the validity of a marriage at the time of the marriage should depend on a future event.[58]

Some judges have applied the 'proper law of the marriage' or **the law with the most real and substantial connection.**[59] This is a flexible solution, but the Law Commission found it to be inherently vague and unpredictable, and unsuitable as a yardstick for future planning.[60] How would spouses know if their marriage would be eventually found valid by the English courts if they had no idea which applicable law would be used to assess its validity?

The Law Commission were most supportive of the application of **the law of each of the spouses' premarital domicile**. The rule preserves equality between the spouses by giving the law of each domicile equal weight. It is also relatively easy to apply and discourages evasion.[61] This choice supports the idea that a person's legal status is a matter of public concern to the country in which he makes his permanent home. However, Hartley and other commentators have criticised the dual-domicile rule because it leans toward invalidity of the marriage.[62] In addition, the spouses may have very little real connection to their premarital domicile.

The Law Commission decided against introducing legislation on applicable law for marriage. It was felt that the common law rules were in a state of development.[63] Flexibility would be lost if the Law Commission introduced strict statutory rules. The failure to introduce legislation means that conflicting case law still exists, suggesting that a different applicable law may be applied depending on the type of invalidity in the formation of the marriage. The weight of authority leans toward the application of the law of each of the premarital domicile[64] – the dual-domicile rule. Section 11(d) of the Matrimonial Causes Act 1973 also supports this approach. Each of the possible invalidities will be examined in turn.

10.6.1 Prohibited degrees of relationship

Most legal systems impose restrictions on marriage between parties who are related by blood or other close personal relationships. The precise scope of the prohibited degrees varies from country to country. In general, the class of prohibited relatives has been reducing, and the European Court of Human Rights (ECtHR) has found such rules to be in conflict with the right to marry under the European Convention on Human Rights.[65]

---

55 Consultation Paper [3.22].
56 Consultation Paper [3.23].
57 *De Reneville v De Reneville* [1948] P 100; *Kenward v Kenward* [1951] P124; *Radwan v Radwan (No 2)* [1973] Fam 35.
58 Consultation Paper [3.35].
59 *Vervaeke v Smith* [1983] 1 AC 145, 166; *Lawrence v Lawrence* [1985] Fam 106.
60 Consultation Paper [3.20].
61 Consultation Paper [3.36].
62 T Hartley, 'The Policy Basis of the English Conflicts of Law of Marriage' (1972) 36 MLR 571.
63 Law Commission Report [2.14].
64 Law Commission Report [2.2].
65 *B and L v UK* [2006] 1 FLR 35.

In *Brook v Brook*,[66] Brook was a widower who married his deceased wife's sister in Denmark in 1850. Both parties were British subjects and domiciled in England. The marriage was valid under Danish law, but void under English law, which at that time prohibited marriage with a deceased wife's sister. The House of Lords held that, as the parties were British subjects and domiciled in England at the time of the marriage, and as England was to be their matrimonial home, the marriage was void.

In *Mette v Mette*,[67] a marriage was celebrated in Germany between a man domiciled in England and his deceased wife's half-sister who was domiciled in Germany. The marriage was void by English law but was valid under German law. It was held that the marriage was void, since there could be no valid contract unless each of the parties was competent to contract with the other. Moreover, the husband 'remained domiciled in this country and the marriage was with a view to subsequent residence in this country'.

Later cases have expressly favoured the dual-domicile rule. In *Re Paine*[68] the wife, a British subject and domiciled in England, visited Germany, where she married her deceased sister's husband, a German subject. This marriage was void in England but valid in Germany. The couple then lived in England until their respective deaths. On the question of whether the surviving daughter was legitimate for the purposes of succession, the court had to decide on the validity of the marriage. Bennett J applied the dual-domicile rule and held that the marriage was void, since the wife lacked capacity to enter into such a marriage under the rule of her premarital domicile.

In *Sottomayor v De Barros (No 1)*[69] the parties to the marriage were Portuguese first cousins. The couple were 16 and 14 at the time of the marriage. Although they had lived in the same house for six years, the marriage had never been consummated. Under Portuguese law the parties lacked capacity to marry each other as they were within the prohibited degrees of relationship. The wife petitioned for a declaration of nullity on the basis of the relationship. The Queen's Proctor intervened and alleged that, at the time of the marriage, the parties were domiciled in England and not in Portugal so the validity of the marriage should be determined by English domestic law.

The Court of Appeal held that the personal capacity of the parties to enter into a marriage must depend on the law of their premarital domicile. In this case Portuguese law rendered the parties incapable of marrying. This case provides express authority for the dual-domicile rule when determining whether a marriage will be invalid due to lack of capacity to marry within the prohibited degrees.

However, when the case was remitted to the Divorce Division in *Sottomayor v De Barros (No 2)*[70] James Hannen P held that while the husband was domiciled in England, the wife was domiciled in Portugal. He declined to give effect to the prohibition imposed on the wife by Portuguese law and was obviously in favour of applying the law of the place of celebration.

This decision has never been overruled and appears to have established an exception to the dual-domicile rule. Where the validity of marriage celebrated in England between persons of whom one has an English domicile and one has a foreign domicile, the incapacity of the foreign domiciliary under foreign law will not exist under the law of England. The Law Commission proposed that this exception to the dual-domicile rule should be abolished.[71] This case can also be explained as being based on English public policy which prevented the foreign law from being applied.[72]

66 (1861) 9 HL Cas 196.
67 (1859) 1 Sw & Tr 416.
68 [1940] Ch 46.
69 (1877) 3 PD 1.
70 [1879] 5 PD 94.
71 Law Commission Report [2.7]–[2.8].
72 C Clarkson, 'Marriage in England: Favouring the *lex fori*' (1990) 10 *Legal Studies* 80–90.

10.6.2 Age

In English law, a person must be 16 in order to marry. In other legal systems the minimum age for marriage can be as low as 12.

The question of whether the English courts should recognise a marriage between an English domiciliary and an underage foreign domiciliary was addressed in *Pugh v Pugh*.[73] In this case, the wife was born in Hungary with a Hungarian domicile of origin. In 1945, she went with her parents to Australia, where she met her husband, a British officer domiciled in England. They were married in Australia in 1946 when she was still 15, and they returned to England in 1950. Soon after their arrival, she petitioned for a decree of nullity on the ground of her lack of age at the time of the marriage. By Hungarian law, the marriage was voidable until the wife's 17th birthday, by Australian law the marriage was valid, and by English law it was void. Pearce J held that the personal status and capacity to marry of each party were governed by the country of domicile. Since the husband could not lawfully enter into a marriage with an underage spouse under his English law of domicile, the marriage was void.[74]

10.6.3 Sex

In *Corbett v Corbett*,[75] Ormrod J held that a marriage which took place in Gibraltar between two English domiciliaries was invalid because at the time of the marriage both parties were men. Mrs Corbett had undergone a sex-change operation in Casablanca but this was not recognised by the courts. Ormrod J held that for the purposes of English law, marriage must be between a man and a woman.[76]

The legal understanding of gender has changed since *Corbett v Corbett* and individuals can now be recognised in their new gender following gender reassignment surgery. The Gender Recognition Act 2004 allows transsexual people to marry in their reassigned gender once a gender recognition certificate has been granted by the Gender Recognition Panel.[77]

Where a person has changed their sex through an overseas gender reassignment, this will only be recognised in the UK in certain circumstances. The application must be considered by the Gender Recognition Panel. If the gender reassignment has been recognised by the law of the country in which the procedure was carried out, and this country has been approved by the Secretary of State, the gender reassignment will be automatically recognised in the UK once all relevant information has been given to the Panel.[78] If the reassignment occurred in a country that has not been approved by the Secretary of State, the application to the Gender Recognition Panel will be treated like a domestic application.

Marriage in England is still limited to marriages between a man and woman. Same-sex marriages are recognised now as civil partnerships.

Section 21(2) of the Gender Recognition Act provides that where an individual has gender reassignment overseas and marries abroad in the new gender, this marriage will not be recognised in the UK until a full gender recognition certificate has been granted.

In *Wilkinson v Kitzinger*[79] two British domiciliaries entered into a same-sex marriage in British Columbia in Canada and returned to live in Britain. They sought to have the relationship recognised

73 [1951] P 482.
74 See also *Mohamed v Knott* [1969] 1 QB 1.
75 [1971] P 83.
76 Ibid 106.
77 S 1(1).
78 S 2(4); Gender Recognition (Approved Countries and Territories) Order 2011/1630. The full list is available online at www.justice.gov.uk/tribunals/gender-recognition-panel/overseas-application-process (accessed 16 May 2013)
79 [2006] EWHC 2022 (Fam).

as a marriage. The court held that this relationship could not be recognised as a marriage as the parties lacked capacity under English law as the law of their domicile to enter into such a marriage. The court held that the couple had entered into an overseas relationship which was recognised in England as a civil partnership under ss 215–217 of the Civil Partnership Act 2004. Sir Mark Potter held that same-sex relationships were in no way inferior to marriage but they were different to marriage under the current definition of marriage in English law.[80] He felt that this difference of treatment could be justified and fell within the margin of appreciation granted to states under the ECHR.

10.6.4 Subsisting marriages and civil partnerships

It is clear that where a person marries a second time without ending a first marriage or civil partnership, the second marriage will not be recognised by English law. For example, in *Whiston v Whiston*[81] a woman married in the Philippines and married a second husband in England. The second husband was granted a decree of nullity under the Matrimonial Causes Act.

Where the person has taken steps to legally end the first marriage by divorce or nullity and the divorce decree or nullity decree is not universally recognised, more complicated conflict-of-laws issues arise. Today, a person whose foreign divorce, decree of nullity, or dissolution of civil partnership is entitled to recognition in England under Brussels II *bis* or the Family Law Act 1986 is entitled to remarry **in England** notwithstanding the fact that the law of the person's domicile does not recognise the divorce and therefore regards the previous marriage as subsisting.[82]

In *Mendal v Mendal*,[83] where the English registry office ceremony occurred four months before the wife's Brazilian divorce was made final, the English wedding was void *ab initio*. In H v H[84] the court held that a marriage held in England after a Japanese divorce was valid.

In contrast, where the English courts are asked to determine the validity of a second marriage that took place **overseas**, the old common law rules will apply. The court must determine two issues. The main question is whether both parties would otherwise have had capacity to enter into the second marriage. The incidental question is whether the subsisting relationship had the effect of removing the spouse's capacity to marry a second time.

A dilemma faced by the English courts is whether the incidental question should be determined by the relevant applicable law as if it was a standalone issue or whether it should be determined by the foreign law which is applied to determine the main question. For example, a Brazilian woman married in Germany and later divorced, but the divorce was not recognised by Brazil. The woman entered into a second marriage in Peru where the divorce was recognised. Should the English courts recognise the second marriage because, under English law, the German divorce has legal effect or should the English courts refuse to recognise the second marriage because the wife had no capacity to marry under the law of her Brazilian domicile? There is no definite rule on the incidental question and case law is not consistent.[85]

For example, in *Lawrence v Lawrence*[86] a man and woman domiciled in Brazil married in Brazil. The wife obtained a divorce in Nevada. This divorce was not recognised in Brazil and therefore the wife did not have capacity to remarry under Brazilian law. The wife married again in Nevada. Her husband was an American who had had acquired an English domicile of choice. The parties set up

---

80 Ibid [121].
81 [1995] Fam 198; see also *Rampal v Rampal (No 2)* [2001] 2 FLR 1179.
82 S 50 Family Law Act 1986.
83 [2007] EWCA Civ 437; *Seiden v Fularon* [2008] EWCA Civ 1548.
84 [2007] 1 FLR 1318.
85 *R v Brentwood Marriage registrar ex p Arias* [1968] 2 QB 956; *Padolecchia v Padolecchia* [1968] P 314; *Perrini v Perrini* [1979] 2 All ER 323.
86 [1985] FLR 1097.

their matrimonial home in England but the wife later returned to Brazil. On a petition for a declaration as to the validity of the marriage celebrated in Nevada, Lincoln J held that although the divorce would not be recognised by the law of the wife's domicile, at the time of her marriage to the petitioner she had intended to acquire an English domicile and, since the parties had established their matrimonial home in England, the marriage had a real and substantial connection with England. Accordingly, the court would apply English law and declare that the second marriage was a valid and subsisting marriage. When the case went to the Court of Appeal, the validity of the marriage was upheld on the basis that English courts were obliged by statute to recognise the Nevada divorce.

Where a foreign state places restrictions on marriage after a divorce, these may affect a party's capacity to marry again in England.

In *Scott v AG*[87] an Irish couple moved to South Africa, where they were divorced on the ground of the wife's adultery. By the law of South Africa, a person divorced for adultery was prohibited from remarrying as long as their first spouse remained unmarried. After the divorce, the wife and her lover, an English domiciliary, returned to England and married. Her first husband was still unmarried. Sir James Hannen P upheld the remarriage on the ground that the prohibition on the remarriage in South Africa was penal in nature and had no extraterritorial effect.

In *Warter v Warter*[88] a husband, domiciled in England but resident in India, divorced his wife in India for adultery. Both parties were prohibited by Indian law from remarrying for six months from the decree absolute. The wife, prior to the expiry of six months, married an English domiciliary in England. It was held that the English marriage was invalid because of the wife's incapacity under Indian law. The Indian prohibition was given legal effect. In this case, the couple had gone through a second form of marriage after the six-month period had expired. The case concerned which version of their wills was the most authoritative.

10.6.5 Polygamous marriages

Bigamy occurs when a person enters into two concurrent marriages that are intended to be monogamous. A polygamous marriage is one in which it is permissible for a man to take more than one wife.

Hyde v Hyde held that the courts could not grant a divorce where a person had entered into a polygamous marriage. The matrimonial law of England was adapted to a Christian monogamous marriage and could not be applied to polygamous marriages. The husband in *Hyde* had only ever had one wife. However, by marrying in a polygamous faith, the option was open to the husband to take another wife. The court found that the nature of the potentially polygamous commitment was fundamentally different to the English institution of marriage. For example, it would be unfair to grant a divorce on the basis of adultery where a man was permitted to have other wives.

Today, although a polygamous marriage celebrated in England will not be valid,[89] polygamous marriages that have take place abroad are valid in England for most purposes.

The English courts have gradually moved away from the rule in *Hyde*. First, the courts began to recognise polygamous foreign marriages where neither party had English domicile and both parties had the legal capacity to enter into a polygamous marriage. Polygamous marriages were recognised as a basis of liability for maintenance[90] and establishing succession rights.[91] By 1968, in *Mohamed v Knott*,[92] Lord Parker stated that, 'A marriage which is polygamous . . . will be recognised in England as a valid marriage unless there is some strong reason to the contrary.' A polygamous marriage was

87 (1886) 11 PD 128.
88 (1890) LR 15 PD 152.
89 *M v M (Divorce: Jurisdition Validity of Marriage)* [2001] 2 FLR 6.
90 *Iman Din v NAB* [1967] 2 QB 213.
91 *The Sinha Peerage Claim* [1946] 1 All ER 348, (1939) 171 Lord's Journals 350.
92 *Mohamed v Knott* [1969] 1 QB 1, 16.

still not considered to be a marriage for matrimonial relief purposes in England but this was the anomaly and not the rule.[93]

The Matrimonial Proceedings (Polygamous Marriages) Act in 1972 finally permitted the courts to provide matrimonial remedies to those in foreign polygamous marriages.[94] The Act also provided that any polygamous (or potentially polygamous) marriage celebrated abroad by an English domiciliary was void *ab initio*,[95] putting the dual-domicile rule on a statutory footing.

The question of whether a marriage is monogamous was determined by the place of celebration.[96] This meant that any marriage carried out in a country which tolerated polygamy could be viewed as potentially polygamous. The courts held that a potentially polygamous marriage could be converted into a monogamous marriage where the husband became domiciled in a country which tolerated only monogamous marriages.[97]

The fact that the nature of the marriage was determined by the place of celebration, combined with the rule that English domiciliaries were not permitted to enter into polygamous marriages, caused extreme hardship to immigrant communities who had settled in the UK.[98] The custom of arranged marriages persisted within these families and often an English domiciliary would travel to a country such as India to contract an arranged marriage. As polygamy was permitted under the laws of India, these marriages were potentially polygamous in nature, and an English domiciliary did not have the capacity to enter into such a marriage. This rendered all Indian marriages void by English law if one of the spouses was an English domiciliary. This approach was an interference with the customs of ethnic minority communities and had adverse practical consequences on the immigrant community in Britain.[99]

The courts attempted to alleviate the hardship of this rule in two very controversial decisions. In *Radwan v Radwan* (No 2)[100] the husband was an Egyptian domiciliary who married his first wife in Egypt in a valid polygamous ceremony. He took a second wife, an English domiciliary, in a Muslim ceremony in the Egyptian Consulate General in Paris. He divorced the first wife shortly after the second marriage ceremony and took up residence with the second wife in Egypt, until the Suez crisis forced them to move to England. In 1970 the second wife filed for divorce. The question for the courts was whether the parties were actually married. Cumming-Bruce J held that both parties had capacity to enter into a polygamous marriage. Even though the wife was of English domicile it was held that capacity in this case should be determined by reference to the law of the intended matrimonial domicile, which in this case was Egypt.[101] Accordingly this decision seemed to suggest that a woman domiciled in England could enter into an actually or potentially polygamous marriage so long as the intended matrimonial home would be in a country that tolerated polygamy.[102]

In *Hussain v Hussain*[103] a marriage was celebrated in Pakistan between a British domiciliary and a Pakistani woman. The parties set up their home in England. The marriage broke down, and the wife petitioned for judicial separation. The husband claimed that the marriage was void under s 11(d) of the Matrimonial Causes Act 1973. The court held that the marriage was in fact monogamous.

93 This rule was confirmed in *Nachimson v Nachimson* [1930] P 217; *Sowa v Sowa* [1961] 3 All ER 689 (EWCA); *Baindail v Baindail* [1946] P 122 (EWCA).

94 This provision is now found in s 47 of the Matrimonial Causes Act 1973.

95 Section 3 of the Act added a subsection to s 1 of the Nullity of Marriage Act 1971 to this effect. It was later replaced with s 11(d) of the Matrimonial Causes Act 1973.

96 *Quershi v Quershi* [1972] Fam 173; cf *Hussain v Hussain* [1983] Fam 26.

97 *Ali v Ali* [1966] 2 WLR 620; *Onobrauche v Onobrauche* [1978] Fam Law 107.

98 English Law Commission, *Family Law: Report on Polygamous Marriages* (LC 42, 1971).

99 S Poulter, 'Polygamy – New Law Commission Proposals' [1983] *Family Law* 72.

100 [1973] Fam 35.

101 Although the Matrimonial Proceedings (Polygamous Marriages) Act 1972 was in force, the court declared that it was only concerned with the common law status of the parties in 1951.

102 J Murphy, *International Dimensions in Family Law* (Manchester University Press, 2005) 75.

103 *Hussain v Hussain* [1983] Fam 26.

The court held that a marriage was only potentially polygamous if one of the spouses had the capacity to take a second spouse. Here the wife could not take another husband as that was not permitted by Pakistani law, and the husband could not take another wife as he was an English domiciliary and so did not have the capacity. Accordingly the marriage was monogamous and valid.

The unsatisfactory effect of both of these decisions led to the Private International Law (Miscellaneous Provisions) Act 1995, which amended s 11(d) of the Matrimonial Causes Act 1973 so that its operation was specifically limited to actually polygamous marriage.

Today English law permits all English domiciliaries to enter into marriages abroad in countries that tolerate polygamy, and such marriages will be considered to be monogamous in nature by English law. Where an English domiciliary enters into an actually polygamous marriage by taking a second wife, this will not be recognised under English law.[104]

Actually polygamous marriages of foreign domiciliaries who marry in a country that tolerates polygamy and where both parties have the capacity under their *lex domicilii* to enter into a polygamous marriage are recognised in England. These marriages are now recognised for most purposes[105] except immigration[106] and widows' pension rights.[107] This difference in treatment has been justified by the Law Commission as pragmatic: 'It is true that the theory that monogamy and polygamy are separate institutions has now been discredited but it does not follow that our law, based on monogamy, can, with no modification, be applied to polygamy without creating difficulties.'[108]

10.6.6 Foreign impediments to capacity unknown to English law

While the English impediments to marriage are limited to sex, age, prohibited degrees and marital status, other countries may have further restrictions on marriage. The court will have to consider whether this foreign impediment will have any effect on English recognition. Section 14(1) of the Matrimonial Causes Act 1973 suggests that the English courts may annul marriages on grounds which are unknown to English law. However, the case law suggests that these impediments will not be recognised by the English courts, and in the Law Commission Consultation document it was recommended that the English courts should not annul a marriage on a ground unknown to English law.[109]

In *Chetti v Chetti*[110] an Englishwoman married a Hindu man who was temporarily resident in England. The marriage took place at a London registry office. The parties cohabited in England, and a few months later the husband returned to India. The wife petitioned for judicial separation on the ground of desertion, and the husband argued that, at the time of the marriage and at all material times since then, he was a Hindu domiciled in India. He further argued that the marriage was invalid on the basis that, by Hindu religion and law, he could not marry a woman from outside his own caste or one who was not by religion a Hindu. Barnes P was of the view that the marriage was in fact valid in India. He followed the rule in *Sottomayer v De Barros (No 2)* and indicated that if the marriage takes place in England and one of the parties has an English domicile a foreign incapacity will be disregarded.

104 S 11(d) of the Matrimonial Causes Act 1973.
105 Such as domestic violence protection (Family Law Act 1996 s 63(5)), social security benefits (Social Security Contributions and Benefits Act 1992, ss 121(1)(b), 147 (5)) and income tax (*Nabi v Heaton* [1983] 1 WLR 626).
106 S 2(2) Immigration Act 1988.
107 *R v Department of Health, ex p Misra* [1996] 1 FLR 129.
108 Law Commission, *Family Law: Report on Polygamous Marriages* (LC 42, 1971) 786.
109 Consultation Paper [5.48].
110 [1909] P 67.

10.7 Formal validity of marriage

Non-compliance with the formal requirements of the law of the country where a wedding takes place means that no marriage has been formed. It is a well-established principle that formal validity of a marriage depends entirely on the law of the place where the ceremony is performed. This is known as the *lex loci celebrationis*. Formal requirements include the requirement of a civil ceremony, the number of witnesses necessary, licensing, and the necessity of publicity or notice.

In *Berthiaume v Dastous*[111] a French-Canadian woman of the Roman Catholic faith met a French-Canadian man of the same faith in Paris. They were married in France in a Roman Catholic Church. The marriage was not preceded by a civil ceremony as required by French law. On the wife's petition for divorce, the Privy Council held that the marriage was void, on the basis that it did not meet the formal requirement of the law of the place in which it was celebrated. This was irrespective of the law of the domicile of the parties.

In *Starkowski v AG*[112] a wife of Polish domicile entered into her first marriage in a church in Austria in May 1945. At that time in Austria, a religious ceremony did not constitute a valid marriage; a civil ceremony was required. In June 1945, an Austrian decree was passed to the effect that religious marriages celebrated between 1 April 1945 and the date of the decree should be valid as soon as they were registered in the Family Book. The marriage, however, was not registered until July 1949. This was after the wife's second marriage. The House of Lords held that, where there had been retrospective legislation which had the effect of validating an earlier marriage, the balance of justice and convenience was clearly in favour of recognising the validity of such retrospective legislation. Accordingly the first marriage was valid.

When applying the law of the place of the ceremony, the English courts may apply the law of a third country under the doctrine of *renvoi*.[113] For example, in *Hooper v Hooper*[114] the parties, who were English domiciliaries, married in a Church of England ceremony in Baghdad. Under Iraqi law, a marriage between foreign nationals was valid where it complied with the formalities of the national law of the parties. The English courts found the marriage invalid as the parties had knowingly and wilfully married without calling banns.

In 1985, the Law Commission considered the application of *renvoi* to be practically inconvenient. Proof of the choice-of-law rules of the country of celebration is required, and where these point to the domestic law of a third country this can cause additional delays and extra costs to legal proceedings. Where the laws of the third country point to the laws of a fourth country or back to the laws of the first country this causes theoretical difficulties. However, the application of *renvoi* provides greater uniformity of recognition and prevents the creation of a limping status.[115] The Law Commission recommended that the English court should use *renvoi* and apply the choice of law rules of the *lex loci celebrationis* where they point to the law of a third county.

There are three exceptions to the *lex loci celebrationis* rule.

10.7.1 Consular marriage

The Foreign Marriage Act 1892[116] allows a marriage to be solemnised abroad before an English marriage officer in a foreign country, if one of the parties is a UK national. The term 'UK national',

111 [1930] AC 79.
112 [1954] AC 155.
113 See Chapter 1.
114 [1959] 1 WLR 1021.
115 Law Commission & Scottish Law Commission, 'Private International Law: Choice of Law Rules in Marriage' (Cons Memo 64. 1985) [2.39].
116 As amended by the Foreign Marriage Act 1947 and the Foreign Marriage (Amendment) Act 1988.

includes British citizens and Commonwealth citizens.[117] 'Marriage officers' include consular officers, High Commissioners and British Ambassadors, provided they hold a 'marriage warrant' from the Secretary of State.[118] The marriage officer should be satisfied that local facilities are inadequate, that the local authorities will not object to the marriage and that the marriage will be recognised by the laws of each party's domicile.[119] As long as the marriage ceremony complies with the requirements laid down in the Act[120] it will be considered formally valid by the English courts even where it does not comply with the formalities of the law in the place of celebration.

10.7.2 Marriages of members of the British forces serving abroad

Section 22 of the Foreign Marriage Act 1892[121] applies to marriages entered into by members of Her Majesty's British Forces while serving abroad and to civilians who are subject to military, air force or naval law when not on active service.[122] It provides that a marriage solemnised in any foreign territory, apart from the Commonwealth, by a chaplain or an authorised commanding officer of the British naval, military or air forces serving abroad will be regarded as valid in law, as if it had been solemnised in the UK.

10.7.3 Formal requirements of the English common law

Before the Marriage Act of 1753[123] there were no state-imposed formalities to marriage in England. The formal requirements of marriage were governed by the canon law of England and policed by religious authorities. A marriage entered into by mere exchange of promises without any witnesses or clergyman was given some legal effect by the Ecclesiastical Courts or the Temporal Courts.[124]

In 1844, the House of Lords had to review the requirements of the pre-1753 law when assessing the validity of a marriage carried out in Ireland, where the 1753 Act did not apply. This marriage had been carried out by a Presbyterian minister in a Presbyterian church. The House of Lords held that in order for a marriage to be recognised under the common law of England an exchange of promises in the presence of a minister in holy orders was required.[125]

In exceptional circumstances, where there are insurmountable difficulties in complying with local law or where a country is under hostile occupation, a marriage that complies with these bare minimum formalities will be recognised by the English courts.

In *Wolfenden v Wolfenden*[126] the parties, both British subjects, went through a ceremony of marriage in a Scottish Mission Church in a remote part of China. The ceremony was performed by the minister of the Mission without banns or licence. The minister was not episcopally ordained, nor was he authorised to perform such a marriage in accordance with the Foreign Marriage Act 1892. The court held that the requirement of an ordained priest imposed in *R v Millis*[127] applied only to

117 S 1(2).
118 S 11.
119 Foreign Marriage Order 1970 SI 1970/1539.
120 Outlined in s 8.
121 As amended by the Foreign Marriage Act 1947 and the Foreign Marriage (Amendment) Act 1988.
122 Foreign Marriage (Armed Forces) (Amendment No 2) Order 1990/2592.
123 An Act for the Better Preventing of Clandestine Marriage, 26 Geo II c 33.
124 Stone notes that the status of these marriages was rather confused: L Stone, *Road to Divorce: A History of the Making and Breaking of Marriage in England* (OUP, 1995) 11. In R Probert, *Marriage Law and Practice in the Long Eighteenth Century: A Reassessment* (Cambridge University Press, 2009) it is argued that these marriages by exchange of promises were simple betrothals.
125 *R v Millis* (1844) 10 Cl & Fin 534 (House of Lords) [655]. See also Probert, '*R v Millis* reconsidered: Binding contracts and bigamous marriages' (2008) 28 LS 337.
126 [1946] P 61.
127 (1843–44) 10 Cl & Fin 534.

marriages performed in England and Ireland. The marriage was valid based on the mere exchange of promises alone.[128]

Wolfenden was followed in *Penhas v Tan Soo Eng*,[129] where a marriage by exchange of promises performed before a layman in Singapore was held to be valid.

This exception is not confined to marriages of British nationals. The English courts have also used the doctrine to recognise the marriages of foreign nationals who have married in wartime conditions where the place of the marriage was under foreign occupation.

In *Kochanski v Kochanski*[130] the parties, born and domiciled in Poland until 1939, were married in Germany in 1945. The marriage was solemnised by a Roman Catholic priest according to the rite of the Roman Catholic Church. The ceremony did not comply with the formalities required by German law. The parties were living in a displaced persons camp whose occupants did not comply with the German law and led the lives of a separate community. Sachs J held that the presumption that the parties had to subject themselves to German law for the purpose of celebrating their marriage was rebutted. As the ceremony was one which would constitute an English common law marriage by exchange of promises, the marriage was valid.

In *Taczanowska v Taczanowski*[131] the Court of Appeal applied English common law and upheld the formal validity of a marriage in Italy during World War II between two Polish nationals, one of whom was serving as an officer with the British armed forces. The marriage, which was celebrated by a Roman Catholic priest, did not comply with the local forms and was void by Italian domestic law and Polish law.[132]

The common law marriage exception to the *lexi loci celebrationis* rule has been heavily criticised. There is no clear reason why marriages conducted in extenuating circumstances should be held to the formal standards of eighteenth-century England.[133]

10.8 Characterisation of issues

From the examination of the above case law it is clear that where the issue being examined is related to the essential validity of a marriage, the dual-domicile rule will generally be applied to see if the marriage is valid but where the issue relates to formal validity the *lex loci celebrationis* will be used. The court can use expert testimony to establish if the formalities satisfy the requirements of the *lex loci celebrationis*.[134]

The courts must determine whether the relevant issue relates to essential validity or formal validity. This process is known as characterisation.

10.8.1 Consent

A marriage may be flawed due to lack of consent where no consent has actually been given. This is established as a matter of fact.[135] Where consent is given in the wrong form, the matter will be considered to be one of formal validity. Where the parties are considered incapable of giving consent at all, or where the reality of the consent given is in question, this will be a matter of essential validity.[136]

---

128 The Court relied on *Catterall v Catterall* (1847) 1 Rob Eccl 580 and *Maclean v Cristall* (1849) 7 Notes of Case, Supplement 17, 24.
129 [1953] AC 304.
130 [1958] P 147.
131 [1957] P 301.
132 See also *Merker v Merker* [1963] P 283; *Preston v Preston* [1963] P 411.
133 D Mendes Da Costa, 'The Formalities of Marriage in the Conflict of Laws' (1958) 7 ICLQ 217, 226–235; JA Andrews, 'The Common law Marriage' (1959) 22 MLR 396, 403–407.
134 *Alfonso Brown v Milwood* [2006] EWHC 642 (Fam), [2006] 2 FLR 265.
135 Ibid.
136 Consultation Paper [5.7].

10.8.1.1 Form of consent

In *Solomon v Walters*[137] a marriage was celebrated without parental consent. This is not required by English law but was necessary where the marriage was celebrated. The courts characterised this problem as one relating to the formal validity of the marriage. This meant that the courts applied the law of the place where the marriage was celebrated. Accordingly the marriage was held to be voidable.[138]

In *Apt v Apt*[139] the Court of Appeal established that whether or not a marriage by proxy was valid was an issue relating to formal validity. In this case, where the wife was resident and domiciled in England, a ceremony of marriage was celebrated in Buenos Aires between her and her husband, who was domiciled and resident in Argentina. The wife did not make an appearance at the ceremony but she was represented by a person whom, by power of attorney, she named as her representative to contract the marriage. This marriage was valid by Argentinean law but invalid by English law. The Court of Appeal drew a distinction between the method of giving consent and the fact of consent. The method of giving consent is considered to be a marriage of formal validity. As the marriage was formally valid by the law of the place of celebration, it was recognised as valid in England law.

In *McCabe v McCabe*[140] a marriage ceremony was celebrated in Ghana under Akan custom. The man was Irish and the woman was Ghanaian. They lived together in London and neither of them attended the ceremony. He sent £100 and a bottle of gin. Relatives of both parties attended the ceremony, during which the £100 was distributed and the gin was drunk as a blessing of the marriage. On the issue of formal validity the Court of Appeal upheld the marriage, applying Ghanaian law.

10.8.1.2 Reality of consent

There is controversy over whether defects affecting the reality of consent should be classified as relating to formal or essential validity. For many years the English court applied English law as the law of the forum.

In *Buckland v Buckland*[141] the petitioner, a Maltese man, was charged under Maltese law with the corruption of a 15-year-old girl. He claimed that he was innocent but was advised by his solicitor that he would be found guilty and his only alternative to criminal penalties was to marry the girl. He married her at a church in Malta. A few days later, he left for England and never returned. In 1964, he had acquired English domicile and petitioned for an annulment of his Maltese marriage on the basis that it was void for lack of consent. Scarman J, referring only to English domestic law, declared the marriage null and void. The only connection to England was that by the date of the proceedings the petitioner had acquired an English domicile.

Today, it seems that the weight of judicial opinion favours reference of the issue of consent to the law of the domicile of the parties.

In *Way v Way*[142] the husband, a British subject domiciled in England, went through a ceremony of marriage in Russia with his wife, a Russian domiciliary. He believed that he was legally married but certain formalities required by Russian law had not been complied with. Shortly after the marriage, the couple intended to relocate to England. The wife was not permitted to leave Russia.

---

137 [1956] 3 DLR (2d) 78.
138 *Simonin v Mallac* (1860) 2 Sw & Tr 67; *Ogden v Ogden* [1908] P 46.
139 [1948] P 83.
140 [1994] 1 FLR 410.
141 [1968] P 296.
142 [1950] P71.

The husband eventually petitioned the English courts for annulment of the marriage on the basis that it did not comply with formalities required by Russian law. He further contended that his consent to the marriage was defective as he believed at the time of the ceremony that his wife would be allowed to accompany him to England. Hodson J held that, under English law, the law of the domicile of the petitioner, a mistake of this kind was not sufficient to nullify consent. On appeal the marriage was held to be void on the basis of non-compliance with the Russian formalities.

In *Szechter v Szechter*[143] a Polish professor divorced his wife and married the petitioner, who was domiciled in Poland, in order to secure her release from prison, and enable her to escape to the West. On arrival in England, she petitioned for annulment on the ground of duress. Sir Jocelyn P held that it was for Polish law, as the law of the domicile of both parties at the time of the marriage, to determine the validity of that marriage.

In *City of Westminster v IC (By His Friend The Official Solicitor) and KC and NN*[144] the court held that a vulnerable autistic adult did not have the capacity to consent to marriage in English law. He entered into a marriage with a Bangladeshi woman by telephone. The court held that this marriage was not valid as the man did not have capacity to enter into a marriage under the law of his domicile. In addition, refusal of recognition was justified on public policy grounds in order to protect the vulnerable adult from potential abuse.

10.8.2 Non-consummation

In English domestic law, a marriage is voidable if one of the parties is impotent or wilfully refuses to consummate the marriage. In other countries, impotence is a common ground that can render a marriage invalid, but wilful refusal is quite an unusual basis for nullity. In other countries, wilful refusal may be a ground for divorce or may incur no legal relief at all. Neither impotence nor wilful refusal really relates to form or capacity[145] as it can only be determined if the marriage is flawed for failure to consummate after the marriage has taken place. The case law is unclear on how failure to consummate should be characterised and which law should be applied to determine the marriage's validity.

In *Ponticelli v Ponticelli*[146] the parties were married in Italy by proxy. The wife was domiciled in Italy, and the husband was domiciled in England. The husband petitioned for a nullity on the ground of wilful refusal. Wilful refusal was not a ground for annulment under Italian law. Sachs J classified the defect as relating either to the personal capacities of the parties or as a basis for dissolution.[147] He found himself unable to reconcile the authorities[148] but rejected the classification of such a defect as being an issue of form. He held that either the *lex domicilii* of the petitioner or the *lex fori* should be applied. In this case, both factors pointed to English law.[149]

The Law Commission noted the lack of clarity in the law but no clear recommendation was made.[150]

---

143 [1971] P 286.
144 [2008] EWCA Civ 198, [2008] 2 FLR 267.
145 Consultation Paper [5.2].
146 [1958] P 204.
147 Ibid 212.
148 *Way v Way* [1950] P 71; *De Reneville v De Reneville* [1948] P 100; *Robert v Robert* [1947] P 164.
149 *Ponticelli v Ponticelli* [1958] P 204, 215.
150 Consultation Paper [5.33].

Impediment	**Applicable law**	**Special rules where one of the spouses is an English domiciliary**
Prohibited degrees	*Lex domicilii*	Rule in *Sottomayer v De Barros No. 2*
Age	*Lex domicilii*	Rule in *Sottomayer v De Barros No. 2*
Sex	English law applies; a foreign gender reassignment must comply with the Gender Recognition Act	
Subsisting marriage	Where the dissolution of the first marriage is recognised in English law the second marriage will be valid	
Polygamous marriage	*Lex domicilii* and *lex loci*	British domiciliary cannot enter into an actually polygamous marriage. Any potentially polygamous marriage will be recognised as if it were monogamous.
Foreign impediments	*Lex fori* although case law is inconclusive	Rule in *Sottomayer v De Barros No. 2*
Formal validity	*Lex loci* unless the Foreign Marriage Act 1892 applies or it is recognised as complying with the formalities of the English common law	
Capacity to consent	*Lex domicilii*	Rule in *Sottomayer v De Barros No. 2*
Quality of consent	*Lex domicilii*	Rule in *Sottomayer v De Barros No. 2*
Form of consent	*Lex loci*	
Parental consent	*Lex loci*	
Non-consummation	*Lex fori* or *lex domicilii* (case law is unclear)	

Fig 10.2 Applicable law when recognising foreign marriages.

10.9 Public policy issues

The English courts will not enforce or recognise a right or obligation arising under a foreign law if to do so would be contrary to English public policy. It may be that the rule itself is objectionable or that the impact of the rule's recognition in England in the particular case would be objectionable. Where the recognition of a marriage would be contrary to public policy it will be refused recognition.

In *Cheni v Cheni*,[151] Sir Jocelyn Simon P stated that the true test was whether the marriage is 'so offensive to the conscience of the English court' that recognition of a marriage validly created under foreign law should be refused. In deciding that question, the court will seek to exercise common sense, good manners and reasonable tolerance.

The courts must weigh up the implication of refusing recognition against the English policy goals of upholding marriages and the undesirability of creating limping statuses.[152]

10.10 Where a marriage is found to be invalid on the application of foreign law

Where an English marriage is found to be invalid on the application of English law there are three consequences in English law: the marriage may be void, voidable or a non-marriage. Where the English courts find a foreign marriage to be invalid under an applicable foreign law, should the English courts apply the consequences of invalidity as determined by that foreign law or should they apply the law of the forum? For example, in Ireland, lack of consent renders a marriage void, not voidable, and there is no right of ancillary relief once a marriage has been annulled. If an English court declares a marriage to be void for invalid consent on the application of Irish law, is this marriage recognised in England as void *ab initio* or void from the declaration of nullity? Furthermore, should the parties be permitted to apply for ancillary relief in the English courts as a consequence of invalidity?

In *De Reneville*[153] the court considered whether a marriage that had not been consummated should be recognised as void or voidable in England. The court held that the consequences of the impediment should be determined by the applicable law. Here the court declared the marriage to be invalid on the application of French law, therefore French law applied to determine if the marriage was void or voidable. The Law Commission recommended the *De Reneville* approach in determining whether a marriage is void or voidable in the Consultation Paper.[154]

In *Corbett v Corbett* the court stated that the consequences of invalidity are to be determined by the *lex fori*.[155] The Law Commission recommended that the consequences of a nullity decree should be determined by the law of the forum. It is for English law to determine the consequences of its own decrees.[156] In recent cases, the English courts have applied the *lex fori* in determining the legal consequences of a finding of invalidity.

In *Alfonso Brown v Milwood*[157] the court held that a Ghanaian marriage where there was, as a matter of fact, no consent at all was a non-marriage in English law with no legal consequences whatsoever.

In *Burns v Burns*[158] the parties married in California, in a hot-air balloon. Under California law this ceremony would have no legal effect at all as a marriage licence had not been obtained before the ceremony. The wife sought a decree of nullity from the English court. This would entitle her to apply for financial relief. The court held that foreign law was merely the litmus test by which the validity of the marriage was tested. It was for the *lex fori* to decide the implications of invalidity, and to decide what remedies were available to a petitioner. The court could grant a decree of nullity in relation to a foreign marriage where the local law did not categorise the invalid marriage by its own

151 [1965] P 85.
152 *City of Westminster v IC (By His Friend The Official Solicitor) and KC and NN* [2008] EWCA Civ 198, [2008] 2 FLR 267.
153 [1948] P 100.
154 Consultation Paper [5.53].
155 [1971] P 83, 109.
156 Consulatation Paper [5.54]; see also *Pugh v Pugh* [1951] P 482.
157 [2006] EWHC 642 (Fam), [2006] 2 FLR 265.
158 [2008] 1 FLR 813.

terminology as void.[159] This would leave it open to the parties to apply for financial relief from the English courts.

In *Hudson v Leigh*[160] the court held that a marriage ceremony in South Africa which had marriage-like characteristics failed fundamentally in law to effect a marriage. The court held that although this marriage would have been declared void under South African law[161] the English courts should consider the marriage as a non-marriage with no legal consequences.[162]

10.11 Civil partnership

UK law currently recognises certain same sex overseas relationships as civil partnerships.[163] These overseas relationships are recognised where they are specified by the Secretary of State in Sched 20 to the Civil Partnership Act[164] or where they meet the general conditions of s 214 of the Civil Partnership Act 2004. Under the general conditions, the overseas relationship must be one that cannot be entered into if either party is already married or in a similar relationship. The overseas relationship must be monogamous. The relationship must be of indeterminate duration and must have the effect of treating the parties as if they were a married couple.

In addition the overseas relationship must be registered in the UK or in the territory in which it was formed.[165] The parties must be of the same sex under the law of the country where the relationship is registered **and** the law of England.[166] Neither party may be married or in a subsisting civil partnership.[167]

Under Art 215 of the Civil Partnership Act 2004, an overseas relationship between two people is treated in England as a civil partnership where both parties had capacity to enter into the relationship under the *lex loci celebrationis* and the parties had complied with the necessary formalities in the place where the overseas relationship was created. Where either party to the overseas relationship was domiciled in England and Wales, the couple will not be treated as a civil partnership if either party was under 16 or if they were within the English prohibited degrees of relationship.[168]

Norrie argues that it is legitimate to apply the law of the place of celebration to the question of capacity, as many countries do not, as yet, have a concept of civil partnership or same-sex marriage and so the law of the domicile may be silent on the issue. However, the application of English law to the capacity of the foreign civil partner where the other party is domiciled in England and Wales is unprincipled and does not mirror the law for recognition of foreign marriages.[169]

The overseas relationship will not be recognised as a civil partnership if it would be manifestly contrary to public policy to recognise the capacity, under the relevant law, of one or both of the parties to enter into the relationship.[170]

It is also possible for two parties, one of whom is a UK national, to enter into a civil partnership in a foreign territory in the presence of a prescribed officer of Her Majesty's Diplomatic Service.[171] This procedure is very similar to a consular marriage. The parties must be eligible to

159 Ibid [45].
160 [2009] 2 FLR 1129.
161 Ibid [41].
162 Ibid [76].
163 If the Marriage (Same Sex Couples) Bill 2012–13 to 2013–14 (HC Bill 126) is enacted, such relationships will be recognised as marriages.
164 S 213.
165 S 212(1)(b).
166 S 216.
167 S 212(2).
168 S 217.
169 K McK Norrie, 'Recognition of foreign relationships under the Civil Partnership Act 2004' (2006) 2 JPIL 137, 166.
170 S 218.
171 S 210 Civil Partnership Act 2004.

register as civil partners in the UK, the authorities of the foreign territory must not object to the registration, and insufficient facilities must exist for parties to enter into an overseas relationship under the law of that country or territory. The civil partnership will be valid where it complies with the formal requirements of English law. These formalities are outlined in the Civil Partnership (Registration Abroad and Certificates) Order.[172]

Overseas civil partnerships may be carried out by an officer appointed under the Registration of Births, Deaths and Marriages (Special Provisions) Act 1957 where one of the parties is a member Her Majesty's Forces serving in the country or territory. The formalities for such civil partnerships are outlined in the Civil Partnership (Armed Forces) Order.[173] Civil partnerships conducted by a chaplain through a religious ceremony will not be recognised. The parties are treated as if they had registered their civil partnership in the UK.

10.12 Further reading

C Clarkson, 'Marriage in England: favouring the *lex fori*' (1990) 10 *Legal Studies* 80–90.

T Hartley, 'The policy basis of the English conflicts of law of marriage' (1972) 36 MLR 571.

A J E Jaffey, 'The foundations of the rules of choice of laws' (1982) 2 OJLS 368–392.

Law Commission and Scottish Law Commission, 'Private International Law Choice of Law Rules In Marriage' (LC 164, 1987).

Law Commission and Scottish Law Commission, 'Private International Law: Choice of Law Rules in Marriage' (Cons Memo 64, 1985).

JHC Morris, 'De Reneville revisited' (1970) 19 ICLQ 424.

J Murphy, 'Rationality and cultural pluralism in the non-recognition of foreign marriages' (2000) 49 ICLQ 643.

J Murphy, 'The recognition of same sex families in Britain: the role of private international law' (2002) 16 *International Journal of Law, Policy and the Family* 181.

K McK Norrie, 'Recognition of foreign relationships under the Civil Partnership Act 2004' (2006) 2 JPIL 137.

P Shah, 'Attitudes to polygamy in English law' (2003) ICLQ 369.

172 SI 2005/2761.

173 SI 2005/3188.

Chapter 11

Divorce and Financial Relief

Chapter Contents

Key Issues:

- **Jurisdiction** to grant divorce under Brussels II *bis* and English domestic law
- **Recognition** of foreign divorces under Brussels II *bis* and English domestic law
- **Jurisdiction** to grant financial relief under the Maintenance Regulation and English domestic law
- EU regulation of **applicable law** in divorce proceedings
- The legal effect given to foreign prenuptial agreements in the English courts
- Private international law issues relating the dissolution of same sex partnerships

11.1 Introduction

This chapter will examine the conflicts of laws issues involved when a marriage or civil partnership is dissolved through divorce/dissolution. Different countries have different social attitudes to divorce. In some countries, such as Ireland, divorce is permitted only after long periods of living apart and attempts at reconciliation and counselling. In other countries, such as Sweden, the parties can simply end their marriage by agreement. In England, divorce is based on irretrievable breakdown, demonstrated either by living apart for set periods or some evidence of unreasonable behaviour.[1] Where a couple has a connection to more than one Member State it may be easier to get a divorce in some states than in others.

EU regulation Brussels II *bis*[2] determines which EU Member States will have jurisdiction to grant an order ending a marriage.

Brussels II *bis* also provides for the mutual recognition of EU Member State judgments dissolving marriage throughout the EU. Where a divorce, legal separation or decree of nullity has been granted by a non-EU country, the Family Law Act 1986 allows these orders to be recognised by the English courts.

In other EU Member States the law applicable to a grant of divorce or judicial separation is determined by EU regulation Rome III,[3] where the EU Member State has adopted this regulation. The UK has opted out of this regulation, and so the English courts will apply English domestic law to determine if a divorce or judicial separation should be granted.

This chapter will also examine the ability of the English courts to grant financial relief after the dissolution of a relationship. Different courts have different policy objectives when granting financial relief. These reflect the different economic realities in each country. The English courts are perceived to make very favourable orders for the economically weaker spouse.[4]

1 S 1(2) Matrimonial Causes Act 1973.
2 Council Regulation (EC) No 2201/2003 concerning jurisdiction and the recognition and enforcement of judgments in matrimonial matters and the matters of parental responsibility, repealing Regulation (EC) No 1347/2000, 2003 OJ L338/1.
3 Council Regulation (EU) No 1259/2010 implementing enhanced cooperation in the area of the law applicable to divorce and legal separation, 2010 OJ L343/10.
4 R Deech, 'What's a Woman Worth?' [2009] Fam Law 1140; M Thorpe, 'London – the Divorce Capital of the World' [2009] Fam Law 21.

Jurisdiction and enforcement for maintenance issues are now governed by the Maintenance Regulation.[5] The Maintenance Regulation allows for a common approach to applicable law in maintenance cases in other EU Member States through the Hague Protocol 2007.[6] The English courts continue to apply domestic law to maintenance disputes.

In most European countries, a distinction is made between determination of property ownership after the dissolution of marriage and awarding financial support in the form of maintenance. English law does not have this distinction, and, as part of financial relief, the English court can adjust the ownership of property. Two draft EU regulations[7] have been proposed to regulate decisions relating to matrimonial property. These proposals allow spouses or civil partners to choose the law applicable to the property consequences of their marriages.

England has opted out of these regulations and will continue to apply English law to issues of matrimonial property. How the English courts should treat foreign matrimonial property agreements in financial relief cases has been the subject of recent controversy.

11.2 Jurisdiction to grant a divorce, annulment or judicial separation

In most cases, the jurisdiction of the English courts to grant divorces, judicial separations or annulments is established using EU regulation Brussels II *bis*, which is binding on all EU Member States except Denmark. A small number of cases fall outside Brussels II *bis* and are governed solely by national rules. Domestic rules apply only where a person, domiciled or habitually resident in England, seeks to divorce a spouse who is not habitually resident in an EU Member State and is not a national or domiciliary of an EU Member State and no Member State has jurisdiction under Brussels II *bis*.

11.2.1 Jurisdiction under Brussels II *bis*

Brussels II *bis* originated from plans to extend the Brussels Convention to cover matrimonial matters. An explanatory report based on this version of the regulation is available and may aid in the interpretation of the current regulation.[8] After the Treaty of Amsterdam, regulation of matrimonial matters took the form of a binding EU regulation.

EU regulation Brussels II[9] entered into force on 1 March 2001. This regulation established when EU Member States had the jurisdiction to hear proceedings relating to matrimonial status and provided that a judgment given by a court with jurisdiction would be recognised in all other Member States.

In 2003, Brussels II was repealed by Brussels II *bis*, which added a range of rules on the mutual enforcement of judgments relating to parental responsibility for children.[10] No amendments were made to the measures on nullity, divorce and separation except some renumbering of the articles.[11]

---

5 Council Regulation (EC) No 4/2009 on jurisdiction, applicable law, recognition and enforcement of decisions and cooperation in matters relating to maintenance obligations [2008] OJ L 7/1.

6 Hague Protocol on the Law Applicable to Maintenance Obligations, 2007 available at www.hcch.net/index_en.php?act=Conventions.status&cid=133 (accessed 16 May 2013).

7 Proposal for a Council Regulation on jurisdiction, applicable law and the recognition and enforcement of decisions in matters of matrimonial property regimes COM (2011) 126 final; Proposal for a Council Regulation on jurisdiction, applicable law and the recognition and enforcement of decisions regarding the property consequences of registered partnerships COM (2011) 127 final.

8 A Borrás, *Explanatory Report on the Convention, Drawn up on the Basis of Art K.3 of the Treaty on European Union, on Jurisdiction and the Recognition and Enforcement of Judgments in Matrimonial Matters* [1998] OJ C221/27 (Borrás Report).

9 Council Regulation (EC) No 1347/2000 of 29 May 2000 OJ L160/30.

10 These rules are explored in Chapter 13.

11 Annex V of Reg 2201/2003 shows the correspondence between articles of Brussels II and Brussels II *bis*.

Denmark has opted out of the regulation and is not obliged to apply Brussels II *bis*. Brussels II *bis* was given effect in England and Wales by the European Communities (Jurisdiction and Judgments in Matrimonial Matters and Matters of Parental Responsibility) Regulation 2005[12] and applies from 1 March 2005. Judgments granted under the rules of Brussels II are recognisable under Brussels II *bis*.[13]

Brussels II *bis* applies to civil proceedings relating to divorce, legal separation or the annulment of a marriage.[14] These proceedings relate to a change in legal status. A marriage is dissolved either through divorce or a decree of nullity which allows the parties to marry again. Legal separation has the same meaning as a decree of judicial separation. This does not dissolve the marriage or enable either party to remarry but it entitles the spouses to live apart.

Seven alternative bases of jurisdiction are found in Art 3 of Brussels II *bis*.

Under the general rule jurisdiction will lie with:

- the court of the Member State in which both spouses are habitually resident, **or**
- the court of the Member State where the spouses were last jointly habitually resident, if one of them still resides there, **or**
- the court of the Member State where the respondent is habitually resident, **or**
- the court of the Member State where either of the spouses is habitually residence if a **joint application** is made, **or**
- the court of the Member State where the applicant is habitually resident if he has resided there for at least a year immediately before the application was made, **or**
- the court of the Member State where the applicant is habitually resident if he has resided there for at least six months immediately before the application was made and is a national of the Member State in question; if the applicant is habitually resident in the United Kingdom or Ireland, this will apply where the applicant has his 'domicile', **or**
- the Member State of which both spouses are nationals or, in the case of the United Kingdom or Ireland, where both spouses are domiciled.

The rules of Brussels II *bis* also apply to intra-UK jurisdictional issues.[15]

The notion of domicile is intended to be used interchangeably with nationality depending on the internal system of the Member State. Civil law countries such as Spain are more comfortable in claiming jurisdiction based on common nationality, whereas in England or Ireland dual domicile is preferred.[16] Domicile is given its common law meaning as understood in the legal systems of England and Ireland.[17]

Habitual residence is not defined in the regulation but must be given an autonomous EU meaning which focuses on a 'centre of interests'.[18] In *Z v Z (Divorce Proceedings)*[19] a French couple had moved to London on an open-ended relocation package provided by the husband's French employer. They left their Paris property vacant in case they wanted to return, but their children were enrolled in London schools. After a year, the couple broke up and the wife petitioned the English courts for divorce. The court held that the couple were habitually resident in England within the meaning of Art 3.[20]

---

12 SI 2005/265.
13 Art 64 Brussels II *bis*.
14 Art 1(a).
15 Art 66.
16 Borrás Report, 27.
17 Art 7(2).
18 *Swaddling v Adjudication Officer* [1999] ECR 1–1075, *V v V (Divorce: Jurisdiction)* [2011] EWHC 1190 (Fam), [2011] 2 FLR 778; [2011] 2 FLR 778 See Chapter 2.
19 [2009] EWHC 2626 (Fam), [2010] 1 FLR 694.
20 See also *L-K v K (No 2)* [2006] EWHC 3280 (Fam), [2007] 2 FLR 729.

In *Hadadi v Hadadi*[21] the couple were Hungarian nationals who had later both acquired French nationality. The ECJ confirmed that both the French courts and the Hungarian courts had jurisdiction under Art 3(1)(b) and the couple could choose between them.

Under Art 5, a court of a Member State that has granted a legal separation retains jurisdiction to convert a legal separation into a divorce if such a procedure is possible under the law of that Member State. This creates an additional basis of jurisdiction. In some Member States, legal separation is a necessary step prior to divorce, and a stated period must pass where reconciliation can be encouraged. Other states have no institution of legal separation.

There is no hierarchy to the grounds in Art 3, and a couple may well have a basis to bring a petition for divorce in more than one Member State. For example, a French husband and his German wife lived in Sweden for several years. When the marriage broke up, the husband returned to France, and the German wife remained in Sweden. Six months later, it was possible for either party to bring proceedings in Sweden as the Member State where the couple were last habitually resident together because the wife was still resident there. It was also possible for the wife to bring proceedings in France as the husband is habitually resident there. The husband could also bring proceedings in France as he was habitually resident there and a French national.

Article 19 of Brussels II *bis* creates a strict, first in time, *lis pendens* rule. Where proceedings relating to divorce, legal separation or marriage annulment between the same parties are brought before courts of different Member States, the court second seised must stay its proceedings until such time as the jurisdiction of the court first seised is established.[22] If the court first seised establishes jurisdiction, the court second seised must decline jurisdiction in favour of that court.

There is no provision in Brussels II *bis* to allow a Member State court which has jurisdiction to transfer a case relating to matrimonial proceedings to another court within the EU.

Where more than one jurisdiction is available, the first spouse to seise a court with jurisdiction will determine where many of the issues are heard. This potential 'race to court' has been criticised for pitting spouses against each other, undermining the possibility of reconciliation and allowing one spouse to take advantage of a more preferential system.[23] No empirical evidence of this rush to court has yet been put forward.[24] Article 3 ensures that the jurisdiction in which proceedings are brought has some connection to the marriage. It is not possible for one spouse to merely travel to another Member State to take advantage of an easier divorce regime. Neither is it possible to avoid judicially directed reconciliation.

In *Chorley v Chorley*,[25] a French husband had commenced divorce proceedings in France which involved a period for reconciliation. During that period, the wife petitioned the English courts for divorce. The Court of Appeal granted a stay, under the Brussels II equivalent of Art 19, in order for the French court to determine whether the judicially directed reconciliation procedures had seised French jurisdiction.[26]

Article 18 of Brussels II *bis* also allows the court to stay proceedings to allow a respondent, habitually resident in another Member State, sufficient time to prepare for the hearing.[27]

Article 6 of Brussels II *bis* confirms that the jurisdictional rules of Brussels II *bis* are exclusive where the person being divorced has a connection to an EU Member State by being habitually resident in a Member State or a national or domiciliary of an EU Member State. For example, the

21 C168/08 [2009] ECR I-6871, [2011] ILPr 15.
22 Art 19(1); *L-K v K (Brussels II Revised: Maintenance Pending Suit)* [2006] EWHC 153 (Fam), [2006] 2 FLR 1113.
23 *Golubovich v Golubovich* [2010] EWCA Civ 810, [2010] 2 FLR 1614.
24 K Boele-Woelki, 'For Better or Worse: The Europeanization of International Divorce Law, *Yearbook of Private International Law*, Vol 12 (2010), 1–26.
25 [2005] EWCA Civ 68.
26 See also *Re N* [2007] EWHC 1274 (Fam).
27 Art 18(1).

rules of Brussels II *bis* will apply where an application is made to an EU Member State court to divorce a Japanese spouse habitually resident in the Netherlands or a German spouse who is habitually resident in California. Where the court does not have jurisdiction under Brussels II *bis* it must decline to hear such cases.

In *Sundelind Lopez v Lopez Lizazo*[28] a Swedish woman issued divorce proceedings against her Cuban husband. The couple had been habitually resident in France but at the end of the marriage the husband had returned to Cuba. The wife tried to bring proceedings in Sweden, basing jurisdiction solely on her Swedish nationality. The Swedish courts held that they were precluded from hearing the petition as the French courts had jurisdiction over the case under Art 3 of Brussels II *bis* as the courts of the couple's last habitual residence. However, the husband was no longer habitually resident in the EU and had no EU nationality.

The ECJ held that where the respondent is not resident in an EU Member State and is not a national of an EU Member State, the courts of a Member State are still bound by the rules of Brussels II *bis*. It is only possible to base jurisdiction to hear the petition on purely national law if no other Member State has jurisdiction under Art 3 of Brussels II *bis*.

11.2.1.1 Provisional and protective measures

Article 20 allows courts to take provisional and protective measures in respect of persons or assets in that state even if it has no jurisdiction over the divorce. Such measures must be urgent, provisional and taken in respect of persons or assets present in the Member State ordering the provisional measure.[29] In *Wermuth v Wermuth* (No 2)[30] the Court of Appeal held that an order for maintenance pending suit cannot be considered as a provisional or protective measure as its effects were likely to impact on the application for divorce.[31]

11.2.1.2 No Jurisdiction under Brussels II *bis* for ancillary relief

Brussels II *bis* governs jurisdiction for proceedings to dissolve a marriage. It contains no rules regarding jurisdiction to determine the financial consequences of divorce. In many legal systems divorce and the financial consequences of divorce will be dealt with in the same set of proceedings, but these proceedings may also be free standing.[32] A court which is competent pursuant to Brussels II *bis* will have jurisdiction to grant financial relief under both the Maintenance Regulation and English domestic law.

11.2.2 Jurisdiction under the Domicile and Matrimonial Proceedings Act 1973

Article 7 of Brussels II *bis* provides that jurisdiction may be based solely on national law where no other Member State has jurisdiction under Brussels II *bis*. Article 7(2) specifically provides that national rules of jurisdiction can be used when the respondent is not habitually resident in, a national of or domiciled in an EU Member State.[33] For example, English rules determining jurisdiction will apply where a husband habitually resident or domiciled in England applies to the English courts to divorce his Russian wife who is habitually resident in Russia and no other EU Member State has jurisdiction under Brussels II *bis*.

---

28 C68/07 *Sundelind Lopez v Lopez Lizazo* [2007] ECR I-10403; [2008] 1 FLR 582.
29 C523/07 *Re A* [2009] ECR I-2805, [2009] 2 FLR 1.
30 [2002] EWCA Civ 50, [2003] 1 FLR 1029.
31 Ibid [32], [33].
32 *Moore v Moore* [2007] EWCA Civ 361 [2007] 2 FLR 339.
33 Art 7(2).

The Domicile and Matrimonial Proceedings Act 1973 allows the English courts to hear proceedings for divorce, nullity or judicial separation based on domicile of either party where no court has jurisdiction under Brussels II *bis*.[34] Where an application to annul a marriage is made after the death of either spouse to the marriage, the English courts will have jurisdiction to hear the nullity petition where the deceased spouse was domiciled in England and Wales at death or had been habitually resident in England and Wales throughout the period of one year ending with the date of death.[35]

11.2.2.1 Staying proceedings under the Domicile and Matrimonial Proceedings Act 1973

The English court is required to stay divorce proceedings, if divorce or nullity proceedings relating to the same marriage are pending elsewhere in the British Islands[36] and the parties have a strong connection to this other jurisdiction.[37] This connection exists where the parties to the marriage both resided in that jurisdiction before the English proceedings began or had their last place of joint residence in that other jurisdiction. One of the parties must have been habitually resident in that jurisdiction for at least a year when the period of joint residence ended.

The English courts also have a discretionary power to stay any 'matrimonial proceedings' other than proceedings governed by Brussels II *bis*, where proceedings are pending in a jurisdiction outside the British Islands which are capable of affecting the validity of the same marriage.[38] 'Matrimonial proceedings' include a declaration as to the validity and subsistence of a marriage, nullity, divorce and judicial separation.[39] Free-standing applications for custody or financial relief are not 'matrimonial proceedings'.[40]

The discretion of the court is to be exercised where it appears, on the balance of fairness and convenience, that it is appropriate to deal with the foreign proceedings before future steps are taken in England. The court may order the foreign proceedings to be stayed pending a decision by the English court or stay the English proceedings pending a decision by the foreign court.[41] The court will decide which forum is the most appropriate to hear the dispute. The court must have regard to all the relevant factors, including the convenience of witnesses and delay or expense likely to result from the English proceedings being stayed.[42] When exercising its discretion, the court may consider the effect that a stay on matrimonial proceedings will have on ancillary financial relief proceedings.

In *De Dampierre v De Dampierre*[43] the House of Lords held that the courts should apply the same principles as the common law doctrine of *forum non conveniens*[44] when deciding whether to grant a discretionary stay under the Domicile and Matrimonial Proceedings Act 1973. The court should not grant a stay merely on the basis that English proceedings would be more advantageous, as long as substantial justice would be done in the overseas forum. In *De Dampierre*, divorce proceedings were pending in both England and France. The husband applied to have the proceedings in England stayed. The wife was likely to receive more favourable financial provision after divorce in England. However, the House of Lords held that France was the most natural forum for the divorce proceedings and there was no reason to believe that justice would not be done in France.

34 Ss 5(2)–(3); *M v M (Divorce: Domicile)* [2010] EWHC 982 (Fam)
35 S 5(3).
36 Scotland, Northern Ireland, Jersey, Guernsey and the Isle of Man.
37 Sched 1 para 8, Domicile and Matrimonial Proceedings Act 1973.
38 Sched 1 para 9, Domicile and Matrimonial Proceedings Act 1973.
39 Sched 1 para 2, Domicile and Matrimonial Proceedings Act 1973.
40 *Thyssen-Bornemisza v Thyssen-Bornemisza* [1985] 2 WLR 715.
41 Sched 1, para 9(1) Domicile and Matrimonial Proceedings Act 1973.
42 Sched 1, para 9(2) Domicile and Matrimonial Proceedings Act 1973.
43 [1988] AC 92, [1987] 2 FLR 300; *M v M (Divorce: Domicile)* [2010] EWHC 982 (Fam).
44 See Chapter 4.

In *O v O (Appeal Against Stay: Divorce Petition)*[45] a couple had married in Nigeria. The wife had taken divorce proceedings in England on the basis of her habitual residence. The husband issued divorce proceedings in Nigeria and applied to have the English proceedings stayed. Some issues arose as to the validity of the marriage, and the court of first instance held that the Nigerian court might be better placed to decide on this issue and granted a stay. The Court of Appeal reversed the decision, holding that there was no strong case for nullity and that greater consideration should be given to the jurisdiction first seised – in this case England. The Court drew attention to the fact that most of the husband's financial assets were in London and allowing the stay would cause manifest unfairness to the wife.

The existence of a prenuptial agreement can influence the court in deciding whether to order a stay of English proceedings. For example, in *S v S*[46] the couple had entered into a binding prenuptial agreement that New York law would govern any future divorce. The wife brought proceedings in the English courts. Concurrent proceedings were taken in New York, and the husband applied to have the English proceedings stayed. The court held that the prenuptial agreement connected the proceedings to New York and was a significant factor in the court's consideration of whether it was fair to stay the English proceedings. The court was satisfied that substantial justice would be done in New York and ordered the stay.[47]

In *Ella v Ella*[48] a couple had dual British and Israeli nationality. They married in Israel. Before the marriage they entered into a prenuptial agreement stating that the law of Israel would apply to questions involving the ownership of property between the spouses. On the breakdown of the marriage, concurrent proceedings for divorce were brought in London and Tel Aviv. Jurisdiction in London was based on the spouses' joint habitual residence. The husband applied for the English proceedings to be stayed under the Domicile and Matrimonial Proceedings Act 1973. The stay was granted as the wife had made no effort to have the Tel Aviv proceedings stayed and to deny the husband's stay would lead to two possibly conflicting judgments.[49] Charles J held that the existence of the prenuptial agreement was also a strong connecting factor to Israel.[50]

From the wording of Sched 1 para 9, it would appear that discretional stays are not available where the English jurisdiction is based on Brussels II *bis*. However, the English courts have continued to stay proceedings in such circumstances, where the competing jurisdiction is a non-Member State. This seems incompatible with the limits placed on national rules of jurisdiction by the ECJ in *Sundelind Lopez v Lopez Lizazo*.[51]

The issue of whether such stays were still compatible with Brussels II *bis* was considered in *JKN v JCN*.[52] The wife took proceedings for divorce in England as the country of the spouses' former joint habitual residence, where she still resided. Her husband brought divorce proceedings in New York and sought a stay of the English proceedings under the Domicile and Matrimonial Proceedings Act 1973. This case fell squarely within the remit of Brussels II *bis*, and the court considered whether it had retained discretion to stay proceedings in favour of the New York proceedings.

The court considered the meaning of the phrase 'other than proceedings governed by the Council Regulation' in Sched I para 9 and held that this only limited the power to grant a stay where the competing proceedings were in another Member State.[53]

---

45 [2003] 1 FLR 192.
46 [1997] 2 FLR 100.
47 See further *C v C* [2001] 1 FLR 264; and *K v K* [2003] 1 FLR 120.
48 [2007] EWCA Civ 99, [2007] 2 FLR 35.
49 Ibid [27].
50 Ibid [42].
51 [2008] 1 FLR 582.
52 [2010] EWHC 843 (Fam).
53 Ibid [147] (vii).

In *Owusu v Jackson*[54] the ECJ held that where the courts have jurisdiction under Brussels I there is no discretion to grant a stay on the basis of *forum non conveniens*.[55] The court considered whether the same rule applied where the court had jurisdiction under Brussels II *bis*. The court held that *Owusu* did not apply to situations where there are concurrent proceedings. In addition, Brussels II *bis* did not have the same mandatory language as Brussels I, and if the stay was refused this would increase the chances of conflicting judgments.[56]

The decision in *JKN* has been criticised.[57] However, it is clear that the extension of *Owusu* to family matters would be very unpopular with many practitioners and with members of the judiciary who feel that a strict first in time rule is inappropriate in family matters.[58]

11.2.2.2 Common law powers to restrain oppressive and vexatious proceedings abroad

A common law power exists to allow the English courts to restrain oppressive and vexatious proceedings abroad by way of an anti-suit or *Hemain* injunction. This power should be used very rarely, with caution, and only where the action abroad is vexatious or useless.[59]

In *R v R*,[60] the husband issued separation proceedings in Denmark. He did not inform his wife, which was a necessary step in issuing proceedings in Denmark. She took proceedings in England and then received notice of the Danish proceedings. The husband sought a stay of the English proceedings. The wife sought an English injunction to restrain the Danish proceedings. The husband withdrew his application for stay of English proceedings but continued to challenge English jurisdiction.

The court held that the purpose of a *Hemain* injunction was to prevent one party from manipulating two sets of concurrent proceedings to take advantage of the other party, for example, by seeking to litigate the substantive issues in the foreign court while actively preventing the other party litigating the substantive issues in the English court. In this case, the husband had managed to delay English proceedings while actively pursuing Danish proceedings. This had left the wife with inadequate time to prepare for the Danish proceedings. The court granted a *Hemain* injunction until such a time as the English court had ruled on jurisdiction.

In *S v S*[61] the court emphasised that a *Hemain* injunction should only be granted where it had been demonstrated that the respondent had acted unconscionably, oppressively or vexatiously by disputing that England was the appropriate forum and holding up the English proceedings while at the same time pursuing his own proceedings abroad.

11.3 Applicable law in applications for divorce

Brussels II *bis* contains no provisions on applicable law. This means that a court with jurisdiction under Brussels II *bis* is free to apply its own domestic law as *lex fori*, or to use national rules to determine applicable law. In 2006, the Commission proposed that Brussels II *bis* should be reformed and that the substantive divorce law governing the end of the marriage would be designated by common

54 C281/02 *Owusu v Jackson* [2005] ECR I–553, [2005] 2 All ER (Comm) 577.
55 See Chapter 4.
56 *JKN v SCN* [2010] EWHC 843 (Fam)[149].
57 S Jarmain, 'Staying Matrimonial Proceedings – a Thing of the Past?' [2007] Fam Law 429.
58 I Karsten, 'The State of International Family Law Issues: A View from London' [2009] *International Family Law* 35; T Amlot and K Longmate, 'Forum Shopping: *JKN v JCN*' [2010] Fam Law 990.
59 [1988] 2 FLR 388.
60 [2003] EWHC 2113.
61 [2010] EWHC 3224 (Fam), [2010] 2 FLR 502.

rules.[62] This would eliminate forum shopping and reduce the need for the parties to rush to court. The same law would be applied no matter where the case was heard.

The reception to the proposal was mixed and the unanimity required to adopt the Regulation was not achieved.[63] Several Member States indicated to the Commission that they wished to establish enhanced co-operation in the area of applicable law to matrimonial matters. The Council authorised enhanced co-operation in this area.[64] Rome III[65] was adopted in December 2010 and came into force on 21 June 2012. The enhanced co-operation measure does not affect the operation of Brussels II *bis* and concerns only applicable law. Fourteen Member States[66] have signed up to enhanced co-operation, which means that Rome III will apply to determine the applicable law in divorce and separation proceedings in those states. Thirteen Member States, including the UK, will continue to use their own domestic rules to determine the law applicable to divorce or legal separation. Rome III does not apply to applications for nullity.[67]

Article 5 of Rome III allows spouses to choose the law applicable to their divorce proceedings. This choice is limited to the law of states that are closely connected to marriage. The connections are very similar to the bases of jurisdiction under Brussels II *bis*. The parties may choose the law of the state where the couple were habitually resident when the divorce was concluded, the law of the state where the couple were last habitually resident when the divorce was concluded if one of them still lives there at the time of the conclusion of the agreement, the law of the country of the nationality of either spouse, or the law of the forum.

In the absence of choice, the provisions of Art 8 determine the law that will apply. The law applicable will be the law of the spouses' joint habitual residence at the time the court is seised. **Failing that**, the law applicable is the law of the last joint habitual residence of the spouses, providing that one spouse still lives there and both spouses lived there less than one year before the proceedings started. **Failing that**, the law applicable is the law of the country where both spouses are nationals, and **failing that**, the law applicable is that of the forum. There is a strict hierarchy to the rules under Art 8.

Under Art 8, when the couple changes joint habitual residence, the law applicable to their divorce will also change. The applicable law can be that of a Member State that has not signed up to Rome III.[68] This means that a court that has signed up to enhanced co-operation could be mandated to apply English law to divorce proceedings under Rome III.

As the UK has opted out of Rome III, the English courts will apply English law as the *lex fori* where the English court has jurisdiction to hear divorce or separation hearings. Under the Matrimonial Causes Act 1973 there is no statutory choice-of-law rule, but it is clear that the Law Commission intended English law to apply to all cases where the English courts have jurisdiction.[69]

11.4 Recognition of foreign judgments

Brussels II *bis* governs the recognition of orders dissolving marital status given in EU Member States. This allows divorces to be recognised in other Member States so that the ex-spouses can marry

62 Proposal for a Council Regulation Amending Regulation (EC) No 2201/2003 as Regards Jurisdiction and Introducing Rules Concerning Applicable Law in Matrimonial Matters. Brussels 17 July 2006 COM (2006) 399 final.

63 K Boele-Woelki, 'For Better or Worse: The Europeanization of International Divorce Law' (2010) 12 *Yearbook of Private International Law* 1–26.

64 Council Decision of 12 July 2010 authorising enhanced cooperation in the area of the law applicable to divorce and legal separation (2010/405/EU) OJ L189/12.

65 Council Regulation (EU) No 1259/2010 implementing enhanced cooperation in the area of the law applicable to divorce and legal separation [2010] OJ L343/10.

66 Greece withdrew its request in 2010.

67 Art 1, Rome III.

68 Art 4, Rome III.

69 Law Commission, *Report on Jurisdiction in Matrimonial Causes* (LC No 48, 1972).

again if they should wish to do so. Recognition is not limited to court judgments. Agreements between the parties that are considered to be enforceable in one Member State are recognisable throughout the EU, as authentic instruments.[70] Brussels II *bis* does not contain any enforcement provisions on financial relief. Such judgments are enforceable under the Maintenance Regulation.

Where an order relating to marital status is made by a non-EU Member State or Denmark, domestic English law will govern recognition of that foreign order in England.

11.4.1 Recognition under Brussels II *bis*

Article 21 of Brussels II *bis* provides for automatic recognition of orders relating to marital status granted in an EU Member State. No special process is required to update civil status records; a final decree or authentic instrument from another Member State is sufficient.[71] It is not possible to review the substance of the decision,[72] nor can the jurisdiction of the Member State which gave the judgment be reviewed.[73] Article 25 expressly provides that recognition cannot be refused where the Member State in which recognition is sought would not allow divorce, legal separation or annulment on the same facts. This means that a conservative state where divorce is only permissible after a long period of living apart cannot refuse to recognise a divorce granted in another Member State merely because that state does not require the couple to live apart or seek reconciliation.

Article 22 provides that non-recognition is permitted where such recognition is manifestly contrary to the public policy of the Member State in which recognition is sought.[74] This exception is to be used in very exceptional circumstances[75] as non-recognition of a divorce will create a limping status where the couple will be considered married in one Member State but divorced in all other Member States. This is highly undesirable. Recognition can also be refused where the respondent was not made aware of the divorce proceedings or given sufficient time to arrange for defence.[76] Recognition can be refused where the judgment is irreconcilable with a judgment given between the same parties in the Member State in which recognition is sought or if it is irreconcilable with an earlier judgment given in another Member State.[77]

11.4.2 Recognition under English Law – the Family Law Act 1986

Section 44 of the Family Law Act 1986 provides that divorces, annulments or legal separations obtained by a civil court in the British Islands shall be recognised throughout the British Islands. This means that religious divorces such as a *talaq* or *get* which are obtained in the UK will not be recognised as ending a marriage.[78] Instead, the Divorce (Religious Marriages) Act 2002 enables British courts to take account of the desirability for a religious divorce in a particular case by refusing to make a decree absolute unless a declaration has been made by both parties that they have taken such steps as are required to dissolve the marriage in religious terms.[79]

Overseas divorces, annulments and separations which are granted in countries outside the EU are recognised in England and Wales if certain conditions are satisfied. Two different regimes apply depending on whether the order was obtained by means of 'proceedings' or 'otherwise than by

70 Recital 22.
71 Art 21(2).
72 Art 26.
73 Art 24.
74 Art 21(a).
75 Recital 21.
76 Art 22(b).
77 Arts 22(c)–(d).
78 S 44(1).
79 See also *A v T* [2004] 1 FLR 977.

proceedings'. The meaning of 'proceedings' is much broader than a decree from a court of civil jurisdiction. A divorce obtained by means of proceedings includes any divorce where a formal process is required that involves state officials or a recognised agency.[80] This means that the Family Law Act 1986 will allow some overseas religious divorces to be recognised in England and Wales as divorces granted by 'proceedings'.

By ancient Islamic law, which is still in force in some countries, a husband can divorce his wife simply by pronouncing the word *talaq* three times. The procedure required for a *talaq* differs according to the country in which it occurs and the school of Islamic law that applies. In some cases, the husband does not have to give a reason for the *talaq*, which can be pronounced in the wife's absence. In other countries the *talaq* must be witnessed and registered with a tribunal or authority.

In *El Fadl v El Fadl*[81] a *talaq* divorce was held to constitute 'proceedings' under s 46(1) of the Family Law Act 1986 where the *talaq* had been registered in a Sharia court according to Lebanese law. A mere oral delivery of a *talaq* declared without witnesses or registration will not be considered to be a divorce by proceedings.[82]

Under Jewish law, a divorce is obtained through a consensual process, usually presided over by a Beth Din in a rabbinical court. A *get* or divorce document must be presented by a husband to his wife in order to fully effect the divorce and allow her to remarry. A Jewish *get*, which involves the active participation of members of the Rabbinical Council, is considered to be proceedings.[83]

In *Wicken v Wicken*[84] the court found that a mere 'letter of divorce', sent by a husband in Gambia to his wife in Gambia, evidenced a divorce which was by means 'otherwise than by proceedings'.

11.4.2.1 Recognition of overseas orders by means of proceedings

Section 46 of the Family Law Act 1986 sets out the rules for recognition of decrees granted by means of proceedings outside the British Islands. Such a divorce, separation or annulment will be recognised in England and Wales if it is effective under the law of the state in which it was obtained[85] **and**, on the date of the commencement of foreign proceedings, either party to the marriage was habitually resident or domiciled there or a national of the country granting the judgment.[86]

If an annulment was obtained after the death of one of the spouses, it will be recognisable if the dead spouse had been habitually resident or domiciled in the foreign country, or a national of that country at the time of his death.[87]

A foreign divorce will **not** be recognised if either party to the marriage was habitually resident in the United Kingdom throughout the period of one year immediately preceding the commencement of foreign proceedings.[88]

11.4.2.2 Recognition of overseas orders 'otherwise than by proceedings'

Section 46(2) of the Family Law Act 1986 allows foreign divorces, annulments or legal separations granted with no formal proceedings of any kind to be recognised if more stringent conditions are met. Such divorces, annulments or legal separations are recognised only if they are effective under the law of the country in which they were obtained[89] **and** at the relevant date each party to the

80 *Chaudhary v Chaudhary* [1985] FLR 476; *H v H (Validity of Japanese Divorce)* [2006] EWHC 2989 (Fam), [2007] 1 FLR 1318.
81 [2000] 1 FLR 175; *H v H* [2007] EWHC 2945 (Fam), [2008] 2 FLR 857.
82 *H v S (Recognition of Overseas Divorce)* [2012] 2 FLR 157 [63].
83 *Berkovits v Grinberg* [1995] 1 FLR 477, 486.
84 [1999] Fam 224.
85 S 46(1)(a); *Kellman v Kellman* [2000] 1 FLR 785.
86 S 46(1)(b).
87 S 46(4).
88 S 46(2)(c).
89 S 46(2)(a).

marriage was domiciled in the country or one party was domiciled[90] in that country and the other party was domiciled in another country in which the divorce, annulment or legal separation is recognised as valid. Again, such a divorce will not be recognised where either party to the marriage was habitually resident in the UK throughout the period of one year immediately preceding that date.

Although a divorce obtained 'otherwise than by proceedings' can be recognised in England, no right to apply to English courts for subsequent financial relief will exist under the Matrimonial and Family Proceedings Act 1984.

The s 46(2) procedure was applied in *Wicken v Wicken*.[91]

11.4.2.3 Grounds for non-recognition

Section 51 of the Family Law Act 1986 gives the English courts a discretionary power to refuse to recognise divorces, annulments or judicial separations that would otherwise be recognised under the Family Law Act 1986 in certain circumstances.

The recognition of a divorce, annulment or judicial separation can be refused on the basis of *res judicata* if the order is incompatible with a prior decision on the validity of the marriage.[92] Recognition can also be refused if, at the time that the foreign order was granted, no valid marriage existed under English law.[93] So, for example, if an English brother and sister married abroad and later divorced, the English courts would not recognise the divorce or the marriage. These provisions apply both to overseas orders and to orders granted by a civil jurisdiction within the British Islands.

The English court has further discretion to refuse to recognise overseas orders. Orders granted 'by means of proceedings' may be refused recognition where no proper notice of the proceeding has been given to a party to the marriage or they have not been given an opportunity to take part in proceedings.[94] For example, in *D v D*[95] both parties came from Ghana, where they were validly married pursuant to Ghanaian custom in 1977. A few years later, they came to reside in England. In 1990, the husband left his wife in England and went to Ghana, where he obtained an order dissolving the marriage in proceedings held before the Customary Arbitration Tribunal. He did not inform his wife of the proceedings and named his mother-in-law as the defendant. It was held that because the wife had no knowledge of the proceedings and the mother-in-law had objected to taking part, the divorce would not be recognised for want of proper notice of proceedings.

Orders obtained 'otherwise than by proceedings' may be refused where there is no official document certifying that the divorce was effective under the law of the country in which it was obtained, or that it is recognised as valid in another country in which either party was domiciled.[96]

All overseas divorces, annulments or legal separations can be refused recognition where recognition would be contrary to public policy.[97] This discretion is used sparingly, and the court must weigh up the unconscionability of the order against the need to respect the processes of the other country.[98]

In *Kendall v Kendall*,[99] the husband and wife had their matrimonial home in England. In 1972, the husband was posted by his employers to Bolivia. In 1973, the wife joined him. In 1974, she returned to England with the children. Before she left Bolivia, she was induced by the husband to

90 This can be under the common law definition of domicile or domicile as understood in the foreign country: S 46(5).
91 [1999] Fam 224.
92 S 51(1); *Vervaeke v Smith* [1981] Fam 77.
93 S 51(2). This includes a marriage recognised under the rules of English private international law; see Chapter 10.
94 S 51(3)(a); *A v L* [2010] EWHC 460 (Fam), [2010] 2 FLR 1418.
95 [1994] 1 FLR 38; *Duhur-Johnson v Duhur-Johnson* [2005] 2 FLR 1042.
96 S 51(3)(b).
97 S 51(3)(c).
98 *Eroglu v Eroglu* [1994] 2 FLR 287; *Golubovich v Golubovich* [2010] EWCA Civ 810, [2010] 2 FLR 1614.
99 [1977] 3 ALL ER 471.

sign some papers in Spanish, a language she did not understand. The papers asked for a divorce, which she did not want. The husband told her that her signature was necessary to enable the children to leave the country. In 1975, the Bolivian court granted a divorce. This was refused recognition in England on public policy grounds as the divorce was obtained by deception.

11.4.2.4 Transnational divorces

The Family Law Act 1986 makes a distinction between orders made in the British Islands, which will only be recognised if granted by a court of civil jurisdiction, and orders made overseas, which will be recognised according to the more flexible rules outlined above. Where all parts of a foreign divorce, annulment or separation have not taken place in the same foreign country the order cannot be recognised in the UK.

In *R v Secretary of State for the Home Department ex p Fatima*[100] the husband was a Pakistani national who married there in 1968 and had lived in England ever since. In 1978 he tried to divorce his wife by *talaq*. He pronounced the *talaq* in England and made a statutory declaration to that effect to an English solicitor. Copies of this were sent to Pakistan to both the wife and to the chairman of the local council. The House of Lords held that the pronouncement of the *talaq* by the husband was the first step in the proceedings, which were completed by registration in Pakistan. The proceedings had taken place partly in England and partly in Pakistan. The *talaq* was not recognisable under English law as it was not an overseas divorce.

In *Berkovits v Grinberg*,[101] a Jewish *get* written in London and delivered to the wife at the Rabbinical Court in Israel was considered to be a transnational divorce where the process began in England and finished in Israel.[102] The court held that transnational divorces cannot be recognised under the Family Law Act 1986.[103]

11.5 Financial relief after divorce

In most divorce proceedings, the courts deal with related issues to ascertain who should own the marital home and other financial assets and whether the needs of the dependent spouse and children should be provided for.

In most European systems, getting married has the legal effect of changing how property is owned after the couple have married. This is called a matrimonial property regime. Couples are generally permitted to choose the type of regime that will apply to their marriage, but where no choice is made, a regime will operate by force of law. Some regimes (separate property systems) allow the couple to continue to acquire and own property as two individuals, while other regimes (community property systems) provide that all property acquired after the marriage is owned jointly, subject to minor exceptions. This means that in most EU countries the dissolution of a marriage has three clear stages. The courts will declare that the marriage has ended and the parties are free to remarry. The court will then apply the rules of the relevant matrimonial property regime to determine who owns what out of the matrimonial property; and finally the court will consider whether maintenance (monetary payments) should be ordered to compensate or support the economically weaker spouse.

Under the English common law system, getting married has no effect on property ownership. However, when a marriage is dissolved, the English courts have broad discretionary powers under

---

100 [1986] 2 All ER 32.
101 [1995] 1 FLR 477.
102 Ibid 486.
103 Ibid 493.

the Matrimonial Causes Act 1973 to redistribute any available property in a fair manner and order financial payments when necessary. This means that there is no clear distinction in English law between the division of matrimonial property and the granting of maintenance. Property rights and support obligations are dealt with together in a 'package solution', and there is no real concept of a matrimonial property regime.

Jurisdiction to make maintenance orders and the rules for the recognition and enforcement of maintenance orders are governed by the Maintenance Regulation.[104] Jurisdiction to make matrimonial property orders and recognition and enforcement of matrimonial property orders is currently left to national law, although there are plans for future EU regulation.[105] The characterisation of these EU regulations, which divide financial relief after divorce into a maintenance stage and a matrimonial property stage, is an uncomfortable fit for the English divorce process.[106]

The EU has also provided for the harmonisation of applicable law in maintenance proceedings, and there are proposals to harmonise applicable law in proceedings relating to matrimonial property rights and property rights that arise from registered partnerships. The UK has opted out of all such instruments, and the English court will continue to apply its highly discretional *lex fori* to such cases.[107]

11.5.1 Jurisdiction to grant maintenance under the Maintenance Regulation

The rules relating to jurisdiction to grant maintenance orders and the recognition and enforcement of maintenance orders were originally covered by Brussels I.[108] In 2011, the Maintenance Regulation[109] came into force, which simplifies the recognition and enforcement of maintenance claims throughout the EU. The Maintenance Regulation goes further than Brussels I, laying down rules of jurisdiction and recognition and enforcement for maintenance orders but also establishing rules of applicable law. The Regulation sets up a system of Central Authorities to promote co-operation between the Member States in relation to maintenance issues.[110]

The Maintenance Regulation binds all EU Member States except Denmark, which has only adopted the new Maintenance Regulation to the extent that it changes the rules imposed by Brussels I. Denmark has not signed up to the new provisions on applicable law and central authorities.[111] The Maintenance Regulation is implemented in England by the Civil Jurisdiction and Judgments (Maintenance) Regulations 2011.[112] The Regulation applies to proceedings from 18 June 2011.[113]

The Maintenance Regulation applies to all maintenance obligations arising from a family relationship,[114] including those that arise on divorce, legal separation or nullity proceeding. In *Van den Boogaard v Laumen*[115] the ECJ distinguished between 'maintenance' and 'matrimonial property' for the

---

104 Council Regulation (EC) No 4/2009 on jurisdiction, applicable law, recognition and enforcement of decisions and cooperation in matters relating to maintenance obligations, [2008] OJ L7/1.

105 Proposal for a Council Regulation on jurisdiction, applicable law and the recognition and enforcement of decisions in matters of matrimonial property regimes COM (2011) (Rome IV); Proposal for a Council Regulation on jurisdiction, applicable law and the recognition and enforcement of decisions regarding the property consequences of registered partnerships COM (2011) 127 (Rome IVb).

106 See M Harding, 'The harmonisation of private international law in Europe: taking the character out of family law?' (2011) 7 *Journal of Private International Law*, 203–229.

107 Hansard HC Deb, 30 June 2011, Vol 530, Col 68WS.

108 Council Regulation (EC) 44/2001, Art 5(2).

109 Council Regulation (EC) No 4/2009 on jurisdiction, applicable law, recognition and enforcement of decisions and cooperation in matters relating to maintenance obligations, [2008] OJ L7/1.

110 Arts 49–63.

111 Agreement between the European Community and the Kingdom of Denmark on jurisdiction and the recognition and enforcement of judgments in civil and commercial matters, [2009] OJ L149/80.

112 SI 2011/1484.

113 Art 76.

114 Art 1, Recital 11

115 C220/95 *Boogaard v Laumen* [1997] ECR I-1147, [1997] QB 759.

purposes of EU regulation. Maintenance is designed to enable one spouse to provide for themselves, and the needs and resources of each of the spouses are taken into consideration in determining the amount payable. Where the court is solely concerned with dividing property between the spouses, it is a matter relating to matrimonial property and falls outside the scope of maintenance.[116]

Article 4 of the Maintenance Regulation allows the parties to choose which court shall have jurisdiction to decide their maintenance dispute. This choice must be expressed in writing.[117] The choice is limited to four courts that are connected to the dispute. The couple can choose either the court of the defendant's habitual residence or the court of the creditor's[118] habitual residence.[119] It is also possible to choose the court with jurisdiction to grant a related divorce or parental responsibility order as long as that jurisdiction is not based solely on one party's nationality or domicile.[120] Parties are not permitted to choose jurisdiction where the maintenance obligation is owed to a person under 18.[121]

Where no choice is made, the general rules of Art 3 of the Maintenance Regulation grant jurisdiction to all four alternative courts: the court of the defendant's habitual residence **or** the court of the creditor's habitual residence[122] **or** the court with jurisdiction to grant a related divorce **or** parental responsibility order, as long as that jurisdiction is not based solely on one party's nationality or domicile.[123]

Under Art 12, a strict, first in time, *lis pendens* rule applies. The court second seised with the same cause of action must decline jurisdiction where the first court has established jurisdiction. Article 13 allows courts seised with related issues to stay proceedings until the first court has determined matters, to avoid the risk of irreconcilable judgments.

Where no court has jurisdiction under Art 3 or 4, Art 6 grants jurisdiction to the court of common nationality or domicile[124] of the parties. Article 7 allows any Member State with a connection to the case to hear a maintenance dispute in exceptional circumstances where no other court has jurisdiction under the Regulation and proceedings cannot reasonably be brought in any connected third State.

Article 14 grants jurisdiction to all Member State courts to take provisional and protective measures where necessary.

Where a decision relating to maintenance has been made by the Member State in which the creditor is habitually resident, that court retains exclusive jurisdiction over the matter while the creditor remains habitually resident there.[125] The debtor cannot bring proceedings for a new decision or to amend the decision without the permission of the creditor by agreement or submission to the new jurisdiction.[126]

11.5.1.1 Jurisdiction to rule on matrimonial property matters – Proposed Rome IV

The UK has indicated that it will not be taking part in this regulation.

In the proposed regulation on jurisdiction, applicable law and the recognition and enforcement of decisions in matters of matrimonial property regimes – Rome IV – the court with jurisdiction to

116 See also C143/78 *De Cavel v De Cavel (No 1)* [1979] ECR 1055; C120/79 *De Cavel v De Cavel (No 2)* [1980] ECR 731; C25/81 *CHW v GJH* [1982] ECR 1189.
117 Art 4(2).
118 This is the person to whom maintenance is owed.
119 Arts 4(a)–(b).
120 Arts 4(c)–(d).
121 Art 4(3).
122 Arts 4(a)–(b).
123 Arts 4(c)–(d).
124 Recital (18).
125 Art 8.
126 Art 8(2).

hear substantive proceedings in relation to divorce, nullity or separation under Brussels II *bis* will also have jurisdiction to determine matters relating to matrimonial property where both spouses have consented to this.[127] The spouses can also agree that the state whose law governs their chosen matrimonial property regime shall have jurisdiction to apply that matrimonial property regime.[128]

Where there is no agreement, the general rules of Art 5 provide that the court of the spouses' joint habitual residence will have jurisdiction, or **failing that** the court of the spouses' last joint habitual residence if one of them still lives there, or **failing that** the court of the habitual residence of the defendant, or **failing that** the court of the spouses' joint nationality or domicile.

11.5.2 Jurisdiction to grant financial relief – the English rules

Under the Matrimonial Causes Act 1973, the English courts have jurisdiction to make orders for financial provision whenever a decree of divorce, maintenance or judicial separation is granted by the English court.[129] The English courts can also grant property adjustment orders in the same circumstances.[130]

11.5.2.1 Transfer of proceedings

The English court is not obliged to exercise its jurisdiction to grant financial relief after a divorce, if it feels that another court is better placed to rule on this issue.

In *D v P*,[131] a case before the implementation of Brussels II *bis* or the Maintenance Regulation, a Dutch husband and his Italian wife lived in Italy. The couple separated and came to an agreement on division of property which was ratified by the Italian court. The husband moved to England for work reasons and applied for a divorce from the English courts. The English High Court granted a stay to ancillary relief hearings, declining jurisdiction on the basis of *forum non conveniens*. Applying the principles of *The Spiliada*,[132] the court found that that the Italian court was better placed to deal with financial relief issues as the wife and children lived in Italy and the court had dealt with judicial separation and child maintenance.

In *Krenge v Krenge*,[133] Holman J held that the court retained a power under inherent jurisdiction to stay an application for ancillary relief after granting a decree absolute, on the basis of *forum non conveniens*. In this case Germany was clearly the more appropriate forum.

It is unclear whether the court retains the power to transfer proceedings relating to financial relief on the basis of *forum non conveniens* since the implementation of the Maintenance Regulation. *JKN v JCN*[134] suggests that such a solution is possible where jurisdiction to the claim for maintenance is dependent on the court's jurisdiction to hear a divorce or where there are concurrent proceedings in a non-Member State. It is clear from s 16(3) of the Matrimonial and Family Proceedings Act 1984 that a free-standing application for financial relief after a foreign divorce cannot be transferred if the court had jurisdiction to hear the claim under the Maintenance Regulation.

11.5.2.2 Jurisdiction to grant financial relief after a foreign order

Part III of the Matrimonial and Family Proceedings Act 1984 allows the English court to grant financial relief on the basis of a foreign divorce, separation or annulment which has been recognised in

127 Art 4.
128 Art 5(2).
129 S 23 Matrimonial Causes Act 1973.
130 S 24 Matrimonial Causes Act 1973.
131 *D v P* [1998] 2 FLR 25.
132 See Chapter 4.
133 [1999] 1 FLR 969.
134 [2010] EWHC 843 (Fam).

the English courts.[135] This Act was introduced following proposals put forward by the Law Commission.[136] The purpose of this Act was to give financial relief to destitute women who had been divorced abroad without any financial relief. In such cases, the English courts could not compel the former husband to support his wife, as no marriage existed. Neither could the English courts order financial relief. The Act has retroactive effect.

If one of the parties has remarried, that party cannot apply for financial relief.[137] No financial relief is available if the foreign divorce has been recognised as one 'otherwise than by proceedings'.[138]

The English courts will have jurisdiction to hear the application for financial relief if the situation falls outside the Maintenance Regulation[139] **and** the parties have a close connection with England. This connection will be established where either of the parties was domiciled in England on the date of the application for leave or on the date when the foreign decree took effect.[140] The connection will also be satisfied where either party to the marriage had been habitually resident in England for one year on the date that the foreign decree took effect[141] or if the parties had ever had a matrimonial home in England and on the date of the application for leave either of the parties retains a property interest in that house.[142]

In *Moore v Moore*[143] the courts considered whether they were precluded from granting relief where the Spanish courts had already been seised under Brussels I. In this case, a very wealthy English couple had emigrated to Spain to avoid tax. The husband applied to the Spanish courts for a divorce but did not initially seek a ruling on financial relief from the Spanish courts. His wife applied for divorce and financial relief in the English courts but her petition was refused as her husband's petition to the Spanish courts was first in time and Brussels II gave this priority. During the process of the Spanish divorce, the couple attempted to come to a private settlement but this was not successful. After the divorce had been granted, the husband applied to the Spanish courts for a determination of financial claims.[144] The wife obtained leave to apply for additional financial relief following an overseas divorce in England under s 13 of the Matrimonial and Family Proceedings Act 1984.[145] The husband applied to have his wife's application to the English courts set aside on the basis that this was a maintenance claim and the Spanish courts had jurisdiction under Brussels I.

The Court of Appeal held that whether or not the pending claim in the Spanish court constituted maintenance was to be determined according to the autonomous meaning of maintenance. They looked to the wording of the husband's petition to apply the *Van den Boogaard* test. As the husband had applied for 'wealth adjustment' this was deemed to be a case of property division rather than maintenance.[146] This meant that the English court was not precluded from hearing the wife's application by the *lis pendens* rule of Brussels I. The reasoning of this case could allow the English courts some flexibility to characterise cases as relating to marital property where they would be barred from granting financial relief under the *lis pendens* rule of the Maintenance Regulation.

There is no automatic right to apply for financial relief from the English courts after a foreign order. The parties must apply to the court for leave to apply for financial relief under s 13. The court

135 Where the court does not recognise the dissolution, no financial relief is available: *Dukali v Lamrani* [2012] EWHC 1748 (Fam).
136 Law Commission, *Financial Relief after Foreign Divorce* (LC No 117, 1982).
137 Ss 12(2) and (3).
138 Under s 46(2) of the Family Law Act 1986.
139 S 15(1)(a).
140 S 15(1)(a).
141 S 15(1)(b).
142 S 15(1)(c).
143 [2007] EWCA Civ 361.
144 Ibid [19].
145 Ibid [21].
146 Ibid [88]–[90].

will not grant leave unless it considers that a substantial ground to allow the application exists.[147] This means that the applicant must have a solid arguable case for financial relief.[148] Section 13(2) states that leave can be granted even where an order for financial relief has already been made by the foreign court. Where leave to apply for financial relief is granted it may be limited to allow only certain issues to be heard. Section 13 acts as a filter to prevent the threat of an application for financial relief from the English courts from being used to gain an unfair advantage where the parties attempt a settlement.

During the substantive hearing, the courts can make orders both for financial provision and for property adjustment.[149] The court must consider whether England is an appropriate forum to make such an order in the circumstances of the case. If the court is not satisfied it must dismiss the application.[150] When conducting this exercise, the court does not apply the classic *forum non conveniens* test to see if England is the most natural forum.[151] Instead the court must simply decide if England is an appropriate forum. The court will consider the connection the parties have with England and the connection the parties have with the country in which their marriage was dissolved and other countries.[152] The courts will also consider the financial relief available to the applicant by operation of foreign law.[153] If a foreign order for financial relief has already been made the courts will consider how likely that order is to be complied with.[154] The courts will consider the enforceability of any English order and the availability in England of property in respect of which an order could be made.[155] Finally the courts will consider the length of time that has elapsed since the making of the order of dissolution.

Where the English courts have jurisdiction to hear a maintenance claim under the Maintenance Regulation, a free-standing claim under the Matrimonial and Family Proceedings Act 1984 must be heard, and the court has no discretion to dismiss the application.[156]

Once the court has decided that it is appropriate to make financial and/or property adjustment orders it will exercise its discretion according to s 18 of the Matrimonial and Family Proceedings Act 1984, which requires the court to give first consideration to the welfare of any child of the marriage and promote a clean break. The court must take into account all relevant matters outlined by ss 25 and 25A of the Matrimonial Causes Act 1973.

In *Agbaje v Agbaje*[157] the UK Supreme Court considered the application of Part III of the Matrimonial and Family Proceedings Act 1984. In this case, a couple with dual Nigerian and English nationality were divorced in Nigeria and the Nigerian courts made an order granting the wife a lump sum and a house in Nigeria. The wife, who was habitually resident in England, applied for financial relief from the English courts. The English court ordered that the wife should relinquish the house in Nigeria in return for a lump sum payable from the sale of the house in England. The husband appealed.

Lord Collins warned that it is not the purpose of Part III to allow a spouse with some English connections to take advantage of a more generous approach in England to financial provision.[158] The amount of financial provision awarded depends on all the circumstances of the case. There is no rule that it should be limited to the minimum amount required to overcome injustice, but

147 S 13(1).
148 *Traversa v Freddi* [2011] EWCA Civ 81 [14]
149 S 17 MFPA 1984.
150 S 16(1).
151 *Agbaje v Agbaje* [2010] UKSC 13 [49].
152 Ss 16(2)(a)–(c).
153 Ss 16(2)(d) and (f).
154 S 16(2)(e).
155 Ss 16(2)(g)–(i). *Golubovich v Golubovich* [2011] EWCA Civ 479, [2011] 2 FLR 1193.
156 S 16(3).
157 [2010] UKSC 13.
158 Ibid [72].

neither should the courts automatically treat the case in exactly the same fashion as an application for financial relief after an English divorce. Under no circumstances should the applicant be awarded more than would be the case in purely domestic proceedings for financial relief.

11.5.3 Recognition and enforcement of maintenance orders under EU law

There are two procedures for recognising and enforcing maintenance orders by court decision, agreement or authentic instrument[159] under the Maintenance Regulation, depending on whether the Member State issuing the decision is bound by the Hague Protocol 2007.

Decisions given by a Member State that is bound by the Hague Protocol 2007 will be automatically recognised in another Member State without any special procedure, and it is not possible to oppose recognition.[160] These decisions are enforceable without any further procedure being necessary.[161] Such decisions can be reviewed only where the defendant did not enter an appearance in the state of origin.[162] This means that, in England, decisions given by all other Member States, except Denmark, are enforceable in the same manner as an order for maintenance made in proceedings in England and Wales; there is no need for registration.[163]

Decisions that are made by a State which has not signed up to the Hague Protocol 2007 (i.e. the UK and Denmark) are recognised automatically.[164] However, such a decision will only be enforceable in other Member States if declared enforceable there.[165] Recognition can be refused where the decision is manifestly contrary to public policy,[166] where the defendant did not have a proper opportunity to arrange defence,[167] or if it is irreconcilable with an earlier decision.[168] The decision on enforceability can be appealed by either party.[169] In the UK, maintenance orders from Denmark require registration before they can be enforced.[170]

Thus, maintenance orders made by states which are signed up to the Hague Protocol are more easily recognised across the EU than orders from Denmark and the UK, which are not signatories of the Hague Protocol 2007.

The question of whether an order is characterised as relating to ownership of matrimonial property or maintenance is important when it comes to the enforcement of orders under the Maintenance Regulation. In *Van den Boogaard v Laumen*[171] the wife sought to enforce financial relief orders from the English courts in the Netherlands. In order to facilitate a clean break, the English courts had ordered that property should be transferred to the wife. The ECJ ruled that where the provision awarded is solely concerned with dividing property between the spouses, the decision will not be enforceable as maintenance.[172] In the case of a mixed order, the part relating to maintenance would be enforceable.

159 Art 48.
160 Art 17(1).
161 Art 17(2).
162 Art 19.
163 Practice Direction 34C – *Applications for Recognition and Enforcement to or from European Union Member States* [2012] 1 FLR 1075 [3.1].
164 Art 23.
165 Art 26.
166 Art 24(a).
167 Art 24(b).
168 Arts 24(c)–(d).
169 Art 32.
170 Practice Direction 34C – *Applications for Recognition and Enforcement to or from European Union Member States* [2012] 1 FLR 1075 [3.2].
171 C220/95 *Boogaard v Laumen* [1997] ECR I-1147, [1997] QB 759.
172 Ibid [22].

11.5.4 Recognition of maintenance orders under English law

The Maintenance Orders Act 1950 provides for the recognition and enforcement of orders relating to maintenance and property readjustment[173] made in one part of the UK in the other parts of the UK. This Act applies to the recognition and enforcement of orders made in respect of the dissolution of marriage and civil partnership, as well as maintenance payable to children. Orders are enforceable where they have been registered in the part of the UK where enforcement is sought.[174]

The UK has reciprocal international agreements with many other countries relating to the recognition and enforcement of maintenance orders, including the 1956 United Nations Convention on the Recovery Abroad of Maintenance, the 1973 Hague Convention on the Recognition and Enforcement of Decisions Relating to Maintenance Obligations and a number of individual reciprocal agreements.[175] If a reciprocal agreement is in place, maintenance orders made in the UK can be registered and enforced in the other country, and orders made in the foreign country can be registered and enforced in the UK.

The Maintenance Orders (Reciprocal Enforcement) Act 1972 has incorporated many of these international agreements into UK law[176] and lays down the procedure for registration and enforcement. Section 40 of the Maintenance Orders Act 1972 allows new reciprocal agreements to be made. The procedure for recognition and enforcement will apply once the new country is named in an Order of Council. For example, the Reciprocal Enforcement of Maintenance Orders (United States of America) Order[177] designated the United States as a reciprocal country for the enforcement and recognition of maintenance claims. The procedure under the Maintenance Orders Act 1972 is now applied to allow for reciprocal recognition and enforcement between the UK and Commonwealth countries, which was previously governed by the Maintenance Orders (Facilities for Enforcement) Act 1920.[178]

11.6 Applicable law in financial relief disputes

Recent EU reform has called for increased harmonisation of the law applicable to maintenance and matrimonial property. **The English courts will continue to apply domestic law to applications for financial relief for the foreseeable future**.

The Maintenance Regulation does not provide for rules of applicable law but Art 15 refers to the Hague Protocol on the Law Applicable to Maintenance Obligations,[179] which has been signed and ratified by the EU.[180] The Hague Protocol 2007 allows the parties to choose the law of a country to which they have a close connection to govern the dispute.[181] In the absence of choice, the general rule under the Hague Protocol 2007 is that the applicable law is the law of the habitual residence of the creditor.[182] England has not adopted the Hague Protocol 2007, and so Art 15 of the Maintenance Regulation on applicable law is not binding on the English courts.

In the proposed Rome IV, the couple have a limited choice to choose the law applicable to their matrimonial property regime.[183] Where no choice is made, the general rule of Art 17 provides that

173 S 16(2).
174 Arts 16 and 17.
175 The full list of agreements is available on the website of the Official Solicitor. Available at www.justice.gov.uk/protecting-the-vulnerable/official-solicitor (accessed 24 May 2013).
176 S 25.
177 SI 2007/2005.
178 Art 4, Reciprocal Enforcement of Maintenance Orders (Designation of Reciprocating Countries) Order 2002/788.
179 Art 15.
180 Council Decision 2009/941/EC of 30 November 2009 on the conclusion by the European Community of the Hague Protocol of 23 November 2007 on the Law Applicable to Maintenance Obligations OJ L331/17.
181 Art 8.
182 Art 3.
183 Arts 16 and 18.

the law of the spouses' first joint habitual residence after their marriage will apply. The UK has indicated that it will not be participating in Rome IV.

English courts will apply English domestic law as the *lex fori* even if the parties are resident or domiciled in another country. Under English domestic law, where the court is petitioned for financial relief under the Matrimonial Causes Act 1973 or the Matrimonial and Family Proceedings Act 1984, the courts will make orders for both financial provision and the readjustment of matrimonial property to achieve fairness between the parties.

The English courts have considerable discretion in making this assessment, and the outcome is difficult to predict. The court must take into account all the circumstances of the case, giving first consideration to the welfare of any child of the family.[184] Section 25 of the Matrimonial Causes Act 1973 outlines a checklist of factors that the court should consider. Under s 25A of the Matrimonial Causes Act the courts are required to prioritise a 'clean break' between the parties where possible. This means that English courts are more likely to order lump sum payments and property transfers where possible rather than periodic monetary payments. The courts have developed guiding principles for how discretion should be exercised. In *Miller v Miller; McFarlane v McFarlane*[185] the House of Lords stated that the elements of needs, compensation and sharing should be separately considered. The court must strive to use the orders available to satisfy the needs of the family and compensate the weaker party for any economic detriment suffered due to the marriage. If there are marital assets left over these will be shared equally between the parties unless there is reason to depart from equality.[186]

11.6.1 Prenuptial agreements

The English legal system does not recognise prenuptial agreements as legally binding contracts. Instead, the presence of a prenuptial agreement is just evidence to be considered as part of the court's consideration under s 25 of the Matrimonial Causes Act. The court may give effect to the prenuptial agreement if it is fair to do so. The weight given to the prenuptial agreement in any particular case is completely up to the discretion of the English courts. In some cases, the agreement would be largely irrelevant (for example where all property assets are needed to provide for the children); in other cases it could have magnetic importance (such as when both parties are very well off and much of the wealth has been generated by one party).

In contrast, autonomy is highly valued in most European countries and in EU regulation of the law applicable to financial relief after marriage. This leads to a conflict when the English court is asked to grant financial relief where a prenuptial agreement exists that would be legally binding in the country in which it was made. For example, if two German spouses divorce in England, the English courts will apply English law to the issue of financial relief. If the German couple have an agreement that a German separation of goods property regime will apply, this is not binding unless the English court finds that it is appropriate to give the agreement effect under its discretionary s 25 powers.

The courts may deal with this situation by transferring the proceedings relating to ancillary relief to another jurisdiction if possible.[187] Where no transfer is possible, the court must consider what weight, if any, to give the foreign agreement.

In *Radmacher v Granatino*,[188] a German heiress and her French husband had signed a prenuptial agreement in Germany, stating that their property would remain separate and that neither would

184 S 25 Matrimonial Causes Act 1973.
185 [2006] UKHL 24, [2006] 2 AC 618.
186 *Charman v Charman* [2007] EWCA Civ 503 [64]–[65].
187 See above.
188 [2010] UKSC 42.

make a claim on the other's property in the case of divorce. The agreement was binding in Germany. The couple later divorced in London. The Supreme Court considered the effect of the foreign agreement. It held that the discretionary powers exercised by the court when discharging its duties under Part II of the Matrimonial Causes Act 1973 are given to the court by English law. The jurisdiction to grant financial relief after granting an English divorce cannot be bargained away by the parties.[189] The court cannot give effect to foreign jurisdiction clauses or apply foreign law.[190]

The majority held that a prenuptial agreement, freely entered into and intended to have effect, should be given decisive weight unless it was not fair to hold the parties to the agreement in the circumstances before the court at the time of the application for ancillary relief. The fact that such an agreement was entered into in a foreign country, where such agreements were commonplace, would be a relevant factor in determining that the parties had intended the agreement to have effect.

The decision in *Radmacher* renders it a little easier to predict the outcome of financial relief proceedings in England where a prenuptial agreement exists.[191] It is still impossible for a party to be certain that a prenuptial agreement will protect their assets against court redistribution. The agreement will be ignored where the assets are needed to satisfy the needs of the other spouse and children or for compensation. However, where the agreement makes fair provision for the children and a dependent spouse or where both spouses are in a position to meet their own needs, it is likely to be given effect. Scherpe argues that *Radmacher* achieves the correct balance between predictability and allowing the court the flexibility needed to achieve fairness.[192] The Law Commission is currently reviewing the domestic law of matrimonial property agreements in the UK.[193]

Radmacher was applied in *V v V*,[194] where financial relief was awarded based mainly on need, but the presence of a specifically negotiated Swedish prenuptial agreement altered the award that would have been given if there had been no agreement. In Z v Z[195] *Radmacher* was applied to give effect to a French agreement to apply a separation of property regime to matrimonial assets.

In B v S,[196] a Spanish couple had tacitly agreed to the separation of property, as they had taken no steps to choose an alternative matrimonial property regime before their marriage in Spain. Mostyn J considered whether the principles in *Radmacher* applied to matrimonial property regimes chosen by default. Mostyn J emphasised that the English courts did not apply foreign law when awarding financial relief.[197] In this case, no weight was given to the matrimonial property regime as there was no indication that both parties had intended the agreement to have effect.

11.7 EU regulation of cross border aspects of same-sex marriage/partnership

There is no express EU regulation of jurisdiction, applicable law or recognition and enforcement of dissolution proceedings relating to same-sex marriage or civil partnership. The process of reform which led to Brussels II *bis* occurred at a time when same-sex marriage was unknown in the EU.

---

189 *Hyman v Hyman* [1929] AC 601.
190 [2010] UKSC 42, [74].
191 P Pavlou, 'Pre-nuptial agreements: back where we were? *Kremen v Agrest*' [2012] Fam Law 957–962; P Harris, 'With this Ring I Thee Wed (Terms and Conditions Apply),' [2011] Fam Law 367–373.
192 J Scherpe, 'Fairness, freedom and foreign elements – marital agreements in England and Wales after *Radmacher v Granatino*', (2011) 23 CFLQ 513–526.
193 Law Commission, *Marital Property Agreements: A Consultation Paper* (LC consultation paper No 198, 2011).
194 [2011] EWHC 3230 (Fam), [2012] 1 FLR 1315.
195 [2011] EWHC 2878 (Fam), [2012] 1 FLR 1100.
196 [2012] EWHC 265 (Fam).
197 Ibid [10].

While the rules of Brussels II *bis* apply to civil matters relating to 'divorce, legal separation or marriage annulment', it is open to national interpretation whether this includes same-sex marriage. As yet, the EU has never defined marriage for the purpose of private international law but has instead left this definition up to individual Member States. Article 13 of Rome III specifically states that the regulation should not oblige courts to provide for divorce where their law does not deem the marriage in question valid for the purposes of divorce proceedings.

It seems at present that it is open to the Member States to recognise same-sex marriage as marriage under their own national law.[198] Where they recognise same-sex marriage as marriage they may apply Brussels II *bis* and Rome III (if they have opted into this regulation).[199] Where same-sex marriage is not recognised as marriage, but rather as civil partnership or some other type of registered partnership, Brussels II *bis* and Rome III will have no direct application and the private international aspects of such relationships will be governed by national law. This means that the recognition of the dissolution of a same-sex partnership across EU Member States is not as straightforward as the recognition of the dissolution of a marriage.

The Maintenance Regulation will apply to maintenance claims arising from the dissolution of a same-sex partnership, as its scope includes all maintenance claims arising from a family relationship.[200] In the proposed EU regulation of property disputes between spouses, two regulations have been proposed – one relating to marital property (Rome IV) and one relating to property consequences of registered partnerships (Rome IVb). The Commission's justification for having two regulations is that different legal consequences flow from the different types of registered partnerships that exist throughout the EU.[201] However, where a state recognises same-sex marriage, it is arguably open to them to apply Rome IV to the property consequence of such a marriage.

11.8 Cross-border aspects of civil partnership in English law

As examined in Chapter 10, same-sex marriage is not currently recognised in England as marriage. Instead, foreign same-sex marriages and registered partnerships are recognised in England as civil partnerships under s 215 of the Civil Partnership Act 2004. The UK courts have jurisdiction to grant a dissolution of a foreign same-sex partnership where it has been recognised in the UK as equivalent to civil partnership.

The English laws relating to jurisdiction and recognition for the dissolution of civil partnership are nearly identical to the laws relating to divorce. The English courts have the same jurisdiction to dissolve civil partnerships as they do to dissolve marriages.[202] English regulations have been made to mirror the jurisdictional grounds of Brussels II *bis* for dissolution of civil partnerships.[203] Thus the English courts will have jurisdiction to grant a dissolution of a civil partnership where one of the bases of jurisdiction in Art 3 of Brussels II *bis* is satisfied.

Section 221 of the Civil Partnership Act extends the rules of jurisdiction under the Domicile and Matrimonial Proceedings Act 1973 to the dissolution of civil partnerships. The powers of the

198 K Boele-Woelki, 'For Better or Worse: The Europeanization of International Divorce Law' (2010) 12 *Yearbook of Private International Law*, 1–26; I Curry- Sumner, 'Same-Sex Relationships In Europe: Trends Towards Tolerance?' (2011) 3 *Amsterdam Law Forum*, 43.

199 See further K: Boele-Woelki & C. Gonzalez-Beilfuss, *Brussels II-bis. Its Impact and Application in the Member States* (Antwerp: Intersentia 2007).

200 Art 1(1).

201 Rome IV b, 3.

202 S 37 Civil Partnership Act 2004.

203 Civil Partnership (Jurisdiction and Recognition of Judgments) Regulations 2005 SI 2005/3334.

court to stay and transfer proceedings relating to the dissolution of civil partnership are mirrored by the Family Procedure (Civil Partnership: Staying of Proceedings) Rules 2010.[204]

The grounds for dissolution of civil partnership are very similar to those for divorce. Dissolution will be permitted where irretrievable breakdown is demonstrated by unreasonable behaviour or periods of living apart.[205]

Dissolutions of civil partnerships granted by a court of civil jurisdiction in one part of the United Kingdom are effective in all parts of the United Kingdom.[206] Dissolutions of civil partnerships granted by EU Member States are automatically recognised in the UK in an identical fashion to foreign judgments recognised under Brussels II *bis*.[207] The basis and procedure for the recognition of overseas dissolutions is identical to the procedure for orders relating to matrimonial proceedings under the Family Law Act 1986.[208]

Civil partners are entitled to financial relief after the dissolution of their civil partnership in the UK, in the same way as married couples.[209] The courts may order financial relief and property redistribution.[210]

Finally, ex-civil partners are entitled to apply to the English courts for financial relief after an overseas dissolution of their civil partnerships, subject to conditions identical to those placed on spouses under the Matrimonial and Family Proceedings Act 1984.[211]

11.9 Further reading

P Beaumont, 'International Family Law in Europe – The Maintenance Project, the Hague Conference and the EC: a triumph of reverse subsidiarity' (2009) 73 RabelsZ Bd 545.

K Boele-Woelki, 'For better or worse: The Europeanization of international divorce law' (2010) 12 *Yearbook of Private International Law*, 1–26.

A Borrás, 'Explanatory Report on the Convention, drawn up on the basis of Article K.3 of the Treaty on European Union, on Jurisdiction and the Recognition and Enforcement of Judgments in Matrimonial Matters' [1998] OJ C221.

C Clarkson, 'Matrimonial property on divorce: all change in Europe' (2008) 2 *Journal of Private International Law*, 421–442.

P Fiorini, 'Rome III – A Step Too Far in the Europeanisation of Private International Law?' (2008) 22 *International Journal of Law, Policy and the Family*, 178–205.

M Harding, 'The harmonisation of private international law in Europe: taking the character out of family law?' (2011) 7 *Journal of Private International Law*, 203–229.

W Healing, 'The Matrimonial and Family Proceedings Act after *Agbaje*' [2011] Fam Law 631–634.

P McEleavy, 'Brussels II *bis*: matrimonial matters, parental responsibility, child abduction and mutual recognition' [2004] ICLQ 503.

P McEleavy, 'The communitarization of divorce law – what impact for English and Scottish law?' [2004] ICLQ 605.

J Scherpe, 'Fairness, freedom and foreign elements – marital agreements in England and Wales after *Radmacher v Granatino*' (2011) 23 CFLQ 513–526.

P Smart, 'The recognition of extra-judicial divorce in the UK' (1985) 34 ICLQ 392.

M Thorpe, 'London – the divorce capital of the world' [2009] Fam Law 21.

---

204 SI 2010/2986.
205 S 44(5) Civil Partnership Act 2004.
206 S 233 Civil Partnership Act 2004.
207 Civil Partnership (Jurisdiction and Recognition of Judgments) Regulations 2005 SI 2005/3334.
208 Ss 234–236 Civil Partnership Act 2004.
209 Sched 5 Civil Partnership Act 2004.
210 *Lawrence v Gallagher* [2012] EWCA Civ 394.
211 Sched 7 Civil Partnership Act 2004.

Chapter 12

Parentage and Adoption

Chapter Contents

Key Issues:

- Establishing legal parentage in an age of artificial reproduction
- Conflict of law problems caused by cross border surrogacy
- Recognition of intercountry adoption under the Hague Adoption Convention
- Restrictions on bringing children into the UK for adoption under the Adoption and Children Act 2002

12.1 Introduction

This chapter will explore the conflict of law issues when the English court is required to determine the legal parentage of a child who has been born abroad. In English conflict of law cases, the determination of parenthood was traditionally considered as matter of **fact**, based on genetic ties. Since the development of assisted reproductive technology, legal recognition of parenthood has become detached from genetic links and become a matter of **law**. In English domestic law, a different system of rules now determines parenthood for children born using assisted reproduction – the Human Fertilisation and Embryology Acts 1990 and 2008. Where children are born abroad using assisted reproduction to English parents who seek recognition of parental status in England, real conflict of laws issues arise. The foreign country may not regulate the parenthood of children born through assisted reproduction, or may have different substantive rules of parenthood to those used in England. English courts determine the parenthood of such children according to English law. This may leave a child without any legally recognised parents. The English law on parenthood will be examined in this chapter in order to explain how such conflicts arise and to what extent they can be resolved by the English courts.

English law recognises adoptive parents as the legal parents of children. In England, the rules of domestic adoption are found in the Adoption of Children Act (ACA) 2002. English law only permits adoption in certain circumstances. Where a child is adopted abroad and brought to England, the foreign adoption may or may not be recognised in English law. The recognition of intercountry adoptions is governed by the Hague Adoption Convention.[1] Where a foreign adoption falls outside the Hague Adoption Convention it may be recognisable as an overseas adoption under English law or may be given recognition under English common law rules. These three possibilities will be examined in this chapter.

12.2 Legal parenthood

In English domestic law, **two different sets of rules** govern the determination of legal parenthood. Rules based on the common law principles of legitimacy[2] apply where a child has been conceived naturally. However, where a child has been conceived using **assisted** reproductive technology, legal

1 The Hague Convention of 29 May 1993 on Protection of Children and Co-operation in Respect of Intercountry Adoption. Text available at www.hcch.net/upload/conventions/txt33en.pdf (accessed 17 May 2013).

2 See further D Lazok, 'Legitimation, Recognition and Affiliation Proceedings' (1961) 10 ICLQ 124.

parenthood is determined according to the Human Fertilisation and Embryology Acts 1990 and 2008. Determining legal parenthood is very important when enforcing maintenance obligations, or establishing inheritance rights, nationality, common law domicile or immigration status.

12.2.1 Naturally conceived children

In England, the rules establishing parenthood are based on the old common law rules relating to legitimacy. They pre-date modern genetic testing and rely on a series of presumptions. This means that parentage can be based on scientific fact or legal fiction depending on the circumstances.

The mother of a child is the woman who gives birth to that child.[3] This will be recorded on a child's birth certificate. The father of a child is determined by a series of legal presumptions. Where the mother of a child is married, her husband will be presumed to be the father of the child.[4] Where the presumption is unchallenged, the father is recorded on a child's birth certificate without any need to prove a genetic link. Where a child is born to unmarried parents there will be no legal recognition of the child's father unless he is registered on the child's birth certificate,[5] which is done after the filing of legal declarations, or named as the father in legal proceedings.[6] The man named on the birth certificate is presumed to be the child's father.[7]

Presumptions of parenthood can be rebutted in court on the balance of probabilities.[8] This might occur where a declaration of paternity is sought[9] or within a contested case over child support or child care. In such cases, the court may give a direction for genetic tests to assist in its determination.[10] A DNA sample can be taken from a child without parental consent where the court considers that it would be in the child's best interests for the sample to be taken.[11] The English courts have generally held that the use of genetic testing to establish parentage is in the best interests of children.[12] Where an adult has refused to take a DNA test, the court may draw inferences from the other evidence before the court.[13]

12.2.2 Assisted reproduction

The Human Fertilisation and Embryology Acts (HFEA) regulate the parentage of children born following assisted reproduction. Assisted reproduction is defined in s 34 of the 2008 Act as the placing in a woman of an embryo or of sperm and eggs or her artificial insemination. The rules replicate the common law presumptions but with one important difference. Genetic testing cannot be used to rebut presumptions of parentage. The HFEA specifically creates a legal parent/child relationship between two genetically unrelated individuals to facilitate the use of donor sperm or eggs.

Section 33 of the HFEA 2008 states that the woman who carries a child (the gestational mother) is to be treated as the legal mother, if the child is born as a result of assisted reproduction. This applies regardless of where in the world the assisted reproduction treatment was carried out.[14]

---

3 *Ampthill Peerage Case* [1977] AC 547, 577.
4 *Banbury Peerage Case* (1811) 1 Sim & St 153 HL.
5 S 10 Births and Deaths Registration Act 1953.
6 This can be made under s 55A of the Family Law Act 1986 or as part of legal proceedings where paternity is in issue, usually maintenance or parental responsibility disputes. See *L v X* [2010] EWCA Civ 1149, [2011] 1 FLR 708.
7 *Brierley v Brierley & Williams* [1918] P 257.
8 S 26 Family Law Reform Act 1969; *S v S* [1972] AC 24.
9 S 55A Family Law Act 1986.
10 S 20 Family Law Reform Act 1969.
11 S 21(3)(b) Family Law Reform Act 1969.
12 *S v S* [1972] AC 24; *Re H and A (paternity: blood tests)* [2002] EWCA Civ 383. See *contra Re K* [1999] 2 FLR 280; *Re D* [2006] EWHC 3545 (Fam); *Re L* [2009] EWCA Civ 1239; J Fortin, 'Children's right to know their origins – too far, too fast?' (2009) 21 CFLQ 336–355.
13 *F v Child Support Act* [1999] 2 FLR 244.
14 S 33(3) HFEA 2008.

Where the gestational mother is married or in a civil partnership at the time of treatment, her husband[15] or civil partner[16] will be considered under English law to be the child's second parent, even if they are not genetically linked to the child. This rule applies regardless of where the artificial reproductive treatment was carried out.[17] This means that if a mother has treatment by donor sperm abroad, her husband or civil partner will be the child's second parent unless the husband or civil partner can show that he/she did not consent to the assisted reproduction.[18]

Sections 36 and 44 of the HFEA 2008 allow a mother's unmarried partner to be considered as the child's second parent in English law. This is possible either where the couple are a same-sex couple or an opposite sex couple. In order for these provisions to apply, the mother must be unmarried.[19] Both the mother and the partner must give written notice that they want the partner to be treated in law as the child's parent.[20] The mother and her partner must not be within the prohibited degrees of relationship.[21] The agreed parenthood conditions **do not** apply to assisted reproductive treatment carried out abroad.[22] Where the gestational mother is unmarried and the agreed parenthood conditions are not satisfied the child will have only one legal parent under English law.

Section 41 of the HFEA 2008 states that any man who donates sperm in accordance with the conditions of Sched 3 of the HFEA 1990 is not the father of any child born using that sperm under English law. This provision only applies where sperm is donated at a UK licensed clinic. Generally, where a man informally donates his sperm he will be considered by English law to be the father of the child and liable for child maintenance.[23]

The English courts will apply English law to the question of parentage regardless of where the child was conceived or born. This means that where a child has been conceived abroad using a foreign sperm donor, the husband or civil partner of the gestational mother will be considered in English law to be the second legal parent under s 35 of the HFEA 2008. However, if the spouse or civil partner did not give consent to the use of the donor sperm in such circumstances, s/he will not be considered the legal parent under s 35 of the 2008 Act. In such a case, the foreign sperm donor may be considered to be the second legal parent. This is because the donor sperm used may not have been donated in accordance with the conditions of the HFEA 1990.

The agreed parenthood conditions do not apply where assisted reproductive treatment has been carried out abroad. This means that where the mother is unmarried, the sperm donor may be considered to be the legal father under English law regardless of the intention of the parties or the law of the place where insemination was carried out. For example, in *U v W*,[24] where an unmarried couple underwent assisted reproduction using donor sperm in Italy, the court noted that the anonymous sperm donor could have been considered the legal father as consent within the meaning of the 1990 Act had not been given.[25]

Section 47 of the HFEA 2008 states that an egg donor cannot be considered to be the legal parent of a child carried by another woman under English law unless other conditions of parenthood under the HFEA are satisfied. This might occur where the egg donor is the civil partner of the gestational mother. This means that the genetic link between egg donor and child is not relevant in English law regardless of the law of the country where the assisted reproduction took place.

15 S 35 HFEA 2008.
16 S 42 HFEA 2008.
17 S 35(2) HFEA 2008; s42(2) HFEA 2008.
18 Ss 35 and 42 HFEA 2008.
19 S 38(2) means that where the gestational mother is married, the legal presumption that her husband is the father of the child must be rebutted by DNA evidence before the agreed parenthood conditions can be applied.
20 Ss 37 and 44 HFEA 2008.
21 Ss 37(1)(e) and 44(1)(e) HFEA 2008.
22 *U v W (Attorney General Intervening)* [1997] 2 FLR 282; S 36(a) HFEA 2008.
23 *Re D* [2006] EWHC 2 (Fam); *Re G* [2008] 1 FLR 1056.
24 *U v W (Attorney General Intervening)* [1997] 2 FLR 282.
25 Ibid 292.

The rules establishing legal parenthood under the HFEA are quite technical and complicated. As there is no provision in the HFEA to recognise foreign rules of legal parentage, where parents go abroad for artificial reproductive treatments they need to be careful that the parent–child link that they intend to create will be recognised by English law.

12.3 Orders transferring legal parenthood

There are two methods of transferring legal parenthood from one individual to another under English domestic law. Where a child has been born through a surrogacy arrangement, the English court can transfer legal parenthood from the surrogate mother to the intentional parents if the conditions of s 54 of the HFEA 2008 are satisfied. This is known as a **parental order**.

An **adoption order** allows the court to transfer legal parentage from birth parents to adoptive parents if the conditions of the Adoption of Children Act 2002 are satisfied. In both cases, the legal obligations of the birth parents cease, and the new parents are treated in law as the child's parents.

The Hague Adoption Convention allows the English courts to recognise foreign adoption orders and have English adoption orders recognised in other countries. No such regulation exists in relation to cross-border surrogacy agreements. The Hague Conference on Private International Law has identified cross-border surrogacy as an area in need of urgent reform.[26] The lack of international regulation has caused significant problems in recognising the legal status of parents and children who have used foreign surrogacy services. In some cases this has deprived the children of legal parents or a nationality and left them in a very vulnerable position.

12.3.1 Parental orders

Section 54 of the HFEA 2008 allows the English courts to make a parental order so that a child born through surrogacy can be treated as the child of the intentional parents. Such an order can be made where the child was born using assisted reproduction[27] whether in the UK or abroad[28] and at least one of the intentional parents is **genetically related** to the child.[29] Such orders may only be made on application by a couple – either husband and wife, civil partners or persons in an enduring family relationship.[30] Both applicants must be over the age of 18.[31] Parental orders are subject to a number of further conditions which have limited the courts' ability to regulate the legal parenthood of children born through cross-border surrogacy arrangements.

12.3.1.1 Domicile

At least one of the applicants must be domiciled in the United Kingdom, the Isle of Man or the Channel Islands at the time that the court is asked to make the parental order.[32] Where this is not the case, the UK courts will have no jurisdiction to make a parental order. The common law meaning of domicile is used.

For example, in *Re G*[33] a Turkish couple, domiciled in Turkey, had a child in England using an English surrogate. As neither of the applicants were UK domiciliaries, the court had no jurisdiction

---

26 HCCH, 'A Preliminary Report On The Issues Arising From International Surrogacy Arrangements', March 2012 available at www.hcch.net/upload/wop/gap2012pd10en.pdf (accessed 17 May 2013).

27 S 54(1)(a) HFEA 2008.

28 S 54(10) HFEA 2008.

29 S 54(1)(b) HFEA 2008.

30 The death of one of the applicants prior to the hearing will not prevent the court from granting the order: *A v P* [2011] EWHC 1738 (Fam).

31 S 54(5) HFEA 2008.

32 S 54(4)(b) HFEA 2008.

33 [2007] EWHC 2814 (Fam).

to grant the parental order. In *Z v C*,[34] a same-sex couple from Israel who had moved to the UK applied for a parental order. Their surrogate was from Israel, and the assisted reproduction services were carried out at a clinic in India. The court held that the applicants had acquired a domicile of choice in England and so the court had jurisdiction to hear their application for a parental order.

12.3.1.2 Consent and time limits

Several of the conditions of s 54 are designed to protect the interests of the surrogate mother. The court must be satisfied that the surrogate mother has given free, unconditional consent to the making of the order with full understanding of what is involved.[35] Consent cannot be given by the surrogate mother until six weeks after the child's birth.[36] This means that entering into the surrogacy agreement in the first place will not necessarily count as valid consent for a parental order to be made. Surrogacy agreements are unenforceable as legal contracts in English law.[37] An application for a parental order must be made within six months after the birth of the child.[38]

At the time of the application and the making of the order the child must be living with the intentional parents.[39] This means that if the child is still living with the surrogate mother, no parental order will be possible. For example, in *Re TT*[40] the surrogate mother changed her mind and retained the child. No parental order was possible, and, on the facts, the court ordered that the child should remain with the surrogate and that contact with the genetic father should be facilitated.

12.3.1.3 Prohibition on commercial surrogacy

Commercial surrogacy is not permitted in the UK, and anyone who negotiates a surrogacy agreement between a surrogate and intentional parents on a commercial basis within the UK is guilty of a summary offence.[41] The Warnock Committee, which first considered legalising surrogacy in England, considered that the introduction of commercial surrogacy would create a serious risk that women would be exploited. [42] Section 54(8) of the HFEA 2008 upholds this policy objective, stating that the court must be satisfied when making a parental order that no money or other benefit has been given or received by either of the applicants in relation to the surrogacy arrangement. However, parents are permitted to pay the reasonable expenses of the surrogate, and the court can also authorise additional payments and benefits in certain cases.

The prevention of commercial surrogacy is not the only policy concern the court must have in mind when deciding whether or not to make a parental order. The Human Fertilisation and Embryology (Parental Orders) Regulations 2010[43] now require the court to consider the child's welfare as a paramount concern when making a parental order.[44] This creates a conflict of interest where the court is asked to make a parental order in favour of a couple who have availed themselves of overseas commercial surrogacy services. The court has to weigh up conflicting policy considerations – the welfare of the child and the prevention of commercial surrogacy. In most cases, the courts have reluctantly authorised reasonably high payments to the surrogate as this is the best way to regularise the child's parentage and is ultimately in the child's best interests.

---

34 [2011] EWHC 3181 (Fam).
35 S 54(6) HFEA 2008.
36 S 54(7) HFEA 2008.
37 S 1a Surrogacy Arrangements Act 1985
38 S 54(3).
39 S 54(4).
40 [2011] EWHC 33 (Fam)
41 S 2 Surrogacy Arrangements Act 1985.
42 Warnock, 'Report of the Committee of Inquiry into Human Fertilisation and Embryology' (Cmnd 9314, HMSO, London 1984) [8.18].
43 SI 2010/985.
44 S 1(2).

In *Re X and Y*[45] the British intentional parents engaged two surrogate mothers in India after being advised that there was a shortage of surrogate mothers in England. A contract was signed in India stating that the surrogate mothers gave up all parental rights to the children. In return, the intentional parents were to meet all medical expenses, and the surrogates also received payments of approximately £27,405.22. Both surrogates became pregnant using the intentional father's sperm and donor eggs in a clinic in India, and the children were born in India. Upon return to England the parents applied for a parental order. Sir Nicholas Wall P held that the expenses paid went beyond reasonable expenses[46] but that the children's welfare required the orders to be made. The court held that, as a public policy consideration, the sums paid to the surrogates should be examined to see if they were of such magnitude as to overbear the wills of the surrogates and amount to the mere purchase of a child from overseas.

In *Re L*[47] payments made under a commercial surrogacy agreement entered into in Illinois, USA, were retrospectively validated by the English court. Hedley J noted that when weighing up policy considerations, the balance should be heavily in favour of the child's welfare and orders would be withheld only in extreme cases. If controls on commercial surrogacy arrangements were to be effective they needed to operate before the court process was initiated.[48]

A similar approach was taken in *Re S*,[49] *Re IJ*[50] and *Re X and Y*,[51] where Hedley J commented on the unsuitability of s 54 to deal with cross-border commercial surrogacy and recommended Parliamentary reform.

12.3.2 Conflict of laws issues in surrogacy cases

Conflicting national laws on parenthood can cause serious problems in cross-border surrogacy cases. The English courts will always apply English law to the question of parentage. Intentional parents who have attempted to have a child through surrogacy may not have considered English law at all and instead complied with the requirements of the foreign law of the state of the child's birth. The potential conflict between the two different laws may cause a number of legal difficulties for the child and intentional parents. In some cases these can be resolved where the English courts make a parental order. However, in some cases it will not be possible for the English court to make a parental order, and this will leave the child legally parentless.

In *Re X and Y*[52] an English couple entered into a commercial surrogacy agreement in Ukraine with a Ukrainian surrogate mother. Twins were born in Ukraine after treatment there using donor eggs and the intentional father's sperm. Under English law, without a parental order, the Ukrainian surrogate and her husband were considered to be the legal parents of the children under s 35 of the HFEA 2008. The surrogate's husband had consented to the treatment and the surrogate was the gestational mother. Under Ukrainian law, neither the surrogate nor her husband was considered to have the status of parent and the intentional English parents had been registered on the children's birth certificates. As a result, the children had no legal parents. This left them stateless, with no rights of residence or citizenship in Ukraine and no right of entry into the UK.[53] In the end, the intentional father proved to the immigration authorities by DNA testing that he was the biological father of both children. The children were given discretionary leave to enter the UK 'outside the rules' in order to regularise their status under English law by means of a parental order.

---

45 [2011] EWHC 3147 (Fam).
46 Ibid [33].
47 [2010] EWHC 3146 (Fam).
48 Ibid [10].
49 [2009] EWHC 2977 (Fam).
50 [2011] EWHC 921 (Fam).
51 [2008] EWHC 3030 (Fam).
52 Ibid.
53 Ibid [9].

In *Re IJ*[54] a similar situation arose. The intentional parents were English; the child was conceived and born in Ukraine using donor eggs and sperm from the English intentional father. In Ukrainian law the intentional English parents were considered to be the legal parents. In English law, under s 35 of the HFEA 2008, the legal parents were the Ukrainian surrogate and her husband until a parental order was granted. The intentional mother was married and her husband had agreed to the treatment. Real problems were encountered in bringing IJ into the UK. Hedley J urged parents to seek proper legal advice before embarking on such a journey.[55]

In *Re K*[56] twins were born in India following a commercial surrogacy agreement between an English couple and an Indian married couple. Again the same problem arose. Indian law considered the children to have English parents. English law considered the children to have an Indian mother and father under s 35 of the HFEA 2008. The parents applied for a parental order, but without the children being present in England the order could not be processed.[57] The parents applied for entry clearance to bring the children to England. Entry clearance is an executive rather than judicial decision. Entry in this case was only granted if a parental order was likely to be granted by the English courts. The court held that no such indication could be made.

Under para 8.7 of the Human Fertilisation and Embryology (Parental Orders) Regulations 2010, where a parental order is made in the UK and one or both of the intentional parents are British citizens, the child will become a British citizen.[58] However, problems are still encountered in bringing such children into the UK so that the parental order can be made. The UK Border Agency has now issued guidance known as 'Inter-Country Surrogacy and the Immigration Rules'.[59]

Where a parental order cannot be made because the s 54 checklist is not satisfied, the English court will only be able to regulate the child's parenthood through an adoption order. This brings its own difficulties and may not be successful in all surrogacy cases.

In *Re MW*[60] a couple entered into a surrogacy agreement before the implementation of the 1990 HFEA. The surrogate mother was impregnated using the intentional father's sperm. She was to receive £7,500 upon handing over the child as compensation for lost earnings. The child was handed over after birth, and the intentional parents applied to adopt the child. The surrogate objected to the adoption as she wanted to maintain contact with the child. Three barriers to the proposed adoption existed under the Adoption Act 1976. Section 11(1) provided that a person, other than an adoption agency, shall not make arrangements for the adoption of a child, or place a child for adoption, unless the proposed adopter is a relative of the child. The court held that there had been a breach of this section but it was not precluded from making an order.[61] The payment made to the surrogate breached s 57 of the Adoption Act 1967. The court held that it had the power to retroactively authorise the payments.[62] The final problem was that the mother withheld consent. In this case the court was willing to override the mother's consent.[63]

Where the surrogacy situation cannot be resolved through adoption, the court will have to resort to s 8 orders under the Children Act 1989[64] or wardship proceedings to resolve the situation.[65]

54 [2011] EWHC 921 (Fam).
55 Ibid [4].
56 [2010] EWHC 1180 (Fam).
57 Ibid [6].
58 SI 2010/985. Sched 4 of the Regulations amends ss 1(5)(a) and (5A)(a) of the British Nationality Act 1981.
59 Available at www.ukba.homeoffice.gov.uk/sitecontent/documents/residency/Intercountry-surrogacy-leaflet (accessed 17 May 2013).
60 [1995] 2 FLR 759.
61 Ibid 763.
62 Ibid 764.
63 Ibid 765.
64 *A v C* [1985] FLR 445.
65 *Re C* [1985] FLR 846.

12.3.3 Proposals for reform

The unsuitability of s 54 of the HFEA 2008 to regulate cross-border surrogacy has been highlighted by the High Court, and there has been call for Parliamentary reform. Commercial surrogacy has been unenforceable in the UK since 1985.[66] While cross-border surrogacy treatments have become much more desirable since 1985, the law tackling commercial surrogacy has not greatly developed. Subsequent reviews in 1997[67] and 2005[68] only made minor changes to the law regulating surrogacy. It is clear that a sustained review that goes back to first principles and re-examines the ban on commercial surrogacy is now required.[69]

At an international level, the Hague Conference has suggested that a co-operation system should be put in place modelled on the Hague Adoption Convention. This would have minimum safeguards to prevent abuses while ensuring predictability for parents and children.[70] The Hague Conference is due to publish a final report in March 2014.[71] Trimmings and Beaumont argue that the regulation of cross-border surrogacy is the only way forward to safeguard children and that any workable system will have to recognise commercial surrogacy.[72]

12.4 Adoption

The second way in which the English courts can transfer the status of parent from one person to another is through an adoption order. Unlike the parental order, which is limited to parents with a genetic link to the child, an adoption order is usually made in favour of unrelated adults. Adoption is designed to find a child a new family where the birth family cannot provide the care needed. It is a drastic measure that severs the legal relationship between birth parent and child[73] and interferes with the child's right to family life with his birth family under Art 8 of the European Convention on Human Rights.

In England and Wales, the adoption of children is regulated by the Adoption of Children Act (ACA) 2002, which provides that adoption requires a court order. A court will only make an adoption order if there is no realistic hope that the child will be able to live with his birth family. Birth parents must consent to the adoption, or the court must have decided to dispense with that consent.[74] The adoption order must promote the welfare of the child throughout his life.[75]

The adoption process in England has several stages and is a highly regulated process. In order to decide whether adoption would be in the best interests of the child, investigations are carried out by skilled experts at each stage, and these assessments are made available to the courts. It is important that these assessments are accurate and objective, and so all adoption agencies in the UK are voluntary[76] and must be registered with the local authority.[77] Private or commercial adoption agencies are not permitted.

66 Surrogacy Arrangements Act 1985.
67 Surrogacy: Review for Health Ministers of Current Arrangements for Payments and Regulation, Report of the Review Team Cm 4068 (HMSO, London 1998).
68 Department of Health, Review of the Human Fertilisation and Embryology Act: A Public Consultation (DoH, London 2005).
69 K Horsey and S Sheldon, 'Still hazy after all these years: the law regulating surrogacy' (2012) 20 *Med L Rev* 67–89.
70 HCCH, 'A Preliminary Report On The Issues Arising From International Surrogacy Arrangements' March 2012 [62]–[63].
71 Ibid [66]; HCCH, 'Council on General Affairs and Policy of the Conference' (9–11 April 2013) [10].
72 K Trimmings and P Beaumont, 'International surrogacy arrangements: an urgent need for legal regulation at the international level' (2011) 7 *Journal of Private International Law* 627–647.
73 *Down Lisburn and Social Services v H* [2006] UKHL 36 [34].
74 S 47 ACA 2002.
75 S 1(4) Adoption and Children Act 2002.
76 S 2 ACA 2002.
77 Part II Care Standards Act 2000.

The adoption agency will identify potential adopters and assess them for suitability.[78] The agency considers whether the adoptive parents and the child will be an appropriate match. An adoption order is made only after a trial placement. The placement is reviewed periodically by the adoption agency.

An adoption order can be made by the courts at the end of the relevant placement period.[79] The court will make an adoption order if it is in the best interests of the child, and the requisite consents have been given. Once such an order is made, the adopted child will be treated as the legitimate child of the adopters[80] and parental responsibility is given to the adopters.[81] Adoption by a British citizen confers British citizenship on a child by virtue of s 1(5) of the British Nationality Act 1981.[82] Where the motive behind the adoption is to circumvent immigration controls, the application will be treated as a sham.[83]

Adoption in England is traditionally a closed process. Although the ACA 2002 permits post-adoption contact with the birth family, the courts have been reluctant to make orders to maintain contact between the child and his birth family.[84] In England only people under 19 may be adopted.[85]

12.4.1 Adoption of foreign children

The opening up of formerly communist Eastern Europe in the 1990s led to considerable growth in intercountry adoption. Television documentaries about the deplorable conditions in Romanian orphanages led to an increase in foreign adoptions by British citizens.[86] Initially, many of these adoptions were entirely unregulated, much as cross-border surrogacy is today.

Until 2003, there were only two ways to adopt a foreign child and have that adoption recognised in the UK. A foreign adoption would be recognised by the English courts as an overseas adoption if it had been made in a country listed on the Adoption (Designation of Overseas Adoptions) Order 1973.[87] Alternatively the child could be brought to the UK and adopted using a domestic adoption order under the Adoption Act 1976.

Other countries may have different adoption laws that require less rigorous procedures and enquiries to be completed prior to adoption. The limited regulation of overseas adoption led to some abuses of the English adoptive system. Children were sometimes removed from their state of origin without any formalities. Parents who had been rejected as unsuitable adopters commissioned private adoptability reports called home study reports which they then used to adopt children overseas from private adoption agencies to which they paid large fees. There were concerns that the international adoption process could be used as a cover for child trafficking.

The Adoption Act 1976 prohibited payments in relation to adoption[88] and also prohibited making private arrangements for adoption.[89] However, these prohibitions had few teeth as they could be dispensed with by the court on a 'best interests of the child' basis.[90] Although such actions

78 Suitability of Adopters Regulations SI 2005/1712.
79 S 42 ACA 2002.
80 S 67 (1) ACA 2002.
81 S 46(1) ACA 2002.
82 For more information see Home Office, 'Intercountry adoption and Immigration rules' 2008 available at www.bia.homeoffice.gov.uk/sitecontent/documents/residency/intercountryadoption.pdf (accessed 17 May 2013).
83 *Re B (Adoption Order: Nationality)* [1999] 1 FLR 907
84 *Re J (A Child) (Adopted Child: Contact)* [2010] EWCA Civ 581; see further K Hughes and B Sloan, 'Post-adoption photographs: welfare, rights and judicial reasoning' [2011] CFLQ 393; *R and H v United Kingdom* (App No 35348/06) [2011] 2 FLR 1236.
85 S 47(9) ACA 2002.
86 J Murphy, *International Dimensions in Family Law* (Manchester University Press, 2005) 194–196.
87 SI 1973/19.
88 S 57.
89 S 11.
90 *Re A (Adoption: Placement)* [1988] 2 FLR 133, [1988] 1 WLR 229, FD

carried criminal penalties, there were rarely any convictions as proceedings had to be brought within six months and the infractions were rarely detected during this period.[91]

For example, in *Re C (Adoption: Legality)*[92] a single woman, who had been rejected by English adoption services as a potential adopter, adopted a child from Guatemala. In order to obtain the adoption she commissioned a home study report for £300. She had never been to Guatemala but merely sent the home study report to adoption services in Guatemala and picked up the child in Amsterdam. The adoption order was made in Guatemala in 1996. She returned to England and informed social services that she wished to adopt the child.

Johnson J held that the mother in this case had committed a criminal offence by making arrangements for the adoption and also by paying for the home study report.[93] He exercised his discretion to make the adoption order in the best interests of the child in spite of these infractions.[94] However, he expressed concern that by retroactively validating such adoptions in the best interests of the child the English domestic system was effectively providing a lower standard of protection for foreign children than those adopted in the UK under the standard adoption processes. He called for stricter regulation of adoptions with a foreign element.[95]

Today there is much greater regulation of intercountry adoption. The Hague Convention on Protection of Children and Co-operation in Respect of Intercountry Adoption 2003 (Hague Adoption Convention) came into force in England and Wales in 2003[96] and creates a uniform system of safeguards for adoptions in Contracting States. Such adoption orders are automatically recognised in the UK subject to public policy exceptions.

Chapter 6 of the Adoption of Children Act 2002 now imposes restrictions on bringing a child into the United Kingdom for the purpose of domestic adoption by a British resident.[97] It is also a criminal offence under the Act for a British resident to bring a child who is habitually resident outside the British Islands and has been adopted abroad in the last six months into the UK unless the individual has complied with prescribed requirements.

The Adoption of Children Act 2002 provides for review of overseas adoptions[98] and imposes stronger restrictions on the preparation of reports related to adoption to ensure that only professionally qualified staff carry out assessments.[99] It also renders it a criminal offence to make payments in relation to adoption[100] and for a private agency to arrange an adoption.[101]

The provisions of the Hague Adoption Convention are examined below. The English rules for recognition of non-Hague adoptions will then be outlined, followed by a review of the restrictions on bringing children into the UK laid down in the Adoption of Children Act 2002.

12.5 The Hague Adoption Convention

The Hague Adoption Convention was drawn up to regulate intercountry adoption in 1993. The Hague Adoption Convention recognises that intercountry adoption can offer a child a permanent

91 *Re C* [1999] 1 FLR 370.
92 [1999] 1 FLR 370; *Re JS (Private International Adoption)* [2000] 2 FLR 638.
93 *Re C (Adoption: Legality)* [1999] 1 FLR 370 379.
94 Ibid 382.
95 Ibid 377. See also *Re A (Adoption: Placement)* [1988] 2 FLR 133, [1988] 1 WLR 229, FD; *Re Note: Adoption Application (Non-Patrial: Breach of Procedures)* [1993] 1 FLR 947; *Re AN* [1992] 1 FLR 341, FD; *Re AW (Adoption Application)* [1993] 1 FLR 62.
96 Adoption (Intercountry Aspects) Act 1999, brought into force by Adoption (Intercountry Aspects) Act 1999 (Commencement No 8) Order 2003 SI 2003/198. The provisions of the Adoption (Intercountry Aspects) Act 1999 have now been re-enacted in the Adoption and Children Act 2002, which came into force on 30 December 2005.
97 S 83 ACA 2002.
98 S 87 ACA 2002.
99 S 94 ACA 2002.
100 S 95 ACA 2002.
101 S 92 ACA 2002.

family where no suitable family is available in his home country.[102] Intercountry adoption is promoted only in certain circumstances, and the Convention acknowledges that, where possible, states should take measures to ensure that the child remains with his own birth family.[103] The 2010 Hague Special Commission[104] noted that in disaster situations efforts to reunite a displaced child with his or her parents or family members must take priority. Unregulated attempts to organise the adoption of such a child abroad should be avoided.[105] The main objective of the Convention is to ensure that intercountry adoptions are made in the best interests of the child.[106]

The Convention creates a uniform system for recognition of adoption orders between Contracting States.[107] The Convention does not require national adoption laws of the Contracting States to be the same but does impose minimum safeguards to prevent child abduction and human trafficking.[108]

As a method of intergovernmental regulation, the Hague Convention comes into force in a Contracting State when it is signed and ratified by domestic legislation. The Convention came into effect in English law in 2003.[109] Article 44 of the Hague Adoption Convention allows signatories to the Convention to raise objections to the accession of new countries. Where an objection is in place, the Convention does not enter into force between the acceding state and the objecting state. There are currently 88 Contracting States to the Convention.[110] The United Kingdom has lodged objections to two Contracting States.[111] An explanatory report giving guidance on how the Convention should be interpreted is available from the Hague Conference website[112] as well as a best practice guide.[113]

The rules of the Convention apply where a child who is habitually resident in one Contracting State is moved to another Contracting State either before or after an adoption order is made.[114] The adoption order can be made either in the state of origin or by the receiving state. The potential adopters must be habitually resident in the receiving state.[115] Therefore the Convention would apply where a person habitually resident in England adopted a child from Romania under Romanian law and brought the child to live in England. It would also apply where an English resident brought a child from Romania to England for the purpose of adoption. In such a case Romania would be the child's **state of origin**, and England would be the **receiving state**. The Convention applies only to adoptions that create a permanent parent/child relationship and not to fostering.[116]

12.5.1 The role of Central Authorities

The Hague Adoption Convention requires the creation of Central Authorities in each Contracting State. The Central Authorities ensure that the safeguards set out in the Convention are observed.

102 Preamble.
103 Preamble.
104 HCCH, 'Conclusions and Recommendations and Report of the Special Commission of June 2010' (2011) [38], available at www.hcch.net/index_en.php?act=publications.details&pid=5458&dtid=2 (accessed 17 May 2013).
105 Ibid.
106 Arts 1(a) and 1(b).
107 Art 1(c).
108 Art 1(b).
109 Adoption (Intercountry Aspects) Act 1999, brought into force by Adoption (Intercountry Aspects) Act 1999 (Commencement No 8) Order 2003 SI 2003/198. The provisions of the Adoption (Intercountry Aspects) Act 1999 have now been re-enacted in the Adoption and Children Act 2002.
110 www.hcch.net/index_en.php?act=conventions.status&cid=69 (accessed 17 May 2013).
111 Cambodia and Guatemala.
112 G Parra-Aranguren, 'Explanatory report on the Convention on protection of children and co-operation in respect of intercountry adoption' (1992), available at www.hcch.net/upload/expl33e.pdf (accessed 17 May 2013).
113 HCCH, 'The Implementation and Operation of the 1993 Intercountry Adoption Convention: Guide to Good Practice' (2008), available at www.hcch.net/index_en.php?act=publications.details&pid=4388&dtid=3 (accessed 17 May 2013).
114 Art 2(1).
115 Art 2(1).
116 Art 2(2).

Central Authorities also transfer information between the Contracting States to remove any obstacles to the child's migration. In England, Part 3 of the Adoptions with a Foreign Element Regulations 2005[117] outlines the procedure to be taken for intercountry adoption under the Hague Convention. Central Authorities must act promptly when engaged in the intercountry adoption; process and delays should be minimised.[118]

It is a requirement of the Hague Adoption Convention that the Central Authorities are central authorities or accredited public bodies.[119] All Hague adoptions must go through the Central Authorities, and parents are not permitted to act for themselves or go through private adoption agencies.[120]

Where prospective adopters wish to adopt from another Contracting State, they apply to the Central Authority in their own state. The Central Authority will prepare a report on the prospective parents and send it to the Central Authority of the other state, which is the state of origin of the child.[121]

The state of origin will check its register of adoptable children[122] and see if a match can be found.[123] The Central Authority in the child's state of origin will transmit a report to the receiving state.[124] The Central Authorities in the receiving state must accept the match and ensure that the parents agree to the proposed placement.[125]

Both states are required to ensure that all relevant parties have received counselling.[126] Both states must ensure that the child is authorised to enter the receiving state and reside there permanently.[127] This ensures that the child is not left stateless, as adoption usually ends the child's nationality of birth. Both states must ensure that the transfer takes place in secure and appropriate circumstances.[128]

The actual adoption order may be made in the state of origin or in the receiving state. This will depend on the adoption law of the state of origin.[129] Where the adoption order is to be made in the state of origin all legal procedures must be complete before the child leaves the state of origin.

If the adoption order is to be made in the receiving state, the Central Authority of the receiving state must monitor the placement of the child with the prospective adopters. If it is decided that the adoption order will not be in the child's best interests, the child may be adopted by another family in the receiving state or returned to the state of origin as a last resort. The Central Authority of the State of origin must be kept informed.[130]

12.5.2 Applicable law and the minimum standards of the Hague Adoption Convention

The Hague Adoption Convention does not require the national adoption laws of the Contracting States to be the same. However, minimum standards and safeguards are laid down in Chapter II of

117 SI 2005/392.
118 Art 35.
119 Art 22(2).
120 Art 14. HCCH, 'The Implementation and Operation of the 1993 Intercountry Adoption Convention: Guide to Good Practice No 1' 2008 [626]. P Pfund, 'Intercountry adoption: The 1993 Hague Convention: its purpose, implementation, and promise' (1994) 28 *Family Law Quarterly* 53–88, 61–64. See also: HCCH, 'Draft – Accreditation and Adoption Accredited Bodies: General Principles and Guide to Good Practice, Guide No 2', 2012.
121 Art 15.
122 Art 4.
123 'Guide to Good Practice No 1' [318].
124 Art 16.
125 Art 17.
126 Arts 4(c) and 5(b).
127 Art 18.
128 Art 19(2).
129 Art 28.
130 Art 21.

the Convention. The Contracting States may put in place more stringent systems of safeguards and procedures than those provided for in the Convention in order to combat child trafficking and child abduction and promote the best interests of the child.[131]

Each Contracting State will apply its own national adoption law when asked to make determinations or assessments under the Hague Adoption Convention. This will occur when the state is asked to make a determination of adoptability or a declaration that potential adopters are eligible to adopt. When the state is asked to make an adoption order it will do so according to its national law.

Conflicts may exist between the adoption law of the state of origin and the adoption law of the receiving state. For example, the state of origin may declare a child adoptable where the child has been abandoned by his married parents. The receiving state may not permit the adoption of marital children. The Hague Adoption Convention lays down minimum standards and provides that further conflicts should be resolved by communication and co-operation between Central Authorities.

12.5.3.1 Eligibility to adopt

The Central Authority in the receiving state is required to determine that adoptive parents are eligible and suitable to adopt.[132] It is open to the Contracting State to stipulate its own rules of eligibility and suitability. It has been suggested that the Convention does not recognise same-sex partners and unmarried couples as suitable adopters as Art 2 refers only to adoptions by spouses or individuals.[133] In 1993, when the Convention was written, it was not common for unmarried couples or same-sex couples to be permitted to adopt. Wardle suggests that adoption by same-sex couples or unmarried couples is not precluded by the Hague Adoption Convention but that such adoptions run the risk of non-recognition in other states on the basis of public policy.[134]

Ideally, conflicts over eligibility should be sorted out between the Central Authorities of the state of origin and the receiving state. The receiving state must provide a report on the parents' suitability to the state of origin.[135] The authorities in the receiving state should ensure that the prospective adoptive parents meet the requirements of a state of origin before sending their file to that country.[136] As it is up to the state of origin to make a determination that a child should be placed with the particular adoptive family,[137] prospective parents who are ineligible under the law of the state of origin are unlikely to be matched.

12.5.3.2 Adoptability

The determination of 'adoptable' is left up to the domestic law of the state of origin. However, Art 17(c) of the Convention states that the adoption may not proceed unless the requirements of the laws of both countries have been met. This allows the authorities of the receiving state to insist that their requirements as to adoptability are met. It is recommended that any potential conflicts are picked up by the Central Authorities early in the process.[138] When the court of the receiving state makes the final adoption order it will apply national law. This may mean that the court will find that the child is not adoptable under the national law of the receiving state.

131 'Guide to Good Practice No 1' [136]–[137].
132 Art 5(a).
133 J Murphy, *International Dimensions in Family Law* (Manchester University Press, 2005) 192.
134 L Wardle, 'The Hague Convention on Intercountry Adoption and American Implementing Law: implications for international adoptions by gay and lesbian couples or partners' (2008) 18 *Indiana International & Comparative Law Review* 134–141.
135 Art 15.
136 'Guide to Good Practice No 1' [332].
137 Art 16(1).
138 'Guide to Good Practice No 1' [331].

12.5.3.3 Consent

The state of origin must ensure that the birth parents consent freely to the adoption.[139] The level of consent required is determined by the applicable law of the state of origin.

Under the requirements of the Hague Adoption Convention, a birth mother cannot give consent to the adoption before the child has been born.[140] The Convention also rules out commercial adoptions, and the state of origin is required to ensure that the adoption has not been induced by compensation or payment of any kind.[141] Reasonable expenses can be reimbursed as long as this payment has not been made to ensure consent.[142]

Article 29 of the Hague Adoption Convention prohibits any contact between the prospective adoptive parents and any person whose consent might be influenced, intentionally or otherwise, by the adoptive parents.

The state of origin submits proof to the receiving state that such consents have been obtained.[143] Under Art 17(c), the receiving state can require future assurances that the law of the receiving state has been complied with as regards consent.

12.5.3.4 Wishes of the child

The Hague Adoption Convention provides that the wishes and views of the child must be taken into consideration throughout the adoption process having regard to the child's age and understanding.[144]

12.5.3.5 Identifying the birth parents

Article 30 ensures that information concerning the child's origin, the identity of his or her birth parents, and the child's medical history is preserved. However, the rights of the child to access this information are governed by the law of the Contracting State that holds the information.[145]

12.5.3 Recognition of Hague Convention adoption orders

An adoption made in compliance with the Hague Adoption Convention, and certified under Art 23, is automatically recognised in all other Contracting States. The Central Authority of the Contracting State in which the adoption order is made will certify the adoption. An Art 23 certificate of conformity facilitates recognition of the adoption if the child and his new family move to another Contracting State in later years. Where the adoption order does not meet the minimum standards of the Hague Adoption Convention and has not been certified under Art 23 it cannot be recognised under the mechanisms of the Hague Adoption Convention.

Article 24 provides that the recognition of a Hague Convention adoption can be refused if it is manifestly contrary to public policy.[146] In making this decision, the best interests of the child concerned must be considered. This is designed to be a very narrow exception.

The recognition of an intercountry adoption order means that the child shall be treated in the recognising state as having rights equivalent to those resulting from domestic adoptions there.[147]

---

139 Art 4(c).
140 Art 4(c)(4).
141 Art 4(d).
142 See Art 8 and Art 32.
143 Art 16(2).
144 Art 4.
145 Art 30(1).
146 S 89(1) of the ACA 2002 provides that the High Court may annul a Convention adoption or Convention adoption order on the ground that the adoption is contrary to public policy.
147 Art 26.

This includes the recognition of a legal parent/child relationship between the child and his adoptive parents and granting parental responsibility to the adoptive parents.[148] Recognition also means the termination of the legal relationship between the child and his birth parents if that is the effect of adoption in the state in which the adoption order was made.[149]

In some countries adoption does not terminate the rights and obligations of the birth parents entirely. This type of adoption, which maintains a legal relationship between the child and his birth parents, is known as simple adoption. Article 26(1) requires that a simple adoption certified under Art 23 by the state of origin is recognised in all other Contracting States, with the effects that the simple adoption has under the laws of the state of origin. Article 26(3) allows the recognising state to give additional legal effects to the simple adoption, as long as these rights are in the best interests of the child, for example citizenship rights or rights of inheritance. Article 27 allows a simple adoption to be converted into a full adoption. The birth parents must give consent to the full adoption under Art 4.

Where the UK is the receiving state, the Central Authority will seek to obtain the consent of the birth parents to a full adoption. Where England is asked to recognise a simple adoption that has already been recognised by another Contracting State the adoption will generally be treated as a full adoption by operation of law. However, if it is felt that it would be more favourable to the child to treat the adoption otherwise than as a full adoption, an application may be made to the High Court under s 88 of the Adoption of Children Act 2002 to allow directions to be made.

12.6 Foreign adoption outside the Hague Adoption Convention

It is possible for a British resident to adopt a child who is habitually resident in a country which is not a contracting party to the Hague Adoption Convention. Any person who takes this option must comply with the procedures of the Adoptions with a Foreign Element Regulations 2005[150] or face criminal penalties. These regulations ensure that all such adoptions go through an English adoption agency and that the child is known to the local authorities.

One option is to adopt the child in the country of habitual residence and apply to have the foreign adoption order recognised in the UK. Another option is to bring the child into the UK and apply for a domestic adoption order.

12.6.1 Recognition of non-Hague foreign adoption orders

Where the Hague Adoption Convention does not apply, a foreign adoption order can be recognised in England by one of two methods.

The adoption can be recognised as an 'overseas' adoption.[151] This is an adoption from a country specified in an order made by the Secretary of State and includes adoptions designated in the Adoption (Designation of Overseas Adoptions) Order 1973.[152] Overseas adoptions are automatically recognised in the UK, but s 89 of the ACA 2002 allows for non-recognition where the adoption is contrary to public policy.

148 Art 26(1).

149 Art 26 (2) & (3).

150 SI 2005/392.

151 S 87(1) ACA 2002.

152 SI 1973/19. The current list is available at www.education.gov.uk/vocabularies/educationtermsandtags/5571 (accessed 17 May 2013).

Where the foreign adoption is not recognised as an overseas adoption it may still be recognised at common law. The basis of such recognition is a statement by Lord Denning MR in *Re Valentine's Settlement*.[153]

> Our courts should recognise a jurisdiction which *mutatis mutandis* they claim for themselves . . . We claim jurisdiction to make an adoption order when the adopting parents are domiciled in this country and the child is resident here. So also, out of the comity of nations, we should recognise an adoption order made by another country when the adopting parents are domiciled there and the child is resident there.[154]

It has been suggested that the common law could recognise a foreign adoption if the adopters have been habitually resident in the country of adoption for at least one year as this would mirror the domestic jurisdiction rule of s 49(2) of the ACA 2002.[155] The court must be satisfied that the adoption order was obtained lawfully in the foreign jurisdiction, the concept of adoption must substantially conform to the English concept and recognition must not be contrary to public policy such as the buying and selling of children irrespective of welfare needs.[156]

In *D v D (Foreign Adoption)*[157] an Indian couple who divided their time between India and the UK adopted two Indian children under the Hindu Adoption and Maintenance Act 1956 in India. They applied to have the adoption orders recognised in the UK. The adoptions were not Hague Convention adoptions as the couple had been habitually resident in India at the time of the adoptions. Nor were the adoptions recognised as overseas adoptions. The court recognised the adoption orders as being similar to English adoption. The parents had made every effort to comply with the law of India. Moreover, the orders were held to be in the best interests of the children. A similar approach was taken in *Re T and M (Adoption)*.[158]

In *Re G*[159] an English couple attempted to adopt a child in Paraguay. The Paraguay courts adopted a 'simple adoption' order which does not sever legal ties between the birth mother and child completely but is revocable. The couple sought recognition of the adoption order in England. This adoption pre-dated the Hague Adoption Convention and was not recognised as an overseas adoption. Johnson J held that the 'simple adoption' order could not be recognised under English common law principles as it was not a type of order recognised in England.[160] He further held that the mother's consent to the simple adoption order was not sufficient to grant an English adoption order.

In some cases it may be necessary to apply for a domestic English adoption order. Under the Adoption of Children Act 2002, the English court has jurisdiction to determine an adoption application if the prospective adopter or one of the prospective adopters is domiciled in 'part of the British Islands'[161] or has been habitually resident there for no less than 'one year ending with the date of the application'.[162]

There is no statutory requirement that the child to be adopted should be a British citizen or that he should be domiciled or habitually resident in the British Islands. This means that the English court has jurisdiction in relation to the adoption of a 'foreign child' who is present in England, but

153 [1965] Ch 831.
154 Ibid 842.
155 J Murphy, *International Dimensions in Family Law* (Manchester University Press, 2005), 202.
156 *Re T and M* [2010] EWHC 964 (Fam) [13].
157 [2008] EWHC 403 (Fam), [2008] 1 FLR 1475.
158 [2010] EWHC 964 (Fam), [2011] 1 FLR 1487. See also *Re J (A Child)* [2012] EWHC 3353 (Fam).
159 [1995] 2 FLR 534.
160 Ibid 537.
161 This includes the UK and Guernsey, Jersey and the Isle of Man.
162 S 49 ACA 2002.

may have a foreign domicile or foreign nationality. All the requirements of English domestic adoption law must be satisfied for the order to be made.[163]

12.6.2 Restrictions on bringing children into the UK

Anyone who intends to bring a child into the UK for the purposes of adoption must comply with the Adoptions with a Foreign Element Regulations 2005.[164] The regulations also apply where the intention is to bring the child into the UK after a foreign non-Hague adoption. Failure to comply with these regulations is a criminal offence punishable by up to 12 months' imprisonment.[165] This is to deter prospective adopters from trying to circumvent proper processes.

The Foreign Element Adoption Regulations require the prospective adopters to be assessed for suitability by an adoption agency prior to bringing the child into the country.[166] The Secretary of State must provide a certificate to the foreign authorities that the prospective adopters are eligible and that the child is authorised to enter the UK and remain indefinitely.[167] The prospective adopters must also visit the child in the state of origin.[168] The parents must inform the local authority once the child has been brought into the UK.[169]

When dealing with infractions of the Foreign Element Adoption Regulations 2005 the courts must view the welfare of the child as the paramount consideration and this may take priority over immigration policy.[170]

In *ASB and KBS v MQS (Secretary of State for the Home Department Intervening)*[171] two British citizens of Pakistani origin decided to adopt one of the wife's nephews in Pakistan. The child was brought to England on a visitor visa, which expired. The husband and wife applied for an adoption order. The local authority and the guardian supported the making of an adoption order. The Secretary of State for the Home Department intervened and opposed the order on the basis that the husband and wife had deceived the immigration authorities. Bennett J considered the court's obligation to ensure the best interests of the child. He held that where the application for an adoption order is designed merely to grant the child British nationality and not to exercise parental authority such action is most unlikely to be in the child's best interests.[172] In this case it was held that the adoption would confer real benefits to the child throughout his life, and the adoption was ordered.

Part 2 of the Children and Adoption Act 2006[173] allows the Secretary of State to place further restrictions on bringing children into the United Kingdom from particular countries if it is considered to be contrary to public policy. This Act was passed after the ruling in *R (Thomson and others) v Secretary of State for Education and Skills*,[174] where the Secretary of State suspended adoptions from Cambodia because there was information to suggest that children were being adopted without proper consents and that individuals involved in the adoption process were making improper financial gain.

---

163 *Re C* [2006] 1 FLR 318; *Re A (Adoption of a Russian Child)* [2000] 1 FLR 539; *Re WM* [1997] 1 FLR 132.
164 SI 2005/392.
165 S 83 ACA 2002.
166 Reg 3, SI 2005/392.
167 Reg 4(2)(a).
168 Reg 4(2)(c).
169 Reg 4(4).
170 See also *Re N* [2010] 1 FLR 1102; *MN v Entry Clearance Officer* [2008] EWCA Civ 38, [2008] 2 FLR 87; *Flintshire County Council v K* [2001] 2 FLR 476.
171 [2009] EWHC 2491 (Fam); [2010] 1 FLR 748; see also *Re H* [1996] 1 FLR 717.
172 *ASB and KBS v MQS (Secretary of State for the Home Department Intervening)* [2009] EWHC 2491 (Fam); [2010] 1 FLR 748 [38].
173 As implemented by the Adoptions with a Foreign Element (Special Restrictions on Adoptions from Abroad) Regulations 2008/1807.
174 [2005] EWHC 1378 (Admin), [2006] 1 FLR 175; See P Cordery, 'Further suspension by the UK of intercountry adoptions' [2006] IFLJ 39.

A number of regulations have been made restricting adoptions from Nepal, Cambodia, Haiti and Guatemala.[175] Guatemala and Cambodia are signatories to the Hague Adoption Convention but the UK has lodged objections to their accession under Art 44(3) of the Hague Convention, and so the Hague Convention does not govern intercountry adoption between England and Guatemala or Cambodia. Such a moratorium is also permitted under the Hague Abduction Convention where it is for child protection reasons.[176]

12.7 Further reading

P Cordery, 'Further suspension by the UK of intercountry adoptions' [2006] IFLJ 39.

N Gamble and L Ghevaert, 'The chosen middle ground: England, surrogacy law and the international arena' [2008] IFLJ 223–227.

A Hutchinson and H Khan, 'International surrogacy arrangements: time for a multi-lateral Convention?' [2011]; IFLJ 303–307.

I Iusmanm, 'The EU and international adoption from Romania' (2013) 27 Int J Law Policy Family 1–27.

P Pfund, 'Intercountry adoption: The 1993 Hague Convention: its purpose, implementation, and promise' (1994) 28 *Family Law Quarterly* 53–88.

D Ranton, 'Striking the balance – intercountry adoption in England and Wales' [2001] *International Fam Law* 35.

E Ryan, 'For the best interests of the children: why the Hague Convention on Intercountry Adoption needs to go farther' (2006) 29 *Boston College International and Comparative Law Review* 353.

K Trimmings and P Beaumont, 'International surrogacy arrangements: an urgent need for legal regulation at the international level' (2011) 7 JPIL 627–647.

175 Special Restrictions on Adoptions from Abroad (Cambodia) Order 2008/1808; Special Restrictions on Adoptions from Abroad (Guatemala) Order 2008/1809; Special Restrictions on Adoptions from Abroad (Haiti) Order 2010/2265; Special Restrictions on Adoptions from Abroad (Nepal) Order 2010/951,

176 'Guide to Good Practice No 1' [457]–[459].

Chapter 13

Parental Responsibility Disputes and Child Abduction

Chapter Contents

Key Issues

- The rules of **jurisdiction** under Brussels II *bis*, the Hague Child Protection Convention and English domestic law
- The effect of the Hague Convention on Child Protection on the rules of **applicable law**
- The **enforceability** of foreign decisions on contact, residence and parental responsibility
- The treatment of **child abduction** under the Hague Abduction Convention and the added protections of Brussels II *bis*

13.1 Introduction

This chapter will examine the situation in which the court is asked to make a determination about the future care and upbringing of a child. Most cases involve a dispute between separated parents who may live in different countries. Where the child has connections to more than one country the court most appropriate to determine the child's future must be established. In general, it is accepted that the most appropriate court to make a decision about a child's future upbringing is the court of the child's habitual residence. The rules of jurisdiction for such cases are governed by EU regulation Brussels II *bis*.[1]

Most legal systems prioritise the best interests of the child principle when making decisions about the child's future upbringing. This approach is required by Art 3 of the UN Convention on the Rights of the Child. However, different legal systems will assess the best interests of the child in various different ways in light of their own cultural and social values. The rules regarding enforcement of judgments throughout the EU is governed by EU regulation Brussels II *bis*. The Hague Child Protection Convention regulates the enforcement of such decisions between Contracting States.[2]

A further issue in child care disputes occurs where one parent takes the child abroad in order to get away from the other parent or to escape the ruling of the court of habitual residence of the child. This is often done in violation of the rights of the parent left behind. This problem is known as international child abduction. In such cases, the courts will determine whether the child should be returned to their home country for the resolution of the dispute or remain in the country to which they have been abducted. In general, there is a presumption that such children should be returned immediately to their country of habitual residence so that the court there can deal with the dispute. This area of law is regulated by the Hague Child Abduction Convention.[3] The provisions of the Hague Child Abduction Convention are given added force in cases involving two EU Member States by EU regulation Brussels II *bis*.

---

1 Council Regulation (EC) No 2201/2003 concerning jurisdiction and the recognition and enforcement of judgments in matrimonial matters and the matters of parental responsibility, repealing Regulation (EC) No 1347/2000, 2003 OJ L338/1.

2 The Convention of 19 October 1996 on Jurisdiction, Applicable Law, Recognition, Enforcement and Co-operation in respect of Parental Responsibility and Measures for the Protection of Children. Text available at www.hcch.net/index_en.php?act=conventions.text&cid=70 (accessed 17 May 2013).

3 Hague Convention of 25 October 1980 on the Civil Aspects of International Child Abduction, text available at www.hcch.net/index_en.php?act=conventions.text&cid=24 (accessed 17 May 2013).

13.2 Parental responsibility, rights of custody and access

Brussels II *bis* applies to any disputes relating to parental responsibility.[4] Parental responsibility is defined under Brussels II *bis* as 'all rights and duties relating to the person or the property of a child which are given to a natural or legal person by judgment, by operation of law or by an agreement having legal effect'.[5] This broad autonomous term encompasses many different types of orders in national law, including those that relate to **rights of custody** and **rights of access** and guardianship.[6] Similar concepts of parental responsibility, rights of custody and rights of access are used in the Hague Abduction Convention[7] and the Hague Child Protection Convention.[8]

Rights of custody include the rights and duties relating to the care of the child and in particular the right to determine the child's place of residence.[9] In contrast, rights of access include the right to take the child to a place other than his habitual residence for a limited time.[10] The distinction between rights of custody and rights of access is very important within the framework of Brussels II *bis* when it comes to enforcement procedures. The distinction is also crucial when deciding whether the Hague Abduction Convention will apply.[11]

English domestic law uses slightly different terminology from Brussels II *bis* and the Hague Conventions. Parental responsibility is a broad concept which includes the right to make decisions regarding the upbringing of a child.[12] In English law, married parents have automatic parental responsibility to look after their children and make decisions on their behalf.[13] If parents are not married, the mother will have automatic parental responsibility[14] but the unmarried father must acquire parental responsibility. This can be done by registered agreement with the mother or by a court order.[15] A holder of parental responsibility in the English system has rights of custody within the meaning of Brussels II *bis* and the Hague Conventions.

Parents living together share the day-to-day care of a child and make decisions together about that child's upbringing. Where parents separate and disagree over who should care for their child, a number of orders are available to the English courts under s 8 of the Children Act 1989. When making s 8 orders or any orders regarding the upbringing of a child the English court must be guided by the best interests of the child in that particular case.[16] This is a very flexible and highly discretionary test and allows the court to individually tailor solutions to the particular dispute. The court can make an order as to where a child should live, known as a **residence order**. The person with whom the child lives under the residence order will also have custody rights.

A common solution is for the child to live with one parent. In such cases the court will usually make an order regulating how often the child sees the other parent. A **contact order** requires the person with whom a child lives to allow the child to visit or stay with the person named in the order or otherwise have contact. This may be done by face-to-face visits, supervised visits, Skype, telephone, email or post. Contact orders are equivalent to rights of access.[17]

A recent tendency in private child care disputes is for the courts to order shared residence or joint custody in order to facilitate shared parenting and to ensure that contact is maintained. A

4 Art 1(1)(b).
5 Art 2(7).
6 Arts 1(2)(a)–(b).
7 Art 1(b).
8 Art 3.
9 Art 2(9).
10 Art 2(10).
11 See below
12 S 3 Children Act 1989.
13 S 2 Children Act 1989.
14 S 2 Children Act 1989.
15 S 4 Children Act 1989.
16 S 1(1) Children Act 1989.
17 S 27(4) Child Abduction and Custody Act 1985.

person who has a shared residence order in their favour will have custody rights. Article 2(11)(b) of Brussels II *bis* states that parents will be considered to have joint custody when one holder of parental responsibility cannot decide on the child's place of residence without the consent of another holder of parental responsibility. In some cases it can be difficult to tell if a shared care order gives both parents rights of custody.[18] In *Re DF (Children)*[19] Thorpe LJ noted the importance of keeping the concepts of residence and contact distinct in international cases.

In English law, unmarried fathers with rights of contact who have not acquired parental responsibility have no 'custody rights'. This has been upheld by the European Court of Human Rights (ECtHR) as being in compliance with Art 8(2) of the European Convention on Human Rights (ECHR).[20] In *J McB v LE*[21] the European Court of Justice (ECJ) held that although the term 'custody rights' under Art 2(11) of Brussels II *bis* was an autonomous concept, national law determined the conditions under which a father acquired custody rights. National law was not precluded from requiring a father to obtain a court order or agreement.[22] Articles 7 and 24 of the Charter of Fundamental Rights did not require the father to have automatic parental rights under Brussels II *bis* as long as the father had a right to apply for rights of custody before the child's removal.[23] This decision has been criticised by some commentators as discriminatory against unmarried fathers.[24]

13.3 Jurisdiction under Brussels II *bis*

Brussels II *bis* came into effect on 1 March 2005. The regulation is binding on all EU Member States except Denmark.[25] Brussels II *bis* was implemented in England and Wales by the European Communities (Jurisdiction and Judgments in Matrimonial and Parental Responsibility Matters) Regulations 2005.[26]

Brussels II *bis* replaces Council Regulation (EC) No 1347/2000 of 29 May 2000 on Jurisdiction and the Recognition and Enforcement of Judgments in Matrimonial Matters and in Matters of Parental Responsibility for Children of Both Spouses (Brussels II). Brussels II only regulated parental responsibility decisions made by courts during the dissolution of marriage. Brussels II *bis* has a much greater scope and governs jurisdiction of courts in all 'matters relating to parental responsibility'.[27] The regulation applies whenever the English court is asked to make a s 8 order under the Children Act 1989.

Although Art 1(1) of the regulation limits Brussels II *bis* to 'civil matters', in *Re C*[28] the ECJ held that the decision to take a child into care falls within the scope of the Regulation.[29] The court held that the term 'civil matters' must be interpreted with regard to the objectives of Brussels II *bis*. The Regulation applies to a decision to take a child into care; even there this is regulated by public law as it affects parental responsibility and rights of custody. The Regulation does not apply in cases to determine the child's legal parentage or in adoption proceedings.[30]

18 A Schulz, 'The 1980 Hague Convention and the European Convention on Human Rights' [2002] *Transnational Law & Contemporary Problems* 379–380.
19 [2011] EWCA Civ 963; *T and J (Abduction: Recognition of Foreign Judgment)* [2012] EWHC 983 (Fam) [7]–[8].
20 *Balbontin v United Kingdom*, no 39067/97, [2000] 1 FLR 1.
21 C400/10 PPU, *J McB v LE* [2010] ECR I–0000, [2011] 1 FLR 518.
22 Ibid [41]–[44].
23 Ibid [59].
24 PJ Blanco, 'Unmarried fathers and child abduction in European Union Law' (2012) 8 *Journal of Private International Law* 135–157.
25 Recital (31).
26 SI 2005/265.
27 Art 1(1)(b).
28 C435/06 [2007] ECR 1–1014.
29 Ibid [29]–[37]. See also recital (5).
30 Art 1(3)

Brussels II *bis* requires Member States to designate a Central Authority to assist with the application of the Regulation in matters of parental responsibility.[31] The authorities communicate and co-operate using the European Judicial Network.[32] This can be helpful in establishing the content of foreign law or the intentions of another court or in resolving delays. The Office of the Head of International Family Justice deals with these issues in England and Wales.[33] The authorities also provide information for specific cases and facilitate co-operation between holders of parental responsibility.[34] For example, requests for voluntary co-operation and mediation can be made before requiring court intervention.

As Brussels II *bis* is an EU regulation, its terms have autonomous meanings, and questions of interpretation are referred to the Court of Justice of the European Union (CJEU). Many of the parental responsibility cases have been referred to the ECJ under the new urgent procedure for preliminary rulings introduced in 2008.[35]

The rules determining jurisdiction as between different parts of the UK also reflect the provision of Brussels II *bis*.[36]

13.3.1 Rules of jurisdiction under Brussels II *bis*

Brussels II *bis* grants jurisdiction for matters involving parental responsibility to the courts of the Member State where the child is habitually resident at the time the court is seised.[37] The child's habitual residence is the country in which the child is integrated in a social and family environment.[38]

In *Re H-K (Habitual Residence)*[39] an Australian family moved to the UK for a year with the intention of returning home. The English court held that the children were habitually resident in England as all of the indicators of integration into a social and family environment were present in this case: the family lived in a house owned by the mother; her family was nearby and supportive; the parents worked when they could; they sought and obtained social security benefit; and the older child was established in school. Presence of a certain permanency had been obtained.[40]

Habitual residence can be difficult to determine where a shared residence order is in place and the child divides his or her time between two jurisdictions. Brussels II *bis* only envisages a child having one habitual residence at the time the court was seised.[41] This may mean that a child with shared residence alternates habitual residence between the two jurisdictions, so the presence of the child in one or the other at the time the court is seised will be crucial.

Article 13 applies where the child's habitual residence cannot be established. In such a case the Member State where the child is present shall have jurisdiction.[42]

Parties to a dispute have a limited ability to choose another court's jurisdiction. Article 12(1) gives jurisdiction to the Member State where a divorce or separation is being heard to deal with

---

31 Art 53.

32 Decision No 2001/470/EC

33 See www.judiciary.gov.uk/about-the-judiciary/international/international-family-justice (accessed 17 May 2013).

34 Art 55.

35 Council Decision of 20 December 2007 ((2008) OJ L 24/42); Amendments to the Rules of Procedure of the Court of Justice adopted by the court on 15 January 2008 ((2008) OJ L 24/39); see C Kumar, 'A fast track to Europe: the urgent procedure for preliminary rulings' [2008] IFL 180.

36 Art 66 Brussels II *bis* and s 2 Family Law Act 1986 as amended.

37 Art 8(1).

38 C497/10 PPU *Mercredi v Chaffe* [2011] 1 FLR 1293 [47]. The meaning of habitual residence under Brussels II *bis* is examined in Chapter 2.

39 [2011] EWCA Civ 1100, [2012] 1 FLR 436.

40 A similar approach was taken in *FVS v MGS (Habitual Residence)* [2011] EWHC 3139 (Fam), [2012] 1 FLR 1184.

41 C523/07 *Re A* [2009] ECR I-2805,[2009] 2FLR 1; *HA v MB (Brussels II Revised: Article 11(7) Application)* [2007] EWHC 2016 (Fam), [2008] 1 FLR 289; *Re H-K (Habitual Residence)* [2011] EWCA Civ 1100, [2012] 1 FLR 436 [101].

42 Art 13.

related matters of parental responsibility. The parties must have agreed to the jurisdiction, and it must be in the superior interests of the child. This jurisdiction ceases when the matrimonial proceedings have come to an end.[43]

Article 12(3) allows all parties to a parental responsibility dispute to accept the jurisdiction of any Member State where it is in the best interests of the child and the child has a substantial connection with that Member State. Such a connection exists if one of the holders of parental responsibility is habitually resident in that Member State or if the child is a national of that Member State. Acceptance must be express or unequivocally expressed.

Where a child is **lawfully moved**[44] from one Member State to another, the courts of the child's old habitual residence retain jurisdiction for three months after the move for the purposes of amending orders regarding access rights.[45] The jurisdiction lapses if the access rights holder accepts the new jurisdiction.

Under Art 10, where a child is **unlawfully removed** from one Member State to another, the Member State in which the child was habitually resident before the removal retains jurisdiction until the child has acquired a new habitual residence in the state of abduction and all holders of parental responsibility acquiesce to removal or where no application for return has been made within a year or where the possibility of an order for return has been conclusively rejected.[46]

13.3.2 Staying and declining jurisdiction (Art 19)

Once the court of one Member State is seised of proceedings relating to parental responsibility, it is not possible to bring parallel proceedings in another Member State. A court is seised when documents are lodged with the court.[47] If proceedings regarding the same cause of action and the same child are then brought in a second Member State, the second court must stay proceedings until the court first seised has established jurisdiction.[48] If the court first seised accepts jurisdiction, the court second seised must decline on its own motion.[49]

In *Mercredi v Chaffe*[50] the ECJ ruled that where the second seised court did not decline proceedings its judgment could have no effect on the ruling of the court of the state with jurisdiction, over the substance of the dispute.[51]

13.3.3 Transferring jurisdiction (Art 15)

Article 15 allows the courts of a Member State with jurisdiction to transfer proceedings relating to parental responsibility to the courts of another Member State better placed to hear the case. The child must have a 'particular connection' to the state as outlined by Art 15(3). For example, it is the place of the child's nationality or former habitual residence. The transfer must also be in the best interests of the child. Under Art 15 the court may stay proceedings and request a court in another Member State to assume jurisdiction. This can be done on the application of either party to the dispute, on the court's own motion or in response to a request from the courts of another Member State.

---

43 Art 12(2).
44 This applies where a parent has been granted permission to bring the child to live abroad either by a court or by the other parent.
45 Art 9(1)
46 Art 10(b).
47 Art 16
48 C296/10 *Purrucker v Vallés Pérez (No 2)* [2012] 1 FLR 925.
49 Art 19. See *Re I* [2011] EWHC 2752 (Fam), [2012] 1 FLR 768.
50 [2011] 1 FLR 1293.
51 Ibid [70].

In *AB v JLB (Brussels II Revised: Article 15)*[52] an English couple worked in the Netherlands, and had a child born in the Netherlands. In 2008, the marriage broke down, and both parties filed for divorce. The mother issued a divorce petition in England and based jurisdiction on her English domicile. The father took proceedings in the Netherlands seeking care of the child and some ancillary relief. The mother made an application for residence in the English courts. The father conceded that the divorce proceedings should continue in England. The Dutch courts granted the father temporary care of the child and exclusive use of the family home. The Dutch court declined to transfer jurisdiction to the English courts as the child's habitual residence was in the Netherlands. The mother applied again to the English courts for a residence order and requested the English court to have the case transferred to England under Art 15 as divorce proceedings were ongoing. The English court rejected the application as the mother had not shown any reasonable prospect of persuading the Dutch court to come to a different decision. The court stayed the applications for residence and contact pending the decision of the Dutch court.

13.3.4 Provisional and protective measures under Art 20

Article 20 of Brussels II *bis* allows the court to take provisional or protective measures in urgent cases even where another court has jurisdiction over the substantive parental responsibility dispute.

A judgment is considered to be provisional where it satisfies the test laid down in *Re A*.[53] The measure must be urgent, it must be taken in respect of persons present in that Member State and it must be provisional.[54] The court must inform the courts of the Member State with jurisdiction over the substance of the dispute that provisional measures have been taken.[55]

In *Deticek v Scueglia*,[56] an Italian father and Slovenian mother lived in Italy with their child. The couple split up, and the Italian courts provisionally granted custody to the father and ordered that the child be placed temporarily in a children's home pending further reports. The father took enforcement proceedings in Slovenia. The mother obtained provisional and protective measures from the Slovenian courts granting her sole custody.

The ECJ examined the validity of the provisional measures granted by Slovenia. Applying the three-part test from *Re A*, the court held that in this case the measures were not urgent.[57] The child's gradual integration with the social and family environment in Slovenia could not be considered to be an urgent reason to make Art 20(1) orders. To do so would allow a court to block enforcement where there was any delay in finalising matters in the Member State with jurisdiction over the matter. In addition, the father was not present in Slovenia when the order was made, which deprived him of his custody rights.[58]

Where a court has been seised only for the purpose of making provisional measures under Art 20, a second court with jurisdiction over the substance of the matter does not have to stay proceedings under Art 19(2).[59] It must be manifestly clear from the facts that the action before the first court contains no ground on which the first court might claim jurisdiction over the substance of the dispute. If it is unclear whether action before the first court is limited to provisional measures, the second court is under an obligation to make enquiries of the first court.[60]

52 [2008] EWHC 2965 (Fam), [2009] 1 FLR 517.
53 C523/07 *Re A* [2009] ECR I–2805, [2009] 2 FLR 1.
54 Ibid [65].
55 Ibid [66].
56 C403/09 PPU *Deticek v Scueglia* [2010] 1 FLR 1381.
57 Ibid [39]–[40].
58 Ibid [50]–[52].
59 C296/10 *Purrucker v Vallés Pérez (No 2)* [2012] 1 FLR 925 [77].
60 Ibid [82]–[83].

Provisional measures cease to apply once the Member State with jurisdiction has decided on the substance of the case.[61]

In *Purrucker v Vallés Pérez (No 1)*[62] a German mother and Spanish father were living in Spain when their twins were born. The parents had a joint custody agreement which outlined that the mother would return to Germany with one of the twins and the other would follow when released from hospital. After the mother left for Germany, the father took provisional proceedings for custody of the twins in the Spanish courts. The courts awarded the father sole custody and ordered the mother to return the child from Germany. The father sought enforcement of the order in Germany.

The ECJ held that provisional judgments under Art 20 are not enforceable with extraterritorial effect under Brussels II *bis*.[63] The enforcement of such judgments, which are not based on the jurisdictional grounds of Brussels II *bis*, would circumvent the jurisdictional rules under Brussels II *bis*.[64]

13.3.5 Jurisdiction outside the remit of Brussels II *bis*

Jurisdiction is not governed by Brussels II *bis* where the habitual residence of the child is a third state and the parties have not accepted the jurisdiction of an EU Member State under Art 12.[65] If that third state is a contracting party to the Hague Child Protection Convention 1996 and the state determining jurisdiction is also a party to that Convention, jurisdiction will be determined according to the rules of the Hague Child Protection Convention.

If the child is habitually resident in a state that is not a party to the Hague Child Protection Convention, the parties may accept the jurisdiction of an EU Member State, and this will be presumed to be in the child's best interest. For example, in *Re I (A Child)*[66] the father was given leave to take his child to Pakistan after giving undertakings that he would return the child to England if asked to do so. The mother applied to facilitate contact rights. On appeal she argued that the English courts retained jurisdiction under Art 12(4). The court held that Art 12 could apply to children habitually resident in a non-EU State. The court examined the need for jurisdiction to be in the best interests of the child and held that in this case the requirement was satisfied as contact was to take place in England.[67]

If there is no acceptance of the jurisdiction of an EU Member State and the child is habitually resident in a third-country state that is not a Contracting State to the Hague Child Protection Convention, national rules of jurisdiction may be used.[68]

13.4 The Hague Child Protection Convention 1996

The Convention on Jurisdiction, Applicable Law, Recognition, Enforcement and Cooperation in respect of Parental Responsibility and Measures for the Protection of Children was concluded on 19 October 1996 and came into force in 2002. The Hague Child Protection Convention is designed to promote international co-operation to protect children, and it prioritises the best interests of the child.[69] The Convention applies to cases involving questions of parental responsibility. 'Parental responsibility' includes parental authority, or any analogous relationship of authority determining

61 Art 20 (2).
62 C256/09 *Purrucker v Vallés Pérez* (No 1) [2012] 1 FLR 903.
63 Ibid [87].
64 Ibid [100].
65 I.e. a state that is not an EU Member State.
66 [2009] UKSC 10.
67 Ibid [37]–[38].
68 Art 14.
69 Preamble.

the rights, powers and responsibilities of parents, guardians or other legal representatives in relation to the person or the property of the child.[70] Like Brussels II *bis*, the Convention applies to decisions on rights of custody, access and guardianship.[71] The Convention contains rules to establish jurisdiction, and it regulates the recognition and enforcement of parental responsibility decisions across international borders. Unlike Brussels II *bis*, the Convention also determines applicable law for disputes involving parental responsibility rights.

The Convention uses a system of Central Authorities to facilitate the exchange of information between Contracting States, assist in the location of children and facilitate conciliation between the parties and the protection of children across borders.[72] A practical handbook on the application of the Convention has been published by the Hague Conference.[73]

The EU Council has authorised Member States to sign the Hague Child Protection Convention.[74] There are 39 signatories to the Convention, including the EU States, Australia and the USA. The Convention does not come into force in each state until it is ratified.[75] The UK has put measures in place to implement the Convention[76] and the Convention came into force in the UK on 1 November 2012. The rules of Brussels II *bis* take priority over the Hague Child Protection Convention when establishing jurisdiction in a Member State or when recognising and enforcing judgments from other Member States.[77]

13.4.1 Jurisdiction under the Hague Child Protection Convention 1996

The rules of jurisdiction of the Hague Child Protection Convention are very similar to those of Brussels II *bis*. The general rule is that the court where the child is habitually resident will have jurisdiction to take measures directed to the protection of the child's person or property.[78] If the child's habitual residence cannot be ascertained, the Contracting State in which the child is present will have jurisdiction.[79] A court with jurisdiction over dissolution of marriage will have jurisdiction over related parental responsibility matters under the Hague Child Protection Convention.[80]

Courts may also take urgent protective measures where a child is present on their territory.[81] These provisions lapse if a court with jurisdiction under the Convention takes measures.

Once a court has been seised under the Hague Child Abduction Convention, other courts must stay proceedings until the first court has determined jurisdiction.[82]

A court with jurisdiction under the Hague Child Protection Convention can transfer jurisdiction to a more appropriate court in another Contracting State in much the same way as under Brussels II *bis*.[83] Transfer can be requested if the other Contracting State has a substantial connection to the child and it is considered to be in the child's best interests.

70 Art 1(2).
71 Arts 3 and 4.
72 Arts 29–31.
73 HCCH, 'Revised draft Practical Handbook on the operation of the 1996 Hague Protection of Children Convention (Prel. Doc. No 4 of May 2011)' available at www.hcch.net/index_en.php?act=publications.details&pid=5535&dtid=2 (accessed 17 May 2015).
74 Council Decision 2003/93/EC of 19 December 2002.
75 Art 61.
76 Parental Responsibility and Measures for the Protection of Children (International Obligations) (England and Wales and Northern Ireland) Regulations 2010/1898.
77 Art 61 Brussels II *bis*.
78 Art 5.
79 Art 6.
80 Art 10.
81 Arts 11 and 12.
82 Art 13.
83 Arts 8 & 9.

13.4.2 Jurisdiction under UK domestic rules

Article 14 of Brussels II *bis* allows jurisdiction to be determined by UK rules where no Member State has jurisdiction under Arts 8–13.

Jurisdiction is governed by s 2 of the Family Law Act (FLA) 1986. The English court has jurisdiction to grant s 8 orders where the order is related to matrimonial or civil partnership proceedings[84] or if the child is present in England and Wales but not habitually resident in another part of the UK.[85] Section 2A gives the English courts discretion not to make orders relating to children in matrimonial proceedings if such matters could be dealt with more appropriately elsewhere.

In addition, the English courts can exercise the inherent jurisdiction of the High Court or wardship proceedings to give care of a child to any person or to provide for contact or a child's education where the child concerned is present in England and Wales on the relevant date and the court considers that the immediate exercise of its powers is necessary for his protection.[86] In *H v H (Jurisdiction to Grant Wardship)*[87] the court considered its jurisdiction to grant wardship. In this case the

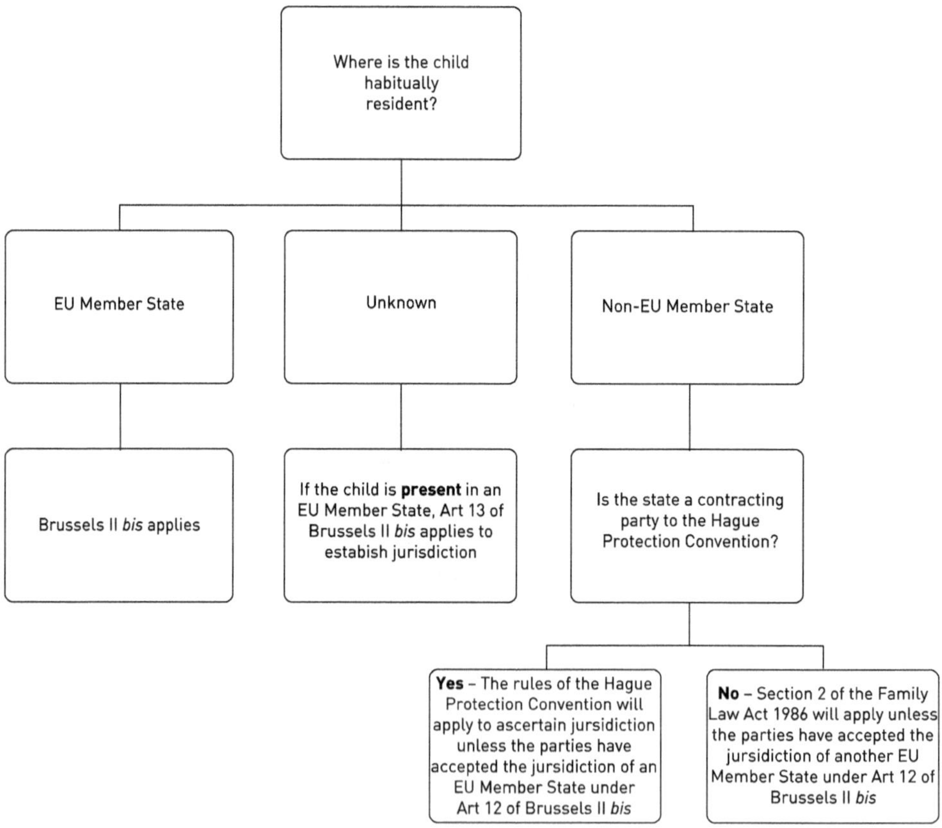

Fig 13.1 Jurisdiction: which instrument to use?

84 S 1(b)(i).
85 S 1(b)(ii).
86 S 2(3)(ii).
87 [2011] EWCA Civ 796, [2012] 1 FLR 23.

father had married an Afghanistani woman in Afghanistan. She had a child there and left him in the care of an uncle before joining her husband in England. The marriage broke down. The child went missing from the uncle's care. The mother believed that the father had abducted the child and issued wardship proceedings. The father challenged the jurisdiction of the English court. On appeal the Court of Appeal held that the English court had no wardship jurisdiction over a child who had never been present in the country and where jurisdiction had not been conceded.

If Brussels II *bis* does not apply to the case, an English court can decline to exercise jurisdiction[88] if the issue has already been determined elsewhere. It may also stay its proceedings on a *forum non conveniens* basis by virtue of s 5(2) of the FLA 1986.[89]

13.5 Recognition and enforcement of orders relating to parental responsibility

An order made by a court in one part of the UK is recognised in any other part of the UK under the Family Law Act (FLA) 1986.[90] If these orders are breached, a parent can apply to the local court to have the order registered and enforced under ss 27 and 29 of the FLA 1986.[91]

Article 21 of Brussels II *bis* provides for automatic recognition in all Member States (except Denmark) of judgments given in a Member State relating to parental responsibility. The Regulation promotes the principle of mutual trust and so the grounds for non-recognition are minimal.[92] Article 24 precludes a Member State from reviewing another Member State's assessment of its jurisdiction under Brussels II *bis*. Article 26 forbids Members States from reviewing the substance of another Member State's judgment.

13.5.1 Grounds for non-recognition

Non-recognition is permitted where the judgment is manifestly contrary to public policy, taking into consideration the best interests of the child.[93] The meaning of the phrase 'manifestly contrary to public policy' was examined in *Re S (Brussels II: Recognition: Best interests of child) (No 1)*.[94] Holman J stressed that the use of the word 'manifestly' was a very high hurdle. Here, although the order was not, in Holman J's opinion, in the child's best interest, this was not to such a degree as to be manifestly contrary to public policy.[95] An in-depth investigation of the child's best interest would amount to reviewing the judgment of a court of another Member State, which is prohibited by the Regulation.[96]

In *AB v KB (Abduction: Brussels II Revised)*[97] the Spanish court issued a residence order in favour of the mother. The father retained the children in England and appealed. Three years later the mother registered the Spanish residence order under Art 28(2). The father argued that the order was now so old that it was manifestly contrary to public policy to have the order enforced. The court held that although it was possible for an order of a foreign court to be so strongly contrary to the welfare of the child that its recognition was manifestly contrary to the public policy of England, such cases

88 S 5(1) Family Law Act 1986.
89 *Re V (Forum conveniens)* [2005] 1 FLR 718.
90 S 25 Family Law Act 1986.
91 *Re M* [1992] 2 FLR 382, 386–7.
92 Recital (21).
93 Art 23(a).
94 [2003] EWHC 2115 (Fam), [2004] 1 FLR 571.
95 Ibid [32].
96 Ibid [29]–[31].
97 [2009] EWHC 2243 (Fam), [2010] 2 FLR 1664.

would be extremely rare.[98] When asked to enforce a judgment under Brussels II *bis*, the court did not reopen the question of the best interests of the child. Instead there was an overriding duty to enforce, subject only to public policy concerns.[99] Welfare is not paramount in enforcement proceedings.[100]

Non-recognition is also permitted where parties to the dispute, including the child, have not been given the right to be heard[101] or where the judgment is irreconcilable with a later judgment by the Member State in which recognition is sought or a later judgment of another Member State with jurisdiction.[102]

In *Re LSdC (BIIR)*[103] the court refused to recognise an order on the basis of public policy. The family had lived in Portugal but when the relationship broke down the mother attempted to leave Portugal with the child and was stopped by authorities at the airport. An agreement was negotiated between the parents in the presence of police officers.[104] This was ratified by the Portuguese court. The agreement was for the child to share residence between the parents and between England and Portugal on a two-month rotation basis until the child turned three. The mother contested recognition of the judgment under Art 23. The court found that the mother had been very depressed when the agreement was made,[105] the views and interests of the child had not been taken into account and the emphasis of the agreement was on adult agreement.[106] This was enough to justify non-recognition on public policy grounds under Art 23(a).

13.5.2 Enforcement procedures under Brussels II *bis*

There are two enforcement procedures under Brussels II *bis*. The ordinary procedure under s 2 (Arts 28–33) applies to judgments relating to parental responsibility and orders for return of a child under the Hague Convention. An expedited procedure under s 4 (Arts 40–45) is for judgments relating to rights of access and particular orders for return of the child under the Hague Convention granted according to Art 11(8) of Brussels II *bis*.[107]

In order to enforce a judgment relating to parental responsibility in another Member State, the judgment must be served and declared enforceable there.[108] In the UK the judgment must be registered for enforcement in the part of the United Kingdom where it is to be enforced.[109] When deciding whether the judgment is enforceable, the court is required to give its judgment without delay. The prohibition on reviewing the judgment is reiterated.[110] Enforcement can only be refused on the same grounds as recognition. A declaration of enforceability can be appealed by either party within one month of service.[111]

Section 4 of Brussels II *bis* lays out an expedited method of enforcement for judgments concerning rights of access and particular orders requiring the return of a child under Art 11(8).[112] Under Art 41, a judgment for rights of access is enforceable without a declaration of enforceability

98 Ibid [32].
99 Ibid [33]–[34].
100 Ibid [35].
101 Arts 23(b)–(c).
102 Arts 23(e)–(f).
103 [2012] EWHC 983 (Fam).
104 Ibid [18]–[19].
105 Ibid [21]–[26].
106 Ibid [37]–[38].
107 See below.
108 Art 28.
109 Art 28(2).
110 Art 31.
111 Art 33; *Re S (Foreign Contact Order)* [2009] EWCA Civ 993, [2010] 1 FLR 982; *Re D (Brussels II Revised: Contact)* [2007] EWHC 822 (Fam), [2008] 1 FLR 516.
112 Art 40.

if the judgment has been certified in the Member State of origin. This is a highly effective way for non-resident parents to enforce access rights.[113] This certificate will not be granted unless all parties were appropriately served and given an opportunity to be heard. This expedited procedure means that the state which issues the judgment ensures compliance, rather than the state of enforcement. Under Art 42, the same procedure applies for judgments for return under Art 11(8). Certificates are automatically enforceable and not subject to review of any kind by the state of enforcement, not even on welfare[114] or human rights grounds.

In *Aguirre Zarraga v Simone Pelzi*,[115] an Art 42 certificate had been issued. The mother applied for non-recognition of the certificate on the basis that the child's right to be heard had been violated. The German court referred the case to the ECJ, asking if was possible to review an Art 42 certificate where a particularly serious infringement of a fundamental right had occurred. The ECJ held that a certified judgment is enforceable and no review is possible.[116] There is no appeal against the issuing of a certificate but certificates can be rectified by the state of origin.[117]

13.5.3 Facilitating access under Art 48 Brussels II *bis*

Article 48 allows the courts of the Member State of enforcement to make practical arrangements for organising the exercise of rights of access. For example, Spain, as the court of habitual residence of the child, may order the child to have overnight contact with his father in England. The English courts will have to facilitate the smooth operation of contact. The courts of the state of enforcement must respect the substance of original order.[118]

In *Re G (Foreign Contact Order: Enforcement)*, a case under Brussels II, Thorpe LJ noted that contact orders are particularly subject to change, and some flexibility is required when making detailed arrangements for contact in order to ensure that the orders made by the foreign court are followed.[119]

In *Re S (Brussels II: Recognition: Best interests of child) (No 2)*[120] a father sought to enforce an order for contact to have his three-year-old son travel to Belgium for fortnightly periods. The child had not yet stayed overnight with the father and could not remember him. Holman J held that although the enforcement of access rights was left to English law, this did not mean that English principles could be used to justify non-enforcement.[121] The court must make the foreign judgment happen as soon as it can be legitimately achieved; welfare is not paramount or the primary concern.[122] Here the court ordered a gradual introduction of contact to the levels ordered by the Belgian court.[123]

Only the court with jurisdiction over access rights can change the substance of the rights of access order. This will usually be the court of the child's habitual residence.

In *Re S (Brussels II Revised: Enforcement of Contact Order)*[124] the mother and father both lived in Poland. The Polish court granted sole residence to the mother and ordered that the children spend every other weekend staying overnight with their father and half the holidays with him. The mother relocated to England, and the father sought to enforce his contact order. As the children were now habitually resident in England and had been for over three months, the English court now had

113 *Re DF (Children)* [2011] EWCA Civ 963.
114 C211/10 PPU *Povse v Alpago* [2010] ECR I–000, [2010] 2 FLR 1343.
115 C491/10 PPU *Aguirre Zarraga v Simone Pelzi* [2010] ECR I–14247.
116 Ibid [51].
117 Art 43.
118 Art 48.
119 *Re G (Foreign Contact Order: Enforcement)* [2003] EWCA Civ 1607, [2004] 1 WLR 521, [2004] 1 FLR 378 [27].
120 [2003] EWHC 2974 (Fam), [2004] 1 FLR 582.
121 Ibid [10].
122 Ibid [14].
123 Ibid [16] and [17].
124 [2008] 2 FLR 1358.

jurisdiction over contact and refused to enforce the old order as it was no longer in the best interests of the child. Instead the court made new contact orders.

13.5.4 Recognition and enforcement of measures of protection under the Hague Child Protection Convention

If the judgment to be enforced comes from an EU Member State, the rules of Brussels II *bis* apply to enforcement. If a judgment comes from a Contracting State to the Hague Child Protection Convention which is not an EU State, the rules of the Hague Child Protection Convention will apply to its recognition and enforcement.

Under Art 23, a measure of protection given by a Contracting State must be recognised in other Contracting States. Recognition can only be refused in certain cases which are similar to the grounds for non-recognition under Brussels II *bis*.[125] The jurisdiction of the state which took the measure can be reviewed, but the court is bound by findings of fact from the first court.[126] There can be no review of the merits of the measure taken.[127]

Measures of protection must be enforced, but the procedure for enforcement is up to the law of the enforcing state. The Convention states only that it must be a simple and rapid procedure.[128] Measures of protection are defined in Art 3 as measures involving the creation, exercise, termination or restriction of parental responsibility, rights of custody, rights of access and guardianship. Measures of protection also include the placement of a child into state care.

13.5.5 Recognition and enforcement of judgments from other states

Where a judgment relating to the custody and upbringing of a child is made by a state that is not a party to Brussels II *bis* or the Hague Child Protection Convention, it will not preclude an English court making a determination of the issues based solely on the best interests of the child.[129] In such a case the substance of the foreign order will only be enforced if it accords with the English court's estimation of what is in the best interests of the child.

13.6 Applicable law

Brussels II *bis* does not regulate the law applicable to parental responsibility disputes. It merely designates which court has jurisdiction to hear the dispute. The courts use their own rules to determine applicable law. In most cases this will be domestic law but some states apply the personal law of the child, which is based on the child's domicile or nationality.[130] In English law there is no 'proper law' of the child. If the English court has jurisdiction to hear a parental responsibility dispute it will decide the case on the basis of English law, which amounts to an application of the best interests of the child principle as outlined by s 1(1) of the Children Act 1989.[131]

125 Art 23.
126 Art 25.
127 Art 27.
128 Art 26.
129 *J and Another v C and Others* [1970] AC 668, (1969) FLR Rep 360.
130 *Re JB (Child Abduction) (Rights of Custody: Spain)* [2003] EWHC 2130 (Fam); *Kennedy v Kennedy* [2009] EWCA CIV 986, [2010] 1 FLR 782.
131 *Re J* [2005] UKHL 40, [2006] 1 AC 80, [2005] 2 FLR 802 [19].

13.6.1 Applicable law under the Hague Convention 1996

Articles 16 to 18 of the Hague Convention 1996 create a special regime of applicable law for parental responsibility. This departs somewhat from the former English approach. Where parental responsibility rights are created by court order, Art 15 states that the country exercising its jurisdiction may apply its own domestic law.[132] Foreign law may be taken into account in exceptional circumstances, provided that this is in the best interests of the child.[133] However, where parental responsibility rights are created automatically by the operation of law or by agreement, the applicable law is the state of the child's habitual residence.[134] Lowe notes that the Hague Child Protection Convention gives priority to a substantive rule imposing parental responsibility whenever possible.[135]

The effect of Art 16 is that parental responsibility rights can be acquired by changing a child's habitual residence. For example, if an unmarried English mother with sole parental responsibility moves to a country where natural fathers have automatic parental responsibility, this will give the father parental responsibility rights. Once parental responsibility rights exist under the state of the child's habitual residence they continue to exist when the child changes habitual residence unless the rights are expressly extinguished.[136] This means that if the mother moves back to England at a later date, the father will retain parental responsibility.

However, Art 17 of the Hague Child Protection Convention provides that the exercise of parental responsibility is governed by the state of the child's habitual residence regardless of where the parental responsibility was originally acquired. This may moderate the exercise of rights acquired in another jurisdiction.

The application of the law designated by the Convention can only be refused for public policy reasons, and provided that it is in the best interests of the child.[137] This may affect the recognition of parental responsibility rights of same-sex couples in certain countries.[138]

13.7 Child abduction

When a relationship breaks down, one parent may wish to move to a different country and take the children with them. If one of the parents is a non-national they may wish to return to their home country where they may have more family support to care for the child.

Often the leaving parent acts properly and obtains permission to take the child to live in another country from the other holders of parental responsibility or from the court.[139] Where an English residence order is in place, it is possible to take the named child abroad for up to one month, but longer trips require court permission.[140] In some cases, the court will require an undertaking that the child will be returned.[141]

For example, a Polish mother who has been granted sole residence in England may be granted permission to take her children to live in Poland as long as they return to England each year to

132 *Renvoi* is generally excluded by Art 21 except for the attribution of parental responsibility where the applicable law is that of a non-party state.
133 Art 15(2).
134 Art 16(1)& (2).
135 N Lowe, 'The Applicable Laws Provisions of the 1996 Hague Convention on the Protection of Children and the Impact of the Convention on International Child Abduction' [2010] *International Family Law* 51, 52.
136 Arts 16(3) and 18.
137 Art 22.
138 N Lowe, 'The Applicable Laws Provisions of the 1996 Hague Convention on the Protection of Children and the Impact of the Convention on International Child Abduction' [2010] *International Family Law* 54.
139 In England and Wales such a procedure is governed by s 12 Children Act 1989.
140 S 13(1) Children Act 1989; *Payne v Payne* [2001] EWCA Civ 166 ; *Re K (Children)* [2011] EWCA Civ 793.
141 *Re L (Removal from Jurisdiction: Holiday)* [2001] 1 FLR 241; *Re S* [2001] 2 FLR 507.

spend some time with their English father. If the Polish mother then breaches the English court ruling, the left-behind parent can seek to enforce his order for contact as an order relating to access rights under Art 41. If the arrangements relating to access need to be changed, the English courts will retain jurisdiction to do so for three months after the move.[142] The English courts will no longer have jurisdiction over other parental responsibility issues once the child becomes habitually resident in Poland. However, the father is free to bring new custody proceedings in Poland.

If a parent takes the child out of the country without court approval, or in violation of a court order, this wrongful removal can be treated as international child abduction. In such a case, the absconding parent can be forced to return to the country of origin using the Hague Abduction Convention and the supporting provisions of Brussels II *bis*. However, a better route in most cases is for the parent to apply to have the custody order enforced in the state of abduction under Brussels II *bis*.

For example, a Spanish court makes an order of sole residence for a child to live with his father in Spain. His English mother abducts the child and brings him to England. It is open to the English father to simply apply to have the Spanish order enforced under Brussels II *bis*, which will be nearly automatic and require the return of the child to Spain. This is a much simpler and less expensive process than a Hague Abduction Convention application.[143]

It is also possible to bring enforcement of custody order proceedings where the child is abducted to a non-EU State that is a contracting party to the Hague Child Protection Convention.

It is only necessary to use the Hague Abduction Convention when the child has been wrongfully removed to a non-EU Member State or where no custody order exists to be enforced.

13.7.1 The Hague Convention on International Child Abduction

The United Kingdom is a Contracting State to the Hague Convention on the Civil Aspects of International Child Abduction 1980 (Hague Child Abduction Convention). The Hague Child Abduction Convention imposes obligations on Contracting States to ensure the prompt return of children wrongfully removed or retained, to the country of habitual residence.[144] The Convention promotes the best interests of the child as paramount.[145] There is a presumption within the Convention that the best interests of the child are generally served by prompt return to the country of habitual residence for the determination of parental responsibility disputes. The meaning of habitual residence under the Hague Convention has been addressed in Chapter 2.

The Hague Abduction Convention applies to any child under the age of 16 who is habitually resident in a Contracting State and has been wrongfully removed or wrongfully retained in another Contracting State.[146] An application for assistance in securing the return of such a child may be made by any person.[147] If the application is made within 12 months, the court must order the return of the child.[148]

The Hague Child Abduction Convention depends on Central Authorities in each Contracting State. These authorities co-operate to ensure the prompt return of children to their state of origin.[149] They also assist in locating children who have been wrongfully removed.

142 Art 9(1).

143 *JRG v EB* [2012] EWHC 1863 (Fam); *J v J (Relinquishment of Jurisdiction)* [2011] EWHC 3255 (Fam), [2012] 1 FLR 1259; see also *Re T And J (Abduction: Recognition of Foreign Judgment)* [2006] EWHC 1472 (Fam), [2006] 2 FLR 1290.

144 Art 1(a).

145 Preamble.

146 Art 4.

147 Art 8.

148 Art 12.

149 Arts 6 and 7.

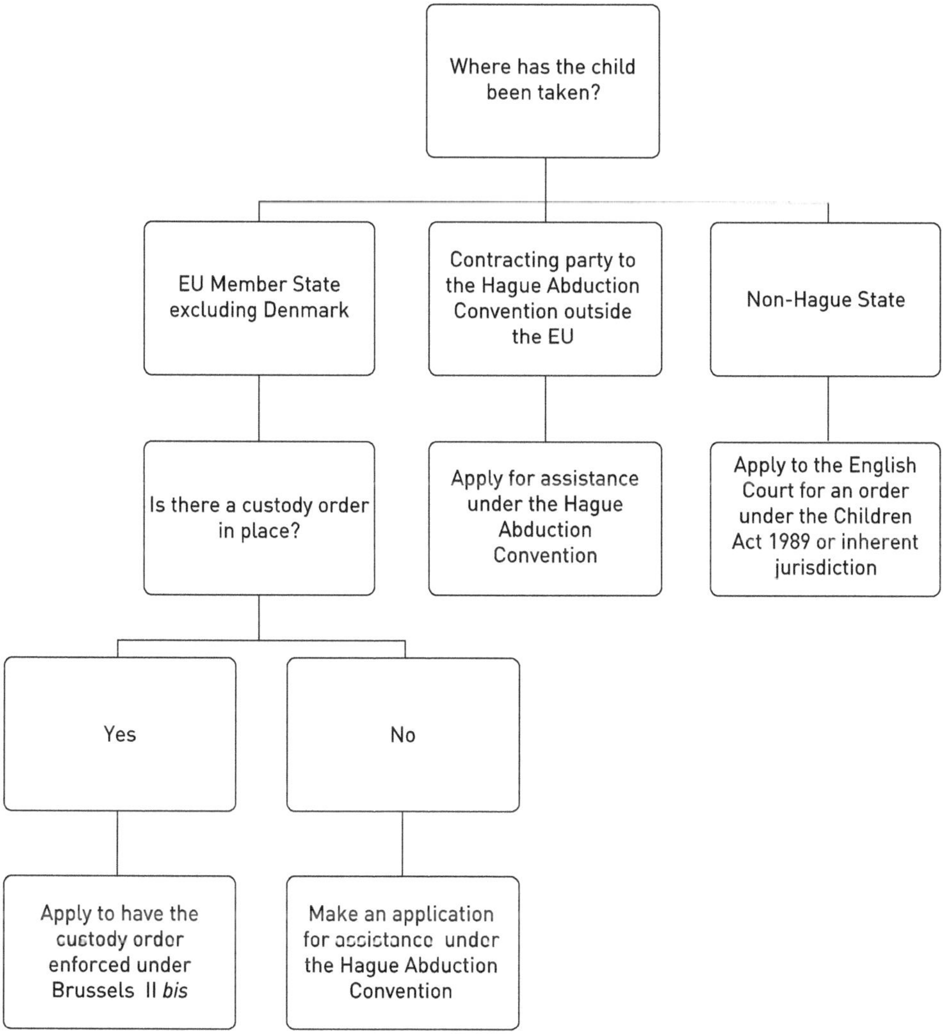

Fig 13.2 Child abduction: which instrument to use where removal is wrongful.

The Hague Abduction Convention is a much narrower mechanism than Brussels II *bis* and only applies in cases of wrongful removal. Although the Hague Abduction Convention aims to ensure that rights of custody and access granted under the law of one Contracting State are respected by other Contracting States,[150] the Convention contains no provision for enforcement of custody or access orders. The state to which the child has been abducted should return the child to the state of habitual residence to determine these issues. The Central Authorities can facilitate voluntary co-operation between the parties and courts.[151]

150 Art 1(b).
151 Art 8 and Art 21.

The Hague Convention is supported by sections of Brussels II *bis*.[152] Where a wrongful removal case involves two EU Member States, Brussels II *bis* provides for closer co-operation between EU Member States than is required under the Hague Convention.[153] Stricter timelines are applied and more power is given to Central Authorities.

The Hague Abduction Convention was incorporated into English law by the Child Abduction and Custody Act 1985. Part 12 of the Family Procedure Rules 2010 outlines English rules of practice and procedure for child abduction cases.

13.7.2 Process

The person seeking return of a child will make an application for assistance in his own state.[154] The Central Authority of that state will transmit the application to the Central Authority in the state where the child is believed to be.[155] The Central Authority in that state must take all appropriate steps to trace the child and secure his prompt voluntary return.[156] If a voluntary return cannot be secured, the authorities of the state in which the child is being held must order the return of the child.[157] This order should be made within six weeks.[158]

The order will not be made unless the child has been wrongfully removed or retained. There are also a number of exceptions outlined in Art 13 where the court can refuse to order the return of the child.

Article 11 of Brussels II *bis* provides several additional procedural safeguards when a child who is habitually resident in one Member State has been wrongfully moved to another Member State. Brussels II *bis* requires that the child is given an opportunity to be heard unless it is inappropriate in the circumstances.[159] The court hearing the application for return is required to act quickly using the most expedient provision of national procedural law.[160] In most cases a judgment is expected within six weeks after the application is lodged.

13.7.3 Wrongful removal and wrongful retention

Wrongful removal and wrongful retention are two mutually exclusive concepts.[161] Wrongful **removal** occurs when a child is removed from his state of habitual residence and the removal is in breach of custody rights. Wrongful **retention** occurs when a child is permitted to leave his state of habitual residence for a set period of time but is not returned at the end of that period.[162]

Retention and removal are only wrongful if in breach of rights of custody under the law of the state where the child was habitually resident before removal[163] **and** if at the time of removal the custody rights were actually exercised.[164] Custody rights can arise by agreement having legal effect or by operation of law or by judicial or administrative decision. Parental responsibility can be

---

152 For a critique of the interaction see P McEleavy, 'The New Child Abduction Regime in the European Community: symbiotic relationship or forced partnership?' (2005) 1 *Journal of Private International Law* 5–34.
153 Art 60 and recital (17) Brussels II *bis*. See also A Schulz, 'Guidance from Luxembourg: First ECJ Judgment clarifying the relationship between the 1980 Hague Convention and Brussels II Revised' [2008] *International Family Law* 221.
154 Art 8.
155 Art 9.
156 Art 10.
157 Art 12.
158 Art 11.
159 Art 11(2).
160 Art 11(3).
161 *Re H* [2000] 1 FLR 374; *Re S (Minors) (Abduction: Custody Rights)* [1991] 2 AC 476, [1991] 2 FLR 262.
162 *Re S (Minors) (Abduction: Custody Rights)* [1991] 2 AC 476, 500, [1991] 2 FLR 262; *Re G* [2007] EWHC 2807.
163 Art 3(a) Hague Abduction Convention; Art 2(11)(a) Brussels II *bis*.
164 Art 3 (b) Hague Abduction Convention; Art 2(11)(b) Brussels II *bis*.

acquired by a change in the child's habitual residence, through the application of the Hague Child Protection Convention.[165]

As examined above, the concept of custody rights includes the English notion of parental responsibility and residence, but mere rights of contact will not amount to custody rights.[166]

If an order stating that the child cannot be taken out of the country is in place, removal in violation of that order is wrongful. In *SH v MM and RM (Prohibited Steps Order: Abduction)*[167] the paternity of a child was in dispute. The court issued a prohibited steps order preventing the mother from removing the child until the matter had been resolved. The mother took the child to Italy. The English court held that the removal was wrongful.[168]

Where a parent has made an application for custody rights and proceedings are pending, the court acquires custody rights. This means that where a parent removes a child before the pending proceedings are decided, removal is wrongful.[169]

In order to decide if there has been wrongful removal or retention, the court must look at the rights of the petitioning parent and decide if they amount to rights of custody.[170] The court can make its own determination of whether or not rights acquired under foreign law constitute custody rights.[171] Article 15 of the Hague Abduction Convention also allows the court to ask the state of the child's habitual residence whether the removal or retention is wrongful for the purposes of the Hague Convention. It is now clear that such a determination from the state of habitual residence is decisive.[172]

13.7.4 Time

Under Art 12 of the Hague Abduction Convention, the court must order return if less than one year has passed since wrongful removal.[173] Where more than one year has passed, the child must be returned unless it can be shown that the child is settled into its new environment.[174] Where the child has become settled, the court can decide whether or not to order return based on the best interests of the child.

In *Re M (Abduction: Zimbabwe)*,[175] two children were born in Zimbabwe. Their parents separated, and the children remained with their father and had contact with their mother. The mother brought them to England and claimed asylum. Two years later the father applied to the Zimbabwean authorities for summary return under the Hague Abduction Convention. The children were now settled in the UK. Article 18 states that the Hague Abduction Convention does not limit the powers of the court to order the return of the child at any time.

The House of Lords considered whether the English court had discretion to return children on summary Hague procedures after they had become settled or if a full merits examination of fact, prioritising the welfare of the child, was then required. In Convention cases, general policy considerations are weighed against the interests of the child in the particular case.[176] The policy goals of the Convention are to deter abduction and ensure both the swift return of children and

165 See further N Lowe, 'The Applicable Laws Provisions of the 1996 Hague Convention on the Protection of Children and the impact of the Convention on international child abduction' [2010] *International Family Law*, 56–57.
166 *D v Romania* [2008] 2 FCR 303; *Re VB* [1999] 2 FLR 192.
167 [2011] EWHC 3314 (Fam), [2012] 1 FLR 837.
168 Ibid [14]. See also *Re D (A Child) (Abduction: Custody Rights)* [2006] UKHL 51, [2007] 1 AC 619, [2007] 1 FLR 961.
169 *Re H* [2000] 1 FLR 374.
170 *Kennedy v Kennedy* [2010] 1 FLR 782.
171 Art 14.
172 *Re D* [2007] 1 FLR 961 overruling *Hunter v Murrow (Abduction: Rights of Custody)* [2005] EWCA Civ 976, [2005] 2 FLR 1119.
173 Art 12.
174 Ibid.
175 [2007] UKHL 55, [2008] 1 AC 1288, [2007] 3 WLR 975, [2008] 1 FLR 251.
176 Ibid [42]

respect for other countries' processes. Where the child has settled, the object of swift return cannot be met. Baroness Hale held, overruling previous case law,[177] that in such cases it can no longer be assumed that the other forum is more appropriate and so the policy of the Convention would not necessarily point to return.[178] The further away the case was from the speedy return envisaged by the Convention, the less weighty the general Convention policy considerations must be and the more emphasis should be given to the best interests of the child in the particular case.[179]

13.7.5 Refusal to return

There is very strong presumption under the Hague Abduction Convention that a child will be returned to the country of his habitual residence. Under the design of the Convention, the court in the state of abduction is prevented from making a decision based on the merits of the case and cannot examine the merits of rights of custody.[180] Decisions regarding custody and future upbringing of the child should be made by the court of the child's habitual residence as the best-placed court to determine these issues. However, there are a number of circumstances in which the court in the state of abduction can refuse to return.[181] The Convention thus contains a thought-out balance between promoting the policy consideration of swift return and respect for other courts and the best interests of the child in any particular case. Where Brussels II *bis* applies, refusal is more limited.

13.7.5.1 Parent has acquiesced: Art 13(a)

Article 13(a) allows return to be refused where the person with care of the child was not exercising custody rights at the time, or had consented or acquiesced to the removal. In such cases, by allowing the move to happen, the parent has acted in such a way that it is unfair to return the child.

Consent to removal must be positive and unequivocal.[182] It will not be valid where it has been given without proper knowledge of the facts.[183] Acquiescence can be inferred from conduct such as delay[184] or failure to take action or by acts inconsistent with an objection to the move. In *Re M*, the father read prospectuses for the child's new school in England and promised to send over Greek language tapes so that the child would not forget her Greek.[185]

In *Re H (Abduction)*[186] the father's failure to take legal action was not considered to be acquiescence as he had consistently objected to the removal of the child and had attempted to settle matters in a Jewish Beth Din court.

13.7.5.2 Grave risk: Art 13(b)

Under Art 13(b), return can be refused where there is grave risk that return would expose the child to physical or psychological harm or otherwise place the child in an intolerable position. A high threshold is used by the English courts; the risk must be grave and the harm must be serious before return will be refused.[187] The situation must be one which the particular child, in particular circumstances before the court, should not be expected to tolerate.[188]

177 *Cannon v Cannon* [2004] EWHC 1245 (Fam), [2005] 1 FLR 127.
178 Ibid [48].
179 Ibid [53].
180 Art 16.
181 *Re M (Abduction: Zimbabwe)* [2007] UKHL 55, [2008] 1 AC 1288, [2007] 3 WLR 975 [2008] 1 FLR 251 [42].
182 *B v D* [2008] EWHC 1246 (Fam); *Re P* [2004] EWCA Civ 971, [2005] Fam 293; *Re K* [1997] 2 FLR 212.
183 *T v T* [1999] 2 FLR 912.
184 *Re S (Child Abduction: Delay)* [1998] 1 FLR 651.
185 *Re M* [1999] 1 FLR 171.
186 *Re H (Abduction: Acquiescence)* [1997] 1 FLR 87.
187 *Re S* [2002] EWCA Civ 908 [40]; *Re H (Abduction)* [2003] EWCA Civ 355; *M v T* [2009] 1 FLR 1309.
188 *Re D* [2006] UKHL 51, [2007] 1 AC 619, [2006] 3 WLR 989, [2007] 1 FLR 961 [52].

In *Re D (Article 13b: non-return)*[189] the children were habitually resident in Venezuela but removed to the UK. Return was ordered but upon return the mother was shot in the face. The mother was given permission to return to England for a holiday, and she remained there. The father sought a return to Venezuela again. The judge found a real risk of physical danger to the children in ordering a return to Venezuela and that their psychological welfare would also be put at risk if the mother returned.

The fact that an order for return will mean separation from the absconding parent does not usually count as constituting an intolerable position. In *Re C*, Butler Sloss LJ held that if the refusal of a mother to accompany her child home could be considered a grave risk of psychological risk to the child it would undermine the Convention and be relied on by every absconding parent.[190] However, in *Re S*[191] it was held that if refusal to return with the child was not based on wilful action but due to illness or external circumstances, such as political unrest in the country of return, the psychological risk to the child could be considered as a grave risk. This approach was also followed in *Re E*.[192]

Where Brussels II *bis* applies, the court cannot refuse to return the child on the basis of Art 13b of the Hague Abduction Convention, if adequate arrangements have been made to secure the child's protection after return.[193] In *M v T*[194] the court held that although there was some risk of psychological problems, adequate psychological support and assistance were available in Ibiza to secure the child's protection on return.[195]

Under Brussels II *bis* the court cannot refuse to return the child without giving the person requesting return an opportunity to be heard.[196]

13.7.5.3 The child's objections

Under Art 13, the court can refuse to return based on the child's objections if the child is of sufficient age and understanding. This obligation is bolstered by Art 11(2) of Brussels II *bis*.

In *Re D*[197] the court held that children should be heard more regularly in abduction cases, and this can be done by report by full legal representation of the child or by the judge talking to the child in chambers.[198] Courts must be wary that a parent might encourage or manipulate a child's views.[199]

In *Re M (Abduction: Zimbabwe)*[200] Baroness Hale held that the court should consider the nature and weight of the child's objections and the extent to which they coincided with other considerations relevant to welfare. Refusal based on the child's objections should not be limited to exceptional circumstances.[201]

In *Klentzeris v Klentzeris*[202] the children had been removed to England. The father sought return to Greece under the Hague Abduction Convention. The children strongly objected, and the evidence from the CAFCASS office was unusually forceful. The court held that the exception under Art 13(b) had been made out and return was refused.

189 [2006] EWCA Civ 146, [2006] 2 FLR 305.
190 *Re C* [1989] 1 FLR 403, 410.
191 [2002] EWCA Civ 908 [37].
192 [2009] 2 FLR 485.
193 Art 11(4)
194 [2009] 1 FLR 1309 [48].
195 See also *TB v JB* [2001] 2 FLR 515.
196 Art 11(5).
197 [2006] UKHL 51, [2007] 1 FLR 961.
198 Ibid [59].
199 *Re P* [1998] 2 FLR 825,827.
200 [2007] UKHL 55, [2008] 1 AC 1288, [2007] 3 WLR 975, [2008] 1 FLR 251. Cf *Zaffino v Zaffino (Abduction: Children's Views)* [2005] EWCA Civ 1012, [2006] 1 FLR 410; *Vigreux v Michel* 2006] EWCA Civ 630, [2006] 2 FLR 1180.
201 *Re M (Abduction: Zimbabwe)* [2007] UKHL 55, [2008] 1 AC 1288, [2007] 3 WLR 975, [2008] 1 FLR 251 [47].
202 [2007] EWCA Civ 533, [2007] 2 FLR 996.

13.7.5.4 Article 20

Article 20 allows the court to refuse to return the child where this would not be permitted by the fundamental principles of the requested state relating to the protection of human rights and fundamental freedoms.

13.8 The level of scrutiny required in Hague Abduction proceedings

Article 8 of the European Convention on Human Rights guarantees a right to family life which can only be interfered with where the interference is in accordance with the law, pursues a legitimate aim and is necessary in a democratic society.[203] Where a child is wrongfully removed, this interferes with the relationship between the child and the left-behind parent. The ECtHR has held that where a child has been abducted, Art 8(2) creates a positive obligation on authorities to do everything that can be reasonably expected of them to facilitate reunion in the circumstances, while striking a balance between competing interests.[204] Balancing competing interests in such situations is not easy. Where an order to return is made that has the effect of disrupting a parent/child relationship between the child and the absconding parent, this is an infringement of the right to family life under Art 8(2) of the ECHR. Where an order of non-return is made that effectively severs the relationship between the child and left-behind parent, this is also an infringement of the right to family life under Art 8(2).

Initially the ECtHR found that the proper application of the Hague Abduction Convention achieved the correct balance between competing interests and was compatible with Art 8(2).[205]

In *Paradis v Germany*,[206] a German mother took her children from Canada to Germany and did not return. The German court issued an order of return under the Hague Abduction Convention. The mother complained that implementation of the order would lead to the separation of the children from their mother, violating her Art 8 rights. The ECtHR held that Art 8 must be interpreted in the light of the Hague Abduction Convention and the legitimate aim of protecting children from wrongful removal from the state of their habitual residence. Application of the Hague Abducton Convention was in compliance with the ECHR.

In *Maumousseau and Washington v France*,[207] the French courts initially refused to return a child to New York under Art 13(b) of the Hague Abduction Convention, holding that separating her from her mother would place her in an intolerable position. The order was reversed on appeal. The French court held that the intolerable position was caused solely by the mother's unlawful actions. They assessed the environment and held that there was no indication of grave risk. The mother complained that the child's return to the USA had been enforced in breach of Art 8(2) of the ECHR. The ECtHR expressly condoned the mechanism of the Hague Abduction Convention.[208] The court was satisfied that in this case the French courts had conducted an adequate assessment of the entire family situation and no violation of Art 8(2) was found.[209]

Recent case law from the ECtHR has suggested that the summary procedures of the Hague Abduction Convention are inadequate, and that an in-depth enquiry into the best interests of the

---

203 Art 8(2) ECHR.

204 *Ignaccola-Zenide v Romania* (App No 3169/96) (2001) 31 EHRR 7.

205 *Monory v Hungary & Romania* (App No 71099/01) (2005) 41 EHRR 37; *Carlson v Switzerland* (Application No 49492/06) (unreported) 6 November 2008

206 (App No 4783/03) (2004) 38 EHRR CD13.

207 (App No 39388/05) (2010) 51 EHRR 35.

208 Ibid [69].

209 Ibid [74]–[76].

child must be conducted before making an order of return or non-return. This has been heavily criticised as undermining the whole purpose of the Hague Abduction Convention in ensuring swift return.[210]

In *Neulinger & Shuruk v Switzerland*,[211] an Israeli father and Swiss mother lived in Israel with their son. The relationship broke down and the mother returned to Switzerland with the child. The father issued Hague proceedings but it took over a year to locate the child. The Swiss court dismissed the father's application under Art 13(b) on the basis that there was grave risk if the child were returned to Israel. The Israel authority put safeguards in place and the Swiss authorities later permitted the child to be returned to Israel, accompanied by his mother. The mother applied to the ECtHR that the order for return violated her Art 8 rights. Her claim was initially dismissed, but on appeal to the Grand Chamber it was held that enforcement of the order for the child's return to Israel would involve a violation of Art 8 in respect of both mother and child.

The Grand Chamber held that the child's return could not be ordered automatically or mechanically and Art 13 must be interpreted in compliance with the ECHR. The court held that the best interests of the child, at the time of enforcement, must be assessed in each case.[212]

In *Šneersone and Kampanella v Italy*[213] the ECtHR held that the Italian courts had breached Art 8 by making an order returning a child to Latvia. The ECtHR noted that the Hague Abduction Convention was essentially an instrument of a procedural nature and not a human rights treaty protecting individuals on an objective basis.[214] However, the court held that the Italian authorities had failed to deal with the concerns of the Latvian authorities or the psychological trauma that would inevitably follow a sudden and irreversible severance of the close ties between mother and child. In doing so, the Italian authorities had failed to secure the guarantees put forth in Art 8.

In *Raban v Romania*,[215] the ECtHR upheld an order for non-return by the Romanian courts. The court noted that a child should not be returned automatically or mechanically, and the court must take an *in concreto* approach. In ensuring that the decision-making process was fair, the ECtHR must ascertain whether the domestic courts conducted an in-depth examination of the entire family situation and of a whole series of factors, in particular of a factual, emotional, psychological, material and medical nature, and made a balanced and reasonable assessment of the respective interests of each person, with a constant concern for determining what the best solution would be for the abducted child in the context of an application for his return to his country of origin.[216]

In *X v Latvia*,[217] the ECtHR reiterated this position. In this case a Latvian mother wrongfully removed her three-year-old child from Australia to Latvia. The Australian courts ordered the return of the child. The Latvian courts ordered return in spite of some concerns that there was not adequate information about the situation of the child after she was returned to Australia. The mother claimed that her Art 8 rights had been infringed as the Hague Abduction Convention had been arbitrarily applied and interpreted.

The ECtHR held that a balance between competing rights could only be assured if the courts conducted an in-depth examination of the family situation. The Latvian court had failed to conduct an in depth examination of the entire family situation by disregarding a psychologist's report,

210 See N Lowe, 'A supra-national approach to interpreting the 1980 Hague Child Abduction Convention – a tale of two European courts: Part 2 – the substantive impact of the two European courts' rulings upon the application of the 1980 Convention' [2012] IFL 170–179; L Walker and P Beaumont, 'Shifting the Balance Achieved by the Abduction Convention: The contrasting approaches of the European Court of Human Rights and the European Court of Justice' (2011) 7 *Journal of Private International Law* 231–249; A Schulz, 'The enforcement of child return orders in Europe: where do we go from here?' [2012] IFL 43–47.

211 (App No 41615/07) (2012) 54 EHRR 31, [2011] 1 FLR 122.

212 Ibid [48].

213 (App No 14737/09) [2011] 2 FLR 1322.

214 Ibid [88]–[92].

215 (App No 25437/08) [2011] 1 FLR 1130.

216 Ibid [38]–[39].

217 (App No 27853/09) [2012] 1 FLR 860.

failing to assess the safeguards in place in Australia, failing to consider whether contact between the mother and child could be maintained and failing to examine the child's material well-being if a return order were made. These omissions and failures meant that there had been a disproportional interference with the mother's Art 8 rights.[218]

The UK Supreme Court has held that the summary procedure of the Hague Abduction Convention is sufficient to comply with Art 8. The court has been highly critical of any attempt to introduce a full welfare hearing into abduction proceedings.

In *Re E*,[219] a mother wrongfully removed two children from Norway to England. The English courts accepted undertakings and ordered return in the best interest of the child. The mother argued that the father was abusive, that return posed a grave risk under Art 13(b) and that the level of scrutiny demanded by *Neulinger* had not been applied. The Supreme Court held that national courts did not automatically return children under the Hague Abduction Convention when a question as to safety was raised. Instead, they examined the particular circumstances of the case but without conducting a full-blown review of what arrangements should be made for the child's future.[220]

In *Re S*[221] the Supreme Court reiterated that the very object of the Hague Abduction Convention was to avoid an in-depth examination of the child's future by the court of the state of abduction. The reference to the need for an in-depth examination in the *Neulinger* case should not be taken out of context. It was most unlikely that a proper application of the Hague Convention would infringe the rights of any members of the family under Art 8.[222]

13.9 After return has been refused – Art 11(8) orders

Under the Hague Abduction Convention, if the court of the state of wrongful removal refuses to return the child, the child will stay in a state of abduction and eventually become habitually resident there.

However, under Brussels II *bis* the court of the Member State where the child was habitually resident before the abduction gets to review the situation if the order of non-return was based on the exceptions outlined in Art 13 of the Hague Abduction Convention.[223] In such cases, Brussels II *bis* requires the court of the state of abduction to send all documents relating to the proceedings to the Central Authority of the Member State in which the child was habitually resident before wrongful removal within one month.[224] Article 11(7) requires the court of habitual residence to re-examine the issue of custody in light of the order of non-return. As part of this re-examination, the court of the state of previous habitual residence can order that the child is returned, as part of its welfare analysis. If such an order for return is made, it is automatically enforceable under the certificate procedure of Art 42.[225] This procedure takes priority over the normal enforcement and recognition procedures but is only available if a custody order is made under Art 11(8) after a judgment of non-return.

In *Re A (Custody Decision after Maltese Non-Return Order)*,[226] an English mother based in England and a Maltese father based in Malta had three children. Two lived with their father in Malta and the

218 Ibid [65]–[78].

219 [2011] UKSC 27.

220 Ibid [26].

221 [2012] UKSC 10.

222 Ibid [37]

223 Arts 11(6)–(8) Brussels II *bis*.

224 Art 11(6).

225 See above.

226 [2006] EWHC 3397 (Fam), [2007] 1 FLR 1923; C523/07 *Re A* [2009] ECR I-2805, [2009] 2 FLR 1; *HA v MB (Brussels II Revised: Article 11(7) Application)* [2007] EWHC 2016 (Fam), [2008] 1 FLR 289.

youngest son with his mother in England. The son went on a visit to Malta aged 12 and did not want to return as he was afraid of drug use going on in his mother's house. There was some evidence in this case to suggest that the child was put under pressure to say these things by family members in Malta. The mother took proceedings for return under the Hague Abduction Convention but the Maltese courts refused to order return under Art 13(b). The mother applied to the English courts under Art 11 for an order for the child to be returned to England. The English courts ordered that the child be returned to England and issued an Art 42 certificate to compel the Maltese authorities to do so.

Where refusal to return is based on Art 20 of the Hague Abduction Convention or a finding that retention or removal was not wrongful under Art 12[227] or a finding that the child is now settled in the state of abduction under Art 12(2),[228] no review of custody is possible under Art 11(7). In such cases the state of former habitual residence may retain jurisdiction to review custody under Art 10. These orders are enforceable under the ordinary procedure of Art 28 but not the expedited procedure of Art 42.

In *Povse v Alpago*[229] the mother took her child to Austria in breach of court orders preventing her leaving Italy. The Italian court awarded joint custody and permitted the child to live in Austria until the final order was made. The father took Hague proceedings to have the child returned, but these were dismissed in Austria. A year later the Italian court ordered return of the child to Italy and issued an Art 42 certificate. In the meantime, the Austrian court had concluded that it had jurisdiction and awarded custody to the mother.

The ECJ held that Art 10(b)(iv) should be interpreted strictly. Thus the court with habitual residence before abduction retains jurisdiction until a final judgment on custody is made that does not entail the return of the child.[230] To be final, a judgment must be ordered on the basis of full consideration of the relevant factors. In this case, the Italian court had permitted the child to live in Austria while awaiting an expert report on the relationship of both parents with the child before making final judgment, and so it was not a final judgment.[231] Italy retained jurisdiction to make a custody order.

13.10 Access rights under the Hague Abduction Convention

Article 21 of the Hague Abduction Convention allows the holder of the rights of access to apply to the Central Authority of the state where the child is to take steps to remove obstacles to the exercise of access rights. This is much more limited than the powers to enforce access rights that exist under Brussels II *bis*. The Central Authority is merely required to provide legal aid, if the applicant is eligible, and instruct a solicitor.[232]

13.11 Abduction cases falling outside Brussels II *bis* or the Hague Abduction Convention

Where the child is removed to a state which is not an EU Member State or a party to the Hague Abduction Convention, and the English court is asked to make an order for return, the situation falls

227 *Re RC and BL (Child Abduction) (Brussels II Revised: Art 11(7))* [2009] 1 FLR 574.
228 *Re RD (Child Abduction) (Brussels II Revised: Arts 11(7) and 19)* [2009] 1 FLR 586.
229 C211/10 PPU, *Povse v Alpago* [2010] ECR 1–000, [2010] 2 FLR 1343.
230 Ibid [46].
231 Ibid [49].
232 *Re T and others* [1993] 2 FLR 617; *Re G (A Minor) (Hague Convention: Access)* [1993] 1 FLR 669.

outside the remit of Brussels II *bis* and the Hague Abduction Convention. Such applications are usually made using a specific issue order under s 8 of the Children Act 1989 or under inherent jurisdiction.[233] In such cases the English courts are governed by the welfare principle.[234] This means that the child's welfare or best interests are paramount and should take precedence over conflicting policy goals regarding prompt return of a wrongfully removed child or comity of the courts.

In *Re J (A Child) (Custody Rights: Jurisdiction)*[235] the House of Lords held that there was no reason for Hague principles to be extended to non-Hague countries. The child's welfare was the paramount consideration as in ordinary domestic cases. The specialist rules of the Hague Convention were not to be applied to non-Hague cases.[236] The English court does have the power to order the immediate return of the child to a foreign jurisdiction without conducting a full investigation of the merits if swift return is in the interests of that particular child. There is no presumption in favour of return, and the court should operate on a case-by-case basis.[237]

13.12 Further reading

A E Anton, 'The Hague Convention on International Child Abduction' (1981) 30 ICLQ 537–567.

PJ Blanco, 'Unmarried fathers and child abduction in European Union Law' (2012) 8 *Journal of Private International Law* 135–157.

HCCH, 'Revised draft Practical Handbook on the operation of the 1996 Hague Protection of Children Convention (Prel. Doc. No 4 of May 2011)' available at www.hcch.net/index_en.php?act=;publications.details&pid=5535&dtid=2 (accessed 17 May 2013).

N Lowe, 'The 1996 Hague Convention on the protection of children – a fresh appraisal' (2002) 14 *Child and Family Law Quarterly* 191.

N Lowe, 'The Applicable Laws Provisions of the 1996 Hague Convention on the Protection of Children and the Impact of the Convention on International Child Abduction' [2010] *International Family Law* 51.

N Lowe, 'A supra-national approach to interpreting the 1980 Hague Child Abduction Convention – a tale of two European courts: Part 1 – setting the scene' [2012] IFL 48–52.

N Lowe, 'A supra-national approach to interpreting the 1980 Hague Child Abduction Convention – a tale of two European courts: Part 2 – the substantive impact of the two European courts' rulings upon the application of the 1980 Convention' [2012] IFL 170–179.

P McEleavy, 'Brussels II *bis:* matrimonial matters, parental responsibilities, child abduction and mutual recognition' (2004) 53 ICLQ 503.

P McEleavy, 'The New Child Abduction Regime in the European Community: Symbiotic Relationship or Forced Partnership?' (2005) 1 *Journal of Private International Law* 5–34.

A Schulz, 'The New Brussels II Regulation and the Hague Conventions of 1980 and 1996' [2004] *International Family Law* 22.

A Schulz, 'The enforcement of child return orders in Europe: where do we go from here?' [2012] IFL 43–47.

L Walker and P Beaumont, 'Shifting the balance achieved by the Abduction Convention: The contrasting approaches of the European Court of Human Rights and the European Court of Justice' (2011) 7 *Journal of Private International Law* 231–249.

---

233 *T v R (Abduction: Forum Conveniens)* [2002] 2 FLR 544; *H v H (Jurisdiction to Grant Wardship)* [2011] EWCA Civ 796, [2012] 1 FLR 23.

234 S 1(1) Children Act 1989.

235 [2005] UKHL 40, [2006] 1 AC 80, [2005] 2 FLR 802.

236 Ibid [22]

237 Ibid [28], [38], [39]. See *Re JA (Child Abduction: Non-Convention Country)* [1998] 1 FLR 231.

Index

For Product Safety Concerns and Information please contact our EU
representative GPSR@taylorandfrancis.com
Taylor & Francis Verlag GmbH, Kaufingerstraße 24, 80331 München, Germany

www.ingramcontent.com/pod-product-compliance
Lightning Source LLC
LaVergne TN
LVHW080806011026
849160LV00015B/1545
* 9 7 8 0 4 1 5 6 9 5 0 6 0 *